T0306371

THE WORLD ENCYCLOPEDIA OF RIFLES AND MACHINE GUNS

AN ILLUSTRATED HISTORICAL GUIDE TO OVER 500 MILITARY, LAW ENFORCEMENT AND ANTIQUE FIREARMS

WILL FOWLER & PATRICK SWEENEY,
WITH T. LOGAN METESH

LORENZ BOOKS

This edition is published by Lorenz Books
an imprint of Anness Publishing Ltd
info@anness.com
www.lorenzbooks.com
www.annesspublishing.com

A CIP catalogue record for this book is available from the British Library.

Originally designed and produced for Anness Publishing by THE BRIDGEWATER BOOK COMPANY LIMITED.

Publisher: Joanna Lorenz
Editorial Director: Helen Sudell
Editor: Rosie Gordon
Project Managers: Sarah Doughty & Cath Senker
Photography: Gary Ombler
Designer: Alistair Plumb
Art Director: Michael Whitehead
Production Controller: Ben Worley

Contents

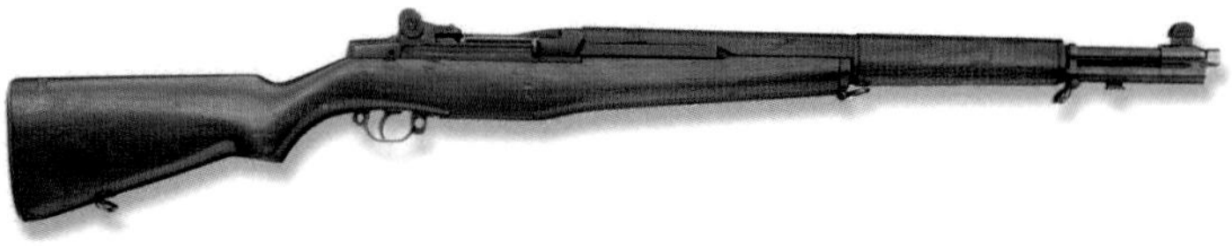

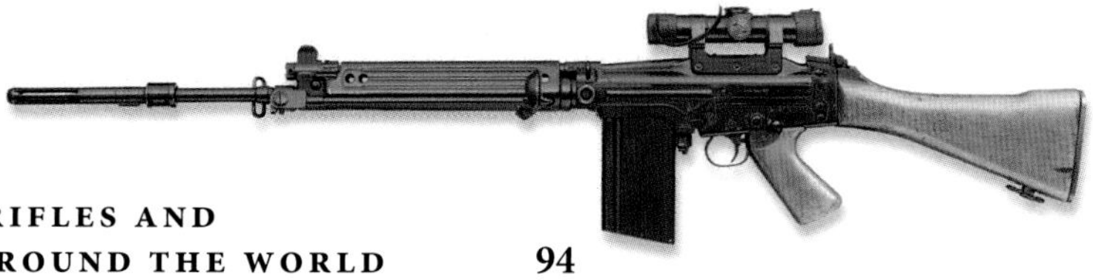

Introduction

Firearms have exerted a fascination since medieval times, and today's weapons are more accurate and effective than the first designers could have imagined. The rifle has been developed for use both in target shooting and for hunting, while the machine gun was exclusively developed for major conflict – and has demonstrated its devastating efficiency.

This book explores the earliest firearms, through to the ultra-modern assault rifles and machine guns of today, and introduces the small arms designers who have shaped history, such as Samuel Colt, Hiram Maxim, Pietro Antonio Beretta and Mikhail Kalashnikov.

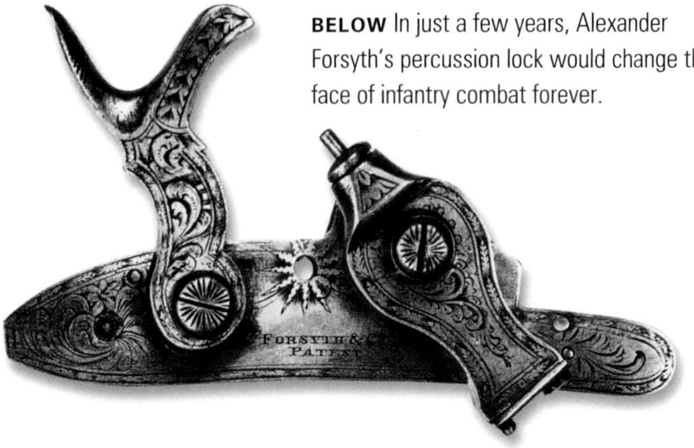

BELOW In just a few years, Alexander Forsyth's percussion lock would change the face of infantry combat forever.

The first muskets

The history of rifle development goes back to 14th-century Europe, when firearms using gunpowder as a propellant first appeared. These hand cannons, which could be loaded and fired by one man, were hazardous and not very effective. In the first section, "Early rifles", discover the designs that were successful and those that failed, and the many developments leading to selection of certain weapons for major conflicts. For example, flintlock muskets and pistols were used during the American Revolutionary Wars of 1775–83 and in the Napoleonic Wars of 1792–1815. Soldiers were drilled to fire in short-range volleys, waiting (often under artillery fire) until they could see the whites of the eyes of the approaching enemy infantry – difficult to imagine today. Following the volley they launched a bayonet charge against their shocked and battered opponents. In the American Civil War (1861–65), M1816 flintlock muskets were still in use with some of the Confederate forces.

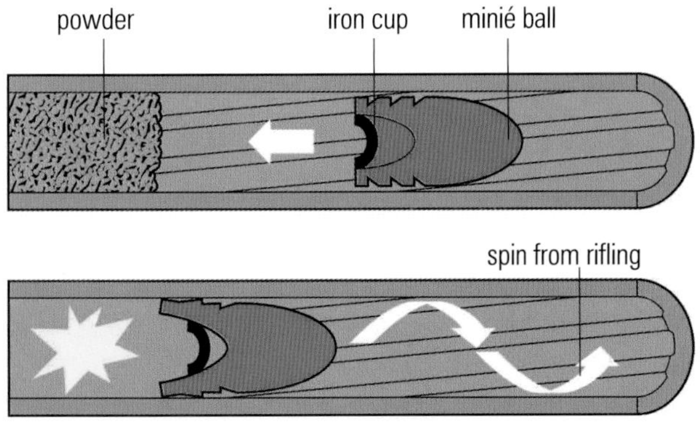

ABOVE The Minié rifle bullet system revolutionized firearm developmment. When the propellant charge exploded, the lead bullet expanded and cut into the twists of the rifling. This produced a spin that made it travel in a straight line and so gave it accuracy over a long range – which had never been achieved before.

From the American Civil War to World War I

Flintlocks may have been an incredible innovation in the 1700s, but as the second section of the book, "Rifles from 1800–2000" shows, 1807 saw a huge step forward. The Reverend Alexander Forsyth developed the first percussion ignition system for sporting guns. Forsyth's system was rather cumbersome, but, unlike flintlock weapons, it was weatherproof. About seven years later an English gunsmith, Joseph Egg of London, invented the percussion cap, which was made of copper and filled with black blasting powder and potassium chlorate. These developments ultimately led to the modern magazine- and belt-fed weapons detailed in these pages. By World War I most combatants had equipped their soldiers with a magazine-fed bolt-action rifle, which could be fired fast, in all weather conditions, from the prone position.

Early machine guns

The inspiration for the world's first machine gun is said to have been a visitor to the Paris Electrical Exhibition of 1881, who said to the American engineer and inventor Hiram Maxim, "If you want to make a lot of money, invent something that will enable these Europeans to cut each other's throats with greater facility." The gun he showed the British Army four years later had the firepower of all the riflemen in an infantry company. The potential of firearms in warfare, which we take for granted today, was just being dreamed of. Section three, "The machine gun age 1883-2000" charts the incredibly fast-paced development of machine guns – once that potential had been spotted, arms manufacture exploded into a race of innovation.

By the end of World War I, the first submachine guns (SMGs) had been developed. These compact, fast-firing weapons fired a pistol-calibre bullet and were ideal for the confined spaces of the trench systems of the Western Front. The book explores the ways that warfare conditions, allies and enemies alike influenced each country's weapons development, coming up with ever more devastating armories – for example, problems with cumbersome SMGs in World War I led the Germans to develop the MG34, the world's first General-Purpose Machine Gun (GPMG). This versatile new weapon was widely copied by all armies after World War II, and classics such as the AAT-52 and RPD are introduced on these pages.

The final development in the story of infantry weapons came just before World War II, but "New developments" shows how modern weapons designers are still drawing upon past guns, such as the Russian PK and the 19th century Gatling, to produce today's awesome fire power.

ABOVE The Maxim gun was the world's first true machine gun. For mobility on the battlefield it could be mounted on a light gun carriage, with the crew protected by a shield.

ABOVE In developing the MG34 (above) between the wars the Germans came up with a wholly new concept – the General-Purpose Machine Gun – a weapon that could be used as a light or medium machine gun. The MG42 that followed was an improvement.

The directories

There are two directories; the first devoted to rifles and carbines from around the world, the second to machine guns. The history of arms manufacture within each country is briefly introduced, then each weapon entry includes a concise description of the firearm and its key specifications, listed by country and manufacturer. Many weapons are pictured.

Readers will discover firearms from the 19th century "Brown Bess" flintlock musket to the Short Magazine Lee-Enfield, which, in the hands of the British Expeditionary Force (BEF) at Mons, shattered German infantry attacks. In the machine gun directory it becomes clear how the World Wars, and warfare generally, were shaped by machine gun development. World War I was dominated by the designs of American Hiram Maxim. Inventive German weapons designers gave the world the assault rifle, an automatic rifle firing intermediate calibre rounds. The directories bring readers right up to date with the weapons used today.

The history section and the detailed directories enable enthusiasts to identify firearms and fully appreciate their unique features, funtionality and designs.

LEFT Cadets of the Confederate Army with the Model 1841 Mississippi rifle, as photographed in 1861. By the end of 1863 most Federal infantrymen were armed with the Mississippi rifle or the Enfield.

Early rifles

The first firearms developed in Europe in the 14th century were hand cannon. These crude weapons were refined during the following century through a series of modifications such as the hackbut and arquebus, some fitted with snapping matchlocks or sear-lock matchlocks. In some regions of the world, including Japan and India's North-West Frontier, matchlocks would survive for centuries, and in the hands of trained marksmen prove very effective weapons. The development of the wheel lock and snaphance in the 16th century led to the production of the flintlock, a weapon that was used until the American Civil War. During this period, sights and rifling were developed, which greatly improved the accuracy of rifles. In the 17th and 18th centuries, new technologies were introduced to allow soldiers to carry gunpowder more safely. The section also covers the muskets of the 18th century, which also saw service in the American Civil War (1861–65) and the British Army in its conquest of colonies around the world.

BELOW The Mauser Model 1871 was the first Mauser rifle to be manufactured in 1871, and after the introduction of an adequate safety, it was adopted by the German Army in 1872. Millions of rifles were subsequently manufactured to the Mauser design.

ABOVE The Remington Model 1871 carbine was a single-shot weapon, which was produced only in the 1870s and early 1880s before the advent of repeating rifles made it obsolete. The advantage of the Remington was its flexibility; it could be adapted to take a variety of rifle cartridges.

Hand cannon

The first firearms that appeared in the late 14th century in Europe were simply miniature cannon that were fired from horseback or from ships and fortifications. They were noisy and had a very short effective range. The invention of gunpowder was the kickstart for this new type of weapon, and although it was only gradually introduced, the use of gunpowder would change the character of war on land and at sea forever.

ABOVE The Welsh longbow (shown without string here) was adopted by the English and used with lethal effect against French mounted knights at the Battle of Agincourt of 1415. The longbow was actually more accurate than most firearms until the introduction of rifled percussion-cap fired weapons in the mid-19th century.

Early combat weapons

Before gunpowder came on the scene, combat weapons were implements that could stab, cleave or batter an enemy to death, and so had to be used at close quarters. The only weapons that allowed combatants to engage at range were the crossbow and longbow. In the 15th century, skilled English and Welsh archers armed with longbows could deliver plunging fire at targets such as massed horsemen at about 180m/200yd. This type of fire was similar to that delivered by a machine gun firing at long range. As the range shortened, the fire would be direct, and the metal arrowhead with the mass of the shaft or stele behind it would take on the characteristics of a modern anti-tank shell with its long rod penetrator.

The invention of gunpowder

In 1242, however, an English monk named Roger Bacon wrote down the formula for the preparation of gunpowder as an anagram or cipher. Not only did Bacon name the ingredients and the proportions then used (saltpetre: charcoal: sulphur 7:5:5) but he also described the explosive properties of the mixture. Although he gave no indication that it could be employed as a propellant, by around 1300 muzzle-loading cannon were beginning to appear. By 1364, there was documented evidence of hand-held firearms in Perugia, Italy; and ten years later firearms had become common in Europe. One of the earliest

BELOW Two early hand cannons. The lip allowed the barrel of the weapon to be hooked over a parapet before it was fired. The upper weapon has a metal hook-type handle, while the lower has a more conventional butt.

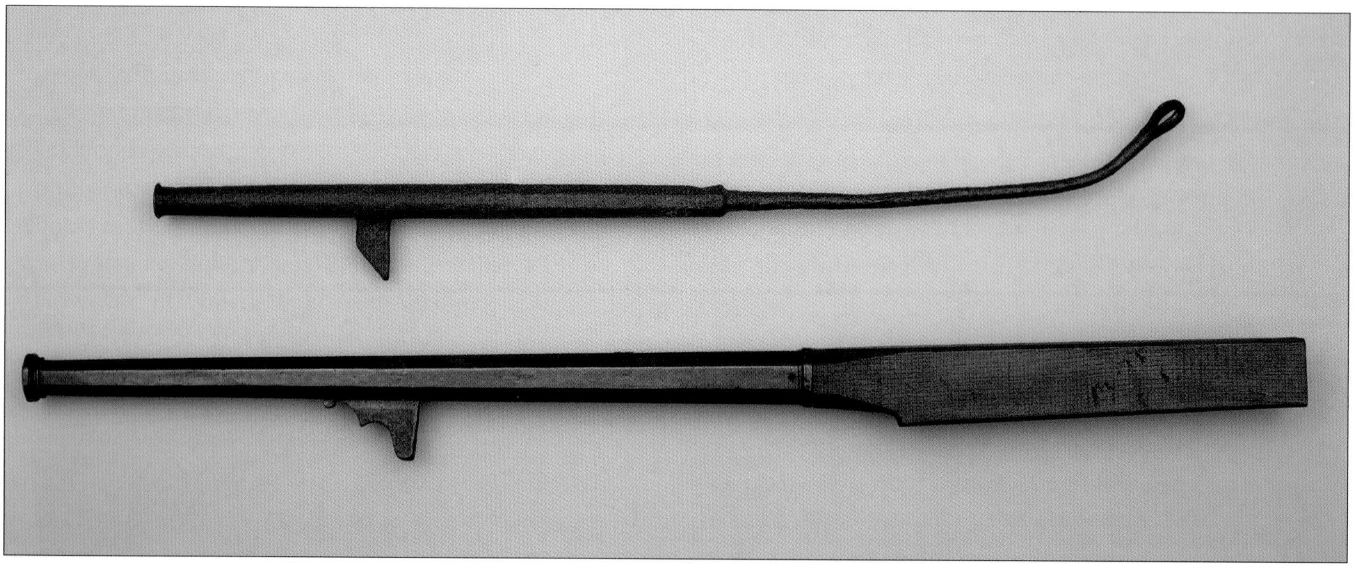

examples is in the Tøjhus Museum in Copenhagen, Denmark. Constructed from iron with a long handle and simple hook, the weapon could be secured to a wall or palisade or even a tripod, so that when the operator fired it the recoil would have been absorbed by the solid structure. Another version, made from iron in the second half of the 15th century (found in the Bernisches Historisches Museum in Switzerland), has both a hook as well as a D-shaped grip for easy carriage and deployment.

Hand cannon design

Early firearms that appeared around 1375 were often called "hand cannon"; they consisted of a simple iron or brass tube with a touchhole at the top fixed in a straight stock of wood, the end of which passed under the right armpit when the gun was ready to be fired. Some versions used by mounted soldiers had a ring at the end of the stock with a cord attached, which allowed the gun to be hung over the shoulder, leaving both hands free. When the rider wished to fire it he used a forked rest, fitted into a ring on the saddle, to steady the gun. When the fork rest was not in use, it hung down in front of the rider's right leg. An example of a cavalry hand cannon dating from 1400–50, and now in the Bernisches Historisches Museum, was found in the River Tiber in Rome. It has a wrought-iron barrel with a ring to allow it to be slung from a strap over the shoulder. The wooden stock had long disappeared and has been restored.

The slow match

The match was made from cotton or loosely spun hemp, which was boiled in a strong solution of saltpetre or in the lees of wine. Kindled by a flint and steel, the match, or slow match, would remain an important piece of equipment while gunpowder weapons were in use. Ideally, the match should not burn quickly or produce sparks, nor should it be blown out by a breeze. Like a conventional cannon, the touchhole was first placed on top of the gun barrel, but afterwards it was moved to the side, with a small pan underneath to hold the priming, and held in place by a pivoted cover.

Firearms training

Although the hand cannons produced a spectacular, and no doubt terrifying bang and cloud of white smoke, the longbow and crossbow were more accurate and deadly – and far less dangerous to use. Yet even early, inaccurate firearms had a distinct advantage: it was easy to train soldiers to use them, whereas the skill of using a longbow could be mastered only after expert tuition and long and regular practice. Soldiers were trained to use firearms by a series of drills, which taught them to load, aim and fire the musket. This ensured that in the smoke, noise and confusion of the battlefield they would keep up a steady volume of fire.

Sometimes in 18th- and 19th-century actions a soldier forgot under pressure that one of the drills was to remove his ramrod after loading his weapon. If the ramrod was fired off, the musket lacked this vital component and became useless. In some European armies there were severe punishments for men who lost their ramrods.

Since muskets were smoothbore (with no rifling to direct the shot) and only accurate over short ranges, soldiers were taught to fire in volleys, at short range, delivering a blast of musket balls that produced an effect similar to a giant shotgun.

ABOVE This early 15th-century illustration depicts the firing of hand cannons in battle. The stock is held firmly under the firer's arm, and the man in the foreground is holding the slow match in his left hand. Burning gas from the gunpowder is emitted from the muzzle and the touchhole.

The matchlock

The 15th century saw improvements in firearm design such as the matchlock, which looked less like a miniature cannon and more like our familiar rifle with a butt and trigger. Further developments in design produced the arquebus, some versions of which were fitted with snapping matchlocks or sear-lock matchlocks.

The matchlock

The first design improvement came in about 1411 with the first matchlock; a simple trigger was linked into a curved metal clamp called a serpentine, which held a match. When the trigger was pressed, the serpentine tipped forwards and pushed the match into the priming pan containing gunpowder. The flash passed through the touchhole to the main charge and the shot was fired. Refinements included a hinged cover for the pan that kept the powder dry and reduced the risk of an accidental discharge. By the late 15th century, these weapons were being fitted with shoulder stocks.

The English idiom "a flash in the pan", to describe an event that looks spectacular but is of no consequence, probably dates from the time of flintlocks (16th century), although men armed with matchlocks would also have been familiar with the phenomenon. Although there would be a flash of exploding powder and a cloud of smoke, the burning gas would not pass into the barrel and set off the main charge because the touchhole was fouled with burned gunpowder residue. It would be a "flash in the pan" or non-event.

The arquebus

The hackbut was the first gun fired from the shoulder. It was a smoothbore matchlock (without rifling) and had a stock resembling that of a modern rifle. The arquebus, invented in Spain in the mid-15th century, was a medium-weight gun that evolved from the heavy and awkward hackbut. Instead of the recoil from firing being directed against the soldier's shoulder, some of it was absorbed by the support; however the hook was needed to prevent the gun sliding off the support. (The name "arquebus" may come from the Low German for "hooked gun".)

The arquebus was the first firearm to resemble a modern gun, with lock, stock and barrel. As technology advanced, the arquebus was fitted with

The gunsmith's craft

Firearms were a "must-have" weapon for the monarchs and rulers of Europe. In addition to their beautifully crafted armour and edged weapons, these leaders had firearms made to order, and gunsmiths came up with some ingenious designs that were pointers to the future. A revolving matchlock was presented to King Louis XIII of France. This gun had multiple chambers, each of which had its own priming pan. To fire it, the user rotated each chamber into place and opened the pan and fired as a conventional matchlock.

King Henry VIII of England had a custom-made breech-loading matchlock. This gun was loaded through the rear by lifting the breech block, placing the shot followed by gunpowder into the barrel and then closing the breech block. The pan was then primed and the gun fired as a conventional matchlock.

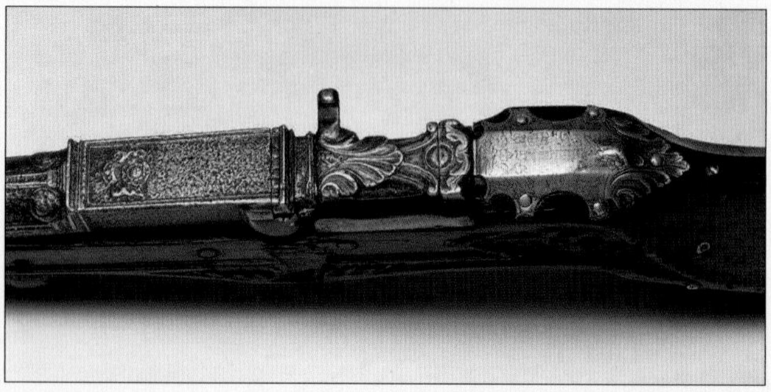

RIGHT The beautifully engraved breech-loading matchlock used by Henry VIII; his crest featuring a rose can be seen on the barrel. The carefully engineered breech was designed to give an effective gas seal for the exploding powder.

more advanced forms of ignition. There were three major types of arquebus: those with serpentine locks, those with snapping matchlocks and those with sear-lock matchlocks. The caliver was a more advanced form of arquebus with a standardized bore size. The caliver used either a trigger lever or a conventional trigger to operate the matchlock mechanism.

ABOVE A good idea of the very short effective range of an arquebus can be gauged from this 15th-century German woodcut. The knights equipped with firearms have sensibly retained their swords. Reloading an arquebus would take up too much time, which would have been in short supply during close combat.

The snapping matchlock

By about 1475 the snapping matchlock had appeared. It was operated by cocking a spring-powered serpentine and pushing a button on the lock plate (a trigger was used on later guns) to release the serpentine, allowing it to snap into the priming pan. This type of matchlock lost popularity in Europe because the slow match was often extinguished when it was snapped hard into the powder. The sear-lock matchlock operated by squeezing a trigger attached to a sprung sear inside the lock, allowing the serpentine to be lowered into the priming pan as the hand squeezed, then retracted when pressure was released.

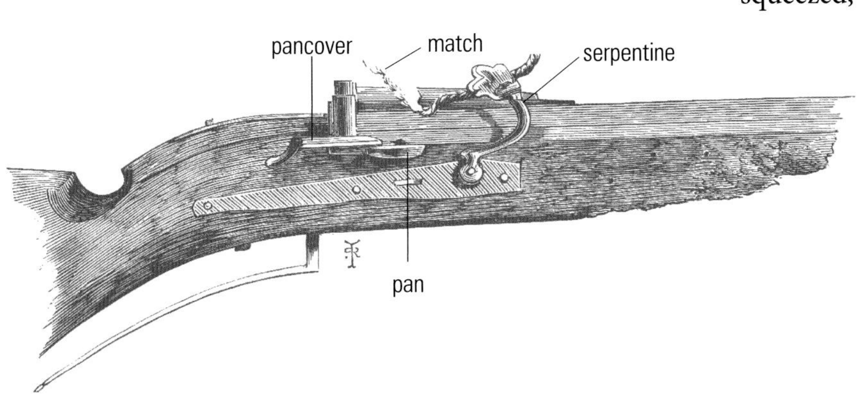

LEFT The slow match smoulders, ready to be lowered into the pan of a caliver. The caliver was an advanced version of the arquebus, which was an improvement on the inaccurate hand cannon.

New users of the matchlock

The simplicity of the matchlock led to its adoption by indigenous warriors wherever it was taken by European traders and soldiers. The Japanese learned how to build matchlocks from Portuguese traders, while the Indians and Afghans adopted the technology from the British. On India's North-West Frontier, warlike tribesmen used their Jezail matchlocks, designed for easy fire from horseback, with ruthless efficiency against the British.

Japanese matchlocks

Although based on matchlocks introduced by the Portuguese traders in 1543, Japanese Tanegashima weapons never progressed beyond the basic snapping matchlock mechanism; most European designs used flintlocks. In the 1860s, percussion locks were imported from the West, and this ignition system was the first departure from the matchlock.

All Japanese matchlocks of this type were handmade, varying greatly in calibre, size, length and styles and rarely had interchangeable parts. Unlike European muskets, the stocks had no shoulder supports with a butt plate, but at the rear they had a distinctive cheek piece, described as a "cheek stock".

ABOVE Warriors on the Afghan–Baluch frontier in the 1890s armed with their Jezail muskets; the stocks and other simple components were often handmade. These men were formidable marksmen, capable of hitting human targets at a considerable range.

In feudal Japan the Tanegashima matchlock styles were classified by the shooting schools where the gun makers taught and worked, and by the fiefdoms of the ruling lords. The country was divided among almost one hundred lords, each with his own distinctive ideas or policies about the manufacture of every kind of civil or military product. Records suggest that in the

LEFT The Japanese had been introduced to the matchlock by Portuguese traders. They were quick to grasp its utility as a weapon. Here, warriors use a modified version; however, like European soldiers they retain their swords for personal protection.

late 18th century there may have about 250 shooting schools in Japan; shooting, or *Houjyutu*, was classed as a martial art along with techniques such as karate.

Indian and Afghan matchlocks

A form of matchlock musket used in India until the 20th century was known as the Bandukh Torador. British soldiers also adopted the name, referring to their rifles as "Bondooks" well into the 20th century.

The Jezail, which came from the area of the Pashto-speaking people of Afghanistan and the North-West Frontier of British India (now Pakistan), was a matchlock or flintlock musket fired from a forked rest. The Jezail used the unusual curved Sind stock, which made the gun easier to fire from horseback. Many of these guns were later converted to percussion. The Jezail, although long and awkward to carry, was reputedly accurate up to 730m/800yd; Afghans picked off sheep and horses at 550m/600yd with a single shot.

In his poem "Arithmetic on the Frontier", Rudyard Kipling writes about the death of a young British officer:

A scrimmage in a Border Station –
A canter down some dark defile –
Two thousand pounds of education
Drops to a ten-rupee jezail –
The Crammer's boast, the Squadron's pride,
Shot like a rabbit in a ride.

War on the North-West Frontier

A series of conflicts known as the Anglo–Afghan Wars took place during the imperialist struggle for domination in Afghanistan between Britain and the Russian Empire in the 19th century.

On 1 January 1842 the besieged British garrison at Kabul, commanded by General William Elphinstone, made an agreement that safe passage for the soldiers and their dependants from Afghanistan would be granted. Five days later, the retreat began. The British column, more than 16,000-strong, was composed of about 4,500 British and Indian soldiers, along with as many as 12,000 camp followers. As they struggled through the snowbound passes, the British were picked off in a series of ambushes by Ghilzay tribesmen armed with Jezails. They were then massacred in close combat while moving through the 50km/30 miles of treacherous gorges and passes lying between Kabul and Gandamak.

After further wars, in 1893 the British succeeded in imposing control up to the Durand Line, a border that ran through the Afghan tribal lands between Afghanistan and what was then British India and thus divided Afghanistan.

BELOW The last stand of the 44th Regiment at Gandamak, during the retreat from Kabul in 1841. Cold was as much a killer as Afghan fire, but together they eventually killed more than 16,000 soldiers and camp followers in what became a Victorian military disaster.

16th-century technology

The 16th century saw great developments in weapons technology, much of which remains in use today. These innovations included the wheel-lock, which was invented around the turn of the century, although the actual inventor is unconfirmed. In addition, sights and rifling were major advances, and ensured that weapons could be aimed accurately and that the bullet had a straight flight path to the target.

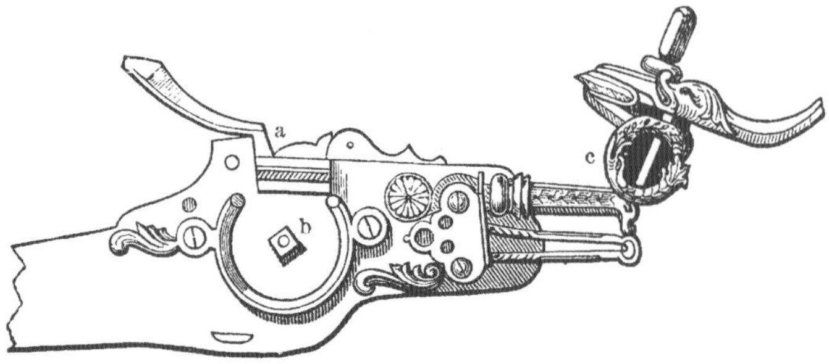

ABOVE The ingenious clockwork mechanism of the wheel-lock introduced in the 16th century was complex, but more reliable than earlier systems. However, the flintlock that would replace it would remain in widespread use for more than two hundred years.

The wheel-lock

Many scholars believe that the Italian genius Leonardo da Vinci invented the wheel-lock, in which a gun's firing mechanism was activated by sparks produced by friction between a small steel wheel and a flint. This belief is based on drawings of a wheel-lock mechanism which da Vinci made between the 1490s and 1510. However, there is a strong possibility that the inventor was actually an unknown German craftsman because a drawing dated 1505 has been found in a German book of inventions as well as a reference in 1507 to the purchase of a wheel lock in Austria.

By 1515 it appears that wheel-locks were in widespread use. A young man from Augsburg in Bavaria, southern Germany is reported to have invited a "handsome whore" to his room where, perhaps showing off his new "self-igniting pistol", he pulled the trigger and it went off, hitting her in the chin. During the plague of 1526 in Italy, Ben Vinito Cellini noted in his diary that he survived by shooting pigeons to eat with his wheel-lock rifle. It was either a good rifle or he was an excellent shot, since he rarely missed.

Across the Atlantic, inventories of public stores from the 1660s and archaeological sites show that a large number of wheel-locks had reached America.

Rifling

The spiral grooving in the bore of a firearm, which was used to spin-stabilize the projectile and so improve its accuracy after leaving the barrel, had been developed by the early 16th century. Rifling can have either an even or odd number of grooves as well as a direction of cut for the grooves that produces either a clockwise or anti-clockwise spin on the projectile. Modern handguns also usually have rifled barrels.

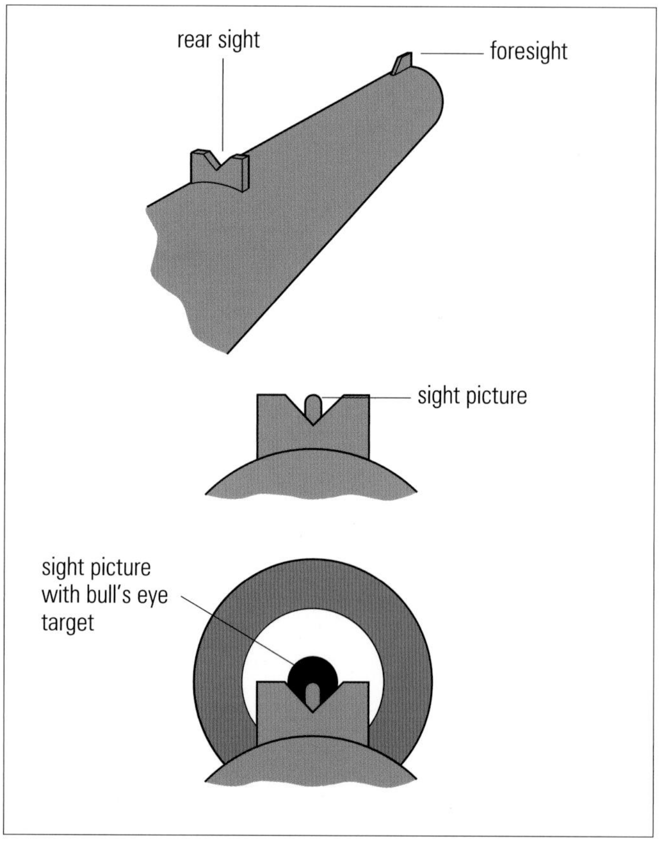

ABOVE The oldest and most basic form of sight consists of a foresight at the end of the barrel and a V-shaped rear sight close to the firer's eye. To aim the weapon, the firer positions the two sights so that the centre of the target is at the top of the foresight, which in turn bisects the V-shaped notch of the rear sight.

Matchlock drill

In 16th-century European armies, there was a strict set of orders for firing a musket. On the command "Handle your piece", the musketeer placed the weapon on the rest, near the point of balance. On receipt of the order "Take forth your match", he transferred the burning match from the left hand to the right hand. On the order "Blow off your coal", he blew off any loose ash from the burning end of the slow match. On the command "Cock your match", he clamped the burning end of the slow match between the jaws of the serpentine.

He flipped the pan cover over the priming powder and on the order "Try your match", operated the serpentine to ensure that the match would hit the powder. On the command "Guard your pan", he placed two fingers over the pan to ensure that random sparks did not fire it prematurely as he followed the order "Blow off the coal". He would then blow the match to make it glow.

On receipt of the last order "Present and give fire", he would swing the stock into his shoulder, open the pan cover and slowly pull the trigger to ensure that the match was not stubbed out as it was lowered into the pan. What followed was a spectacular bang and cloud of white smoke, and the lead ball went on its short and inaccurate journey.

RIGHT This illustration indicates the complexity of firing a 16th-century musket correctly; the musketeer was required to follow no less than 16 precise steps.

Sights

Matchlocks with simple sights appeared around 1537. Sights are the fittings on a firearm that help the user align the weapon accurately when it is pointed at a target. The first sights were in two parts: the foresight, a vertical post mounted at the muzzle, and the rear sight, a V-shaped notch mounted as far to the rear as possible and close to the firer's eye. To aim the weapon, the firer had a sight picture with the foresight in the centre of the notch and the target at the top of the foresight. However, with adjustable sights a weapon could be zeroed or adjusted to suit the individual shooter. With modern adjustable rear sights, to move the shot right, the firer moves the rear sight to the right. The sight is normally adjusted by two screws that can be loosened and tightened. Usually, sights have right-hand threads on their adjusting screws.

With adjustable foresights, the firer moves the sight adjuster in the opposite direction that he or she wishes the shot to go on the target. Optical sights are more accurate since they magnify the sight picture; they may have a crosshair, pointer or dot that the firer should place in the centre of the target.

Although electronic aids have been developed to provide training for soldiers, there is still a place for the range coach – a marksman who can observe a soldier as he or she fires on the range and adjust or zero the sights through various techniques to ensure accurate shooting.

Classic 16th-century designs

In 1517 and 1518, the first gun-control laws were introduced by Holy Roman Emperor Maximilian I, when he attempted to ban the manufacture or possession of matchlocks; being compact and more reliable than earlier firearms, they were seen as an ideal assassin's weapon. The matchlock nevertheless remained popular as a sporting arm and weapon. Meanwhile, the new Spanish musket became a common weapon of war for nearly a century.

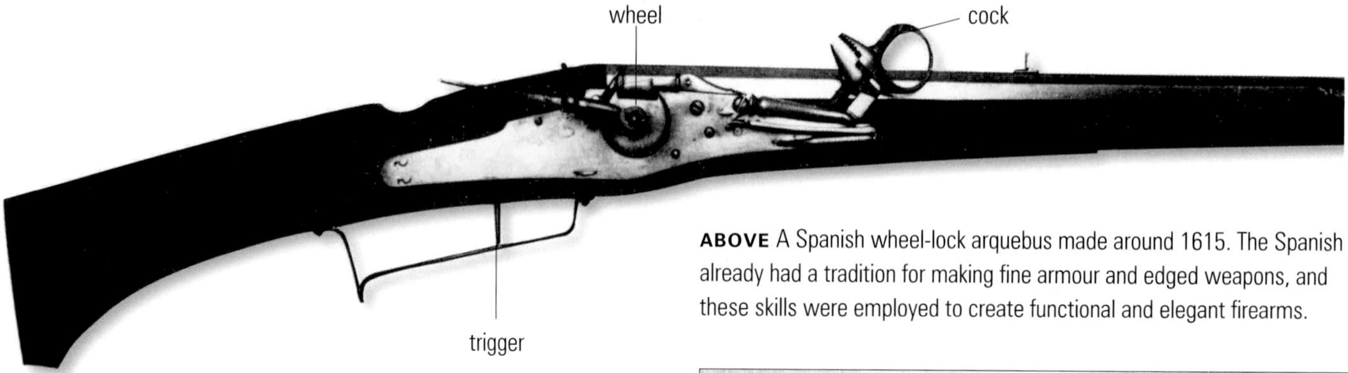

ABOVE A Spanish wheel-lock arquebus made around 1615. The Spanish already had a tradition for making fine armour and edged weapons, and these skills were employed to create functional and elegant firearms.

ABOVE Big men were needed to carry and fire the Spanish musket. It required a forked rest to spread the weight when the musketeer moved it into the aim. The musketeer has gunpowder reloads slung in a bandolier across his chest.

Spanish muskets

Around 1521 the Spaniards constructed the large and heavy musket, which gave them military superiority. The Spanish musket quickly gained popularity throughout Europe owing to its power and reliability. Early types fired a ball about 160m/175yd and were no more accurate than the arquebus. However, later types of Spanish musket proved to be far more lethal weapons than the arquebus at long range, with the ability to reliably penetrate armour at 90m/100yd and kill an unprotected man or horse at 460m/500yd.

This advantage was to some extent gained by sheer size. A 16th-century arquebus was big, weighing around 4.5kg/10lb with a bore diameter of about 60 calibre (sixty-hundredths of an inch). Spanish muskets, however, were even bigger, weighing at least 8.2kg/18lb and with a bore diameter of 70–85 calibre, with some as large as 90 calibre. The large calibres meant that the ammunition was proportionately bigger; while an arquebus fired a ball that weighed about 12g/0.5oz, the musket fired a full 50g/2oz lead ball.

The penalty for firing such a powerful weapon was a huge recoil. Some of this was absorbed by the weight of the weapon. However, to be effective, these muskets required big, muscular men to fire them. This restricted their use and produced a new military elite – the musketeer. The Spanish musket was excellent

Wheel-lock and snaphance

The wheel-lock mechanism used a fluted or grooved steel wheel located above the priming pan and held under tension by a strong spring. The cock was also regulated by a spring and fitted with a piece of iron pyrite. To fire the gun, the lock was wound up with a key, then the cock was let down on the priming pan, so that the pyrite rested on the wheel. To ignite the powder in the pan, the trigger was pressed which caused the wheel to be released and spin round quickly. The sparks produced then ignited the powder. The lock was not only complicated and expensive but also prone to damage, which prevented its wider adoption. Wheel-lock and matchlock combinations were fairly common because many wheel-lock mechanisms were unreliable. Such a gun would function as a regular wheel-lock, but if the wheel-lock broke or malfunctioned the user would still be able to fire the gun using the matchlock.

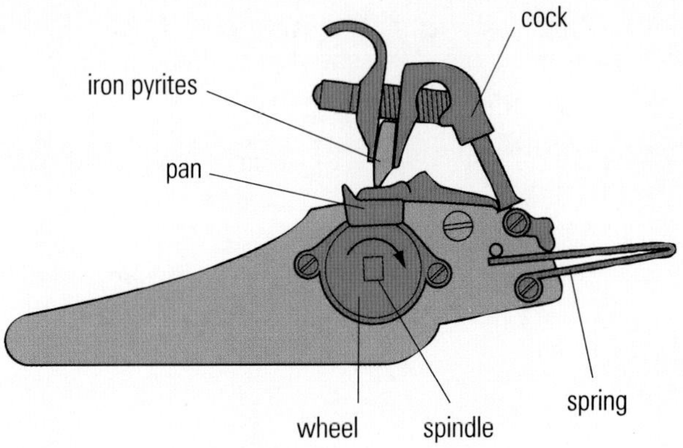

ABOVE The wheel-lock was an efficient but complex mechanism that never entirely replaced the much more basic matchlock in military use. The wheel-lock was popular with aristocratic hunters and sportsmen as an obvious demonstration of their wealth.

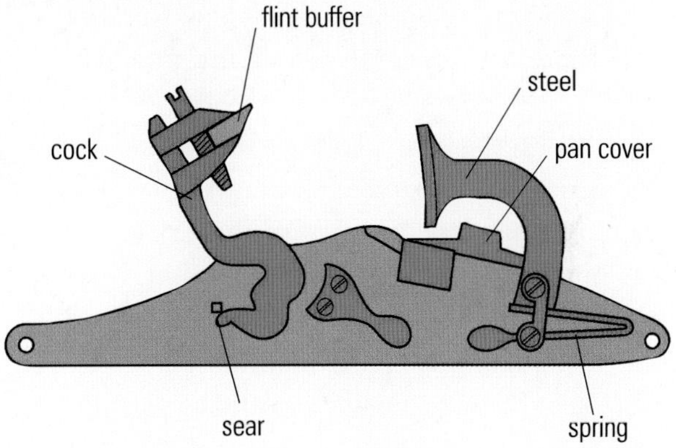

ABOVE The snaphance marked a new innovation since it used flint and steel to ignite the powder. When the trigger was pulled, the pan covering the powder opened mechanically as the flint scraped down the face of the steel to produce sparks.

in siege warfare and aboard ships, where the weight presented less of a problem. (Ottoman shoulder arms, similar in proportion to Spanish muskets, proved very effective in sieges.) The Spanish musket soon came into general use throughout Europe and was introduced into England in the early 16th century.

Elegant wheel-locks

The wheel-lock was first used in action at the siege of Parma in 1521 and was brought to England in 1530, where it continued in partial use until the reign of Charles II (1660–85). It had actually been developed for hunting, and some elegant weapons were made for wealthy clients.

The Metropolitan Museum, New York has an early multi-shot wheel-lock pistol made by Peter Peck of Munich, who worked as a watchmaker and gunsmith between 1503 and 1596. It was made for Emperor Charles V *c.*1540–45. Each barrel had separate ignition which was achieved by two locks being combined in one mechanism. Made from cherry wood, staghorn and steel, the .46-calibre pistol was decorated by Ambrosius Gemlich with the emperor's dynastic and personal emblems: the pillars of Hercules with the Latin motto *Plus ultra* ("More beyond") and the double-headed imperial eagle.

The National Maritime Museum in Greenwich, England has an elegant wheel-lock rifle made in Dresden, Germany in 1664. The stock is made from dark brown wood, partially decorated with inset ivory or bone panels, and the calibre is approximately .33. Utility combines with beauty where, on the right side of the rifle, a sliding trap covers a patch or toolbox let into the side of the butt. The rifle has a horn butt plate and is decorated with pieces of bone or ivory.

Tools of the trade

Men in the 17th and 18th centuries armed with muzzle loaders such as the doglock, miquelet and flintlock required a number of essential pieces of equipment in the field. These would enable them to carry gunpowder securely and maintain their weapons sufficiently when on campaign in all weather conditions.

Powder, flasks and horns

Gunpowder or black powder (also known as *poudre N*, or *poudre noir*) becomes useless with even the slightest amount of moisture, so it had to be kept absolutely dry. It was therefore normally carried in a powder horn or flask often made from a cow's horn. Horn has been described as the equivalent of today's plastic: it was light, strong and completely waterproof.

The flask or horn was designed so that at the wider end black powder could be poured in and then closed off with a cap. At the narrow end there was a spout with a cap. To load his weapon, the muzzle loader tipped the horn forwards to allow sufficient powder into the barrel before ramming wadding and the ball home and then pouring powder into the pan. From around the late 16th century, musketeers carried individual loads in wooden containers attached to a belt slung across their shoulders. Later soldiers carried powder loads in waxed paper cartridges. (Even in the 21st century, good-quality writing paper is still known as cartridge paper.)

Just as many sporting and early military weapons were elaborately engraved, powder flasks and horns were also carved and had elegant metal fittings.

ABOVE A 17th-century musketeer uses his powder horn to load an exact amount of gunpowder into the barrel of his weapon. The powder horn was strong, light and waterproof and could be slung over the soldier's shoulder when not in use.

Bullet moulds and flints

Besides the horn or flask an essential item was a bullet mould. This looked a little like a pair of pliers but had a dimple into which molten lead could be poured. When it had filled the mould the excess was removed with a simple cutter.

Soldiers might also carry a simple metal tool that incorporated several implements for cleaning and servicing their muskets. Today such a tool, called a combination tool, is found in all modern military cleaning kits.

Finally, spare flints were essential, since flint can split or shatter, and without a flint to strike a spark, weapons such as the snaphance, flintlock or miquelet would be useless. Most flints had a useful life of about twenty shots.

The doglock

Named after the dog safety catch behind the cock, the doglock musket replaced the Jacobean English lock of the early 17th century and was a transitional design between the snaphance and flintlock. A "dog" or safety catch was engaged to hold the heel of the hance in a half-cock position.

The doglock entered widespread use around 1640 and was popular with the British Army until about 1715. It remained in use as a regular issued weapon in the Royal Navy for many years after this and eventually evolved into the Sea Service musket of the 1730s. This musket was very popular in the colonies from the Caribbean to Canada. The common early British trade gun with the serpentine side plate was modelled after this musket as well. Many of these rugged muskets were used right up to the Revolutionary War in America by colonial troops as well as Native Americans.

By 1700 the doglock had evolved into a beautiful and sleek weapon complete with brass hardware that was unique to Britain and its colonies. While flintlocks without dog catches started to surface at this time, the doglock would have been one of the principal weapons in Marlborough's army when he defeated the French at the Battles of Blenheim in 1704, Ramillies in 1706, Oudenaarde in 1708 and Malplaquet in 1709, during the War of the Spanish Succession (1701–14).

Excavations of 17th-century Native American burial sites have unearthed doglock muskets. The doglock long fowler – a long-barrelled hunting weapon – was the most popular trade gun from 1625 to 1675. Native Americans valued it not only for hunting but also as a prestige item and for use in self-defence. These later doglocks had vertically attaching sear springs, and often the tumbler had notches for half- and full-cock positions. The cock (or hammer) was long and slender in style.

ABOVE The dog safety catch can be seen holding the cock back on this doglock musket. The hammer that held the flint was called a cock because it looked like a bird's beak and snapped forwards in a pecking action. Even today soldiers "cock" their rifles when they operate the bolt.

The miquelet and flintlock

The miquelet lock was named after Catalan militia leader Miquelot de Prats. Popular in the Mediterranean area from the 16th to 19th centuries, it was a distinctive flint-on-steel ignition mechanism. The design is attributed to an anonymous Italian gunsmith working for a Madrid gunmaker, Pedro Marquart, in the mid-1570s. This prototype was refined by Madrid gunsmiths into the Spanish patilla style now commonly known as the miquelet. A distinctive Italian miquelet lock was also developed.

With its combined battery and pan cover, the miquelet was the final innovative link that would be both the precursor and companion to the flintlock.

The flintlock was a refinement in which the steel and pan cover were made in one piece. When the trigger was pressed, the cock scraped the flint down the length of the steel, simultaneously uncovering the pan and exposing the prime charge to a stream of sparks. It was a simple and effective mechanism that would remain in use for over two centuries.

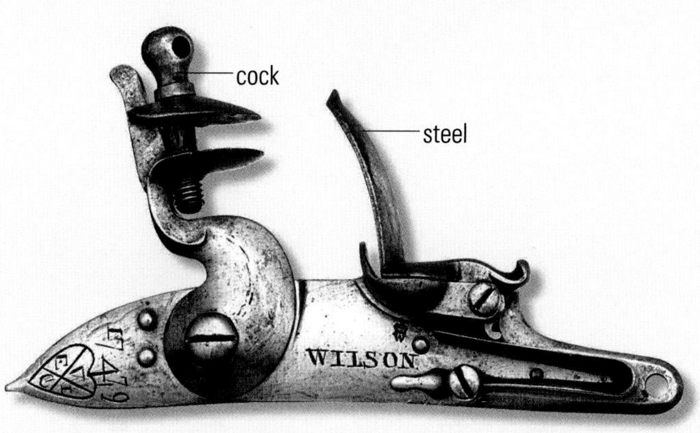

RIGHT A military flintlock from the late 18th century. Though it bears the maker's name and would have been handmade, it was no elaborately engraved work of art but rather a utilitarian weapon suitable for the new mass armies of the Napoleonic Wars.

Three special muskets

The Kentucky rifle was made famous as the weapon carried by "Hawkeye", the colonial trapper Nathaniel Poe, in James Fenimore Cooper's novel *The Last of the Mohicans*. The blunderbuss was a short-range weapon that fired a load of heavy gauge shot (not scrap metal, as has been suggested). In the 18th century the British Army received the "Brown Bess" musket, a reliable weapon that would serve it well through the Napoleonic Wars and the colonial campaigns around the world.

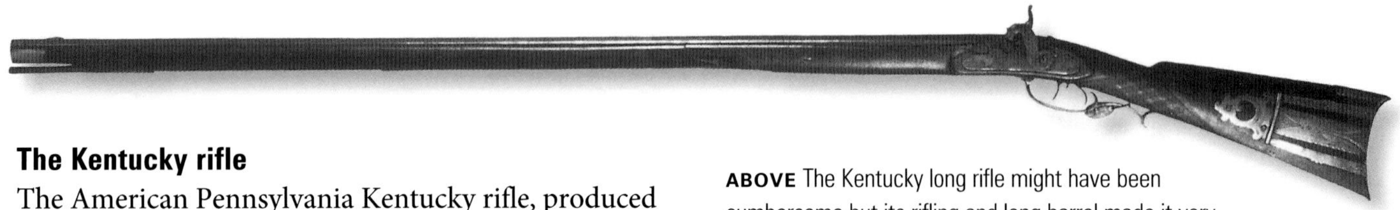

ABOVE The Kentucky long rifle might have been cumbersome but its rifling and long barrel made it very accurate. The settlers in North America found it an invaluable weapon for hunting, though it was also a very effective military arm.

The Kentucky rifle

The American Pennsylvania Kentucky rifle, produced in 1700, was much longer than an ordinary musket and very cumbersome to load while in battle. An expert rifleman could load and fire a shot in 1.5 minutes. However, the rifling provided greater range and accuracy and made the Kentucky ideal for sniping.

The blunderbuss

In the early 18th century, the blunderbuss (also called the blunderbess) was a popular weapon for close range fighting. Like a shot gun, it produced a lethal blast of shot or ball. In the mid-1700s, it was in widespread use by soldiers, sailors and civilians for close-quarter defence and its popularity lasted for nearly forty years. It is reported that George Washington proposed that instead of the carbine, Continental Dragoons should carry a blunderbuss because this weapon was not only easy to handle but actually more accurate with its spread of shot.

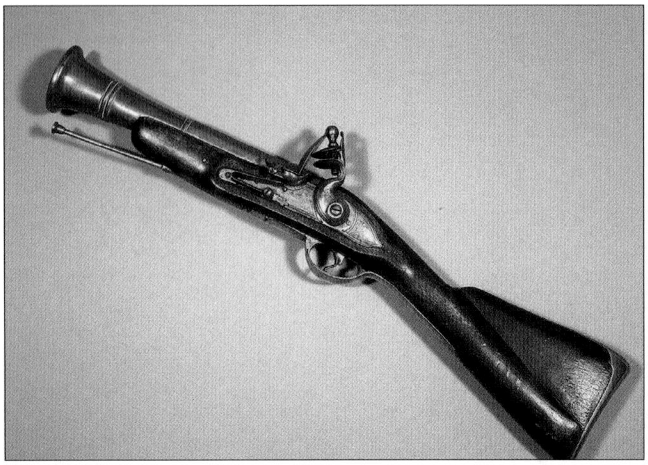

ABOVE The blunderbuss, with its short barrel and bell-shaped muzzle, delivered the same sort of lethal punch as a sawn-off shotgun. As such it was favoured by naval boarding parties for its shock effect at close range.

Blunderbusses were manufactured with both brass and steel barrels during the 18th century. On board ship, often the steel barrels were japanned (covered with a heavy black lacquer); this protected them against salt corrosion. A typical Royal Navy boarding blunderbuss was 775mm/30.5in long with a 370mm/ 14.5in brass barrel, 64mm/2.5in diameter at the muzzle. In the American colonies, settlers armed themselves with blunderbusses. Across the Atlantic, by the late 18th century the blunderbuss had gained fame as the weapon carried by British coachmen to thwart attacks by highwaymen. It was also the weapon of choice of pirates and privateers at sea.

The Brown Bess

The origin of the nickname "Brown Bess" is unknown but it was the affectionate name for the British Army's Land Pattern musket and its derivatives. It entered British service in 1722 and became as important symbolically as it was in practical terms in the field, since this was a period of global expansion. The Long Land Pattern musket and its derivatives, all in .72 and .705 calibre flintlock, were the standard infantry weapons from 1722 until 1838, although there were many incremental changes in its design. These versions include the Sea Service musket, New

ABOVE A re-enactor from the Coldstream Regiment of Foot Guards in the uniform of the late 18th century takes aim with his "Brown Bess" musket. With some minor modifications the Brown Bess would be a great survivor, remaining in service into the early 19th century.

Land Pattern, Short Land Pattern, India Pattern and new Long Land Pattern musket. The earliest models had iron fittings but after 1736 these were replaced by brass, which did not rust. Wooden ramrods were also replaced by more robust iron ones. However, up until 1765, muskets with wooden ramrods were still issued to troops on American service and those fighting for the Crown in the Revolutionary War. Wooden ramrods were also used in the Dragoon version produced from 1744 to 1771 and to reduce problems of corrosion for the Royal Navy and Marine muskets.

Muskets in action

Infantry soldiers were armed with a musket and a bayonet. The musket was muzzle loading with a flintlock mechanism at the butt end of the barrel. The soldier's normal ammunition load was 24 cartridges. Each cartridge contained a single load of gunpowder and a spherical lead ball. When loading, the soldier ripped open the paper cartridge with his teeth and poured a small quantity of powder into the firing pan. He poured the remainder of the charge into the muzzle of the musket, followed by the cartridge paper as a wad, and poked the charge to the bottom of the barrel with the ramrod.

The soldier then put the musket ball into the barrel so that it rolled to the bottom (or he pushed it down with the ramrod), on top of the charge of gunpowder. The soldier cocked the flintlock mechanism, aimed the weapon at the target and pulled the trigger. This caused the flint to strike, producing sparks and igniting the powder in the firing pan, which flashed through the touchhole and set off the charge. The musket discharged the ball with a flash, a considerable quantity of smoke and a roar. A well-trained soldier was able to fire his musket two or three times in a minute.

Guns of the Revolution

In 1776 the United States was locked in war with Britain, the colonial power, and was desperate for muskets. In the spring of that year, the US Congress sent a secret agent to France to ask the king for help in the form of weapons, equipment and financial support. The 1766 musket, shipped over by France, would later be replaced by the home-produced US 1795 musket, made at the Springfield Armory.

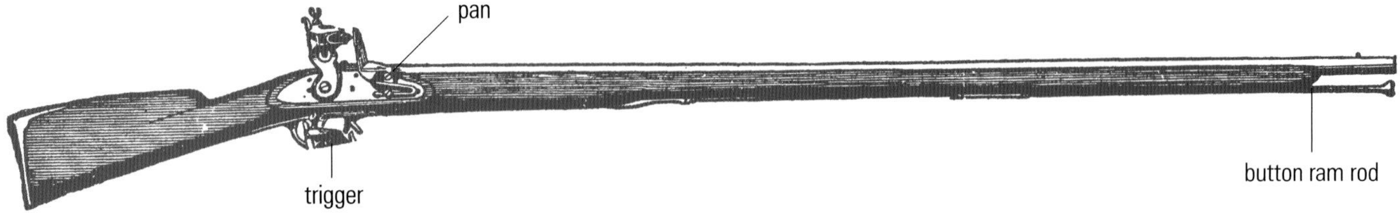

ABOVE The French were responsible for supplying many of the muskets used by the colonists against the British in the American War of Independence. Their Model 1766 was a simple and reliable weapon that was copied by the US Armory at Springfield, Massachusetts.

Safety muskets

On 18 July 1775 the Continental Congress passed the following resolution: "that it be recommended to each colony to appoint a Committee of Safety to superintend and direct all matters necessary for the security and defence of their respective colonies, in the recess of their assemblies and conventions". Several colonies had already begun to acquire muskets from private contractors and builders. Many are signed, and others are attributed to known makers based on similarities to signed muskets or guns made by builders who had connections with the various Committees of Safety.

ABOVE A re-enactor dressed as a civilian soldier in the War of Independence. His simple hunting clothes would have been comfortable and have given him a tactical edge over British troops dressed in the cumbersome uniforms favoured by European armies. He would also have been a skilled hunter and an accurate shot.

Musket drill 1764

Musket drill in the mid-18th century was based around a series of commands. On the order "Poise your Firelocks", the soldier took his musket in his right hand, and turned the lock outwards, while keeping the musket upright. He then swung the musket off his shoulder and grasped it with his left hand just above the lock with the little finger resting upon the spring, and the thumb on the stock.

At the command to "Cock your Firelocks", he turned the barrel towards his face, placed his thumb upon the cock, with his elbow square in this position. He then cocked the action and positioned his thumb on the breech pin and fingers under the trigger guard.

On the command "Present", he moved his right foot about six inches to the rear. At the same time the musket butt was moved to shoulder height, with the left hand on the wooden stock, and the right-hand forefinger on the trigger or "Tricker". The muzzle was lowered a little to compensate for the recoil.

When the order to "Fire" was given, the soldier pulled the trigger. As soon as his musket had fired he moved into the priming position ready to reload.

Genuine Committee of Safety muskets are rare, since they were mostly used up in the early days of the war. During the American War of Independence, a veteran militiaman armed with a Committee of Safety musket could load and fire three shots per minute.

French Model 1766 Musket

Three years after it was introduced in 1763, several modifications were made to the new French Infantry musket to create the French Model 1766 Musket. It was lighter in weight, with a smaller lock and a ramrod shaped like a flat button, known as the button-head ramrod design. Vast numbers of these muskets were produced for the French Army by an arsenal in Charleville in the Champagne–Ardennes region of north-eastern France.

When the request for arms came from the United States, the French, happy to wage a proxy war with Britain, provided the rebellious colonists with shiploads of muskets. Since France was not at war with Britain, various ploys were adopted that now seem very modern: a fake corporation had to be set up to mask the French government's direct involvement; in addition to this, ship's logs were falsified to conceal the ultimate destination of the muskets. Because the Royal Navy dominated the high seas, some French ships sailed to the West Indies and dropped off their cargo of muskets, where American vessels then collected them.

The Model 1766 had a powerful influence on the United States. Most of the surviving French-made muskets that have US markings are the Model 1766 and, in 1795, the United States used this musket as the template when it started mass production of its own at the Springfield arsenal.

The US 1795 musket

Colonel Henry Knox of General George Washington's staff decided that the area near Springfield, Massachusetts would be an ideal location for an ordnance depot to store arms and ammunition during the American Revolution.

A small depot was created in 1776, and Congress established it as a national armoury in 1794. The Springfield Armoury went on to produce arms for the United States for nearly 175 years.

When it began operations, Springfield had only 40 workers available, but in its first year managed to make 245 muskets. The first musket produced was the Model 1795, which was almost a direct copy of the French Model 1766 Charleville musket. Eventually, Springfield Armory would make 80,000 muskets and the armoury at Harpers Ferry in eastern West Virginia a further 70,000. The Model 1795 was carried during the ground-breaking Lewis and Clark expedition in 1803–06 and used in action during the 1812 war between the United States and Britain.

ABOVE At the height of the Napoleonic Wars, a grenadier of Napoleon's Imperial Guard protects the emperor. The grenadier has a Charleville 1777 musket supported in the crook of his arm.

Art and utility

Two types of firearm used in the 19th century are at the extreme end of weapons design. The miquelet, produced in Turkey, was more a work of art than a weapon. By contrast, the Baker rifle, used by British riflemen in the Peninsula War, was a functionally efficient weapon, and the soldiers who used it were trained to make the most of its potential.

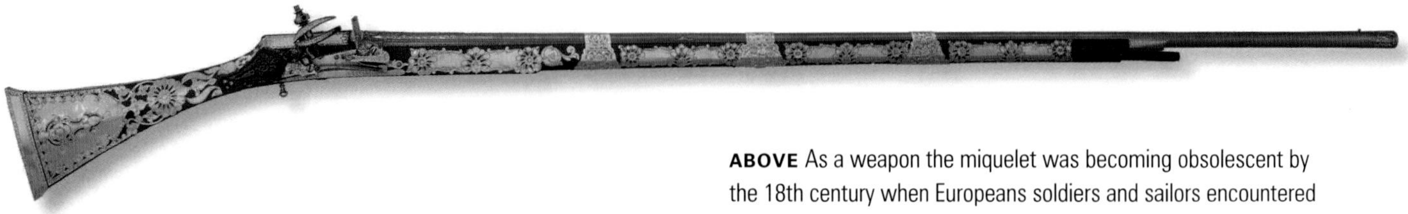

ABOVE As a weapon the miquelet was becoming obsolescent by the 18th century when Europeans soldiers and sailors encountered it. However, as a trophy it was exquisite, since the workmanship and designs were now no longer produced in an increasingly utilitarian European arms industry.

The miquelet

An example of a Turkish miquelet from around 1760 that came up for sale in 2006 on an internet site, with an asking price of £1300 ($2,500), shows how beautiful the work was on these weapons. It has a .60 calibre, 117cm/46in Damascus barrel that has a little silver inlay work. The gunsmith took the Ripoll pistols of Catalonia for his inspiration for the brass overlay decoration of the stock and copied a Spanish mechanism for the lock. Using a punch, the lockplate was signed in Arabic script and was extensively inlaid and overlaid with silver. The barrel may have come from a 17th-century Persian matchlock, since barrels and other parts were often reused. Miquelets like this reached Europe through trading contacts in the Balkans, part of the Ottoman Empire at the time.

A Turkish miquelet was bequeathed by Admiral Lord Nelson to Alexander Davison, his friend and prize agent, together with a water canteen and scimitar. It is a beautiful weapon with an inscription on the butt: "This gun together with a skymetar and canteen were presented by the Grand Signor to Horatio Viscount Nelson and by will bequeathed to his friend Alexander Davidson 10 May 1803." It has a Turkish variant of the Spanish miquelet lock with gold *koftgari* decoration. The stock is ivory and is decorated with silver and gilt studs with bands of gilt brass and mother-of-pearl. It has been suggested that the rifle, scimitar and canteen may have been gifts from the Sultan of Turkey to this successful and charismatic sailor. In 1873 Davison's son gave the rifle to Greenwich Hospital, and it was originally displayed with other Nelson relics in the Painted Hall at the National Maritime Museum in Greenwich, London.

The Baker rifle

This weapon was designed and made by Ezekiel Baker, who was not an innovator but took all the best features in the current European designs. With a seven-groove

LEFT A print produced in 1813 shows riflemen of the 60th and 95th Regiments armed with the superb Baker rifle. Their camouflaged dark-green uniforms and dedicated personal weapon marked them out as an elite within the British Army.

Napoleonic Wars 1792–1815

The wars fought by Britain and European powers against the nationalistic and ambitious French leader Napoleon Bonaparte marked a significant change in the practice of land warfare.

Although there were few innovations in weapons design, the French employed conscription to produce huge armies, and had a flexible form of command that allowed forces to concentrate on the battlefield and achieve overwhelming superiority. The British, who were leaders of the Industrial Revolution, fielded comparatively small armies but had an industrial power base that allowed them to supply arms to many of the allies facing Napoleon. The effects of combining the mass production of weapons and the mass conscription of military-age men began a devastating, grand-scale brand of warfare, which would next be demonstrated in the American Civil War and later in the two world wars.

BELOW The critical moment in the Battle of Waterloo, when Napoleon committed the Old Guard in the last hours of 18 June 1815. Massed volley fire followed by a savage bayonet attack would break their ranks and lead to the British victory.

quarter-turn 76cm/30in rifled barrel, the Baker rifle was robust, soldier-proof and relatively easy to load. The rifle was originally produced in .705, the same calibre as the "Brown Bess" infantry musket in order to standardize ammunition supplies. It was later reduced to .615in, the standard ammunition used for cavalry carbines. This made the rifle lighter and easier to handle. The final innovation was specially designed ball ammunition cartridges.

Most riflemen were permitted to practise with live ammunition. They aimed to accurately fire two shots per minute against human-sized targets at ranges of around 137–183m/150–200yd, a remarkable degree of accuracy given that the ordinary soldier fired his musket in volleys and was not accurate over 68m/75yd. The barrel of the rifle was browned to prevent sunlight reflecting and giving away the camouflaged rifleman's position. In his toolbag, each man carried a supply of cleaning patches, new flints, a worm and tommy bar to service his rifle as well as a turnscrew and ballpuller.

The Baker rifle of the Peninsular War period came with a 60cm-/24in-long sword bayonet. Although handy for camp tasks, it was rarely used in combat.

The last flintlocks

The Prussian Jäger rifle and the Mississippi rifle were examples of weapons built by countries that did not have a large industrial base. The British, by contrast, who were entering the Industrial Revolution, embarked on more systematic weapons production and design rationalization with their Short Land Pattern and India Pattern muskets.

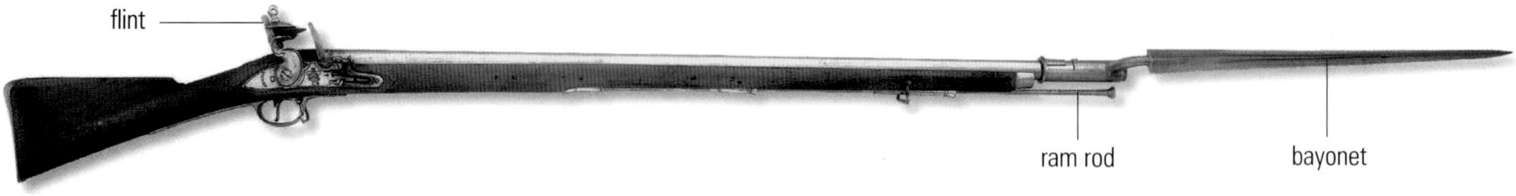

ABOVE The India Pattern musket was a remarkable survivor. Developed in the mid-1790s, it was a good weapon that remained in service with some regiments of the British Army – particularly with the volunteer militia based on the British mainland – as late as the 1850s.

The Prussian Jäger rifle

The German states built their own weapons for their armed forces, and the compact 14.7mm calibre Prussian rifle was widely copied in the 18th century. The Swiss, with a long tradition of marksmanship, produced a longer-barrelled .72 Jäger rifle with two triggers. One was set for accurate shooting and required only the lightest pressure to operate.

The Mississippi rifle

In 1846–48, before the American Civil War, the United States was at war with Mexico. American forces under Zachary Taylor campaigned against substantial Mexican forces, using the Mississippi rifle. Produced around 1841, it would later see service with the Southern armies. It was distinctive as the first rifle, as opposed to musket, to be adopted by the US Army. The first formation to go into action with the rifle was composed of men from Mississippi and so it became known as the Mississippi rifle. One example that came up for sale in 2006 showed that it had enjoyed a varied military career. The lock plate was marked "Tryon U.S.", which indicates manufacture by a private contract rather than at Springfield or Harpers Ferry, and rear of the lock "Philada PA 1847". The gun was in good condition with excellent plum-brown wood with two cartouches, one to indicate it had seen action in the Mexican war, the other the Civil War, as it was altered to a .58in calibre. It had its original sights, and despite some pitting, it had strong rifling.

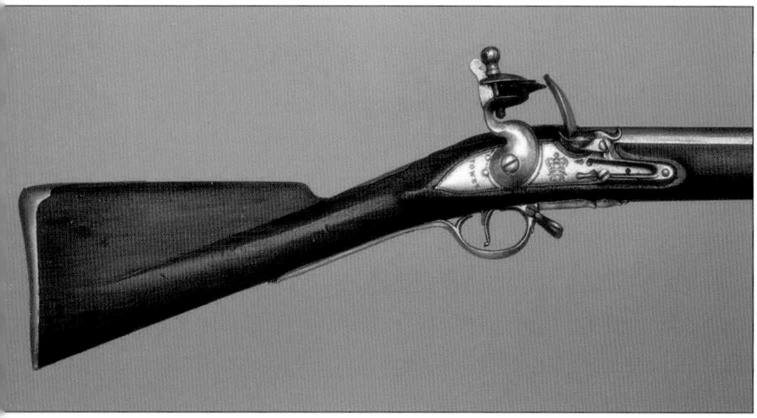

ABOVE The British Short Land Pattern musket was developed as part of a programme of rationalization for kit and clothing for the British Army in the mid-18th century.

Short land and India pattern muskets

In 1768, the Clothing Warrant was introduced to lighten the load that infantrymen had to carry. As a result a new musket called the Short Land Pattern Flintlock was issued to the British Army, which had a shorter overall length of 107cm/42in. In addition, swords were abolished for private soldiers (the exception being the Highland and Grenadier regiments) and uniforms were made less bulky.

The Short Land musket was widely used during the American Revolution and its popularity was such that a number of these black-powder muzzle loaders continued to be used by some regiments until the end of the Napoleonic Wars. Captured weapons were also added to the stocks of the American Continental Army. In addition, it was the most common rifle in the British Army until the 1790s, when it was replaced by the 3rd Model, or India Pattern.

ABOVE A group of Charleston Zouave cadets of the Confederate Army photographed in 1861, armed with the Model 1841 Mississippi rifle. The rifles had already seen service against the Mexicans before it became one of the many weapons fielded in the American Civil War.

Introduced during the mid-1790s, the India Pattern was a new pattern of flintlock musket that was slightly lighter than the Short Land, at under 4kg/9lb, and slightly shorter at 1m/39in. It had no thumb plate, and only three pipes for the ramrod. Developed and adopted by the East India Company in 1795, two years later the India Pattern was accepted by the Board of Ordnance of the British Army. The only modification to the three million or more muskets that were eventually made was the replacement in 1809 of the swan-necked cock by a more robust version. By 1839 the British had adopted a .75-calibre percussion musket, a transitional weapon built mostly from flintlock musket components. However, with so many Short Land and India Pattern muskets having been made, they were still in use by the British Army and the militia as late as 1850.

Volley firing

Throughout the 17th, 18th and 19th centuries, when smoothbore muskets were slow to load and inaccurate, short-range volley firing was an essential tactic. A trained soldier could fire a shot about every twenty seconds but could not expect to hit a human target beyond 73m/80yd. To accommodate this limitation, infantry soldiers fired in closely disciplined volleys, in which one rank would fire while the second reloaded. The firing rank might take place from the standing or kneeling position, while reloading was conducted from a standing position. A variation of this drill had a row of kneeling men with muskets and bayonets at a 45-degree angle, presenting a formidable barrier to enemy infantry or cavalry. A volley could also be fired by all the soldiers simultaneously, producing a crushing weight of fire which would then be followed up with a bayonet charge.

LEFT British soldiers, forming part of the Territorial Army, carrying Lee-Metford rifles just before World War I. In various versions, the Lee-Metford was the British Army's standard service rifle for over 60 years.

Rifles from 1800–2000s

The birth of modern weapons begins with the development of the percussion cap at the start of 19th century. Initially, this did away with the problems of priming with loose powder and the unreliability of the flint striking a steel plate to produce a spark. Paper cartridges had already been developed to hold a fixed charge of gunpowder, and once the first breech-loading system was developed in 1812, the cartridge and percussion cap could be married up with the bullet to produce a self-contained round. This was the work of Frenchman Eugène Lefaucheux with his pinfire cartridge in 1835, and in turn led to efficient feed systems for rifles. Early self-contained rounds weren't as reliable as the more primitive muzzleloading options, but by the third quarter of the 19th century, self-contained rounds had established a foothold that continues into the 21st century. Advancements in powder was the next significant invention. From black powder came smokeless powder, and the battlefield was no longer enveloped in the "fog of war" – clouds of white smoke. Cartridges were loaded with this powder in magazines, fired initially from bolt-action rifles and later from rifles with self-loading mechanisms. This chapter looks at developments in rifles up to the sniper and assault rifles of the late 20th century and into the first quarter of the 21st century.

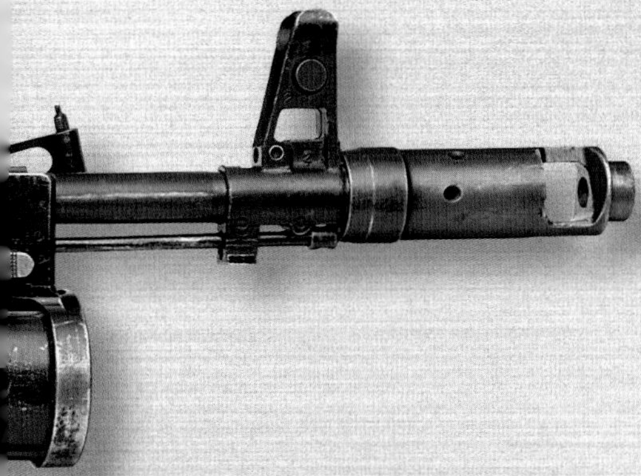

LEFT The AK-74 fitted with a grenade launcher. This enhancement copied from the United States proved very popular during the Soviet intervention in Afghanistan in the latter years of the 20th century.

BELOW The Springfield M1903 would equip the US Army in World War I and many units in World War II. It was one of a range of rifles produced by the Springfield Armory for the US Army that have the generic title Springfield rifle.

An inventive century

The mid-19th century saw two major developments in small arms technology: the Pauly cartridge and the Dreyse needle gun. Just as the percussion cap had advanced weapons technology in its day, so these two inventions would take it further and point to modern small arms of the 20th century. While the British 1853 Enfield rifle did not mark any significant technological advances, it did demonstrate ruthless commercial enterprise, since the British sold it to both sides in the American Civil War.

ABOVE The percussion lock of the British 1853 pattern Enfield rifle musket was used and copied in large numbers by both the Confederate and Union Armies in the American Civil War. The musket fired a big .577 bullet.

Jean-Samuel Pauly

In 1812–16 a Swiss inventor, Jean-Samuel Pauly, experimented with the production of a breech-loading rifle. For some time, firearms designers had hoped to produce an efficient breech-loading mechanism because allowing the soldier to load from the breech end reduces exposure to enemy fire and greatly increases his own rate of fire.

Pauly's solution was to fit a brass base to the cartridge case. This meant the base could expand to seal the breech, then contract when the gas pressure in the barrel fell after firing. The Pauly system was adopted by almost every firearm from the 1850s onwards. It did suffer from some technical problems however; the quality of the seamless drawn-brass cartridge tubing was inconsistent, and the cost made it too expensive except for specialist shooters. Another of his inventions was a centrefire primer, a percussion cap set into the middle of the rear end of the cartridge.

The needle gun

In 1824 Johann Nikolaus von Dreyse, a Prussian inventor, began experiments with breech-loading firearms. Dreyse's solution to the problem was to design the first bolt-action rifle. To load it, the soldier opened the breech to insert a cartridge made of stiff paper, containing a .61-calibre bullet and powder charge. He then closed the bolt home and turned it to lock the breech. When he pulled the trigger, a firing pin about 12mm/0.5in long penetrated the paper cartridge and set off a percussion cap inside it, just below the bullet. It was this firing pin, or needle, that gave the rifle its name.

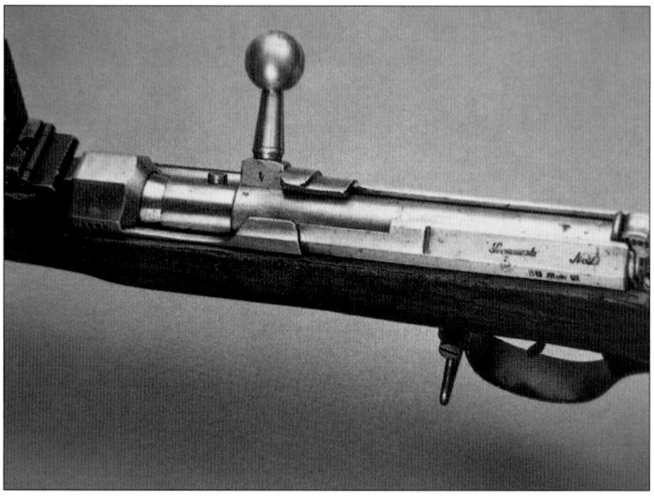

ABOVE The bolt-action, breech-loading rifle developed by the Prussian Nikolaus von Dreyse became widely known as the needle gun. It allowed soldiers to load and fire from the prone position and consequently remain undercover.

1807 percussion cap

One of the problems of flintlock weapons was that sometimes the priming powder didn't ignite because the lock wasn't able to keep it entirely dry. The solution was found in 1807 by Alexander John Forsyth who patented a priming powder made from an unstable mix of chlorate of potash, sulphur and charcoal, which exploded when it was struck. He saw it as a useful development for sportsmen who were wild fowling on wet days. It took 30 years for the technology to be recognized and adopted by the military authorities. In the meantime, it was gradually improved by gunmakers and private individuals, who developed the copper percussion cap.

Conservative Prussian soldiers disliked the new weapon despite its advantages. Unlike a muzzle loader, it did not require a complicated drill to reload. In the pressure of combat, a soldier with a muzzle loader might double load his weapon and then when he fired, it would explode in his face. The Dreyse design made this impossible since two rounds would not fit into the breach. Most significantly, the rate of fire increased from two rounds a minute for a muzzle loader to 10 to 12 rounds per minutes for the needle gun.

In time, weaknesses in the design were revealed. Gas often leaked through the bolt when the needle passed through, and the power of the explosion caused the needle to wear out rapidly or even break.

ABOVE The soldier armed: a New York State militiaman with his percussion lock musket, which has a fixed long-sword bayonet. The bayonet is still issued for modern combat rifles but is now used more as a multi-functional tool.

Made in Britain

In 1842 a new model percussion musket with a block or back sight set for 137m/150yd was issued to the British Army. It weighed 5.17kg/11.4lb, was 1.4m/1.5yd long without bayonet and 1.8m/1.9yd with bayonet fixed. It had a larger calibre than weapons issued to the soldiers of France, Belgium, Russia and Austria, which meant that British troops could fire continental ammunition but European soldiers could not fire British ammunition. The 1842 Pattern percussion musket was the final development of the "Brown Bess," which was used in the British Army until it was completely superseded by the Enfield rifle in 1855.

Although made in Britain, the .577-calibre 1853 Enfield rifle had the distinction of being the second most common infantry weapon of the American Civil War (1861–65). Weighing 4kg/9lb and measuring 140.5cm/55.3in, it was imported by Confederate and Union ordnance officers to meet the sudden increase in demand for small arms at the outbreak of war. It is estimated that 900,000 Enfields were eventually bought by both sides. The rifle was so named because it was originally produced at the Royal Small Arms Factory in Enfield, England, where it was the standard firearm of the British Army at the time. Several contractors later provided arms for export. Its .577 calibre made it compatible with .58-calibre ammunition, which was very common in the American armies.

Mid-19th-century wars

Although the combatants in the American Civil War bought arms from Great Britain, such as the Whitworth .451, they also had stocks of their own weapons, such as the Model 1842 percussion musket and the Model 1865 Spencer carbine. However, it was the bullet designed by Frenchman Claude-Etienne Minié that would play a major part in the war. Meanwhile in France, his fellow national Antoine Alphonse Chassepot had produced the innovative Modèle 1866 breech-loading rifle.

The Model 1842 rifled musket

The Harpers Ferry and Springfield Armories produced large numbers of the robust US Model 1842 rifled Percussion musket between 1844 and 1855. The Model 1842 was the last .69 calibre musket, but in addition it was the first weapon made at both the Harpers Ferry and Springfield Armory that had entirely interchangeable parts – an invaluable feature in the field. Harpers Ferry produced 103,000, while Springfield produced 172,000. As many of the muskets had been delivered to militias in the late 1850s, they were prominent in the early years of the American Civil War. About 14,000 were upgraded between 1856 and 1859 with rifling and around 10,000 were then fitted with rear sights.

The M1855 rifle and rifle-musket produced by the Union was copied by the Confederates at their Fayetteville Armory in North Carolina. The British even produced a version for export to the Union. Designated the P1856, it had a 33-inch long barrel and only two bands to secure the barrel to the stock. The rifles came with a sword rather than a spike bayonet; however as

RIGHT Private Thomas Taylor of the 8th Louisiana Infantry holds his Model 1842 musket. Taylor is well equipped with pack, canteen, ammunition pouches and a Bowie knife tucked into his belt.

BELOW The British Whitworth short rifle enjoyed a reputation for considerable long-range accuracy and was one of the first sniper weapons to be developed fitted with a telescopic sight.

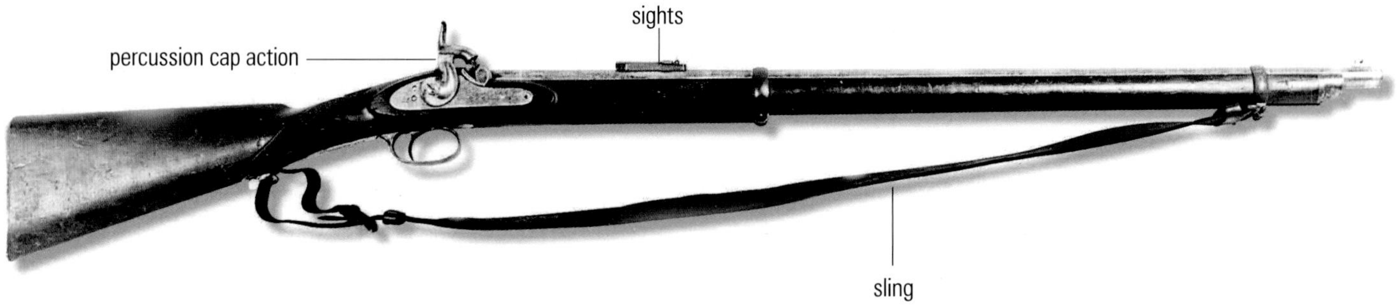

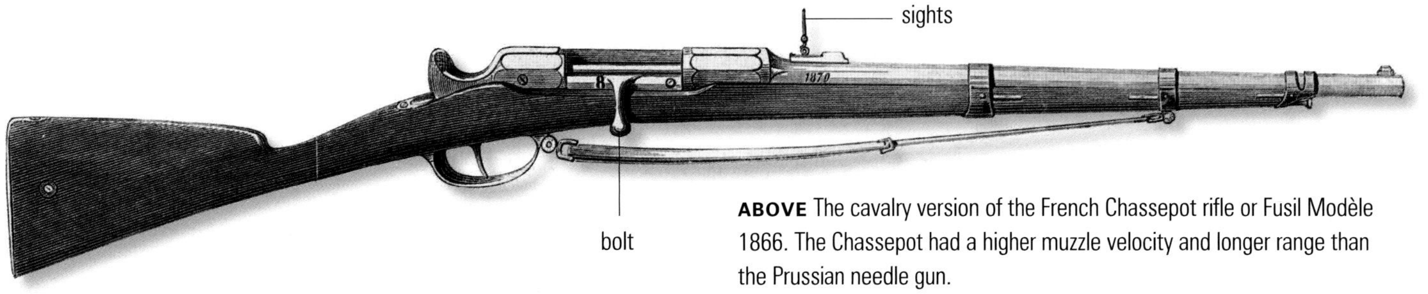

ABOVE The cavalry version of the French Chassepot rifle or Fusil Modèle 1866. The Chassepot had a higher muzzle velocity and longer range than the Prussian needle gun.

the blockade on the Confederacy began to bite, the factory at Fayetteville abandoned the sword bayonet in favour of the spike – a design that harked back to the Napoleonic Wars. The angled spike would survive into the 20th century with the Russian Mosin-Nagant rifle and be revived in a slightly different form with the British Lee-Enfield No. 4 rifle. However, soldiers preferred the sword bayonet, which was a practical tool rather than a weapon, handy for prising open tins and preparing food.

The Whitworth .451 short rifle

In 1863 the British Whitworth .451in short rifle was produced and bought by the Confederate government. It was an unusual weapon with a hexagonal barrel that fired a special hexagonal bullet. This made it more accurate than many modern sniper rifles, with a maximum reported range of around 1,830m/2,000yd. The Whitworth was equipped with a British-made mounted Davidson telescopic sight.

The Model 1865 Spencer carbine

In the Union, Christopher Spencer, noted as one of the leading engineers in the machine-tool industry, produced in 1860 a seven-round carbine that was accurate over long ranges. Spencer asserted that the seven rounds in his percussion carbine models could be loaded and capped and fired in less time than any other rifle. His carbine could fire faster than a revolver and be reloaded in a tenth of the time it would take to reload a Colt revolver. In 1865, Spencer modified and corrected the design flaws in the original weapon and produced the Model 1865 Spencer carbine.

Chassepot Modèle 1866

The "Chassepot", officially known as Fusil Modèle 1866, was the breech-loading rifle with which French forces were equipped in the Franco-Prussian War of 1870–71. It took its name from its inventor, Antoine Alphonse Chassepot (1833–1905), who, from 1857 onwards, had designed and developed various experimental forms of breech loader. The Modèle 1866 became the French service weapon in 1866. At the battlefield at Mentana, Italy on 3 November 1867, soldiers using the Chassepot inflicted severe losses upon the forces of the Italian nationalist leader, Giuseppe Garibaldi. This action fought during the Risorgimento (Italian unification) involved Garibaldi's forces, which had invaded the papal territory, facing the papal army and a French expeditionary force. Napoleon's empress Eugenie was keen on defending the papacy against the Republican threat.

In the Franco-Prussian War the Chassepot proved greatly superior to the Prussian Dreyse needle gun, although it had a smaller calibre of 11mm. The French rifle used more propellant and had a 33 per cent higher muzzle velocity; it also had a longer barrel and thus produced a longer range. The effective range was about 595m/650yd.

1849 Minié bullet

The innovative gunsmith Claude-Etienne Minié was born in 1814 in Paris. After serving as an officer in the French Army, in 1849 he developed the Minié rifle and bullet.

Inaccurately pronounced *minnie* and incorrectly called a ball, the bullet was a cylindro-conoidal (i.e., bullet-shaped) lead projectile fired from a muzzle-loading rifle. It was small enough to fit down the barrel of a rifle even when fouled with burned powder. When the rifle was fired, expanding gases entered the bullet's hollow base, pushing the outer edges into the rifling of the barrel. Since it greatly improved the accuracy, range and rate of small-arms fire, the Minié ball was rapidly adopted by the US Army. During the American Civil War, the Minié became one of the most widely used types of ammunition by the armies of the Confederacy and the Union.

Conversion rifles

The successful Snider P/53 was a converted rifle produced in Enfield from 1866. It was replaced by the 1871 Martini-Henry single-shot rifle, which was used by the British Army for 30 years and could truly be called the gun that served the empire. However, another conversion rifle – the American "trapdoor" Springfield – was a cost-cutting conversion that would prove unsatisfactory when tested in war.

The 1867 Snider rifle

It was an American, Jacob Snider, who invented the .577 weapon adopted by the British Army. The rifle that bore his name was adopted by the British Army to replace the Pattern 1853 rifled musket that had served in the Indian Mutiny and Crimea. However, to keep costs down, the muzzle-loading P/53 was altered to use the Snider system. The modified weapon was more accurate than the P/53 and soldiers could also fire it much faster. The ordnance factory in Enfield, London converted large numbers, beginning with the initial pattern, the Mark I in 1866. The conversion involved fitting a new breech block/receiver assembly but retaining the original iron barrel, furniture, locks and hammer. This rifle was replaced by the Martini-Henry rifle, which was adopted by the British Army in 1871.

The 1871 Martini-Henry

The British had taken an American idea for the Snider and in 1871 would now turn to the Swiss in the shape of Friedrich von Martini. Unlike the Snider-Enfield it replaced, the Martini-Henry rifle was Britain's first service rifle to be designed from the outset as a breech-loading rifle for metallic cartridges. Martini designed the falling block, self-cocking, lever-operated, single-shot action. It was an American, Henry Peabody, who had originally designed this action; however, his had an external hammer that struck the firing pin. Martini's refinement consisted of conversion to an internal

BELOW The 3rd Gurkhas in the 1880s skirmishing with the 1867 Snider-Enfield rifle. Elite troops from Nepal, the Gurkhas would serve with distinction in the British Army.

ABOVE A clear view of the slot through which a round was loaded into the breach in the Martini-Henry action. It allowed trained soldiers to keep up a high rate of fire, providing ammunition was readily available.

coiled spring-activated striker, which was much more soldier-friendly. The barrel used the rifling system designed by Alexander Henry.

It was the Martini-Henry that would save the day at Rorke's Drift on 22 January 1879, when 137 men, largely from the British 24th Regiment, held off about 4,000 Zulu warriors who had just scored a crushing victory over the British at Isandhlwana. The tiny garrison lost 25 men but won 11 Victoria Crosses.

The Springfield Model 1873

At the close of the American Civil War, the US recognized the need to obtain a reliable breech-loading rifle. Funds were tight, however, and the army had huge numbers of muzzle-loading weapons left from the war that it did not want to waste. The "trapdoor" rifle, denoting the method of opening the rifle at the top of the breech to load a cartridge, was developed as a result, and about 30,000 of the left-over rifles were converted to trapdoor models or, as they were more formally known, Allin Conversions.

Smokeless propellants

Poudre B or *poudre blanche* (white powder, to distinguish it from black powder), was the first smokeless propellant, developed around 1885 by Paul Vieille. Made up from nitrocotton and ether-alcohol, unlike black powder it did not produce clouds of white smoke when it was detonated. Subsequently, the prolific Swedish inventor Alfred Nobel added to the growing list of smokeless powders a substance called ballistite.

Ballistite contained two powerful explosives: a low-nitrogen content nitrocotton, gelatinized by nitro-glycerine. Meanwhile in Britain, Sir Frederick Abel and Sir James Dewar used acetone to produce probably the most effective and widely used smokeless powder propellant – cordite made from highly nitrated guncotton and nitro-glycerine. Mineral jelly was added to act as a lubricant. Now when rifles were fired the battlefield would no longer be enveloped in "the fog of war".

By 1868, instead of converting old weapons into trapdoor models, a new rifle was developed using the Allin action. This weapon was designated the Rifle Model 1868. It went through a series of minor modifications (1870, 1873, 1879, 1880, 1884 and 1889, as well as a few more specialized cadet and officer varieties), and was used for 30 years. The modification that represented the major difference between the M1873 and the M1889 was the replacement of the triangular bayonet with a rod bayonet; there were also a few other very minor modifications.

At the outbreak of the Spanish–American War, the current model was the Model 1889, which was used by the volunteer troops, despite being outdated in comparison with the widely available smokeless powder weapons.

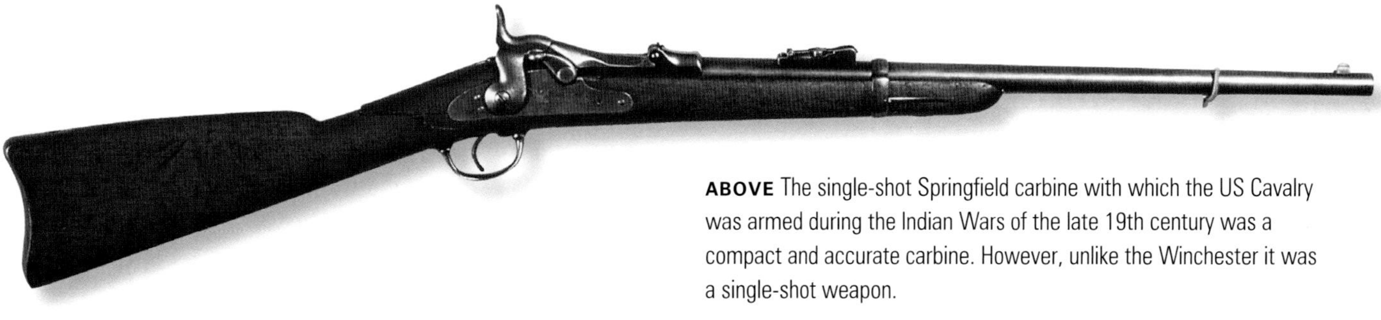

ABOVE The single-shot Springfield carbine with which the US Cavalry was armed during the Indian Wars of the late 19th century was a compact and accurate carbine. However, unlike the Winchester it was a single-shot weapon.

Historic guns

The American Winchester 1873 was not the first gun bearing the Winchester name, but its popularity earned it the nickname of "The Gun That Won the West". The British Lee-Metford had only a short operational life with the British Army, while the Italian Carcano 91/94 had a long and ultimately notorious history, due to its most famous owner. On 22 November 1963, Lee Harvey Oswald used a Mannlicher-Carcano serial number C2766 with an Ordnance Optics 4x18 scope to kill the US President John F. Kennedy in Dallas, Texas.

ABOVE The Mannlicher-Carcano Modello 91 was the standard bolt-action rifle used by the Italian Army in World War I. Like the SMLE with the British, it would carry on with the Italian infantry into World War II.

The Winchester

The first real Winchester was the Model 1866. The major change was the incorporation of a totally round magazine tube. Winchester's plant foreman, Nelson King, designed it to replace the slotted-tube design. There was a marked improvement in the reliability of the rifle since there was no ingress of dirt into the working parts. Frames were initially made of brass for the Model 1866 but when the Model 1873 was introduced, frames were made of steel. The Winchester was popular because the .44-centrefire ammunition was compatible with some handguns, and a man could carry a Winchester and a revolver and use the same rounds of ammunition for both weapons.

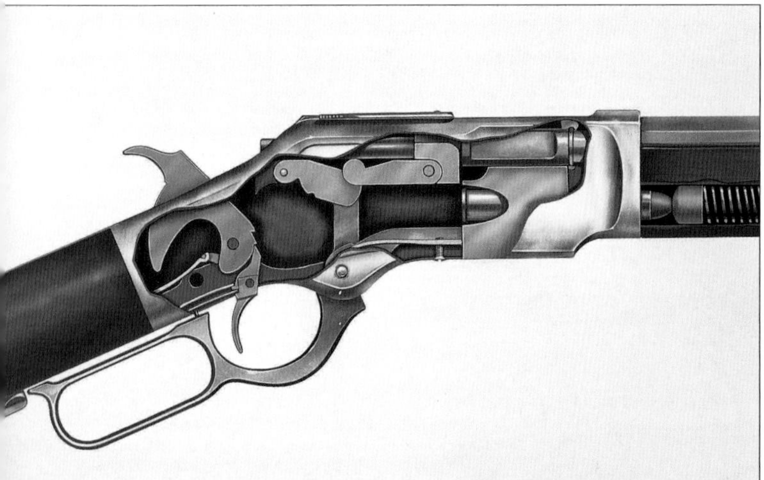

ABOVE The spring-loaded tube magazine on the Winchester Model 1866 fed rounds backwards when the lever was operated and as it was closed loaded them into the breach. It was a quick, reliable mechanism.

The Lee-Metford

Introduced in 1888, the Lee-Metford rifle, also known as the Magazine Lee-Metford or MLM by British soldiers, was a breech-loading service rifle. It combined James Paris Lee's rear-locking bolt system and ten-round magazine with a seven-groove rifled barrel designed by William Ellis Metford. Although nine years of development followed before it replaced the Martini-Henry rifle, it remained in service for only a short time until replaced by the similar Lee-Enfield.

At a time when most military rifles used smokeless powders, the Lee-Metford used a black powder-loaded rimmed .303in cartridge. It had been intended to fire a smokeless cartridge, but this was not available to the War Department when it entered service. The MLM design went through several variations; the main changes were to the magazine (from eight-round single stack to ten-round staggered), sights and safety catch. In 1914 some Territorial Army battalions were still equipped with the MLM.

Mannlicher-Carcano rifles

The Italian Carcano 6.5mm Fucile Modello rifle went through many modifications in the 1890s. The 1892 rifle was the first of the Mannlicher-Carcano rifles to be accepted by the Italian Army. The Mannlicher-

ABOVE Soldiers of the Civil Service Rifles, a British Territorial Army formation, armed with Lee-Metford rifles. The bolt action developed by James Lee would be incorporated into the Lee-Enfield rifle that was in service with the Regular Army.

Carcano system was based on the bolt action of the Mauser Model 1889 with the addition of the Carcano bolt-sleeve mechanism; the Mannlicher six-round clip-loading magazine was retained. The name of General Parravicino is often linked with this rifle; he headed the commission that introduced the rifle to the Italian Army. The Modello 91 was the standard Italian Army rifle during World War I and was still in use in 1940 in large numbers. The Germans took some over in 1943 to arm several of their units in Italy, and these were designated the Gew 214(i). During 1944 some were rebored for the German calibre of 7.92mm/0.31in.

In World War I, Italian soldiers fought Austro-Hungarian forces armed with the Mannlicher Model 1895. Made in Budapest in Hungary as well as Steyr in Austria, the Mannlicher M1895, also known as the Repetier Gewehr M95, was the principal Austro-Hungarian rifle. After World War I, the Italians received large numbers of Mannlichers as reparations from Austria and used them in large numbers. In World War II it was also used by the Bulgarians, Yugoslavs and to some extent by the Greeks.

A Winchester by any other name

In 1848 American small arms designer Walter Hunt developed the concept of the first repeating rifle, giving it the grand name of "Rocket Ball and Volition Repeater." A lever-action, tube-loading repeater, it eventually evolved into the Winchester Model 1873. A US patent was granted in 1849 for an improved design by a machinist named Lewis Jennings and Hunt's partner George Arrowsmith.

A large number of people were involved in improving on the original design, among them Benjamin Tyler Henry and Courtland Palmer. Henry later teamed up with two men whose names would become legendary – Horace Smith and Daniel Wesson of handgun fame – and together they further refined the design. The Volcanic Arms Company was formed in 1855 by Smith, Wesson and Henry to market the rifle. Among their investors was Oliver F. Winchester. He had no knowledge of firearms and was more of an expert on sewing machines. Yet he was a shrewd investor; two years after buying stock he owned the majority holding in Volcanic Arms. So in 1866 the name was officially changed to Winchester Repeating Arms Company and thus Winchester gave his name to "The Gun that Won The West".

World War rifles

The excellent bolt-action rifles produced at the close of the 19th and beginning of the 20th century, such as the German Gewehr 98, British SMLE and American M1903, were used in World War I and, with some modifications, remained in service during World War II.

ABOVE The German Gewehr 98 had an excellent bolt action, but its five-round magazine put a soldier at a disadvantage when he was up against a man armed with the SMLE and its ten-round box magazine.

The Gewehr 1898 and Kar 98k

The 7.92mm Gewehr 98, introduced into service with the Imperial German Army on 5 April 1898, was designed by Paul Mauser and became the standard German infantry weapon in World War I. While the Mauser action is superb (there are about 102 million rifles with the Model 98 bolt action worldwide), the rifle suffered from having a five-round magazine.

Massacre at Mons

In the hands of a trained soldier, the British Short, Magazine-Loaded Lee-Enfield was easily capable of 15 rpm of accurate fire. In the 1930s, a Small Arms School Corps Warrant Officer managed a rate of 37 rpm. This fast rate of fire proved significant in World War I.

Britain declared war on 4 August 1914 and when, by mid-August, the Belgians had been mauled by the German Army, only one intact force stood in the way of the Germans: the British Expeditionary Force (BEF). The first shots fired on 23 August by the BEF were at Malplaquet. The advancing German infantrymen were pulled up short near Mons as the withering rifle fire of the British caused them heavy casualties.

Two days later at Le Cateau the story of Mons was repeated, only on a bloodier scale. Once again the Germans attacked in tightly bunched waves and again they were met with rifle fire so intense that they thought the British were equipped with machine guns.

In 1939 German infantry entered World War II armed with the bolt-action Karabiner 98 kurz (Kar 98k), or Short '98 Carbine, developed from the Gewehr 98. The Kar 98k, first produced in 1935, weighed 3.9kg/8.6lb, was 1.11m/1.21yd long, and in its ten-year production life it was manufactured in its thousands in Germany, by FN in Belgium and Brno in Czechoslovakia.

A trained soldier could fire 15 rounds per minute (rpm) from a Kar 98k. Like all the 7.92mm calibre rifles, the maximum effective range of the Kar 98k was 800m/874yd.

The SMLE

In 1939 the British Army had a rifle with the official designation Short, Magazine-Loaded Lee-Enfield; this cumbersome name was more commonly shortened to SMLE. This weapon had been the standard infantry rifle in World War I and would remain so for much of World War II. A bolt-action weapon that fired a .303-calibre round, the SMLE weighed 3.9kg/8.6lb, was 1.13m/1.23yd long and had a ten-round magazine. Sights were set out to 1,830m/2,000yd.

The sword bayonet fitted to the SMLE had a formidable 43cm/17in blade. In the Sinai and Palestine campaign in World War I, the SMLE bayonet was in fact wielded like a cavalry sabre by the mounted infantrymen of the Australian 4th Light Horse in the Battle of Beersheba on 31 October 1917. In what is often called the last successful cavalry charge, the fast-moving horsemen cleared the Turkish defences in front of the town by stabbing and slashing. At the close of the fighting, the 4th Light Horse Brigade had taken Beersheba and captured 738 Turkish soldiers as well as

ABOVE British infantry in World War I in a secure area behind the front line clean their SMLEs. The rifle was easy to strip, and the mechanism could be operated to clear any dirt that might have fouled it in combat.

four field guns. In the two Australian regiments, only 31 men had been killed and 36 wounded as a result of this unique action.

The M1903

After the Spanish-American War of 1898, Erskine Allin, the Superintendent of the Springfield Arsenal, developed the M1903. It was a magazine-fed rifle that used a modified version of the Mauser Gewehr action and was 1.12m/1.23yd long and weighed 3.6kg/8lb. The M1903 was used by the American Expeditionary Force in France in World War I and continued as the issue US Army rifle until 1936. It was also used in World War II, however, owing to production problems with the M1A1, its intended replacement. It was utilised by snipers as the M1903A4, although because the scope was positioned directly over the action, reloading the magazine with five-round stripper clips was impossible, so rounds had to be loaded singly. The M1903A4 remained in service in World War II and the Korean War.

ABOVE US Infantry in dress blues, the full dress uniform worn in the early 20th century in a garrison base. The men are armed with the modern M1903 rifle, which was introduced following grim combat experience in the Spanish–American War.

Rifles far and wide

At the turn of the twentieth century some international rifle designs were conventional while others were innovative. The Mexican Mondragon was remarkably advanced, as was the philosophy proposed for its tactical employment. In Japan and Russia, two countries that had fought for dominance in the East, two reliable but conventional weapons, the Arisaka and the Mosin-Nagant, were produced for the infantry.

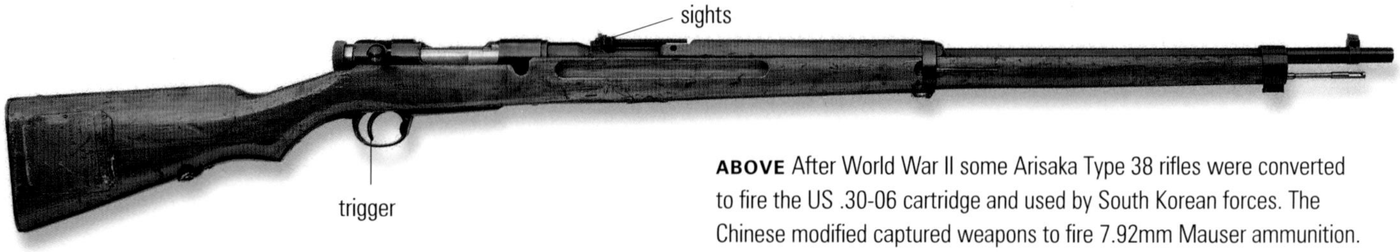

ABOVE After World War II some Arisaka Type 38 rifles were converted to fire the US .30-06 cartridge and used by South Korean forces. The Chinese modified captured weapons to fire 7.92mm Mauser ammunition.

Japanese small arms

The 1905 Japanese 6.5mm Arisaka Rifle Type 38 was a development of the earlier Type 30 rifle designed by Colonel Arisaka and was often referred to by the Japanese as the Arisaka Sampachi (or Sampachi Shiki Hoheiju). It was fundamentally a Mauser rifle based on the Gew 98 but with changes to the safety and cocking mechanisms. The combination of the light cartridge and the long barrel made the Type 38 a very easy rifle to fire because of its low recoil. At 127.5cm/50.2in long, however, it was a difficult rifle for some of the smaller Japanese soldiers to handle, particularly when fitted with its Type 30 sword

Marksmanship in battle

An American hero of World War I, Corporal (later Sergeant) Alvin Cullum York of the 328th Infantry was awarded the Medal of Honor for leading an attack on a German machine-gun nest during the battle of the Meuse-Argonne on 8 October 1918. Armed with the Springfield M1903 bolt-action rifle, he and his section killed 32 German soldiers and captured 132 others as well as 35 German machine guns, and took control of the fortified position.

As a corporal in the 328th Infantry 82nd Division, York had assumed command of his detachment after three NCOs had been killed. A semi-literate backwoodsman from the Tennessee mountains, he was a lay deacon in a Christian pacifist sect. However, he was persuaded that active service was sanctioned by the Bible. While he is sometimes described as acting single-handedly, his official citation says he led seven others in a charge against the machine-gun position.

York's exploit is a clear demonstration that good weapons training and accurate shooting – whatever the weapon – can be devastating in battle. The South African Boers, who were natural marksmen, taught this lesson to the British in the Boer War of 1899–1902. Experienced hunters, they had bought excellent Mausers from Germany and had honed their marksmanship against wildlife targets. The British in turn learnt the lesson and taught it to the Germans in World War I. The accurate fire from their SMLEs did much to slow the German advance.

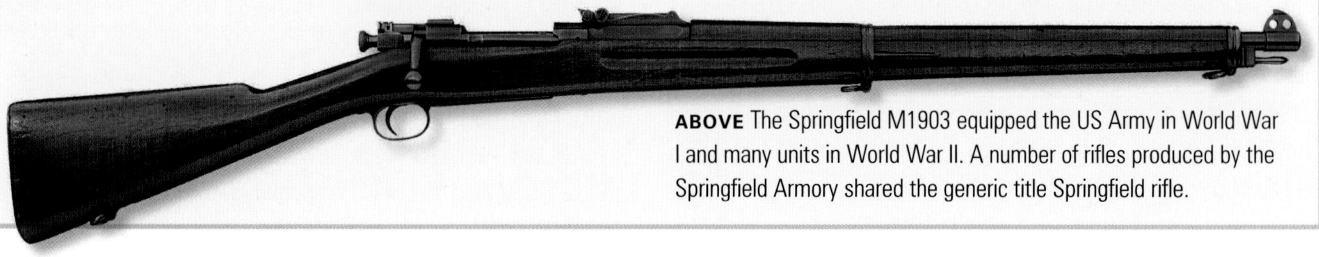

ABOVE The Springfield M1903 equipped the US Army in World War I and many units in World War II. A number of rifles produced by the Springfield Armory shared the generic title Springfield rifle.

bayonet. The Type 38 was exported to Thailand and also used by the Chinese. It had a five-round magazine and weighed 4.2kg/9.3lb. The Type 38 carbine was only 86.9cm/34.2in long, and some were produced with a butt that folded to the right for paratroopers.

ABOVE A German soldier looks down the x 4 P.E. side-mounted telescopic sight on a captured Russian 7.62mm calibre Mosin-Nagant Model 1891/30 rifle during the first days of Operation Barbarossa, the Nazi invasion of the Soviet Union of 1941.

Mexican invention

In the early 1890s the Mexican inventor, engineer and army officer Manuel Mondragon, a graduate of both the Mexican Military Academy at Chapultepec and the French Academy at Saint-Cyr received a request to design an advanced infantry rifle from President Porfirio Diaz.

By the close of 1891, the initial design had been completed and a year later, on 18 October, the first prototypes went for evaluation. The 25th Infantry Battalion received 50 improved versions for troop trials on 27 September 1894. This Model 1894 had a safety catch with three settings: "A" for automatic, "L" for safe and "R" for use in the manual straight-pull bolt-action mode. The rifles were intended to be fired as single-shot weapons but could be switched to automatic in the assault.

The rifles had a fixed eight-round magazine using an enbloc Garand-type clip of special 6.5 x 52mm/ 0.26 x 2in Mondragon cartridges made by SFM in Paris. They were made in Switzerland owing to the lack of indigenous production facilities. However, although the design was advanced, it was also overly complex, not entirely "soldier-proof" and ultimately the weapon was too costly to be issued to the entire Mexican Army.

Old and reliable

The Russian Mosin-Nagant Model 1891/30 bolt-action rifle weighed 4kg/8.8lb empty, had a muzzle velocity of 81m/s (metres per second)/2,661ft/s (feet per second) and, although an old design, was robust and reliable. Until 1930 the iron sights on the rifle were graduated in the archaic linear measurement of *arshins* (0.71m/ 2.3ft), but the Soviet government redesigned the rear sight in metres.

Self-loading rifles

As the prospect of World War II loomed in Europe, designers looked at systems for self-loading or semi-automatic rifles. The most famous and successful was, and remains, the US M1 Garand. However, the Soviet Tokarev 38 and 40 were imaginative designs that impressed the Germans. The French bolt-action MAS 36 would prove a rugged and reliable weapon in some of the toughest campaigns.

The Garand

The US Rifle, Caliber .30, M1 (known as the M1 Garand), designed by John Garand of the Springfield Arsenal in the late 1920s, was adopted by the US Army in 1936. It was a robust, semi-automatic, gas-operated rifle that weighed 4.3kg/9.5lb, was 110cm/43.5in long and had an eight-round box magazine. The effective rate of fire was 16–24 rpm. Sights were set out to 1,100m/1,200yd, but the effective range was 420m/460yd. Although it had the minor tactical drawback that the clip was ejected with a loud "ping" that indicated when the last round had been fired, General George S. Patton described the M1 Garand as "the greatest battle implement ever devised". Over 5,400,000 M1 Garands were manufactured by the Springfield Armory as well as three private contractors, until production stopped in 1957. The Garand was the US infantryman's weapon throughout World War II, the Korean War and in the early years of the Vietnam War.

LEFT Armed with an M1 Garand rifle, a GI looks at the body of a Waffen-SS soldier killed during the break out from Saint-Lô in July 1944, following the Normandy invasion.

The MAS Mle 1936

In World War II the French Army had a rugged bolt-action rifle that fired a 7.5mm round from a five-round magazine built at Manufacture d'Armes de St Etienne (MAS). It was introduced in 1936 and so was designated the Fusil MAS 36. It soldiered on in Vietnam in the 1950s and was still being used during the war in Algeria in the 1960s. It weighed 3.7kg/8.2lb and was 102cm/40in long. A version with a metal folding butt was produced for airborne forces and saw action with French paratroops at the ill-fated battle of Dien Bien Phu in 1954.

The Tokarev SVT 38 and SVT40

It took 20 years of research before the SVT38 (Samozaryadnaya Vintovka Tokarevao 1938g – Tokarev's self-loading rifle) was adopted by the Soviet Army in 1938. The Russian arms designer Fedor Tokarev had developed the 6.5mm Avtomat in 1916, and in 1936 S. G. Simonov had produced the

ABOVE French and Vietnamese paratroopers in dense jungle north of Dien Bien Phu in February 1954. They are armed with the MAS Mle 1936 folding butt bolt-action rifle that was developed for airborne and Alpine troops. Late models of the rifle have an extended barrel with concentric rings to permit the launching of rifle grenades.

John C. Garand

Born on 1 January 1888 on a small farm in Quebec, Canada, John Cantius Garand was working as a floor sweeper at a Connecticut textile mill by the time he was 11, where he was fascinated with the machinery he saw around him. In his spare time, he learnt from the mechanics and by 18 he had taught himself enough to work as a machinist.

Garand had an inventive mind and by November 1919 was working at the Springfield Armory in Massachusetts, where he would eventually become the Chief Civilian Engineer. Garand invented a self-loading .30-calibre rifle, known as the M1 or "the Garand", which was adopted in 1936 after gruelling tests by the US Army. During the time that he took to develop the M1 and other small arms innovations, Garand received no more than his government salary. Some people felt he deserved compensation, yet when a bill was introduced in Congress to grant him $100,000, it did not pass. He received official recognition in the form of a Medal for Meritorious Service in 1941 and in 1944 the Government Medal for Merit. He retired in 1953 and died on 16 February 1974.

select-fire AVS-36. However, the Avtomat used Japanese ammunition, so it was declared obsolete, while the AVS-36 had defects, including dirt ingress and excessive muzzle blast that necessitated fitting a compensator/muzzle brake. Therefore, the SVT38 was adopted. The SVT38 was issued to the Soviet Army, but experience in the Winter War with Finland in 1939–40 led to modifications. In 1940 the updated and re-adapted new rifle went into service as the SVT40.

Like the SVT38, the SVT40 or 7.62mm Samozaryadnaya Vintovka Tokarevao 1940g had a ten-round box magazine. It weighed 3.9kg/8.5lb. Nearly two million SVT40s were manufactured. When German soldiers captured them, they were quick to put them back into use against their former owners, redesignating them A1Gew259(r). The drawback with the SVT40 was that it had heavy recoil. Other versions of the rifle were the SNT sniper's rifle and the fully automatic AKT40. Although it was an innovative design, it demanded too many man-hours from skilled machinists and was phased out in 1943–4.

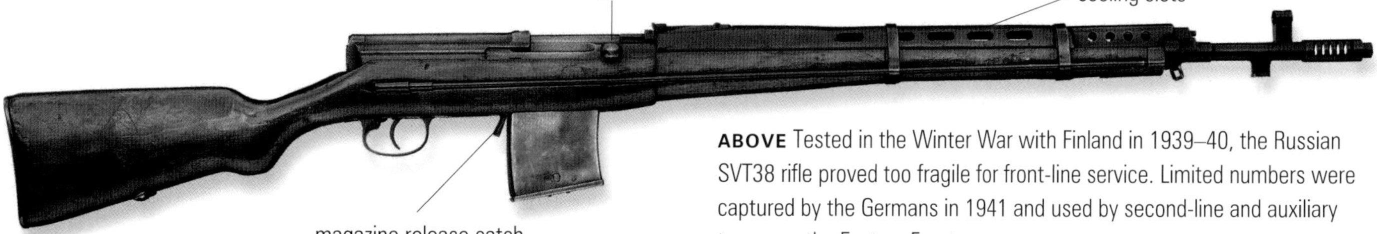

ABOVE Tested in the Winter War with Finland in 1939–40, the Russian SVT38 rifle proved too fragile for front-line service. Limited numbers were captured by the Germans in 1941 and used by second-line and auxiliary troops on the Eastern Front.

The pressure of war

War pressures produced some very successful designs, such as the American M1 carbine; some very innovative designs, such as the German FG42; and some rugged, conventional but battle-worthy weapons, such as the British bolt-action No. 4 rifle. The German Gewehr 41, by contrast, was unreliable and too heavy to be popular.

The M1 Carbine

The American-designed M1 carbine was used in World War II by US forces, by the British in Malaya during the Emergency (1948–60) and by the French in Indo-China in the 1950s. It was described by one veteran as "one of the most appealing of weapons, light, handy, easy to shoot and totally useless over 200 yards [183m] since it fired a pistol bullet". The US Carbine Cal .30 M1 was produced with a folding stock for airborne forces as the M1A1; it weighed 2.7kg/6lb with a loaded magazine and folded down to a compact 630mm/25in. The wooden-stock M1 weighed a little less at 2.5kg/5.5lb, but it folded down to only 890mm/35in. Both weapons had a cyclic rate of 750 rpm and fired from a 15- or 30-round box magazine. A popular practice was to attach a two-magazine webbing pouch to the wooden stock, which gave the soldier two ready-to-use magazines with his weapon.

ABOVE A US Army squad leader briefs his patrol in Normandy. Most of the men are armed with the M1 Carbine, which was a handy weapon although it fired a short range .30 (7.62mm) pistol bullet and was useless at long range.

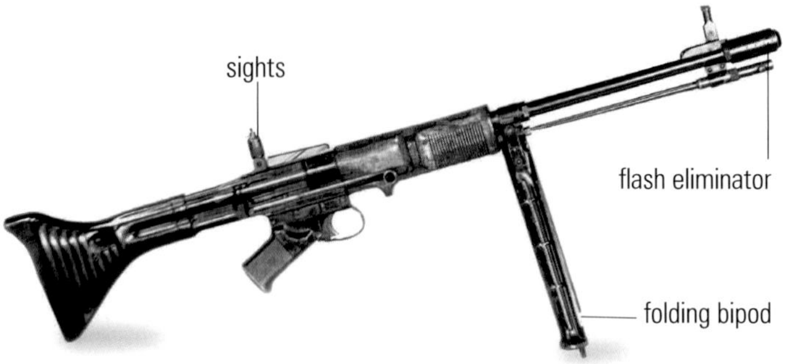

ABOVE The German FG-42 developed for parachute troops was an innovative weapon, but was too light to fire successfully in full automatic mode and too costly to produce.

The Gewehr 41

At the start of World War II, German Army commanders knew that they needed a self-loading semi-automatic rifle to replace the bolt-operated Karabiner 98k. A specification was issued for the weapon in 1940, which resulted in the Mauser Gewehr 41(W). But it was not a success in the field. The main problem was the complex gas-blowback system, which proved unreliable in the dust and dirt of the front line, primarily on the Eastern Front. It was also very heavy, weighing around 5kg/11lb, and the manufacturing costs were unacceptably high.

The paratrooper's rifle

The FG-42 (Fallschirmjägergewehr-42), also known as the Paratrooper's rifle, Model 1942, was designed for German airborne soldiers. Powerful yet light, the FG-42 was air cooled and gas operated, and sturdy – despite the widespread use of stamping and the minimum use of metal to reduce weight. It also had a unique spike bayonet, fitted as an optional extra. The ammunition feed was from a side-mounted 20-round box magazine, which could be loaded separately or from standard five-round Mauser clips with the action open.

No more than 2,000 examples of the original weapon, also known as the FG-42 1st model or FG-42-1, were delivered. This was because the lightweight rifle

ABOVE Allied soldiers in street fighting in north-western Europe. The man in the foreground is armed with a .303in No. 4 rifle while the lance corporal has equipped himself with a captured German MP40 SMG.

Intermediate 7.92mm ammunition

During World War II, German after-action analysis in 1939–40 established that most firefights took place at comparatively short ranges, around 400m/437yd – not the 800–875m/1,005–1,100yd for which weapons such as the Kar 98K rifle had been designed.

Therefore, the ammunition firm Polte developed the 7.92mm K or short round for this type of combat. With a muzzle velocity of 650m/s/2,133ft/s, it was almost twice as powerful as 9mm submachine-gun ammunition. With a round that was more compact and ideal for automatic weapons, the ground had been prepared for the development of the assault rifle.

didn't have enough strength to handle powerful rifle ammunition in full automatic mode. In addition, the manufacturing cost was too high.

A redesigned weapon, the FG-42-2, was introduced in early 1944. It was heavier and longer but even so it was still too light to be fired accurately on full automatic – even from the prone position using the bipod. Just as importantly, it was too expensive, particularly when compared to the StG44 assault rifle. By the end of the war in 1945, some 5,000 FG-42-2 models had been built. The mechanism of the FG-42 reappeared as the basis of another flawed weapon: the US M60 machine gun.

The Lee-Enfield No.4

A new bolt-action rifle, the Lee-Enfield No. 4 replaced the SMLE during World War II, was less expensive to manufacture and had improved tangent sights. The No. 4, which would arm British and Canadian infantry at D-Day and through numerous post-war campaigns including Korea, the Malayan Emergency and Suez, was replaced only in the 1960s, by the 7.62mm SLR. At 3.9ft/1.2m long, the No. 5 or Jungle Carbine was shorter than the No. 4 at 1.4m/1.5yd and lighter at 3kg/6.6lb compared to 4kg/8.8lb. It looked a handsome weapon but suffered from a wandering zero, pronounced kick and a muzzle flash, which made a flash eliminator necessary. As the 7.62mm L42A1 sniper's rifle, the modified No. 4 was used by the British Army until the early 1980s. All weapons had a ten-shot detachable box magazine.

The first assault rifles

In the latter years of World War II, the German small arms industry came up with the assault rifle, which fired an intermediate round – smaller than a rifle round but bigger than a pistol. This was a weapon that would change the whole philosophy of rifle design. Meanwhile, at the end of the war, the AK-47, which would become the weapon of the late 20th century, was designed by Mikhail Kalashnikov.

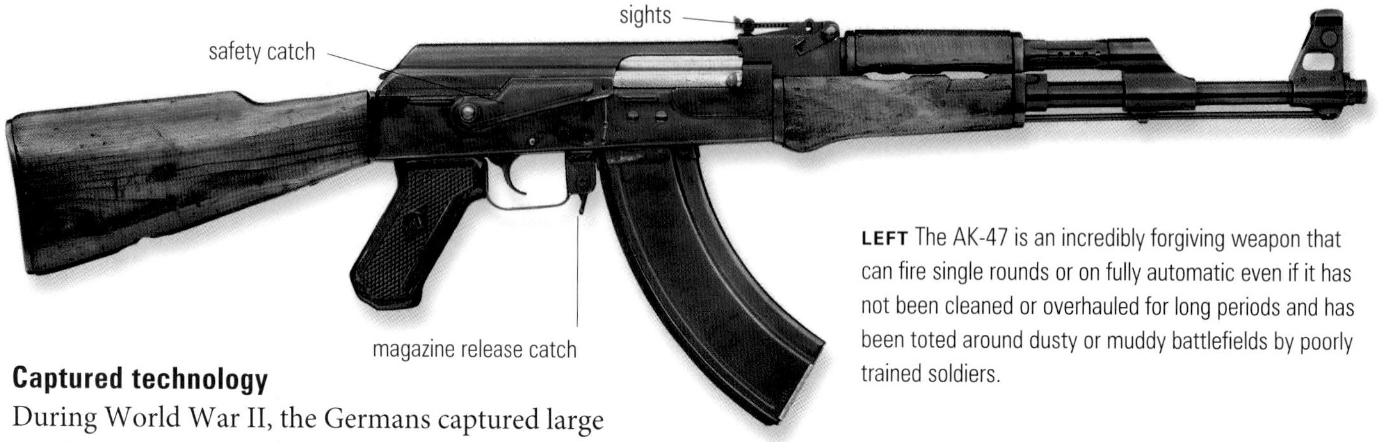

LEFT The AK-47 is an incredibly forgiving weapon that can fire single rounds or on fully automatic even if it has not been cleaned or overhauled for long periods and has been toted around dusty or muddy battlefields by poorly trained soldiers.

Captured technology

During World War II, the Germans captured large numbers of the Soviet Tokarev 7.62mm SVT38 and 40 semi-automatic rifles. The simpler gas-operated bolt system was adapted to the Gewehr 41 and the resulting weapon, the Gew 43, was an immediate success. It weighed 4.4kg/9.6lb and at 1,120mm/44in was slightly shorter than the Gew 41. It was easier to produce and incorporated features such as laminated wood furniture, simple forgings and a minimum of machined parts. The detachable magazine made loading, with two five-round clips, much easier. A bracket for the Zf41 telescopic sight was a standard fitting.

The SturmGewehr-44

In the light of combat experience on the Eastern Front in World War II, the German Army issued a specification to the small arms designers Haenel and Walther for a new machine-carbine. The two resulting gas-operated designs were remarkably similar, using the same straight-line butt and barrel arrangement, pistol grip and curved 30-round box magazine. The Haenel-designed weapon was known as the Maschinkarabiner 42 (H) or MKb42(H) and the Walther as the MKb42(W). Both were designed to be manufactured quickly and cheaply using plastic and stamped and die-cast metal components.

The MKb42(H), which had been designed by the prolific Louis Schmeisser, was 94cm/37in long, weighed 4.9kg/10.8lb and had a cyclic rate of fire of 500 rpm. About 8,000 were produced for troop trials on the Eastern Front, where they were very successful, and this was the weapon selected by the army.

Despite the success of the MKb42(H), Hitler decided that further development of assault rifles should be halted. Fortunately for the soldiers in the field, the German Army and Haenel changed the designation of the improved MKb42(H) to MP43 and so for documentation purposes made the weapon a *Maschinenpistole*, or submachine gun. In this guise it went into mass production. Further modifications to the weapon, including the facility to launch rifle grenades, produced a weapon that weighed 5.2kg/11.5lb and had a cyclic rate of 500 rpm.

When Hitler finally approved the MP43, he gave it a new name, the SturmGewehr-44 (StG-44) or "Assault Rifle". It was a name that would later be used for all post-war infantry automatic weapons designed to fire the compact intermediate cartridge. The total number of German assault rifles of all designs produced was about 500,000.

The Kalashnikov AK-47

The AK-47, in all its numerous versions, is probably the most widely used weapon in the world. The original assault rifle, designed by Mikhail Kalashnikov at the end of World War II, entered service with the Soviet Army in 1951. It was 1.07m/42in long with

Mikhail Timofeyevich Kalashnikov

In 1938 Mikhail Kalashnikov, a self-taught inventor, joined the Soviet Army in Kiev and went to a tank mechanics school. There, among other useful tactical devices for armoured vehicles, he designed a device to count the shots fired by a tank.

Serving as a tank commander, Kalashnikov survived the fierce battles following the German invasion in 1941. Suffering from serious wounds and battle fatigue, he was sent to the rear to recover in hospital. He began to work on the idea of a new lightweight machine gun that could provide a high volume of fire for soldiers in mechanized infantry. While convalescing at Matai he had access to the workshop facilities and began work on the prototype of his weapon. In 1944 his first prototype was accepted for further development, and finally in 1949 the Soviet Army adopted the Automatic Kalashnikov design of 1947 or AK47. To date, an estimated 100 million Kalashnikovs have been made worldwide, with more than half of them being made in countries other than Russia.

a wooden butt. The folding metal-butt version was 870mm/34.2in long open and 635mm/25in closed. It fired a 7.62 x 39mm round weighing 122 grains and had a muzzle velocity of 717m/s/2,352ft/s at a cyclic rate of 600 rpm. The AKM, a modernized version of the AK-47, was lighter and weighed 2.9kg/6.4lb empty or 3.6kg/8lb with a fully loaded 30-round steel magazine. The effective range of both the AK-47 and AKM was 400m/437yd.

The AK family of assault rifles were well designed, easy to use even by unskilled men and had very few working parts. AK weapons were produced throughout the Warsaw Pact countries and in China and North Korea.

ABOVE A German soldier armed with a StG-44 assault rifle plods through mud churned up by tanks on the Eastern Front in the spring of 1945. The StG-44 was a remarkable and very advanced weapon.

LEFT The AKM was essentially an improved lighter version of the AK-47, with the addition of a compensator that reduced muzzle climb when the weapon was fired in full automatic mode.

Post-war assault rifles

In the 1950s new rifles were developed in the United States, Soviet Union and Europe. The American M14 had a short operational life, as did the Soviet SKS. The French MAS-49 soldiered on for many years, but the Belgian FN FAL was a real winner, widely built and used.

The MAS-49

The 7.5mm MAS-49 rifle, developed by the French state arms factory Manufacture Nationale d'Armes de St Etienne (MAS), was based on the direct gas-impingement system developed by the French designer Rossignol early in the 20th century. MAS-1949 (as it was stamped on the receiver) saw heavy combat in French Indo-China and Algeria, where it proved accurate and reliable.

The MAS-1949/56, an improved pattern rifle, was adopted by the Armée de Terre (French Army) in 1956. The MAS-49/56 retained the ten-round magazine but was lighter, had a shorter barrel and forend. It also had different grenade launcher sights and, unlike the MAS-49, the weapon could be fitted with a spike-shaped bayonet. The MAS-49/56 was not replaced in front-line service until 1979, when the French Army adopted the futuristic-looking 5.56mm FAMAS assault rifle.

The SLR

The British 7.62mm L1A1 self-loading rifle (SLR) was based on the Belgian Fabrique Nationale (FN) FAL. It entered service with the British Army in the mid-1960s and remained in use until 1985. Early weapons had wooden furniture, but this was later replaced with black plastic. It was a single-shot gas-operated weapon that had an effective range of 303m/328yd with iron sights. The flow of gas back on to the working parts could be adjusted, so if there was a malfunction, a simple drill was to close down the gas port at the front of the rifle. The cocking handle on the left side allowed the right hand to remain on the trigger.

The Samozaryadnyj Karabin Simonova

The 7.62mm SKS Samozaryadnyj Karabin Simonova, or Simonov Self-loading Carbine, designed by the famous Russian arms designer Simonov in 1949, was

FN Fusil Automatique Léger

Developed by the Belgian Fabrique Nationale company, the FN FAL (Fusil Automatique Léger – light automatic rifle) is one of the most widely known rifle designs of the 20th century. Its popularity is reflected in the fact that more than 70 countries have used it and at least ten countries made it themselves.

Canada was the first country to adopt the FAL in 1955 with a slightly modified version designated the C1. The C1 and heavy-barrelled C2 squad automatic rifles were made at the Canadian Arsenal. Belgium followed in 1956, Britain a year later with the British-built L1A1 SLR (self-loading rifle), which was often issued with a x4 SUIT Trilux optical sight. When Austria adopted the rifle in 1958, it was designated Stg.58 and built at the Steyr arms factory. The FAL was adopted in various types by Argentina, Brazil, Turkey, Australia, Israel, Rhodesia (modern-day Zimbabwe) and South Africa.

RIGHT The FN FAL has the distinction of being adopted by more than ninety countries and has been used in action in almost every continent in the world. Models are available in automatic and semi-automatic fire form.

a gas-operated, magazine-fed, self-loading weapon. It utilized a short-stroke gas piston with its own return spring, and a tilting bolt locking, where a bolt tips down to lock on to the floor of the receiver. The cocking handle was attached to the right side of the bolt carrier and moved when the gun was fired. The receiver was machined from steel. The SKS was fed from the integral ten-round magazine, which could be loaded from the top through the open bolt by loose cartridges or by using special ten-round clips. Adopted by the Soviet Army as the 7.62mm Samozaryadnyj Karabin Simonova obr. 1945 goda – SKS, it entered service alongside the Kalashnikov AK-47.

ABOVE A Royal Marine takes aim with his SLR during arctic warfare training in Norway in the 1970s. This rifle has black plastic furniture but has not been upgraded by being fitted with a SUIT optical sight.

The M14

The M14 rifle, or United States Rifle, Caliber 7.62mm, M14, is a selective-fire 7.62mm rifle that has now been largely superseded in military use by the M16. After trials against other rifles, including the FN FAL, the US Army adopted the M14 in 1957. A production line was set up at the Springfield Armory in 1958, and the first rifles were delivered in 1959. However, owing to long production delays, the 101st Airborne Division was the only army unit fully equipped with the M14 by the end of 1961.

In Vietnam, although its length and weight made it unwieldy in the jungle, the powerful 7.62mm NATO round penetrated cover quite well and had a good range. The weapon also proved to be very reliable and continued to function even under adverse conditions. However, there were several drawbacks to the M14. Soldiers soon realized that in the heavy humidity of the tropics in Vietnam, the wooden stock swelled and expanded, which affected the zeroing on the sights. Fibreglass stocks were developed to compensate for this defect, but by then the M14 had been withdrawn from service. The M14 was replaced by the M16 in Vietnam in 1966–8.

ABOVE The M14 represented a logical development of the M1 Garand, although it fired the NATO standardized 7.62mm round. The M14 saw action in Vietnam before it was replaced by the M16.

Outstanding models

The German G3 rifle is one of the small arms success stories of post-war Europe. An excellent and reliable design, the weapon has been widely exported and manufactured under licence. The American M16 has enjoyed even greater success, and this rifle and its derivatives are in use across most of the world. The Russian SVD's claim to fame is that it is the only semi-automatic sniper's rifle with bayonet fittings.

RIGHT The 7.62mm German Heckler & Koch G3 selective fire rifle has been adopted throughout the world. It is a rugged and reliable weapon that has been made under licence in five countries.

The Heckler & Koch G3

At the close of World War II, engineers at the German Mauser-Werke small arms factory were working on a revolutionary design for a selective-fire, magazine-fed rifle. After the war, the design was refined by CETME in Spain, and in 1959 the Bundeswehr (West German Army) adopted the rifle as the Gewehr 3 or Rifle model 3, better known simply as the G3. In 1959 Germany bought the manufacturing licence for the rifle and transferred it to Heckler & Koch at Oberndorf. The first G3s, although modified, were quite similar to the CETME rifles and until 1961 had CETME stamped on the receiver.

ABOVE Gurkha soldiers board a truck in Borneo in the 1960s. They are armed with the Colt Armalite rifle – at the time it was a unique weapon in the unusual calibre of 5.56mm – it would later become the M16.

The G3 is cheaper to produce than the FAL or M14 since it uses as many stamped parts as possible. To speed production and reduce costs, the rifle uses sheet steel stampings for the receiver, trigger unit and pistol-grip frame. The pistol grip is hinged to the receiver with a cross-pin behind the magazine housing and in front of the trigger unit. The weapons have distinctive drum-type rear diopter sights, marked from 100–400m/109–438yd.

Since its adoption by the Bundeswehr, the G3 in various modifications has gone global. Foreign users include Greece, Iran, Mexico, Norway, Pakistan, Portugal, Sweden and Turkey. In the past forty years more than fifty countries have issued the G3 to their armed forces. The G3 has been manufactured in Greece, Pakistan, Iran, Turkey and Portugal.

The Armalite and M16

The Colt AR-15 Armalite, which became the M16 when it was adopted by the US Army in Vietnam in 1966, was an innovative weapon when it was first introduced. It was made from alloys and plastic and fired an M193 5.56mm round with a 55-grain bullet

M16 controversy

The first M16 rifles, issued to US troops in Vietnam in the mid-60s, were loathed because men were killed or wounded when they jammed in combat. One of the major causes for these malfunctions was that the US Army replaced the originally specified Dupont IMR powder with standard ball powder, used in 7.62 x 51mm NATO ammunition. This produced much more fouling, which rapidly caused the actions of the M16 to jam unless the weapon was cleaned thoroughly. However, the initial M16 rifles had been promoted as "low maintenance", requiring no cleaning, and therefore no cleaning kits were issued and soldiers received no instructions in weapons cleaning.

In 1967–70 new 5.56mm ammunition was loaded using a different propellant. Cleaning kits were produced and issued to troops, and the M16 barrel, chamber and bolt were chrome-lined to enhance their resistance to corrosion. At first, the cleaning kits had to be carried separately from the rifle, but since 1970 a cavity was included in the buttstock of all M16A1 rifles to hold the kit, and 30-round magazines replaced the original 20-round magazines.

RIGHT The M16 in use during the Vietnam War. It has gone through many stages of improvements and remains a general-issue rifle with the US armed forces.

with a muzzle velocity of 975m/s/3,198ft/s. This made the M16 much lighter than big 7.62mm rifles such as the M14 and a more practical weapon for the jungle.

The weapon that is currently in service is the M16A1/2, which is 99cm/39in long, weighs 3.2kg/7lb and fires a 20- or 30-round magazine. On automatic it has a cyclic rate of 700–950 rpm. The M16A1 has a manual bolt-closing device on the right side of the receiver, which allows extra pressure to be applied if there is dirt in the chamber or a cartridge case jams. The M16A2, which fires the NATO SS109 round – a 62-grain bullet with a muzzle velocity of 823 m/s /2,700ft/s – has a heavier barrel and a case deflector. This allows left-handed soldiers to handle the weapon. The M16A3 is an A2 with a removable carrying handle, which, when removed, allows a telescopic sight to be fitted.

The Dragunov SVD

The gas-operated, short-stroke, rotating-bolt, semi-automatic SVD (Snaiperskaya Vintovka Dragunova, or Dragunov Sniper Rifle) was adopted by the Soviet military in 1963. It can use any kind of standard 7.62 x 54R ammunition, but a primary round specially developed for the SVD sniper-grade cartridge has a steel-core bullet. The SVD is extremely reliable in all conditions, and has seen action in Afghanistan and Chechnya. In the mid-2000s, insurgent groups in Iraq and Afghanistan used it against US and Coalition forces. If the PSO-1 optical sight with illuminated reticle is damaged, the soldier has back-up adjustable iron sights. Unusually for a sniper weapon, it takes the standard AK-47 bayonet. The rifle has a ten-round detachable box magazine that gives a maximum rate of fire of 30 rpm or aimed fire of three to five rounds.

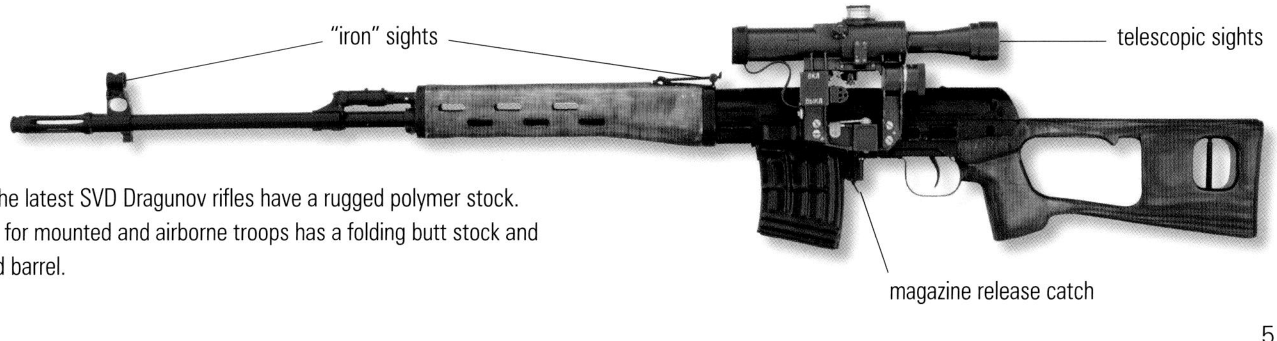

RIGHT The latest SVD Dragunov rifles have a rugged polymer stock. A version for mounted and airborne troops has a folding butt stock and shortened barrel.

Modern assault rifles

Modern assault rifles, such as the Austrian Steyr AUG rifle, are commonly made from polymers and GRP (glass-reinforced plastic, or fibreglass). They are made in weapons "families": individual parts are interchangeable between models, and a rifle can be converted into a light support weapon in minutes. The Israeli Galil came from a different family that took design ideas from the Finnish Valmet, which itself had adopted them from the Soviet AK-47. The Soviet AK-74 is an update on the AK-47.

The Galil

During the late 1960s the Israel Defence Force (IDF) tested two replacements for the FN FAL rifles used by its soldiers. One weapon was designed by Uziel Gal and the other by Israel Galili, chief weapons designer for IMI (Israeli Military Industries). Drawing on the Finnish Valmet Rk 62 assault rifle, an improvement of the Soviet AK-47, Galili placed his rifle in competition with the M16A1, the Stoner 63, the AK-47, the HK 33 and a design by Uziel Gal. Galili's weapon eventually won the competition. It was selected as a new IDF assault rifle in 1973, but the Yom Kippur War of 1973 delayed its introduction.

The Galil is a versatile design that is available in several configurations. The full-sized AR and ARM, the compact SAR carried by vehicle crews and the MAR or Micro-Galil subcompact assault rifle are all in 5.56mm. An AR is available in 7.62mm NATO, while the Galatz is a 7.62mm semi-automatic sniper weapon. Most of the weapons fire at a cyclic rate of 650 rpm, the exception being the MAR, which fires 600–750 rpm. The 7.62mm AR/ARM has an effective range of 500–600m/550–655yd, while that of the 5.56mm AR/ARM is 450m/490yd. The little MAR has an effective range of 150–200m/165–220yd.

Galil rifles were exported to various Central American, African and Asian countries. In the first years of the 21st century, Estonia also took delivery of some Galils. In South Africa, Vektor (part of the DENEL defence and aerospace group) manufactures a modified Galil as the R4 and R5.

The AK-74

Chambered for a smaller 5.45 x 39mm round, the AK-74 is a modernized version of the 7.62mm AKM. Initially, NATO intelligence analysts thought that the AK-74 was a specialist weapon for airborne units of Special Forces. Produced from 1976, it was updated as the AK-74M, with a new muzzle brake and gas return cylinder, and since the early 1990s has been issued to the forces of the Russian Federation.

Like the AK-47 and AKM weapons, the AK-74 is a magazine-fed, selective-fire, intermediate-calibre assault rifle with a rigid-piston gas system and rotating bolt-locking mechanism. In addition, it uses the stamped sheet-metal receiver of the AKM. However, the AK-74 differs from the AKM in several ways, notably with its distinctive muzzle brake, which drastically cuts the already mild recoil and muzzle climb of the AK-74 when it is firing on fully automatic at 600–650 rpm – although the muzzle

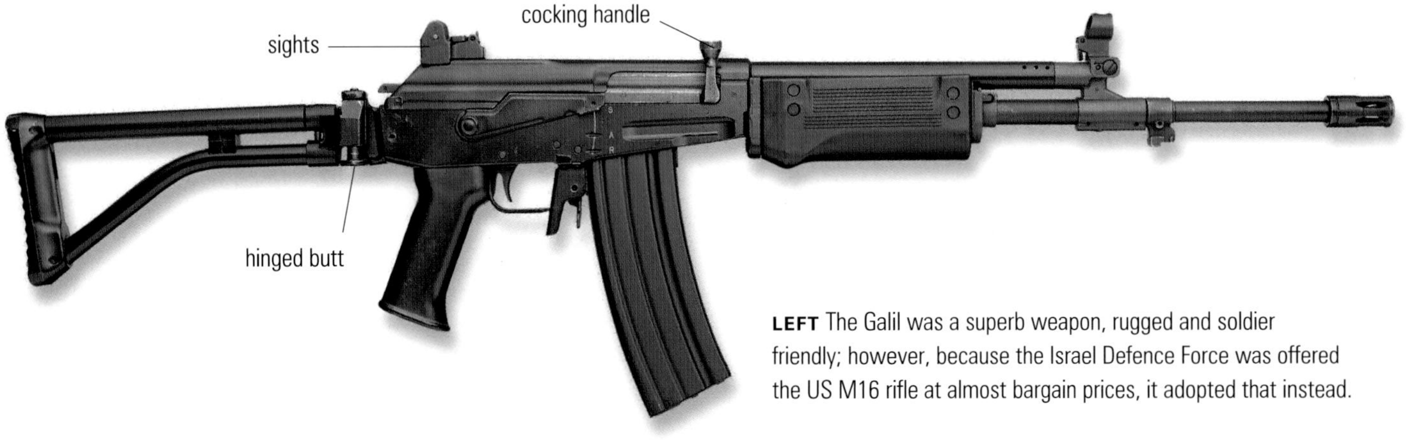

LEFT The Galil was a superb weapon, rugged and soldier friendly; however, because the Israel Defence Force was offered the US M16 rifle at almost bargain prices, it adopted that instead.

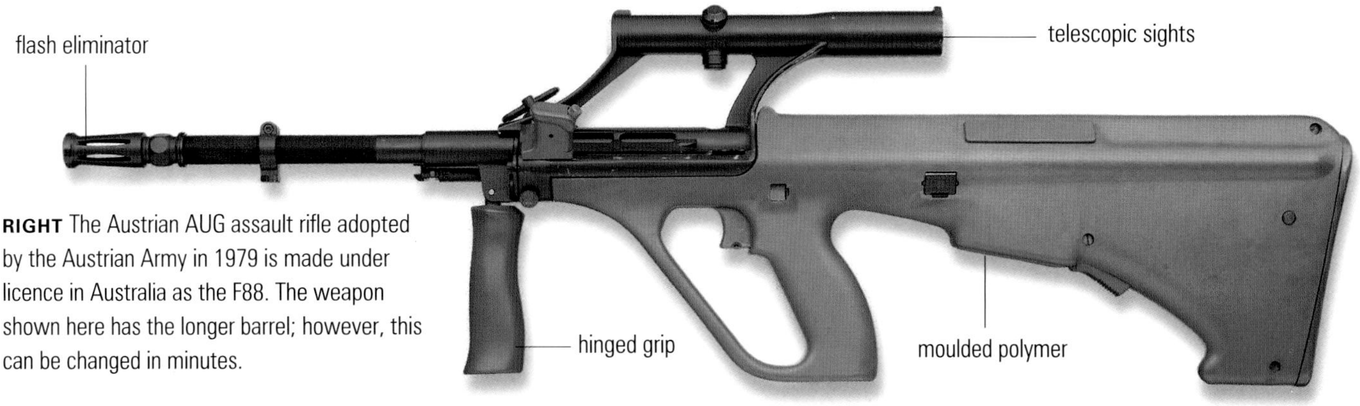

RIGHT The Austrian AUG assault rifle adopted by the Austrian Army in 1979 is made under licence in Australia as the F88. The weapon shown here has the longer barrel; however, this can be changed in minutes.

LEFT The AK-74 fitted with a grenade launcher. This enhancement copied from the United States proved very popular during the Soviet intervention in Afghanistan in the latter years of the 20th century.

brake does increase noise and muzzle blast. Current production versions of the AK-74M have a mounting rail on the left side of the receiver for fixing a telescopic or night-vision sight in place of the adjustable iron sights. It has an effective range of 457m/500yd.

The Steyr AUG

The futuristic-looking Austrian Steyr AUG rifle, with a distinctive green polymer frame and integrated Swarovski x1.5 scope, is actually one of a family of firearms first introduced in 1977 by Steyr Mannlicher. AUG stands for Armée Universal Gewehr, or "Universal Army Rifle", but is often used for the initial version – the 5.56mm NATO bullpup assault rifle. The family includes related weapons such as a submachine gun, sniper's rifle and LMG. Firing from a 30- or 42-round magazine, the rifle has an effective range of 450–500m/490–550yd and a cyclic rate of fire of 650 rpm. The weapon pioneered the use of translucent magazines, which allow the firer to make a quick visual check on how many rounds are available.

The Australian and New Zealand version of the weapon, the F88, fires in semi-automatic mode when the trigger is pressed to a clearly felt point and then in fully automatic when it is fully depressed. Other modifications to the AUG include three-round or fully automatic fire. Besides Austria, Australia and New Zealand, users include Indonesia, Luxembourg, Oman, Pakistan, Republic of Ireland, Saudi Arabia, Tunisia and Malaysia. The AUG has seen action with Australian forces in East Timor, Afghanistan and Iraq.

Plastic guns

Although the Germans had pioneered the use of early plastics such as Bakelite in automatic weapons prior to World War II, it was in the late 1960s that the American M16 rifle first caught the general public's attention. It used black polymers for the "furniture" (the butt and stock), where wood would traditionally have been used. Materials such as polymers and ceramics have considerable advantages over more traditional wood and steel: they do not corrode and deform in wet and humid conditions, which makes them ideal in a maritime or tropical environment; they are often lighter and actually stronger; and polymers can be cast in a colour that suits the theatre in which they are likely to be used – black, sand or olive drab.

France and Britain

While the British L96A1 PM sniper rifle enjoys an excellent reputation, this cannot be said for the L85A1 rifle – the British soldier's issue rifle. The French FAMAS has had its critics too, but it is in wider use around the world. The French FR F2 sniper rifle is well regarded, but lacks the unique features of the L96A1.

ABOVE The French F1 FAMAS is a comfortable weapon to fire with its built-in bipod and ambidextrous cocking handle. It is in service with the French armed forces as well as those of Djibouti, Gabon, Senegal and the United Arab Emirates.

The FAMAS

In 1967, development started on the Fusil d'Assaut de la Manufacture d'Armes de St Etienne or FAMAS. The new weapon was designed to replace both the MAS Mle 49/56 semi-automatic rifle and the veteran MAT-49 submachine gun. Paul Tellie, who headed the design team, came up with a radical design. The first prototype was completed in 1971, trialled in 1972–3 and adopted by the French Army in 1978. It has a delayed blowback action, and although the magazine can hold 30 rounds it is normally loaded with 25 rounds. On automatic it fires at 900–1,000 rpm. The FAMAS has an effective range of 300m/330yd. It has been exported to Djibouti, Gabon, Senegal and the UAE. The FAMAS G2 is intended for export, takes the 3-round M16-type magazine and is rifled for M193 or SS109 ammunition.

The L85A1 rifle SA80

In the late 1960s, the British Army realized it required a new rifle and began the development of the Small Arms for the 80s, or SA 80 system. The system was concentrated on two systems: the Individual Weapon, or SA80 IW and the Light Support Weapon, or LSW. The LSW was mechanically similar to the SA80 but had a bipod and longer barrel.

The L85A1 rifle that finally reached the soldier was not well received. Although it was chambered for 5.56mm, it was the heaviest weapon in this calibre in service. Being a bullpup design, the rifle had a long barrel, but with most of the weight located towards the butt this did not help to control muzzle climb during automatic fire. In the upgrade programme undertaken by Heckler & Koch in 2000–02, about 200,000 rifles were upgraded into the L85A2 configuration out of a total of about 320,000 original L85A1 rifles produced. The rifle is gas-operated with a rotating bolt. It has a 30-round box magazine and a cyclic rate of fire of 650 rpm. In general, the best feature of the L85 is its SUSAT x4 telescopic sight, which allows for accurate shooting out to 500m/550yd.

The L96A1 PM (Precision Marksman) sniper rifle

The Accuracy International, Bolt Action 7.62 x 51mm NATO sniper rifle entered service with the British Army in 1985 and was given the designation L96. With a ten-round box magazine, it is designed to achieve first-round hit at 600m/660yd and harassing fire out to 1,100m/1,200yd. The L96 was upgraded with a new sight and spotting scope to L96A1. The infantry version of the rifle has 6 x 42 Schmidt & Bender

ABOVE Gurkha soldiers armed with the L85A1 rifle and LSW negotiate with Indonesian Special Forces in East Timor in September 1999. The Indonesians are armed with an M16 and a Chinese-made SKS.

telescopic sights as well as iron sights. A covert version of the rifle folds down to fit into a suitcase and is fitted with a suppressed barrel. In ideal conditions the subsonic ammunition is accurate up to 300m/330yd.

Among the distinctive features of the L96A1 are a tool kit of three Allen wrenches and a screwdriver, which means the sniper is able to carry out all but the most major repairs by himself in the field, and a stainless-steel barrel that can be changed in five minutes. The L96A1 is in service with the British Army and with several armies in Africa, the Middle East and Far East.

The FR F2 sniper rifle

The French Army FR F2 sniper rifle is a modernized version of the earlier FR F1. The main differences are that it has been re-chambered from 7.5mm Lebel to 7.62 x 51mm NATO and the barrel design has been changed. FR F2 has a thermal-shielded barrel consisting of a polymer envelope enclosing most of the barrel. This ensures ballistic consistency, since the barrel stays at the same temperature, and it reduces the infrared signature and any heat haze from hot metal that could interfere with target location. FR F2 is a bolt-action weapon with iron sights and a x4 optical sight; it has a ten-round box magazine. It has been in service with the French Army since 1984.

SUSAT

The success story of the L85A1 rifle is the compact Sight Unit Small Arms Trilux (SUSAT), developed by the Royal Armaments and Research Department (RARDE). Weighing 417g/14.5oz, it is only 14.5cm/6in long and can be fitted or removed quickly using its universal mount on rifles, machine guns and recoilless rifles. It has a magnification of x4 and a field of view of ten degrees. The sight has been adopted by several armies including those of Sweden, Oman, Spain, Cameroon and, of course, Britain.

ABOVE Though the L85 rifle has been modified and improved as the L85A1, it still has its critics. Yet the x4 SUSAT sight has proved a huge success and has been adopted by other countries for their rifles.

Classic versus innovation

The United States' M24 sniper weapon and the Beretta SC-70/90 assault rifle are well established, classic designs. By contrast, the Barrett M82 .50in calibre rifle, known as the "Light Fifty", and the Heckler & Koch G-36 are more innovative weapons, and both have attracted great interest outside their countries of origin.

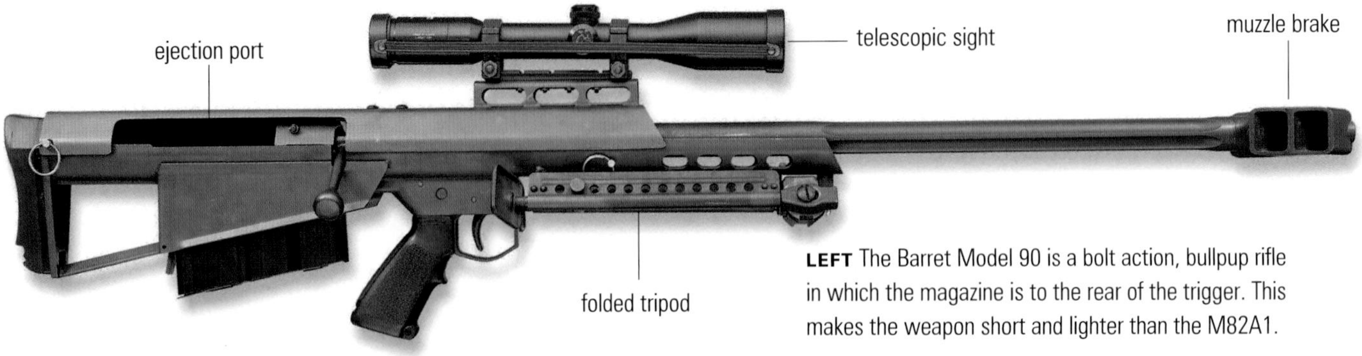

LEFT The Barret Model 90 is a bolt action, bullpup rifle in which the magazine is to the rear of the trigger. This makes the weapon short and lighter than the M82A1.

The Barrett M82 "Light Fifty"

The American Barrett Firearms Company was founded in the early 1980s by Ronnie Barrett, who designed and built semi-automatic rifles chambered for powerful .50BMG ammunition, fired by Browning M2HB heavy machine guns. Barrett's first working rifles were available in 1982; four years later came the improved M82A1 rifle. The semi-automatic rifle has a ten-round detachable box magazine and a x10 scope.

ABOVE The M24 sniper rifle (right), which replaces the M21 rifle seen on the left, is an entirely new system. The M21 is based on the M14 and, despite its vintage, has proved a very effective sniper rifle in numerous conflicts around the world.

At this stage the "Light Fifty" was seen as something of a novelty, but in 1989 the Swedish Army purchased about 100 M82A1s. Major success followed in the US led international operations Desert Shield (1990) and Desert Storm (1991). The US Marine Corps ordered 125 "Light Fifty" rifles, and the US Army and air force also put in orders. It was given the designation SASR – Special Applications Scoped Rifle.

The weapon is used against targets such as the optical equipment on crew-served weapons, radar cabins, trucks and parked aircraft or in an Explosive Ordnance Disposal (EOD) function against unexploded munitions. Its long effective range of 1,800m/1,980yd, powerful muzzle velocity of 854m/s/2,800 ft/sec and capability to use different natures of ammunition such as API make it a potent tool. As with so many concepts, once Barrett had proved the principle of .50 long-range sniping weapons, other small arms manufacturers soon followed suit and produced their own designs.

The M24 sniper weapon

By the mid-1980s, the US Army M21 sniper rifles needed to be replaced, and conflicts in the deserts of the Middle East and mountains of Afghanistan meant that ranges for snipers jumped to distances of up to 1,000m/1,095yd. The US Army set the specifications for a bolt-action rifle, requiring a stainless-steel barrel rifle and a stock made from Kevlar-graphite (a tough man-made material used for body armour). After a final shoot-off between the Steyr SSG rifle and the

Remington model 700BDL, the latter was standardized in 1987 as the US Army's M24 sniper rifle. The M24 fires 7.62 x 51mm NATO from a five-round internal magazine. It has a 10x42 Leupold Ultra M3A telescope sight (Mil-Dots) and detachable emergency iron sights. The maximum effective range is 800m/875yd.

The Beretta SC-70/90

Beretta had already produced the AR70/223, a 5.56mm weapon for the export market, when the Italian Army decided to replace its 7.62mm Beretta BM59 rifles. The AR70/223 had been accepted by Italian Special Forces and exported to several countries including Jordan and Malaysia. Beretta produced an upgraded version in 1985, and following trials against similar calibre rifles, it was accepted as the AR-70/90. A folding butt version, the SC-70/90, was produced for Special Forces and a carbine version with a shorter barrel, the SCP-70/90, was made for paratroops. Finally, a squad automatic, the AS-70/90, was produced with a heavy fixed barrel and detachable bipod. The Beretta AR-70/90 weighs 4kg/9lb empty and has a cyclic rate of 670 rpm. The effective range of the AR-70/90 is 500m/550yd, while for the SCP-70/90 it is 350m/380yd.

The Heckler & Koch G-36

What came into being as the HK-50 project in the early 1990s became the the Heckler & Koch G-36 assault rifle. After the cancellation of the G11 (the futuristic caseless ammunition rifle), the Bundeswehr had no modern 5.56mm NATO-compatible rifle. So Heckler & Koch set out to develop a new assault rifle for the Bundeswehr and export markets. The brief was to produce a new rifle that was flexible, affordable and extremely reliable.

SS109 ammunition

During the 1970s, NATO members signed an agreement to select a smaller-calibre cartridge to replace the 7.62mm round. While there was agreement within NATO on the 5.56mm calibre, the M193 round used by US forces was rejected in favour of the more powerful Belgian FN SS109.

The M193 had proved appropriate for short-range engagements during the Vietnam war, but the SS109 had a heavier bullet but lower muzzle velocity, which gave better performance and greater penetration at the longer ranges likely to be found in Europe. When this powerful round is fired in long bursts from a fully automatic weapon such as the FN Minimi, its destructive power is phenomenal; it is capable of firing holes through brick walls that would not be penetrated by a 7.62mm round.

The G-36 uses a short-stroke gas piston above the barrel, a square-shaped bolt carrier and a rotating bolt with seven locking lugs. In these respects, it has similarities to the American AR-18. However, the receiver and most of the external parts of the G-36 are made from polymers reinforced with steel inserts in load-bearing areas.

The G-36 has a cyclic rate of 750 rpm and even though it can fire from standard M16 30-round magazines, the company has also decided to produce translucent magazines that allow the firer to make a quick visual check of the available ammunition. The rifle has an ambidextrous cocking handle and empty-case deflector for left-handed shooters.

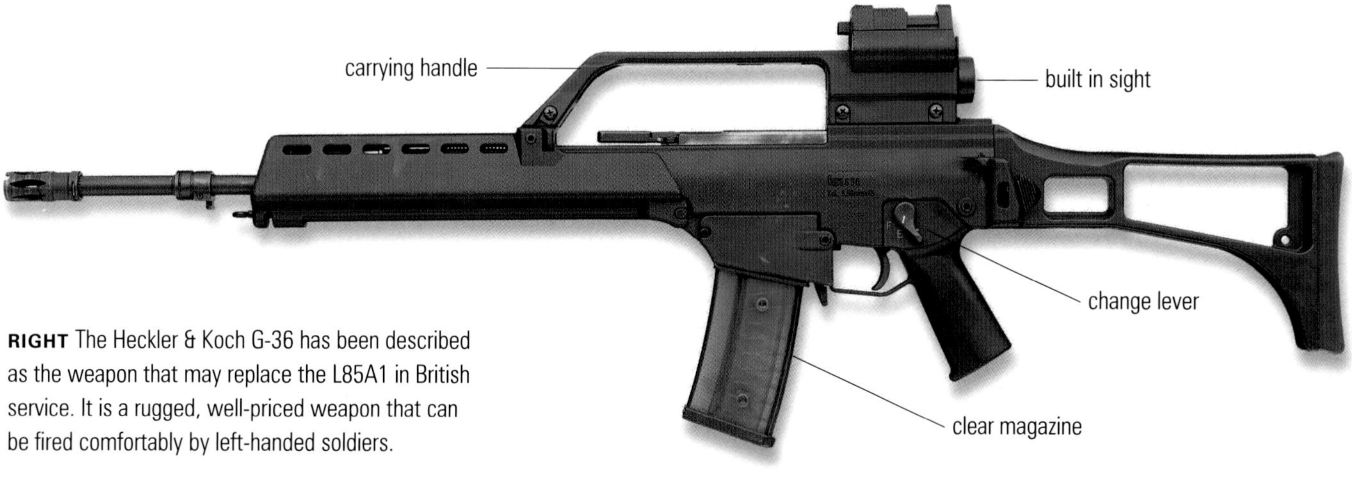

RIGHT The Heckler & Koch G-36 has been described as the weapon that may replace the L85A1 in British service. It is a rugged, well-priced weapon that can be fired comfortably by left-handed soldiers.

ABOVE When the Allies first encountered the superb German MG42 GPMG in Tunisia in 1943, they were intrigued by the stampings and brazings that were used in its construction – these were intended to speed mass production.

ABOVE An American M1917 Browning water-cooled machine gun with the unusual modification of a carrying handle around the water jacket. This allowed the crew to move the complete weapon short distances.

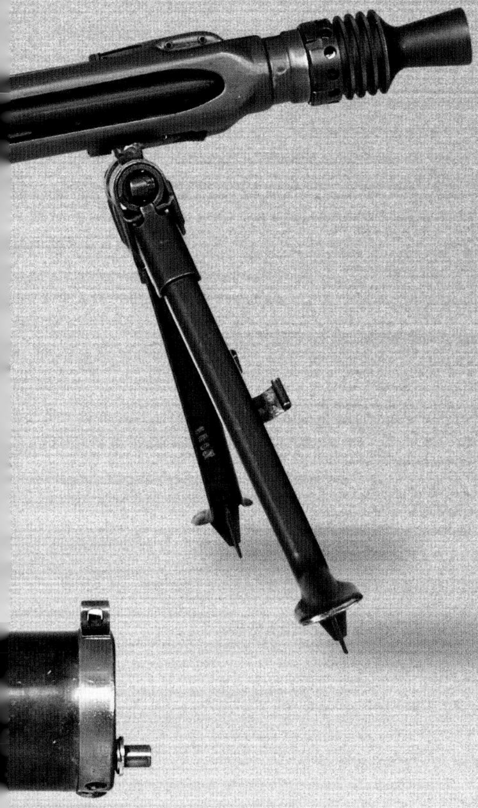

The machine-gun age 1883–2000s

The search for a faster rate of fire led to the machine gun, and this crucial weapon will be covered in this section. Interestingly, prior to the demonstration of a recoil-operated belt-fed machine gun by Hiram Maxim, there had been earlier attempts to produce fast-firing weapons.

Heat is the challenge for all automatic weapons designers. It is generated by the exploding cartridges, by the machinery of the weapon and principally by the rounds passing rapidly up the barrel.

If a weapon overheats it will jam or may become a "runaway gun" that keeps firing even though the trigger is not being pressed. The solution for many machine-gun designs was to enclose the barrel in a water jacket; later weapons had barrels that could be changed quickly so that they did not overheat. It was vital for the machine-gun crew to follow the drills for their weapon as conscientiously as a Napoleonic soldier did for his flintlock musket. Skip a drill or fail to complete it properly and the weapon would malfunction.

ABOVE A German 7.92mm Maschinengewehr 08 water-cooled machine gun in a trench system on the Western Front in the latter years of World War I. The gun commander looks for targets while the crew are ready with belted ammunition.

Machine guns

Without the percussion cap and the self-contained round, the machine gun would never have been developed. As a minister, the Reverend Alexander Forsyth would perhaps have been horrified to discover his major part in this innovation. It was the method of ignition he invented to make wild fowling less vulnerable to the vagaries of the weather that became a key element of the machine gun. Rounds – the bullet and cartridge with its percussion cap and powder – could be fed on a belt or from a spring-loaded magazine into a rapid-firing and brutally effective weapon of war.

The Somme

World War I seems almost synonymous with the machine gun. On 1 July 1916, the first day of the Battle of the Somme, German artillery and machine-gun crews hunched behind their Maxim '08s killed or wounded about 60,000 British soldiers as they advanced across no-man's-land.

However rapid-fire weapons in the shape of multiple-firing flintlocks and muzzle-loaders had existed in the 18th and 19th centuries. The Puckle gun – a sort of large mounted revolver – was introduced in 1718 and was said to have fired 63 shots in seven minutes. In the American Civil War (1861–5), the .50/12mm-calibre Gatling gun (1862) with a reported rate of up to 1,000 rounds per minute (rpm), and the Agar "Coffee Mill" (1860), with a rate of 120 rpm, were used in some numbers. These guns were followed by other hand-cranked multi-barrelled models such as the Gardner, the Lowell and the Nordenfelt. In the period 1870–90 the British and Russian armies adopted the Gatling gun, while the Royal Navy used three makes – the Gatling, the Gardner and the Nordenfelt.

ABOVE The Gardner machine gun looks like a conventional weapon but it was operated by the crank handle on the right-hand side. Ammunition feed was by single rounds fed in from the top.

But none of these weapons was a truly automatic machine gun. All required some form of cranking and/or manipulation; a later model of the Gatling had its barrels rotated by an electric motor. This manipulation, combined with the effect of the recoil, meant that the accuracy of these rapid-firing guns was generally unpredictable. The French and Belgians developed similar weapons – *les mitrailleuses*, the principal product being a 37-barrelled weapon invented in 1870 by Joseph Montigny.

Fully automatic

At the close of the 19th century an American, Hiram Maxim, demonstrated a fully automatic weapon – a machine gun. This weapon would change the character of land warfare and dominate the skies when the first combat aircraft took off in World War I. The machine gun would heavily influence infantry tactics, requiring men to move in short dashes and employ "fire and movement", with the machine gun giving covering fire as rifle-armed soldiers closed with the enemy. As rates of fire increased the infantry would almost become ammunition carriers for the machine gun, advancing with belts or boxes of ammunition.

ABOVE A German MG34 in use in World War II on its sustained fire mount. This turned it from a light machine gun (LMG) into a medium machine gun (MMG), creating the general purpose machine gun (GPMG).

The GPMG

The inter-war years saw German arms designers learn the lessons of World War I and produce a machine gun that fulfilled the functions of both the long-range Medium Machine Gun (MMG) and the Light Machine Gun (LMG). In the MG34 they created the General-Purpose Machine Gun (GPMG). The United States, Great Britain and the USSR fought World War II with both MMGs and LMGs. The British used the superb Bren LMG, a weapon that was still in service with second-line troops in 1990–91 during the First Gulf War. The staggering volume of fire from the MG34 and 42, respectively 900 and 1,500 rpm, was intimidating but could also be inaccurate. A machine gunner would often aim at an area target and produce a lethal "beaten zone" where falling rounds would make movement very risky.

Modern machine guns, such as the Belgian FN 5.56mm Minimi have become lighter and faster firing. Interestingly, the US electrically powered multi-barrelled M134 Minigun and GAU-19/A Gatling-type weapons incorporate technology first used in the designs of the 1860s. However, this development of a proven technology is not new. The Belgian FN MAG – in service with more than eighty armies across the world – uses the double-feed pawl system and the quick-change barrel that replaced the water jackets and cooling fins developed by the Germans for their superb MG42 machine gun in World War II.

BELOW The Belgian FN MAG is the most successful GPMG in service in NATO. It has a rate of fire of around 850 rounds per minute.

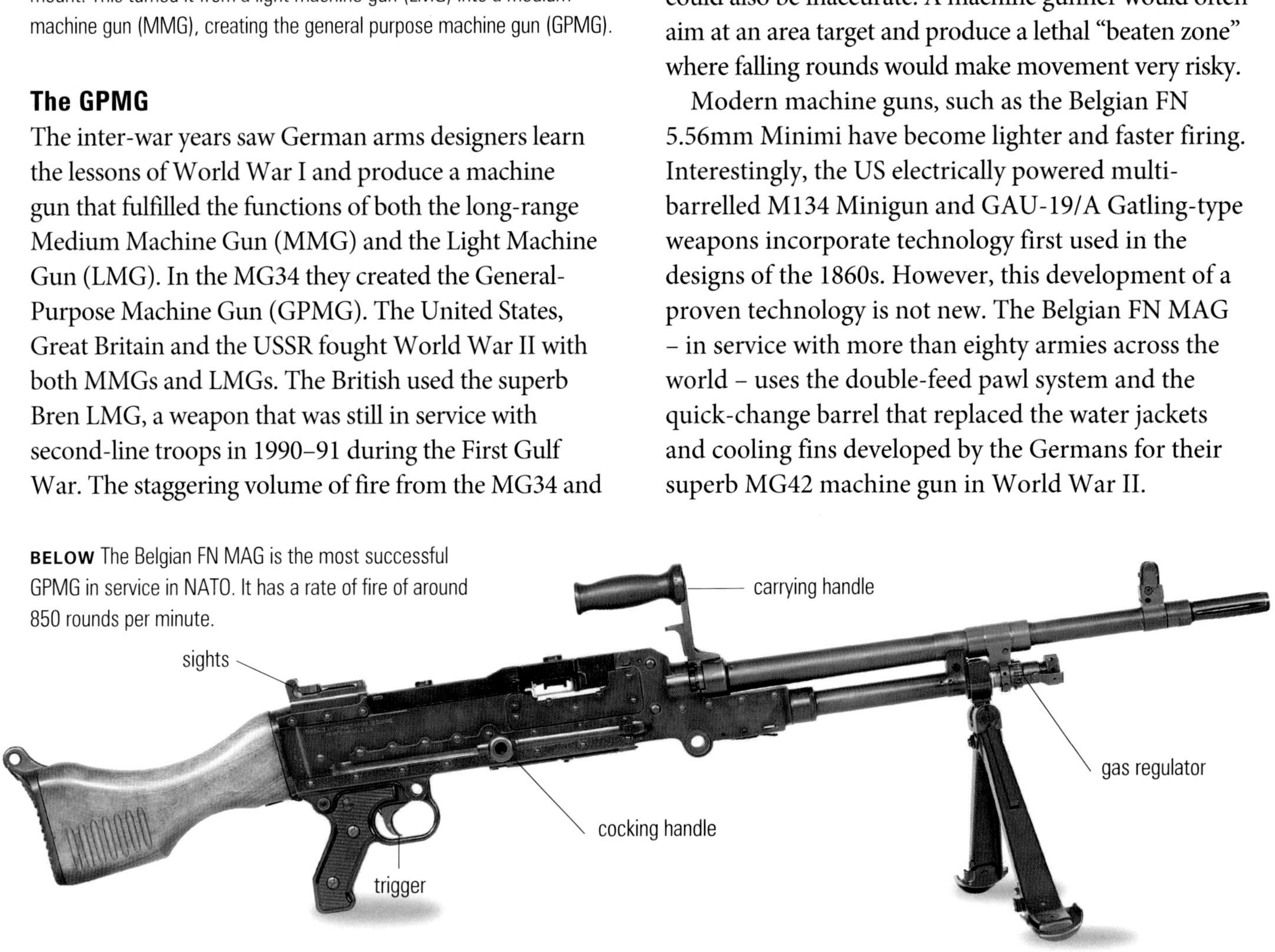

Early multi-shot weapons

The 18th and 19th centuries saw the first multi-shot weapons, such as the English Puckle gun. They were not machine guns, but they pointed to future wars in which heavy volumes of fire could dominate the battlefield. The industrial base of the Union forces in the American Civil War gave inventors the facilities to develop these weapons, notably the multi-barrelled Organ gun and hopper magazine-fed Agar "Coffee Mill".

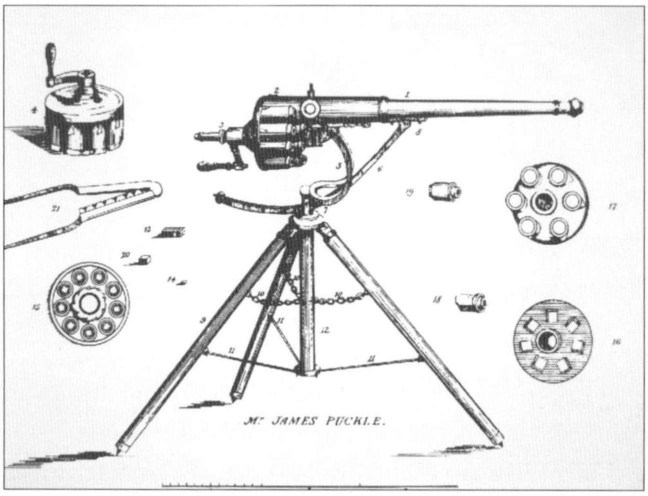

ABOVE The Puckle gun was a futuristic concept in the early 18th century and, unfortunately for its inventor, James Puckle, as was the case with many innovations, conservative British soldiers and government failed to see its military potential.

Puckle's gun

Born in 1667, James Puckle was an English lawyer, inventor and author. He is credited with two military inventions: a sword of which there is no record and his "portable gun or machine called a defence".

The Puckle gun was a tripod-mounted, single-barrelled flintlock gun fitted with a multi-shot revolving cylinder. At a time when a well-trained soldier could fire three shots a minute from his musket, one man with a Puckle gun could fire nine rounds. In a macabre marketing ploy Puckle offered two versions of the basic design. One gun, intended for use against Christian enemies, fired conventional round balls, while the second weapon, to be used against the Muslim Turks, fired square bullets that were believed to cause more severe wounds.

In 1717, after trials at Woolwich in front of senior officers, the gun was rejected by the British Government. Despite this, Puckle obtained a patent on 15 May 1718, and three years later set up a company to market it. An issue of the *Daily Courant* published in March 1722 carried an advertisement for "Several sizes in Brass and Iron of Mr. Puckle's Machine or Gun, called a Defence . . . at the Workshop thereof, in White-Cross-Alley, Middle Moorfields". At the end of the same month the *London Journal* reported that at a demonstration of one of the guns, "one Man discharged it 63 times in seven Minutes, though all the while Raining; and that it throws off either one large or sixteen Musquet Balls at every discharge with very great Force".

Despite the publicity, Puckle failed to attract backers, and when in 1718 his business went bust, a newspaper of the period ruefully noted that "those are only wounded who hold shares therein".

The 1860 Agar "Coffee Mill"

This is the earliest machine gun known to have been used by the United States Army. Designed by Wilson Agar, it was demonstrated to President Lincoln in 1861, and he was so impressed that he ordered ten at a price of $1,300 a gun; 51 were purchased a year later. They are known to have seen action in a limited number of arenas, and those include the battles of Petersburg, Virginia (1864–5). The machine gun earned its nickname from the hopper magazine feed, which resembled the feed for a coffee grinder. The "Coffee Mill" was mounted on a conventional artillery carriage with a small armour plate to protect the gunner. He had to stand, feeding .58in Minié bullets into the magazine and cranking a handle to fire. The weapon had an effective range of 915m/1,000yd and fired at 120 rpm. The gunner could increase this rate by cranking the handle faster, but because the Agar had only one barrel he ran the risk of overheating it. To obviate this, two spare barrels were always carried with the gun.

Billinghurst-Requa battery

Although the Gatling gun, patented on 4 November 1862, would prove a superior weapon, the Billinghurst-Requa battery, an advanced organ gun patented on 16 September 1862, predates it and is widely regarded as the first "practical" machine gun to be used during the American Civil War. It was the invention of the self-contained metal cartridge that made the organ gun (also known as the volley gun) a practical weapon. The cleverly arranged breech, which closed on a piano hinge, allowed for the ammunition strips to be loaded, fired, extracted, and reloaded quickly by the crew of three.

When the side-mounted loading levers were up, the breech was open. A powder train was laid behind the ammunition strip. Pushing the levers forward secured the breech. A musket cap was placed on the central priming nipple and fired with a simple flip-over hammer mechanism. The barrels, each 700mm/24in long, fired sequentially from the centre out with a characteristic rippling effect.

ABOVE A Billinghurst-Requa battery gun from around 1862. The weight of the 25 musket barrels meant that the gun had to be mounted on a light artillery carriage, and many armies therefore mistakenly considered weapons on gun carriages as light artillery and not a support weapon for the infantry. The idea of a multi-barrelled weapon had first appeared in a design by the Italian Leonardo da Vinci in the late 15th century.

ABOVE The Agar "Coffee Mill" was so-named because the ammunition feed was a hopper that looked very like the one that fitted to a coffee mill. It was hand cranked and capable of 120 rounds a minute.

The Organ gun

Also known as a volley gun or ribaldequin, this was a multi-barrelled gun designed to fire a number of shots simultaneously. Some volley guns could also fire their barrels in sequence. They were not machine guns because they did not load and fire automatically and were restricted by the number of barrels bundled together. The weapon was known as an organ gun because the bank of barrels resembled the pipes in a church organ.

In practice, the large organ guns had little more use than as a cannon firing canister or grapeshot. Mounted on a carriage, they were still as hard to aim and manoeuvre as a cannon, and the many barrels took as long or longer to reload. They also tended to be relatively expensive since they were more complex than a cannon; all the barrels had to be individually maintained, cleaned, loaded and primed. Despite this, the Requa battery, a 25-barrel organ gun, was used by Union forces in 1863 in the American Civil War. A three-man crew could fire seven volleys a minute.

Weapons of war

In the mid-19th century, weapons such as the Gatling were used in action by the Americans in the Civil War, while the French used the Montigny mitrailleuse, one of the first secret weapons, in the Franco-Prussian War. The Swedish-designed Nordenfelt was adopted by the British for use by the Royal Navy.

ABOVE The Gatling gun is one of the iconic weapons of the American Civil War. Soldiers were still unsure whether it was an artillery or infantry weapon, and the wheeled carriage makes it look like a field gun.

The Gatling gun

Patented in 1862 by Richard Jordan Gatling, a dentist from North Carolina, this gun was a variation on the revolver principle, with six to ten barrels revolved around a central axis, firing one barrel at a time. The main advantage of having many barrels was that they cooled in between shots, so maintaining their accuracy and preventing "cook-off": the premature ignition of a charge. In 1865 the US Army bought its first Gatling. The first weapons used paper cartridges, but a year later, metallic ones were introduced. Other types of automatic weapons were used in the Civil War but only the Gatling remained in service afterwards.

The Gatling was improved and served with a number of armies around the world as an infantry support or a light artillery weapon. Usually chambered for the contemporary general issue rifle cartridge, some naval Gatlings, however, had calibres up to 1in, and some derivatives, such as the Hotchkiss, were up to 2in in calibre. To fire the Gatling, a handle at the back was cranked, which rotated the barrels and fired them in turn. Each barrel had its own bolt that reloaded with each turn. A competent gunner could reach rates of fire of over 200 rounds a minute – a far higher rate than with a single-shot muzzle-loaded or even magazine-fed bolt-action rifle. By 1890, the first true recoil-operated machine guns had been developed but some Gatlings remained in service until 1914.

ABOVE The mitrailleuse used by the French Army in 1870–71 in the Franco-Prussian War was regarded as light artillery even though it used rifle ammunition. Its lethal potential was not fully realized in that war.

The Montigny mitrailleuse

The mitrailleuse was designed in Belgium by Captain T. H. J. Fafschamps in 1851 and manufactured by Joseph Montigny of Fontaine-l'Evêque near Brussels. It was deployed in Belgium in the 1850s, apparently only on a limited basis as a defensive weapon to protect Belgian fortresses.

The Montigny mitrailleuse entered service with the French Army in 1869. Although it looked similar to a modern machine gun, it was strictly speaking a volley-fire gun. It had 26 barrels enclosed in a brass cylinder. A plate pre-loaded with ammunition was inserted into the breach, and to fire it, the gunner cranked a handle. He could fire all 26 barrels in one blast.

At the outbreak of war between France and Prussia in July 1870, the French Army had approximately 190 of these weapons available. Each division was issued with one battery of six guns, issued as replacement for the *Canon de 4* (86.5mm) battery. However, the tactical philosophy behind the deployment of the mitrailleuse was unsuccessful in practice. The guns were ideal at short range against cavalry and infantry, and on one occasion a single mitrailleuse stopped a charge by 500 Prussian cavalry in a murderous 90-second fusillade. Yet French gunners assumed the mitrailleuse was an artillery piece and attempted to use it in long-range duels with very efficient Prussian artillery, a role for which it was entirely unsuited.

The Nordenfelt

This machine gun was of Swedish design and consisted of four to ten barrels mounted on a tripod and fitted with a hopper magazine, with a hand lever to operate the mechanism. It was adopted by the Royal Navy and used as an anti-torpedo boat weapon and by naval landing parties.

There were several designs, including a ten-barrelled Nordenfelt machine gun in .45 calibre, a four-barrelled Nordenfelt 1in-calibre gun with a rate of 200 rpm (introduced into service by the British in 1880, replacing the Gatling .45-calibre machine gun and five-barrelled Gardner machine gun), and the five-barrelled Nordenfelt .45-calibre, 600-rpm gun introduced in 1882.

Torsten W. Nordenfelt

The Swedish engineer Torsten Wilhelm Nordenfelt (1842–1920) teamed up with his fellow countryman and inventor Palmcrantz to produce the M1877 25mm/1in four-barrelled semi-automatic weapon for the Royal Swedish Navy. The gun was gravity fed and fired at 120 rpm. As the Royal Navy was the largest in the world in the late 19th century, Nordenfelt set up a factory in London to supply guns. He teamed up with Maxim to produce guns that were supplied to the Ottoman and German navies. In 1906 the US Navy adopted its first light automatic anti-aircraft gun, the Maxim-Nordenfelt 1 pdr Mark 6.

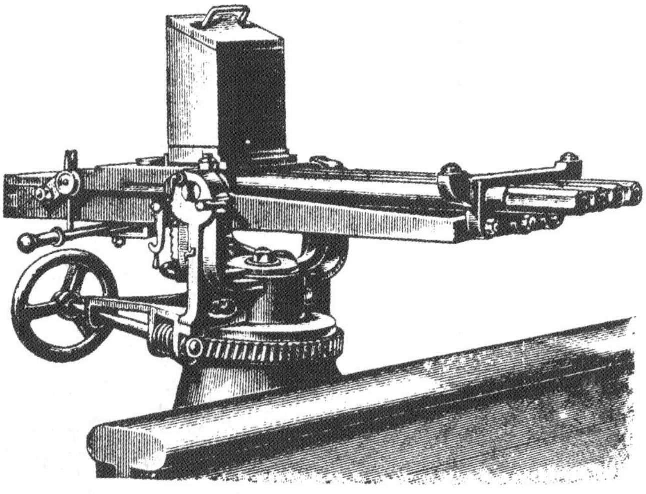

ABOVE The Nordenfelt was produced in several calibres with one to twelve barrels. The weapon shown here is a naval mounting designed to combat torpedo boats.

The first machine guns

Hiram Maxim's invention at the close of the 19th century dominated the 20th century. Colt and Browning, two American small arms giants, combined to produce a machine gun, the Colt-Browning "Potato Digger", while the Danish produced the Madsen – significantly, the first light machine gun (LMG) – which has often been overlooked.

The Maxim machine gun

In 1883–85 US-born Hiram S. Maxim developed the first fully automatic machine gun. After cocking the weapon and pressing the firing button, a round was fired. The recoil energy from firing operated the breech-block; the spent cartridge was expelled, a new round fed into the breech, the firing pin cocked, and a new round fired. As long as the button was depressed a Maxim would fire until the entire ammunition belt was expended. Trials showed that the machine gun could fire 500 rounds per minute. Maxim was knighted for his work after becoming a British citizen.

The Maxim machine gun was adopted by the British Army in 1889. In the following year the Austrian, German, Italian, Swiss and Russian armies also purchased Maxim's gun. The gun was first used by Britain's colonial forces in the Matabele War in southern Africa, in 1893–4. In one engagement, 50 soldiers fought off 5,000 Matabele warriors with just four Maxim guns.

ABOVE The Colt-Browning "Potato Digger" received this nickname during the Irish Civil War in 1922, when combatants likened the action of the swinging lever to a farmer digging for potatoes.

ABOVE Under the watchful eye of a British officer and the inventor Hiram Maxim, Henry M. Stanley experiments with a Maxim gun. Unlike earlier weapons the maxim did not require a hand crank and was belt fed.

The success of the Maxim machine gun inspired other inventors. The German Army's Maschinengewehr and the Russian Pulemyot Maxima were both based on Maxim's invention.

The Colt-Browning "Potato Digger"

The 1895/1914 Colt-Browning .3 machine gun was initially adopted by the American Expeditionary Force (AEF) at the start of World War I pending delivery of other weapons, including the Browning M1917. The Colt-Browning, which weighed a little over

RIGHT Made by the Dansk Rekyt-Riffel Syndikat A/S Madsen in Copenhagen, this LMG was universally known as "the Madsen". It pioneered the overhead magazine that uses gravity as well as a spring to feed rounds.

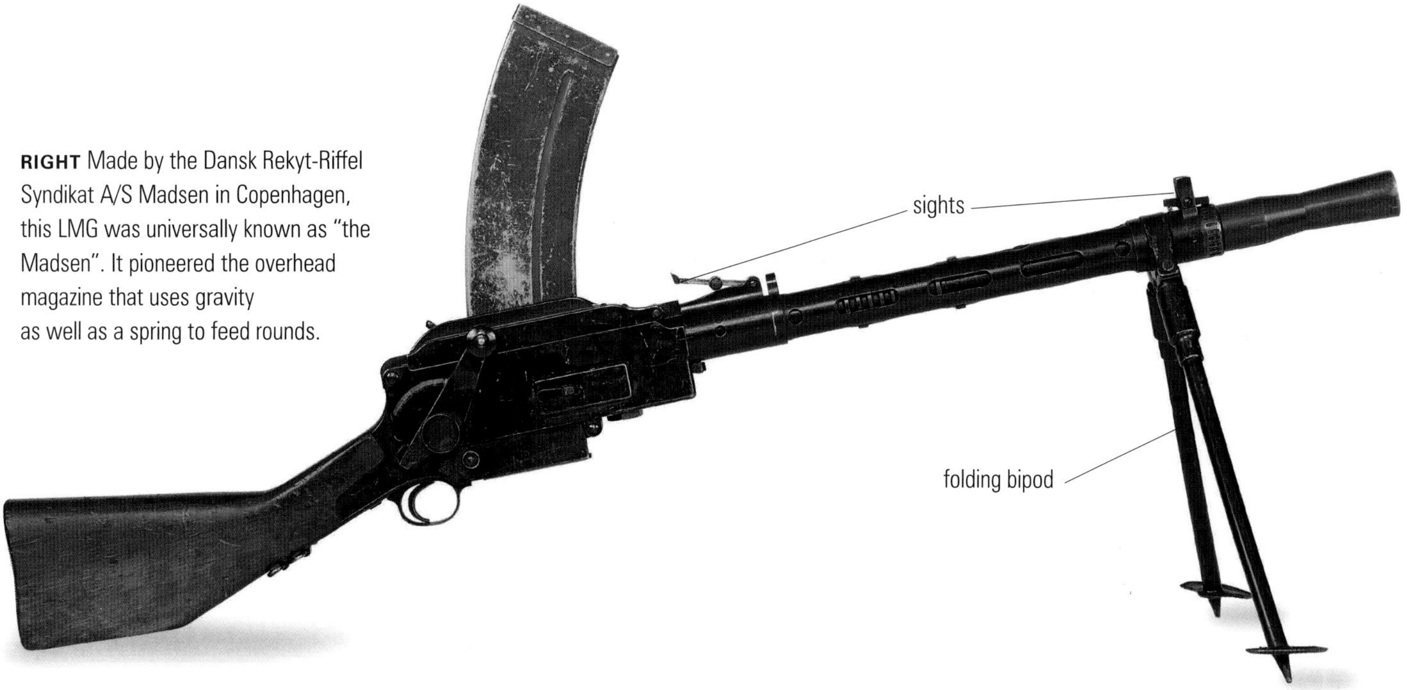

45.9kg/101lb, had a maximum cyclic belt-fed firing rate of 500 rpm. It is regarded as the first successful gas-operated machine gun, designed by John Moses Browning and offered to the Colt company towards the close of 1890.

Originally designed to use .3 Krag Jorgenson cartridges, the gun was modified in 1914 and chambered for .30/60 cartridges. Italy purchased a number of Colt-Browning 1895/1914 guns in 6.5mm calibre for use by its army as a supplement to the home-grown Fiat-Revelli gun. This machine gun got its nickname "potato digger" because of the action of the swinging lever below the gun.

The Madsen LMG

The Danish 8mm Madsen light machine gun (LMG) was first introduced in 1902 and was the first true light machine gun. A recoil-operated weapon, it was fed from a 20-round curved box magazine. It has been said of the Madsen that the remarkable thing about it was not that it worked well, but that it worked at all. It had a complex mechanism built around the Martini breech-block action. The breech was opened by a recoil-driven cam, and then a separate rammer pushed the cartridge into the chamber before it closed and the round was fired. The Madsen has a long operational history; it first saw action with Russian cavalry squadrons in the Russo–Japanese War of 1904–05. In World War I Germany, Britain and France used it in limited numbers. The German Army formed the first light machine-gun units based on the Madsen; the Musketen Battalions. They went into action in the Champagne sector in September 1915. Yet the German Army failed to realize their potential. The three Musketen Battalions were used in a defensive role, and so did not demonstrate the advantages of an LMG in the attack. Later, when the utility of an LMG became apparent, the Germans ignored the Madsen and instead developed the MG08/15 water-cooled gun.

Hiram S. Maxim

Born in Sangersville, Maine, USA in 1840, Hiram Maxim became a coachbuilder in an engineering works in Fitchburg, Massachusetts. When he was 26, he obtained the first of many patents for a hair-curling iron. This was rapidly followed by a machine for producing illuminating gas and a locomotive headlamp.

Maxim was employed by the United States Electric Lighting Company as chief engineer and designed a method of producing carbon filaments. At the Paris Electrical Exhibition in 1881 he found the inspiration to develop a machine gun. Maxim moved to London, and in 1884 produced the first working model of an automatic portable machine gun. His Maxim Gun Company, founded the same year, was later absorbed into Vickers Ltd, and he became a director. Maxim was knighted by Queen Victoria in 1901.

Machine guns of World War I

Prior to World War I, Austria-Hungary had an established small arms industry in what is now the Czech Republic as well as in Austria, where it produced the Schwarzlose MG07/12. In France, Hotchkiss, a firm established by an American, produced two reliable machine guns, while the German Maschinengewehr 08 was used to great effect against British and French forces on the Western Front.

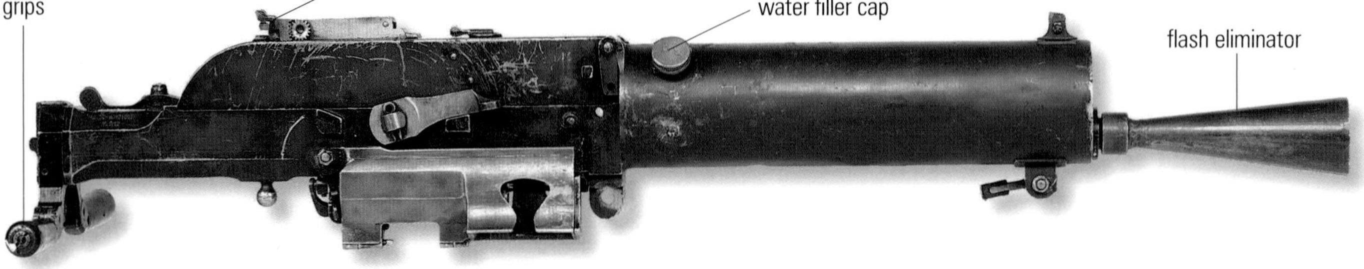

ABOVE The Austrian Schwarzlose MG07, produced by Steyr, was so rugged that guns that were nearly forty years old were still in service in Yugoslavia, Bulgaria, Holland, Romania, Hungary, Italy and Greece as well as Austria at the outbreak of World War II.

The Schwarzlose MG07/12

Designed by Andreas Wilhelm Schwarzlose in 1902, the MG07/12 would be the standard MMG (Medium Machine Gun) with Austro-Hungarian forces during World War I. It was widely sold or delivered as war reparations after 1918. Many were used by the Italians in World War II. The water-cooled machine gun had a distinctive cone-shaped flame damper and pistol grip. It had a cyclic rate of fire of 400–500 rpm and fired from a 250-round fabric belt.

This weapon had a fixed barrel, few moving parts and rugged construction. The breech was at no time truly locked. When the gun fired, the rearward thrust of the exploding gases actually started the action opening at the same instant as it caused the bullet to move down the barrel. However, by using a very short barrel and a combination of extremely heavy recoil parts and springs, Schwarzlose produced a machine gun that permitted the use of powerful military rifle cartridges without an impossibly heavy breech mechanism to absorb the recoil energy from these rounds.

ABOVE A German MG08 machine gun crew in the latter years of World War I. The gun was rugged and reliable, but heavy, which meant that it was not suitable for infantry actions involving the tactics of fire and manoeuvre, and were largely used for defence.

The Maschinengewehr 08

The German Maschinengewehr 08, or MG08, was virtually a direct copy of the 1884 Maxim, and was the German Army's standard machine gun in World War I. At the start of the war, about 12,000 MG08s were available. The British assumed that the Germans had large numbers of guns; in fact they had learned that machine guns proved more effective when concentrated together. The Maschinengewehr 08 remained in service in static positions even after the outbreak of World War II, until it was replaced by the MG34 in about 1942.

ABOVE During a visit by a politician to France in World War I, a Canadian officer explains the workings of the Hotchkiss Mark 1. The gun would remain in service into World War II in light armoured vehicles.

The 7.92mm MG08, based on the 1901 model but named after 1908, its year of adoption, was water cooled by about 4.5 litres/1 gallon of water in a jacket around the barrel. It fired from a 250-round fabric belt and had a cyclic rate of 400 rpm, although sustained firing would lead to overheating. The MG08 had a range of about 2,010m/2,200yd up to a maximum of 3,660m/4,000yd. It was moved on a cart, or dismantled and carried by the crew on their shoulders to a new position.

The Benet-Mercie 1909

The Benet-Mercie Machine Rifle, Calibre .30 US Model of 1909 was a .30 machine gun, adopted by the US Army in 1909 and used throughout World War I. The same basic pattern was also used by the French and British: with the French as the Hotchkiss M1909 chambered for 8mm Lebel ammunition and with the British as the Hotchkiss Mark I. The French and British designs proved longer lived; used in tanks and aircraft, they served on into World War II. The US design was fed from 30-round strips, as were other types, although there were also belt-fed versions and others with enhanced barrel cooling. The US types had a bipod, while some others used a small tripod.

Benjamin Hotchkiss

Born in Watertown, Connecticut, in 1826, Benjamin Berkeley Hotchkiss became a skilled designer in the family's engineering business, working on new weapons designs. When he failed to interest the US Government, he moved to France and set up the Hotchkiss Company in 1867.

Hotchkiss began producing weapons and explosives for the French armed forces at his factory near Paris. After his death in 1885, work continued, and the first working model of an automatic machine gun was produced by 1892.

In 1897 it was adopted by the French Army. A series of improvements and modifications followed, and by 1914 the definitive Hotchkiss gun had been created. Reliable and simple, it became one of the standard gas-operated heavy machine-gun designs to be adopted for use by the British, French and Japanese armies during World War I.

Machine gun veterans

Three machine guns that were the cornerstones of infantry operations in World War I – the Russian PM1910, British Vickers MMG and French Hotchkiss M1914 – were still in use during World War II. Indeed, the Vickers was still in use in the mid-1960s, before the British Army switched to 7.62mm NATO calibre ammunition.

The Pulemyot Maxima PM1910

The Russian Pulemyot Maxima na stanke Sokolova (Maxim's machine gun on Sokolov's mount), was also known as the Maxim machine gun 1910 (or Pulemyot Maxima PM1910). This variant of the Maxim machine gun was chambered for the standard Russian 7.62 x 54mm R ammunition. It served as the medium machine gun in the Imperial Russian Army during World War I and the Red Army during World War II. The gun fired at 600 rounds per minute from a 250-round fabric belt. The water-cooling jacket had a screw cap normally fitted to tractor radiators; it was large enough that snow could be packed into the jacket during the bitter Russian winters when all water was frozen. For a degree of mobility, the M1910 could be installed on the wheeled Sokolov mount. By 1943 it was replaced by the excellent SG-43 Gorunov. Maxims were often bolted together on a high-angle mount as anti-aircraft guns.

ABOVE A sergeant of the British Gloucestershire Regiment, whose ribbons indicate that he is a veteran of World War II, supervises two Vickers MMG detachments in the 1950s in a display of infantry weapons.

ABOVE Soviet sailors fighting as infantry in World War II man a triple PM1910 anti-aircraft machine gun. The guns would have put up 1,800 rpm and made an effective low-altitude anti-aircraft system.

The Vickers MMG

The first Vickers machine gun, the Vickers .303in Medium Machine Gun Mark 1, entered service in 1912 and soldiered on with the British Army until 1974. It was a Maxim mechanism that had been inverted and improved. With water in the cooling jacket, the gun weighed 18kg/40lb and the tripod 22kg/48.5lb, while the total weight of the gun was 40.2kg/88.5lb. The Vickers machine gun had a muzzle velocity of 744m/s/2,440ft/s and a rate of fire of 450–500 rpm, and it was fired from a 250-round fabric belt. The introduction of the Mark 8z round added a further 915m/1,000yd to the 550m/3,600yd maximum range. Using a dial sight, which was introduced in 1942, the gun could be used for indirect fire.

During World War I the Vickers MMG gained a reputation as the "Queen of the battlefield" with men of the British Machine Gun Corps (founded in October 1915). It is a measure of the effectiveness and reliability of the weapon that it would take just three hours and twenty minutes for ten guns to fire one million rounds during World War I. Contemporary and post-war accounts tell of ten guns firing that many rounds on 24 August 1916, but modern research by arms scholars in 2019 have concluded that, while technically possible, the earlier accounts are fabrications due to conflicting evidence regarding the number of guns present and the logistics needed in terms of ammunition and water to pull off such a feat.

The Hotchkiss M1914

The St Etienne Mle 1907 was the standard machine gun of the French Army at the outbreak of World War I. However, it performed badly in the field. It had so many deficiencies that although guns were captured by the Germans and given the designation 8mm sMG256(f), they were never used, even in fixed fortifications.

There were several modifications until the gas-operated, air-cooled Hotchkiss 8mm M1914 machine gun was produced in 1914, when gas operation was still a relatively new concept. It was a very distinctive gun, with five large circular cooling fins and a metal strip ammunition feed. The Hotchkiss became the French army's standard heavy tripod-mounted MMG in World War I. Twelve divisions of the American Expeditionary Forces (AEF) in France were equipped with the Mle 1914 Hotchkiss in 1917–18.

The gun was heavy at 23kg/50lb (44kg/88lb with its mounting), but reliable. The main drawback was the ammunition feed, a cumbersome 24- or 30-round metal magazine strip that fired 8mm Lebel rounds. In 1917 a 250-round belt feed was introduced, enabling effective sustained fire. The Hotchkiss had a muzzle velocity of 701m/s/2,299ft/s and a cyclic rate of 450 rpm.

ABOVE The French mitrailleuse St Etienne Mle 1907 had evolved from the earlier Mle 1905 produced by the State Arsenal Puteaux. It was gradually replaced in service during World War I.

LEFT The French Hotchkiss Mle 1914 was the standard French medium machine gun during World War I. It remained in widespread use during World War II.

Machine-gun tactics in World War I

In 1914 a German Army battalion had six Maxim MG Modell 1908 machine guns; in contrast, a British battalion had only two Vickers Mark 1s, or Maxims. However, from the outset of the fighting, the Germans tactically concentrated these already co-ordinated battalion teams into batteries and thus gave the appearance, and effect, of having even more machine guns than was actually the case. They gave this impression at Loos, where German machine-gun crews opened fire at 1,400m/1,530yd on the advancing British infantry on the afternoon of 26 September 1915. They inflicted 8,000 casualties (50 per cent) on just two British New Army Divisions (21st and 24th). One German single machine-gun crew is said to have fired 12,500 rounds.

In 1917–18 the British and Germans made a change from the defensive to a more offensive role for the machine gun. The British Machine Gun Corps undertook highly co-ordinated offensive and defensive tactics, including barrages. The infantry then concentrated on the deployment, with much success, of the lighter Lewis machine guns at the platoon level.

The good and the bad

The Italian Fiat-Revelli M1914 must have been a gunner's nightmare, with a complex mechanism that was prone to jamming. The unreliable French Chauchat LMG was designed by three men – Chauchat, Suterre and Riberolle – and as such has been called a gun designed by committee. The American-designed British-built Lewis gun, however, would be one of World War I's success stories.

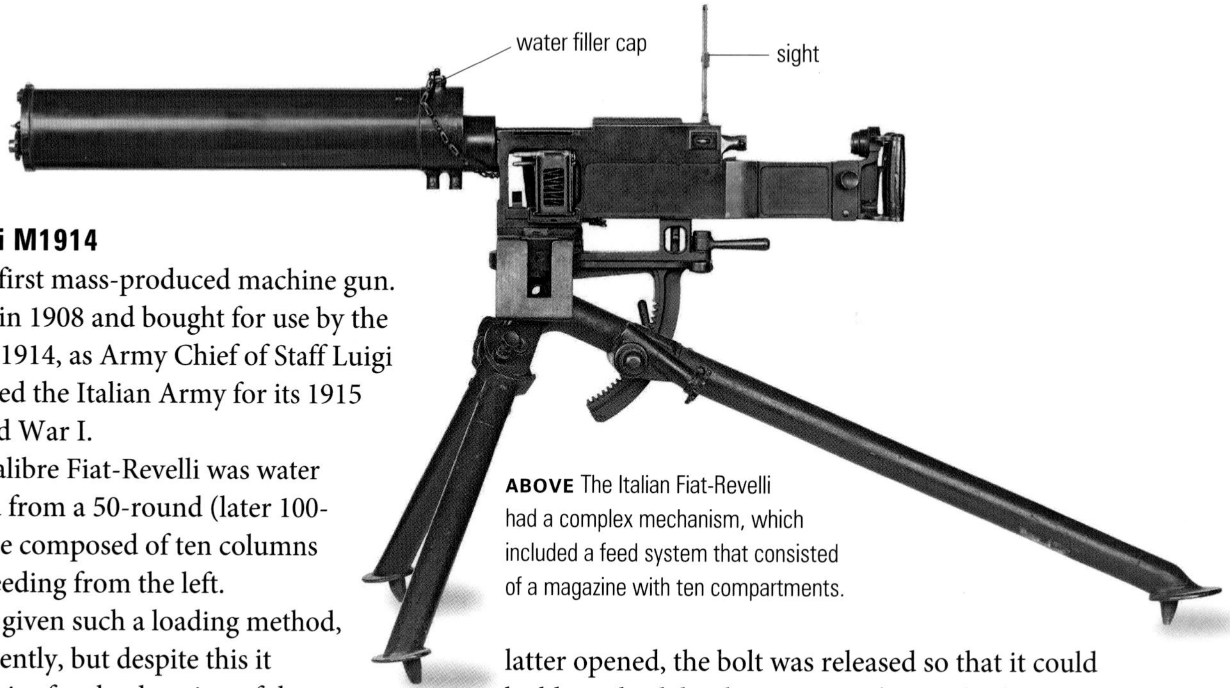

ABOVE The Italian Fiat-Revelli had a complex mechanism, which included a feed system that consisted of a magazine with ten compartments.

The Fiat-Revelli M1914

This was Italy's first mass-produced machine gun. It was designed in 1908 and bought for use by the Italian Army in 1914, as Army Chief of Staff Luigi Cadorna prepared the Italian Army for its 1915 entry into World War I.

The 6.5mm calibre Fiat-Revelli was water cooled and fired from a 50-round (later 100-round) magazine composed of ten columns of five rounds feeding from the left. Unsurprisingly, given such a loading method, it jammed frequently, but despite this it remained in service for the duration of the war.

It bore a superficial resemblance to both the Maxim and Vickers machine guns but had an entirely different mechanism. Using a delayed blowback mechanism, the barrel and bolt recoiled a short distance, held in place by a swinging wedge. As the latter opened, the bolt was released so that it could be blown back by the spent case's recoil. The overly complex design of this mechanism led to cartridge extraction difficulties; consequently, an oil reservoir was used to lubricate cartridges before they were loaded into the gun. However, oil attracts dirt and dirt can jam mechanisms.

Isaac Newton Lewis

In 1911, a serving American officer and amateur inventor, Colonel Isaac Newton Lewis, perfected a light machine gun originally designed by another American, Samuel Maclean. The American Army showed no interest in its production, so Colonel Lewis retired and moved to Belgium in January 1913, where the Belgians undertook its manufacture. Surprisingly, its calibre was 7.7mm or .303, the calibre of the standard British rifle round.

When Germany invaded Belgium in 1914, the German forces who came up against the weapon called it "the Belgian rattlesnake". Many of Lewis's Belgian workers fled to Britain, where they were given employment by the Birmingham Small Arms Company (BSA), which bought the licence to manufacture the gun. From 1915 it entered service in increasing numbers with the British Army. By 1916 approximately 50,000 had been produced. In 1915 each British battalion on the Western Front had just four Lewis guns, but by 1917 each infantry section boasted its own Lewis gunner and number two, with battalions by now deploying 46 Lewis guns.

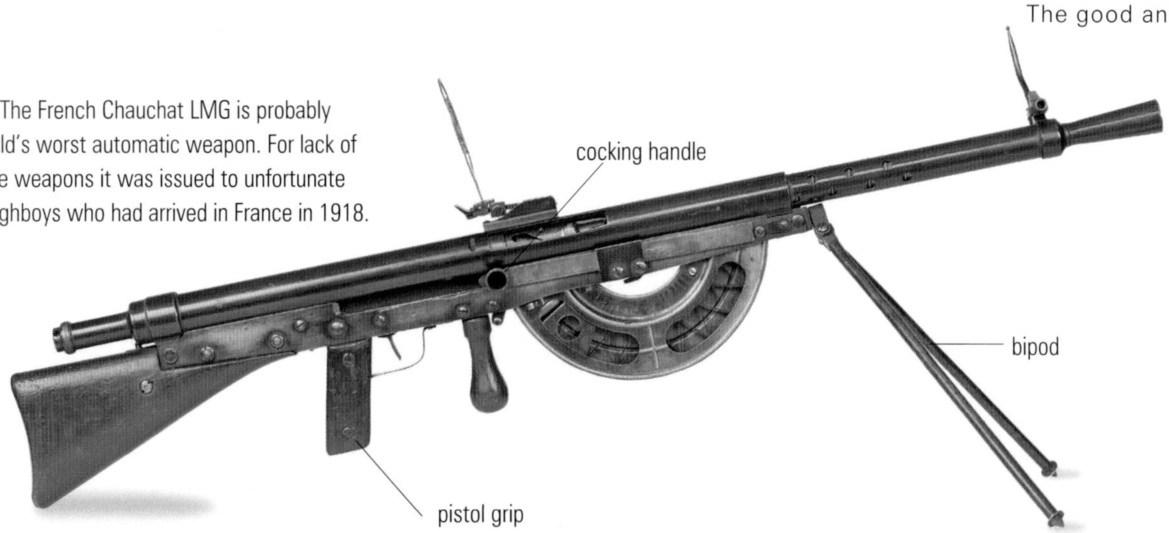

RIGHT The French Chauchat LMG is probably the world's worst automatic weapon. For lack of available weapons it was issued to unfortunate US Doughboys who had arrived in France in 1918.

The Fiat-Revelli was theoretically capable of firing 400–500 rpm out to 1,500m/1,640yd, but in practice it fired approximately 150–200 rpm. It was modified for use in aircraft in 1915 before British-supplied Vickers and Lewis guns were fitted to Italian aircraft in 1917. The Fiat-Revelli nevertheless held a place within the Italian Army's armoury, albeit with modifications including a 300-round belt feed, until the end of World War II.

The Chauchat LMG

The Chauchat was the light machine gun used principally by the French Army and also by seven other nations, including the USA, during and after World War I. Its formal designation in the French Army was Fusil-Mitrailleur Mle 1915 CSRG. It was also known as the CSRG or Gladiator. More than 260,000 were produced, making it the most widely manufactured automatic weapon of World War I. It was among the first light machine-gun designs of the early 1900s, with novel features, such as a pistol grip, an in-line stock and select fire lever, that are now standard in modern assault rifles. To speed production it was made from stampings and tubular and lathe-turned components. It fired from a 20-round magazine at 250 rpm and had a rather complex long barrel recoil and gas-assisted mechanism. The Chauchat was designed and built in a hurry during World War I and had numerous faults, chief among them that it used a magazine with open sides that allowed dust, dirt and other debris to clog it and prevent the gun from firing. As a result, it is recognized today as one of the least reliable automatic weapons ever issued to armed services.

The Lewis LMG

In 1911, Colonel Isaac Lewis of the US Army adapted the complex light machine-gun design of another American engineer, Samuel McLean, and produced the Lewis gun. This early light machine gun was widely adopted by the military forces of Britain and its empire from 1915 onwards. The M1914 air-cooled Lewis gun had a 47-cartridge circular magazine, or a 97-round cartridge for aircraft. The adjustable clockwork recoil spring allowed the gunner to adjust his rate of fire between 500 and 600 rpm, although most gunners preferred to fire short bursts. The gun had adjustable sights and a bipod for firing from the prone position. This gave it an effective range of 600m/655yd.

BELOW Although the Lewis LMG was designed by an American, during the two world wars it became a truly international weapon. Lewis guns accounted for 20 per cent of the Luftwaffe aircraft shot down around London in 1940.

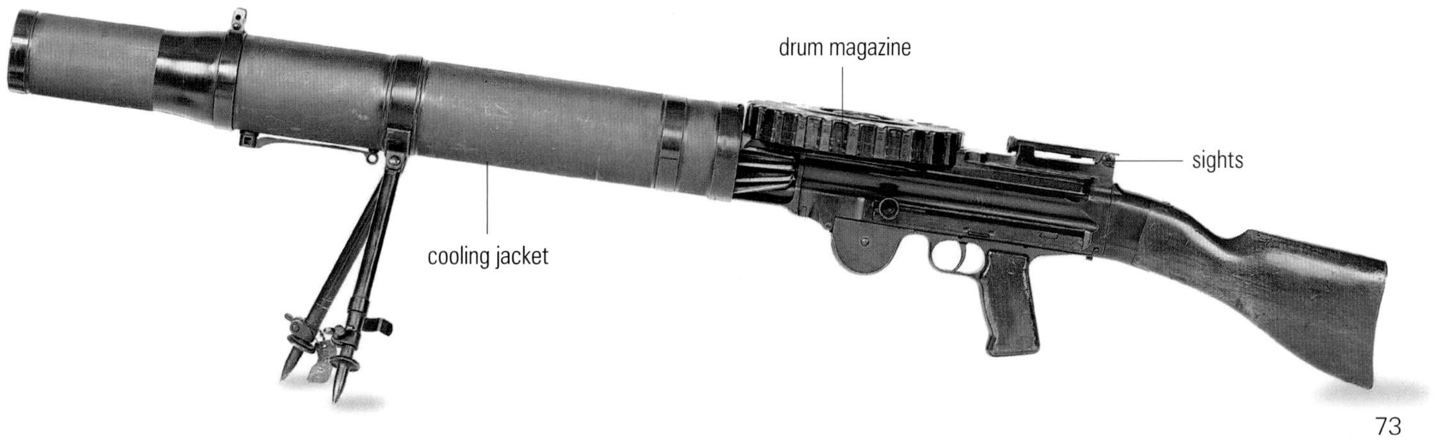

World War I survivors

The heavy weight of the German MG 08/15 (a "light" machine gun) must in part have been the inspiration to produce the genuinely light MG34 and later the well-designed MG42. The American Browning M1917 would serve through two world wars, but the Browning .50 would be a true survivor; it remains in service in the 21st century.

RIGHT The Browning M1917 was under development as far back as the 1890s, but the US Army expressed little interest in it until World War I.

The Browning M1917

Like the MG08 the Browning M1917 was a water-cooled machine gun. It was superficially similar to the Maxim and Vickers machine guns, although its pistol grip and internal mechanism differentiated it from both. It was adopted by the US Army following the entry of the United States into World War I in April 1917. Before the war ended on 11 November 1918, some 57,000 recoil-operated, belt-fed, M1917 machine guns had been manufactured for use by the American Expeditionary Force (AEF). Weighing some 24kg/53lb, the Browning .3 was actually developed in 1910 from an 1890s design. The M1917 fired from a 250-round fabric belt and was capable of firing 450–600 rpm. The basic Browning mechanism in the M1917 would remain virtually unchanged in all future Browning designs.

Immediately following US entry into World War I, the M1917 was not initially available. In the interim, while production was increased, the AEF deployed the French Chauchat LMG. The M1917A1,

The Maschinengewehr MG08/15

The MG08/15 was an attempt by the Germans to produce a lighter version of the MG08 for use by assault troops. It retained the mechanism of the MG08 but in place of the heavy tripod had a bipod with a pistol grip and shoulder stock. Despite this attempt to lighten the gun, it still weighed 18kg/40lb. It fired from 50-, 100- or 250-round fabric belts at 450 rpm. The gun was used by Belgium and Yugoslavia in the inter-war years, and in World War II was still in service with German formations, albeit with second- and third-line units. It was used in an anti-aircraft (AA) role and perhaps most notoriously in the watchtowers of concentration and prisoner-of-war camps. At the close of the war, MG08/15 guns were issued to Volkssturm formations.

LEFT The MG08/15 was an attempt by the Germans to turn the big MG08 into a weapon that could be used as an LMG. The water jacket required to cool the barrel meant that the gun still weighed 18kg/40lb.

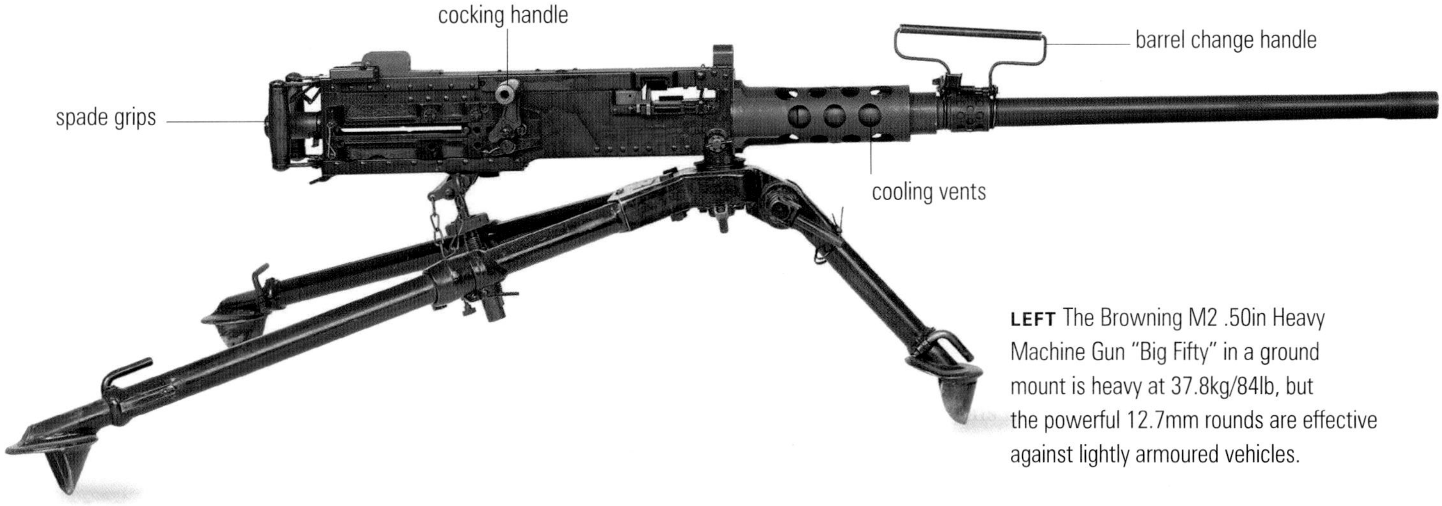

LEFT The Browning M2 .50in Heavy Machine Gun "Big Fifty" in a ground mount is heavy at 37.8kg/84lb, but the powerful 12.7mm rounds are effective against lightly armoured vehicles.

produced in 1936, had changes to the feed, sights and tripod. It continued to be used into World War II with US and Allied forces. A total of 53,854 of these guns were built.

The Browning M2 HMG

The US Browning .50 M2HB machine gun, or "Big Fifty", is one of the longest-serving weapons in the world, having entered service with the US Army in 1923. Some water-cooled guns were produced, but most relied on the heavy barrel to absorb the heat of firing. Although the sights are graduated up to 2,600m/2,845yd the big rounds are effective beyond this range. The M2HB's ammunition was developed from the German anti-tank rifle rounds captured at the end of World War I and is effective against lightly armoured vehicles. The French-made Société Française de Munitions (SFM) armour-piercing ammunition weighs 47.6g/1.68oz and will penetrate 2.49cm/0.98in of steel at 300m/330yd and 1.29cm/0.51in at 1,300m/1,420yd. Among the types available are ball, tracer, incendiary and armour-piercing incendiary. The slow cyclic rate of 450–600 rpm ensures accuracy.

It was firing a Browning M2 HMG mounted on a knocked-out US tank destroyer armoured vehicle that won 21-year-old Lieutenant Audie Murphy the Medal of Honor on 26 January 1945 during the Battle of the Bulge. He pushed the dead tank commander out of the way and used the machine gun to cut down advancing German infantry. At the same time, he called down artillery fire on the tanks supporting them. At one stage, in order to convince the distant gunners that the enemy attack had come dangerously close, he held the field telephone next to the machine gun as he fired.

Post-World War II improvements on the battle-tested Browning .50 include the RAMO and Saco .50 M2HB quick-change kit and the M2 lightweight machine gun, which weighs 27kg/59lb compared to the 38kg/83.7lb of the M2HB. The rate of fire on the lightweight gun can be adjusted from 550–750 rpm to allow it to be used in ground-support or air-defence roles. The quick-change kits only allow hot barrels to be changed quickly and safely after prolonged firing and eliminate the time-consuming task of headspace adjustment.

Machine gun deployment

Machine guns were deployed in three ways in World War I: direct fire, indirect fire and firing from fixed points.

- In direct fire the gunner could clearly see his target and he pressed the trigger, firing bursts of fire in the direction of the enemy infantry.
- Indirect fire was rather like artillery fire with rounds being "dropped" over enemy territory at unseen targets, beyond the effective cone of fire for the weapon. The gunner would adjust the weapon to fire skywards and shoot across the battlefield with a long curving trajectory. Although random, like any harassing fire it could suppress the troops at the other end by killing, injuring or simply dispersing them.
- Firing from fixed points worked by providing a dense, compact cone of fire at the enemy, which could have an end result similar to that of indirect fire.

Browning and Kijiro's designs

The diversity and durability of the small arms designed by John Moses Browning are remarkable. His BAR and M1919 machine gun would see US forces through World War II and the Korean War, and in the case of the M1919, were still used by armies around the world in the 21st century. While never in the Browning league, General Kijiro Nambu was also a very talented designer, producing pistols, rifles and machine guns.

The Browning Automatic Rifle

Late in World War I, John Moses Browning received a request from the US Expeditionary Corps in France to design the 0.3 Browning Automatic Rifle, or BAR. It had a 20-round box magazine and was initially a selective-fire weapon. Since the standard machine guns were heavy and not very manoeuvrable, it was intended for use by infantry firing from the shoulder or the hip when advancing on enemy positions, and to provide mobile firepower to every squad. However, the BAR M1918 proved to be twice as heavy as a bolt-action Springfield M1903 rifle.

In 1939, after several modifications, the final version of the BAR appeared as the M1918A2. Manufactured by Colt, Marlin-Rockwell and Winchester, it became the section or squad automatic weapon for US troops during World War II and the Korean War. M1918A1 guns, converted to M1918A2, had a skid-footed adjustable bipod under the flash hider, M1917 sights, smaller forend and a metal heat shield between barrel and cylinder/spring. The single-shot capability was replaced by two fully automatic modes, with fast at 650 rpm and slow at 450 rpm. The bipod, however, was rather impractical, so many M1918A2 gunners dispensed with it. The BAR remained in service with US Allies into the 1970s.

ABOVE US soldiers in training with the Browning Automatic Rifle (BAR) after World War I. The BAR was a heavy but reliable squad automatic weapon that served through World War II and during the Korean War of 1950–53, with greater range and power than the opponents' weapons.

The M1919 Browning machine gun

The .3in Browning M1919 machine gun was essentially an M1917 but with an air-cooled barrel. The M1919A4 was used on a ground mount by infantry, the M1919A5 worked coaxially in tanks, and the M2 was used in aircraft and as an AA gun by US and Allied forces in World War II. The M1919A6 was fitted with a bipod, butt and carrying handle. As an infantry squad weapon it looked a little odd, but was very popular, and 43,479 were manufactured in World War II. The M1919 remained in service in the Korean War and was even used in Vietnam. Towards the end of the 1960s it began to be superseded by newer designs. Even so, in the late 1990s (as the 7.62mm NATO M2) it formed part of the arsenals of the armies of Canada, Denmark, the Dominican Republic, Guatemala, Haiti, Iran, Israel, Italy, Liberia, Mexico, South Africa, South Korea, Spain, Taiwan and Vietnam. All told, it has been used in more than 75 countries and is still in use in a number of countries a quarter of the way into the 21st century.

US Navy Brownings were converted to 7.62mm during the Vietnam War and designated Mark 21 Mod 0. These guns were fitted to river patrol craft which were operating on the Mekong Delta. A reliable recoil-operated gun, the Mark 21 Mod 0 fired from a 250-round belt at 400–600 rpm. The maximum effective range was 1,370m/1,500yd.

The Type 11 LMG

Commonly known by the Allies as the Japanese Nambu and by the Japanese as the Taisho 11 Nen Shiki Kikanju, the Type 11 LMG was designed by

ABOVE The Browning M1919 machine gun would prove almost as long lived as the bigger .50 Browning. Here it is on an improvised mount on a US jeep in the bitter winter of 1944–45 in Europe.

the prolific General Kijiro Nambu and entered service in 1922. It was the standard light machine gun (LMG) in 1941, although later in the war it was replaced by the Type 96 and the Type 99. It drew on Hotchkiss principles but had an unusual hopper feed mechanism. Up to 30 rounds in standard clips of rifle ammunition could be dropped into it, but the complex mechanism could not handle the powerful rounds, so it required its own lower-powered 6.5mm ammunition to operate. Only capable of automatic fire, the gun fired at 500 rpm.

ABOVE Japanese troops wearing gas masks man a Type 11 LMG during fighting in the streets of Shanghai in the Sino-Japanese War of the 1930s, later becoming part of World War II.

John Moses Browning

The son of a Mormon gunsmith, John Moses Browning was born in Ogden, Utah in 1855. Working with scrap metal, he produced his first gun when he was 13. At the age of 24 he patented a breech-loading single-shot rifle.

In the 1890s Hiram Maxim's invention inspired Browning to develop his own automatic weapon. Instead of using the recoil forces, Browning drilled a hole in the gun barrel and used this to tap some of the gas from the propellants in the cartridge back into a cylinder to drive a piston. This piston extracted the cartridge case, reloaded and fired the gun. In 1895 the Browning machine gun was purchased by the US Navy.

From a slow start, demand for Browning machine guns took off when the USA entered World War I and ordered them for the US Army on active service in France.

Light firepower

Light machine guns developed in the 1930s played a profound part in World War II, as well as in conflicts for years afterwards. The French Chatellerault was fielded by paratroops in the doomed battle of Dien Bien Phu, Vietnam in 1954, while numerous liberation armies in Africa and Asia used the Soviet-supplied DP LMG. The Czech ZB vz/26 was used by all the combatants in World War II and forms the model for the British Bren gun.

The Mitrailleuse de 7.5mm Mle 1924/29

Also known as the Chatellerault, this gas-operated light machine gun was first introduced in 1924 and modified in 1929. It was used by the French armed forces from 1930 until the mid-1950s, when it was replaced by the AAT-F1 light machine gun. Adjusting the gas regulator along with the buffer allowed the gunner to vary his cyclic rate. What set the Chatellerault apart, however, was the new 7.5mm round that it had been developed to fire – a round that was as good as the German 7.92mm. Many Chatelleraults were captured after the fall of France in 1940 and were used by the Germans in coastal defences and in improvised AA mountings.

The M1924/29 had a top-loading 25-round box magazine and a cyclic rate of 500 rpm. It was easy to use in the roles of both LMG and SAW. It had two triggers: the rear one for fully automatic fire and the other for semi-automatic. The Model 31, which had a 150-round drum magazine, was a version of the Chatellerault built specifically for the Maginot Line fortifications.

The ZB vz/26 LMG

Soon after World War I, at the newly formed Czech armaments firm of Ceskoslovenska Zbrojovka at Brno, the talented small arms designer Vaclav Holek was charged by the Czechoslovakian Army to produce a new light machine gun. Holek was assisted by his brother Emmanuel, as well as other experts.

Work on what would become the 7.92mm ZB-vz.26 began in 1923. Within a year Holek's team had produced a prototype light machine gun. Following modifications, the Czechoslovakian Army quickly adopted the ZB as the vz.26, and many other countries later adopted the ZB or similar designs. The main users were China, Czechoslovakia, Lithuania, Yugoslavia, Romania, the Soviet Union, Spain, Sweden, Turkey and Japan. After World War II, guns seized from the Nationalist Chinese by their Communist Chinese opponents entered the arsenal of North Vietnam and were used in the Vietnam War.

The ZB-vz/26 fired from a 20- or 30-round box magazine at 500–550 rpm. It had an effective range of 1,000m/1,095yd.

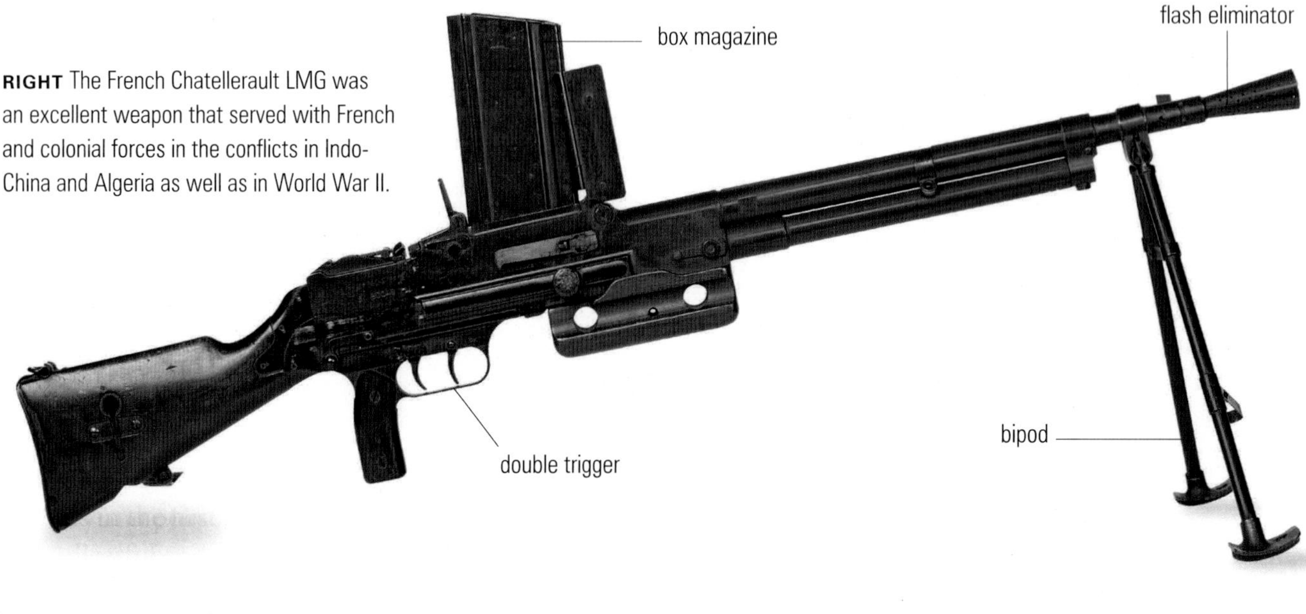

RIGHT The French Chatellerault LMG was an excellent weapon that served with French and colonial forces in the conflicts in Indo-China and Algeria as well as in World War II.

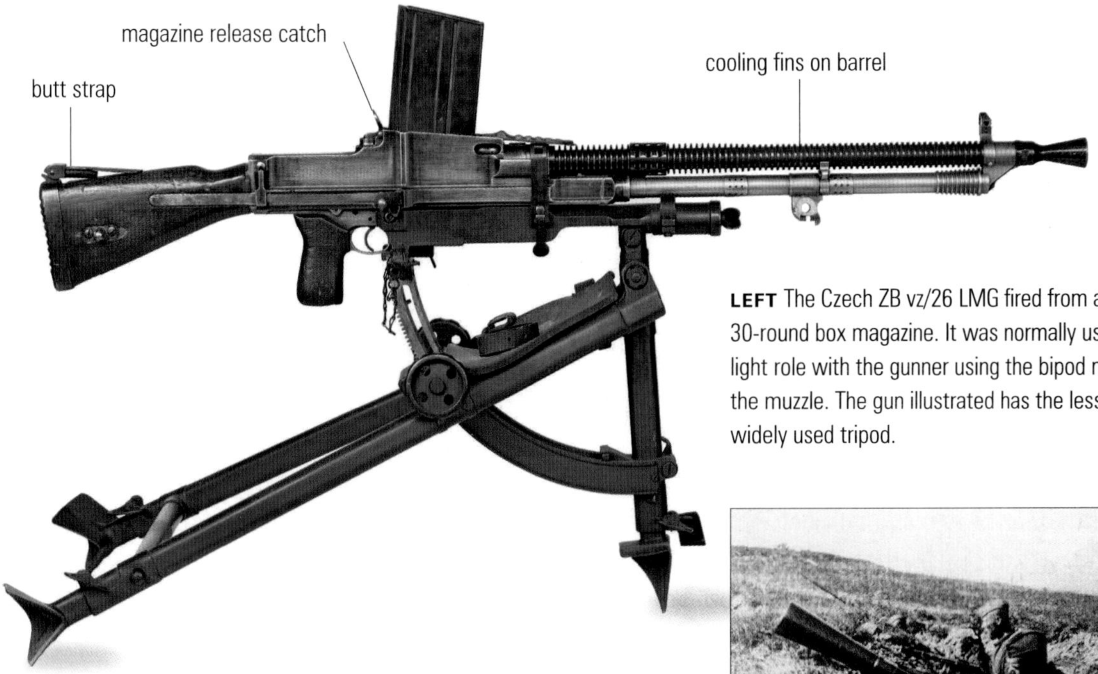

LEFT The Czech ZB vz/26 LMG fired from a 20- or 30-round box magazine. It was normally used in the light role with the gunner using the bipod mounted near the muzzle. The gun illustrated has the less widely used tripod.

RIGHT In the front line in the summer of 1942 a Soviet soldier spoons stew from his mess tin. His DP LMG rests on its bipod, ready to hand. His comrades are armed with the ubiquitous PPSh-41 SMG.

Vasily Alekseyevich Degtyarev

Born on 2 January 1880 at Tula, south of Moscow, Vasily Alekseyevich Degtyarev was to become a prolific Russian weapons engineer. For this work his titles and honours would include Major General of the Engineers and Artillery Service, Doctor of Technical Sciences in 1940, and two weeks after Joseph Stalin had been awarded Hero of Socialist Labour that year, Degtyarev received the second such award in its history. Interestingly for a man so closely involved with the Soviet Union, he did not become a Communist Party member until 1941.

Degtyarev was the first head of a Soviet small arms bureau. The bureau designed and developed the DshK1938 and DT machine guns, the PPD 34/38 and 40 submachine guns and the PTRD-41 anti-tank rifle. For this work Degtyarev received the State Award of the USSR in 1941, 1942 and 1944. He was also awarded the Order of Lenin three times, along with numerous medals and awards. After his death on 16 January 1949 in Moscow, he was posthumously awarded his fourth State Award of the USSR.

The DP LMG

The Ruchnoy Pulemyot Degtyareva pekhotnyi – Degtyarev hand-held infantry machine gun, or simply the DP, was a gas-operated light machine gun adopted by the Red Army in 1928. It fired the powerful 7.62 x 54R round and was cheap and easy to manufacture: early models had fewer than 80 parts and could be built by unskilled labourers. The DP had only six working parts and was especially able to withstand dirt. Indeed, Soviet soldiers joked that the gun fired better if sand were thrown on it. However, the bipod was weak, the pan-shaped drum magazine (normally loaded with 47 rounds) took time to fit on to the gun, and each magazine was slow to load. Its positive points were an inherent lower rate of continuous fire (500–600 rpm), which reduced the risk of the barrel overheating and it had an effective range of 800m/875yd. An improved version of the gun, the DPM, was introduced in 1944, and the gun was not replaced in service until the 1960s, when the PK machine gun was introduced.

Defective designs

The Italian Mitriaglice Fiat 1914/35 has the appearence of a good medium machine gun, just as the Breda Modello 30 has the look of a good light machine gun. However, appearances can be deceptive. Both guns had some troublesome design defects that only came to light when the unfortunate soldiers were in action in the front line. The German Flugzeugmaschinen-gewehr MG 15 and 17 were tested in action in Luftwaffe bombers, before they were modified for a ground role.

The Mitriaglice Fiat 1914/35

From 1935 onwards the Italians modernized the old Fiat 1914. The new machine gun, the Mitriaglice Modello 1914/35, had a 300-round belt feed. The water jacket had been removed and replaced with a heavy air-cooled, quick-change barrel. The gun was rebarreled for the larger calibre of 8mm, and engineers at Fiat hoped that this would mean that they could dispense with the oiler. However, the old violent blow-back mechanism (the way that the recoil from the exploding cartridge pushes back the bolt and a new round is fed in) had been retained from the Revelli-designed Fiat 1914. To reduce wear and tear from this violent action, the oiler had to be reintroduced. Despite all these modifications, the gun was not a success; in fact, many old soldiers said it was worse than the Fiat 1914. Among the undesirable features was the tendency for the barrel to overheat and, as always in the desert, the oiler attracted dust and dirt that clogged the mechanism. The Germans, who were always keen to use any available weapons, gave the Fiat 1914/35 the designation 8mm sMG255(i). Although it was widely available from captured stocks in 1943, they do not appear to have used it. They were probably aware of its deficiencies. The complete gun with its tripod weighed in at 36.6kg/81.25lb. It fired 500 rounds per minute and could be used both in a ground role and as a light anti-aircraft gun.

The Fucile Mitragliatore Breda modello 30

This was the standard light machine gun of the Italian Army during World War II. It was widely regarded as a poor weapon: it had fired the underpowered 6.5 x 52mm cartridge in 20-round clips that were inserted into a fragile hinged magazine, and the gun was prone to jamming. It had a cyclic rate of fire of 450–500 rounds per minute.

LEFT Here the Mitriaglice Fiat 1914/35 appears on a high-angle anti-aircraft mount during the Italian campaign in the Balkans of 1939–41. While one man keeps the mount stable, the other holds the belted ammunition so that it will feed smoothly when the gunner fires.

ABOVE The Italian Fucile Mitragliatori Breda modello 30 was one of the first air-cooled machine guns with a quick-change barrel. It had evolved from the Breda modello 1924 via the modello 1928.

The weapon fired from a closed bolt and had a small lubricating device that sprayed oil on each cartridge as it entered the chamber. However, this caused the chamber and barrel to heat rapidly, which in turn caused rounds to fire prematurely, or "cook off", before they were fully in the chamber. The oil from the lubrication also quickly picked up dust and debris, making the weapon highly prone to jamming during fighting in North Africa.

Some Bredas were modified to fire the new 7.35mm cartridge that was being introduced into service and designated modello 38. However, production problems with the new ammunition meant that this was a short-lived programme.

The Flugzeugmaschinengewehr MG15 and 17

Based on the system of the Rheinmetall MG30, the Flugzeugmaschinengewehr MG15 and MG17 were the standard aircraft machine guns fitted to most German combat aircraft in 1939. The MG15 was developed by Rheinmetall in Borsig as a flexible-mounted defence machine gun for bombers, and the MG17 was the fixed forward-firing armament for fighters such as the Messerschmitt Bf 109E. Both weapons were air cooled and recoil operated. The MG15 firing at 850 rpm was magazine fed from Doppeltrommel (double-drum) magazines containing 75 rounds, while the MG17 was belt fed. Both used Mauser 7.92mm ammunition.

When, later in World War II, the Luftwaffe concentrated on 13 and 15mm machine guns, the MG15 was distributed to ground troops – mainly the field units of the Luftwaffe. Since production of the MG34 and MG42 could never meet the demand from ground forces, reworking the aircraft machine guns for a ground role began in 1942. The modifications involved new sights, a shoulder stock, a tripod or bipod mount, a spent cartridge deflector and a carrying sling. It was widely used in garrison and guard units and issued to formations of the German Volksturm, the home guard, at the end of the war. Four MG17s could be mounted together in an anti-aircraft role, and with a combined rate of fire of 4,400 rpm they were a potent low-level anti-aircraft weapon deployed as a stop-gap in the last two years of the war.

Anti-aircraft ammunition

Machine guns firing rifle-calibre ammunition were only effective against low-flying aircraft if they were used en masse. Weapons such as the heavy Browning .50 and DshK1938 were capable of taking down aircraft. Yet one of the most effective features of these weapons was the deterrent value of the tracer ammunition. For the gunner, the burning tracers allowed him to correct his aim against moving targets. For the pilot of a bomb-laden aircraft diving towards a target on the ground, the sky filled with flashing tracer, which could put him off his aim. Tracers proved effective against aircraft as late as the Falklands War in 1982.

SAS guns

The light .303 drum-fed Vickers-Berthier machine gun would prove an ideal weapon for the Special Air Service Regiment (SAS) jeeps in World War II – armed with these machine guns they caused chaos behind German lines in North Africa and Europe. Sometimes the jeeps came under fire from German MG34s, their weapons firing almost twice as fast as the VB guns. In contrast, the Japanese Type 92 had a slow rate of fire.

ABOVE US Marines on Iwo Jima with a captured Japanese Type 92 machine gun. The 30-round stripper clip feed can be clearly seen.

The Type 92 machine gun

It is unusual for weapons to be given nicknames by the men who are their targets, but the Type 92 Shiki Kikanju Heavy Machine Gun (HMG) had such a low rate of fire at 450–500 rpm and curious stuttering effect that it was known as the "Woodpecker" by Allied soldiers. Allied troops under fire from the Type 92 always recognized it.

In the 1930s, the Japanese had realized that the small 6.5mm round fired by their soldiers was not powerful enough, and a new 7.7mm round was produced. It was introduced into new weapons, including the Type 92, a variation on the Hotchkiss design. Unlike the Hotchkiss, however, the Type 92 was heavy (over 54.5kg/120lb with the tripod; the tripod legs had holes drilled through the "feet" to take poles so that two men could carry it more easily.) The new gun bore was similar to the Type 3, including the oil dispenser required to ensure a smooth feed for the ammunition that was fed from 30 round metal clips.

The Vickers-Berthier

The Vickers "K" or VGO or CO gun was a gas-operated machine gun based on a French Berthier design that Vickers had bought in 1925. It had a cyclic rate of fire of 950–1,000 rpm and a 100-round magazine, although it was normally loaded with 96 rounds to prevent over-compression on the spring. It had a muzzle velocity of 745m/s/2,444ft/s and weighed 11.1kg/24.4lb. The guns were mounted in RAF Hawker Hart aircraft, and when these aircraft became obsolete this was the source of armament for SAS jeeps in North Africa and Europe. K guns were mounted in

ABOVE The Vickers-Berthier K gun had been designed for inter-war RAF fighters. The SAS took surplus weapons and mounted them on jeeps to produce fast, compact vehicles with an awesome firepower.

pairs on the front and rear of SAS jeeps. Such a vehicle therefore had the potential firepower of nearly 4,000 rounds of tracer and ball ammunition per minute.

ABOVE A German grenadier with an MG34 scans the surroundings from a lookout post. The barrel of the gun was air cooled through the holes in the protective metal sleeve, but it could also be changed quickly.

The MG34

To many Allied soldiers the German infantry appeared less as riflemen and more as ammunition carriers for the formidable 7.92mm MG34 machine gun, known by the Allies as the Spandau after its place of manufacture. This gun was 1,220mm/48in long with a 625mm/24.6in barrel, weighed 11.9kg/26.2lb in the light role and 31.1kg/68.5lb on the sustained fire mount. With a muzzle velocity of 755m/s/2,477ft/s, it had a maximum range of 2,000m/2,190yd and a cyclic rate of 800–900 rpm. It fired from a 75-round saddle-drum magazine or 50-round non-disintegrating belts. It was a remarkable design that drew on experience in World War I, during which heavy water-cooled weapons were difficult to handle.

One of the other spurs for the development of the revolutionary air-cooled weapon was accidental. According to the 1919 Treaty of Versailles, Germany was forbidden to construct water-cooled machine guns like the cumbersome MG08.

The MG34 was the world's first General-Purpose Machine Gun (GPMG) that could be used in a light role in the attack and in defence as a medium machine gun. When used in defence, it was mounted on the MG-Lafatte 34, a lightweight folding tripod that could be set at two positions – high and low. The tripod could also be converted into an anti-aircraft mount.

SAS jeep attack

In July 1942, Major David Stirling of the British Special Air Service Regiment (SAS) decided to attack Landing Ground 21, the airfield at Sidi Haneish, Egypt, using a V-shaped formation of two columns of seven jeeps commanded by Earl George Jellicoe and Paddy Mayne, with Stirling leading. They were to drive down the runway, engaging the lines of aircraft with their Vickers K guns, a total firepower of 68. To ensure surprise, the attack would be on a night with a full moon.

On the night of 26 July they set off. They hit the airfield at speed, the machine guns opened fire and Stirling fired a green Very light, the signal for the V formation. Recalling it afterwards, the men told Virginia Cowles, the author of *Phantom Major*: "The planes took longer to catch fire than the men had imagined. It was perhaps thirty seconds before the interior of the aircraft suddenly glowed red, followed by the dull thud of exploding petrol, which turned the whole body into a sheet of flame. Some planes did not burn but seemed literally to crumble and disintegrate as the bullets ploughed into them from less than fifty yards."

A hero's gun

The Japanese Type 96 light machine gun (LMG) drew on some of the design features of the earlier Czech ZB 26. The Bren gun, also based on the Czech ZB 26, became the British and Commonwealth section LMG in World War II. Even as late as 21 November 1965 it was the weapon with which brave junior NCOs such as L. Naik Rambahadur Limbu of the 2/10th Gurkha Rifles won the highest award for gallantry: the Victoria Cross. Another Czech weapon, the ZB vz/53, was fielded by both the Germans and the British in World War II.

The Type 96 LMG

The Japanese 6.5mm Type 96 LMG was introduced in 1936. A number of ideas were taken from the Czechoslovakian ZB 26 (an LMG design manufactured at the small arms factory in Brno, Czechoslovakia) and the Hotchkiss machine gun. The Type 96 LMG had a curved 30-round box magazine and a cyclic rate of 550 rpm. The reduced-power Meiji 30 cartridge produced a muzzle velocity of 730m/s/2,394ft/s; this cartridge should not have caused a feed problem but in fact the gun still needed an oil dispenser to ensure a smooth feed. The Type 96 had a quick-change barrel and drum or telescopic sights. It could be fitted with a Model 30 sword bayonet, although launching a bayonet charge carrying a 9kg/20lb LMG would have been rather challenging to slightly built Japanese soldiers.

ABOVE A Japanese paratrooper armed with the 6.5mm Type 96 LMG. The gun drew on a number of Western design concepts. A typical Japanese feature was that it could be fitted with a bayonet for close combat.

Corporal Tom Hunter VC

In the last weeks of World War II on 2 April 1945, Corporal Tom Hunter's troop from 43 Royal Marine Commando came under heavy and constant fire from three German MG42s dug in close to a group of houses near to Lake Comacchio in northern Italy.

Picking up his Bren gun, Hunter charged the houses single-handedly across 183m/200yd of open ground. He came under intense fire but so determined was his charge that six German gunners surrendered and the rest fled. Changing magazines as he ran, he cleared the house of the enemy. He drew heavy incoming fire but continued until the rest of his troop found safety. Shortly after, Cpl Hunter was killed still firing his Bren gun.

He is buried in the Argenta Gap Cemetery in Emilia-Romagna, Italy.

The Bren gun

The British Bren gun was initially built in 1937 at the Royal Small Arms Factory at Enfield and was based on the Czechoslvakian-designed ZB vz/26 light machine gun. It was tested by British Army officials in the 1930s. A licence to manufacture was obtained and the Czech design modified to British requirements. The two factory names (Brno and Enfield) were combined to produce the name Bren, and the gun continued in use from World War II to the Gulf War of 1991.

The Bren was an air-cooled gas-operated weapon that fired a .303 round from a 30-round box magazine. It had a slow rate of fire – 500 rpm – but was extremely accurate, with sights set out to 1,830m/2,000yd. It was also light, weighing only 10kg/22.1lb, and measured 1,155mm/45.5in in length.

It was easy to strip, and experienced gunners could change magazines or barrels in less than five seconds. Bren guns were also made in Australia, Canada and India during World War II. When, after the war, the British Army standardized its rifle ammunition with NATO and adopted 7.62mm, the versatile Bren was re-engineered to take the cartridge and with it a magazine with a flatter curve that was interchangeable with the L1A1 SLR magazine. This meant that, in a contact, riflemen in a section could resupply ammunition to the LMG crew. The Bren could be mounted on a bipod, tripod or vehicle mounted.

ABOVE The later Bren featured a curved box magazine, conical flash eliminator and barrel that could be quickly changed. In the 1950s the Bren was rebarrelled to accept the 7.62 x 51mm NATO cartridge. It could be fitted on a bipod, or mounted on a vehicle.

BELOW The .303 Bren, with its characteristic curved magazine, remained in service with the British Army after the war. When 7.62mm ammunition was standardized by NATO, the gun was rebarrelled and fitted with a new magazine.

The ZB vz/53 medium machine gun

The Czech ZB vz/53, designed by Vaclav Holek, was first produced in Brno in 1937 and entered service with the Czechoslovakian Army as the Kulomet vz/37. Captured guns were designated by the Germans as the 7.92mm MG 37 (t) and issued widely, often to Waffen-SS units. The British had obtained a production licence before the war and produced it as the Gun, Machine, Besa, building 59,322 of them, which were fitted to tanks. Among the British tanks that fielded the Besa were the Churchill, Valentine, Matilda and Cromwell.

The ZB vz/53 was unusual, with a quick-change barrel (normally fitted to LMGs) and two rates of fire: 500 or 700 rpm, firing from a 100- or 200-round metal link belt. The Besa was a very reliable gun which had a tripod mount that could be adjusted as an AA mount as well as a fortress mount for embrasures in fortifications.

Enduring designs

The German MG42 and Soviet DShk and SG43 are three machine guns that have enjoyed a remarkable operational life. The MG42 has been the basis for numerous automatic weapons and remains the touchstone for all general purpose machine guns.

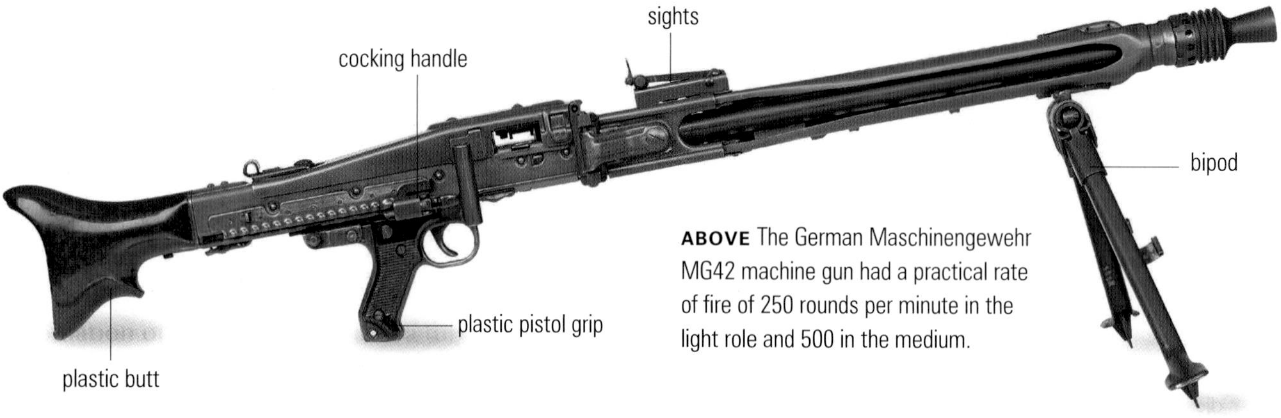

ABOVE The German Maschinengewehr MG42 machine gun had a practical rate of fire of 250 rounds per minute in the light role and 500 in the medium.

The Degtyarev DShk 1938

The large Krupnokaliberny Pulemet Degtyareva-Shpagina, DShK or "Degtyarev-Shpagin, large calibre" 12.7mm/.50 entered service with the Red Army in 1939 and remained in production until 1980. Soviet soldiers nicknamed it the "Dushka". Although it has been compared to the .50 Browning HMG, it was not a recoil-operated gun but used a gas system developed by Georgiy Shpagin that has a three-positions gas regulator. The Dushka was used throughout World War II as an anti-aircraft weapon on tanks like the heavy IS-3, in twin and quad AA mounts and even on river craft. As a formidable heavy infantry support gun it was mounted on a modified version of the Maxim Sokolov mount.

ABOVE The Soviet DshK 1938 12.7mm/.50 in service as an anti-aircraft gun aboard a Soviet naval craft. The gun had an effective range of 1,500m/1,641yd.

After the war, the modernized version DShK Modernized (DShK-M), also known as DShKM-38/46, was mounted on Soviet tanks such as the T-55 and T-62, and armoured reconnaissance vehicles and personnel carriers. The DShKM was also manufactured in China, Iran, Yugoslavia and Pakistan. It was widely used in numerous post-1945 conflicts including Vietnam, the Arab-Israeli wars, and more recently, the Soviet and NATO campaigns in Afghanistan. The DShKM was one of the most successful designs of its time.

The muzzle velocity is 850m/s/2,788ft/s, and the gun fires at 600 rpm from a 50-round belt. The AP rounds can pierce 15mm/0.6in of armour at 500m/547yd.

The MG42

The MG42 replaced the MG34 during World War II. Designed by Dr Grunow of Grossfuss-Werke, it used stamping and spot-welding to speed the manufacturing process. When the Allies captured their first MG42s in Tunisia, they thought that stamping and spot welding indicated a cheap and shoddy weapon. Nothing could have been further from the truth. The MG42 entered service in 1942 and by 1945 some 750,000 had been produced. The gun introduced the quick barrel change that was essential for fast firing air-cooled weapons.

LEFT A Waffen SS soldier cleans his MG34. It has been said that many automatic weapons have been worn out not by constant firing but by constant cleaning; it is essential to keep weapons clean. Gas-operated weapons can foul up with hard carbon that builds up around narrow apertures such as the gas regulator, which can cause stoppages and jams.

The gun was 122cm/48in long with a 53.3cm/21in barrel and weighed 11.8kg/26lb in the light role and 29.7kg/65.3lb on the sustained fire mount. With a muzzle velocity of 755m/s/2,746ft/s, it fired 50- and 250-round metal-belted ammunition and had a maximum range of 2,000m/2,188yd and a cyclic rate of 1,550. A US Army Intelligence Bulletin identified the drawback of this high rate of fire: "the gun has a tendency to 'throw off', so that its fire stays on target for a much briefer time than does that of the slower firing MG34". German gunners were therefore instructed to fire bursts of between five to seven rounds when firing in the light role. The gunners also aimed low and the Intelligence Bulletin noted a comment from a GI who remarked, "German machine gun fire is usually so low – often about a foot and a half above the ground – that we call it 'grass cutting'. "

The SG43 and SGM MMG

In the early 1940s the Red Army realized that the old PM1910 machine gun was being outclassed by the German MG34 and later MG42 machine guns. The need for a new weapon was addressed by the talented Goryunov brothers, who produced the Stankovii Pulemet Goryunova Obrazets 1943G, or simply the SG43. This gun combined in its mechanism features from Degtyarev, Browning and other weapons. It was a robust and reliable weapon that fired at 500–640 rpm to a maximum effective range of 1,000m/1,094yd from a 50-round metal-link belt. The gun was 40.7kg/89.5lb on its two-wheel mount, which compared favourably to the complete weight of a PM1910: a staggering 74kg/163lb.

Among the variants of the SG43 were the SGMT co-axial tank gun and the SGMB vehicle-mounted gun. As late as the mid-1990s the SG43 was still in service in Egypt, China, the Middle East and Southeast Asia.

The MG42 in war

US soldiers who encountered the MG42 in the wooded cover of the bocage of Normandy in June and July 1944 said that the ripping sound of the fast-firing MG42 resembled the sound of a sheet of calico being torn apart.

Sydney Jary, a young British infantry platoon commander in Normandy, recalled "I remember my first reaction to actual infantry warfare in July 1944 was one of amazement at the crushing fire-power of these rapid-firing guns . . . firing long sustained bursts, the object of which seemed to me to keep us pinned to the ground regardless of the ammunition expenditure. Typically German – protracted and discordant."

BELOW The Soviet SGM machine gun developed during World War II could be fired from a wheeled ground mount by infantry or was mounted in armoured fighting vehicles both as a co-axial and an AA gun.

General-Purpose Machine Guns

The GPMG (general-purpose machine gun), which was exemplified by the MG42, would be regarded as an essential weapon by all armies after the war, and widely copied. The French had their AAT-52 and the Belgians their highly successful MAG, while the Russian belt-fed RPD LMG was a step towards the GPMG concept.

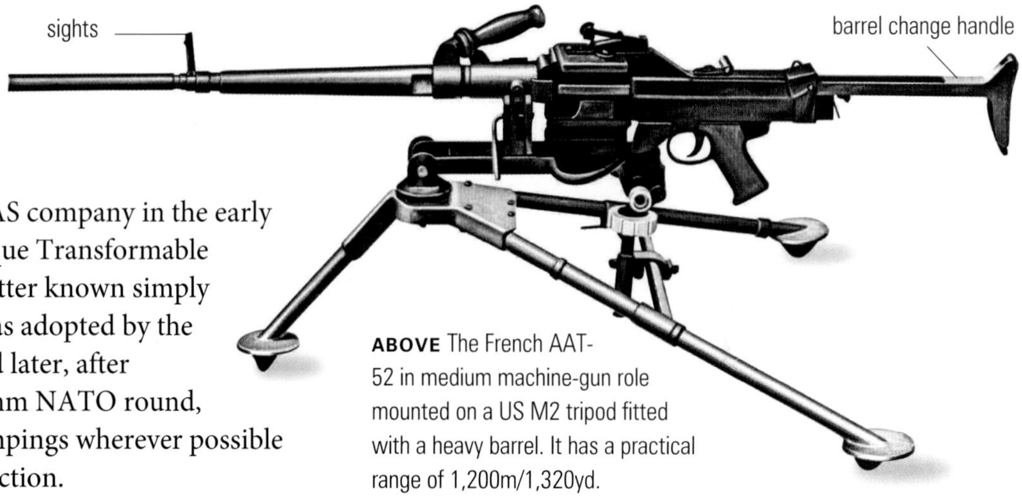

ABOVE The French AAT-52 in medium machine-gun role mounted on a US M2 tripod fitted with a heavy barrel. It has a practical range of 1,200m/1,320yd.

The AAT 52 GPMG

Designed by the French MAS company in the early 1950s, the Arme Automatique Transformable modèle 52 machine gun, better known simply as the "cinquante-deux", was adopted by the French Army in 7.5mm and later, after conversion to fire the 7.62mm NATO round, as the AAT F-1. It uses stampings wherever possible for ease and speed of production.

The AAT-52 uses 50- or 200-round belts and has a delayed blowback action and a rate of fire of 900 rpm. The quick-change barrel has a fluted chamber to assist extraction. In the light role the gun has a 50cm/20in, 2.9kg/6.4lb barrel, while in the sustained fire role it has a heavier 4.3kg/9.5lb barrel that is 60cm/2ft long.

The gun gave good service in Algeria in the 1960s and in numerous operations around the world. It was finally replaced by the FN MAG in the 2010s.

ABOVE An Egyptian soldier taking part in a joint exercise with US Forces takes aim with an RPD LMG fitted with the 100-round magazine. The rugged weapon has performed well in the jungles of Asia as well as in the desert.

The RPD

The RPD 7.62mm light machine gun was designed by Vasily Degtyarev in the USSR in 1943 and introduced into service in the Soviet Army shortly after the end of World War II. It was adopted by Warsaw Pact forces and copied by China as the Type 56 and North Korea as the Type 62. The RPD weighs 7.1kg/15.6lb empty and fires a 7.62 x 39mm round from a 100-round disintegrating link belt housed in a drum clipped below the weapon. It fires only on automatic and has a cyclic rate of 700 rpm and an effective range of 800m/875yd. It works well in adverse conditions and is very easy to strip and assemble.

The FN MAG GPMG

The Belgian 7.62mm FN Mitrailleuse à Gaz, or MAG, is one of the most successful GPMGs to be manufactured since World War II. An FN design, it uses the feed mechanism developed by the Germans for the MG42 during the war. This gives it a rate of fire of 650–1,000 rpm, which can be adjusted by opening or closing the gas regulator controlling the flow of gas from the barrel back on to the cupped piston head. Gunners learn to "balance" their weapon so that this gas flow gives an optimum performance.

The MAG can be used in the light role with a bipod or on a sustained fire (SF) spring-buffered tripod.

ABOVE An Israeli soldier in Lebanon in 1984 lounges by an M151 fitted with two MAGs. The one in the rear has had the butt removed and replaced with the butt plate for ease of operation in limited space.

In the SF role a butt plate is fitted, and the rear sight flips up and shows ranges of 800–1,800m/875–1,970yd. An optical sight, similar to that on a mortar, can also be fitted; this allows the gun to be fired on pre-registered targets that may be obscured by darkness or smoke. In the light role the sights lie flat and are graduated between 200–800m/220–875 yards in 100m/110-yd intervals. The GPMG/MAG weighs 11.7kg/25.7lb empty and has an overall length of 126cm/50in. The rate of fire is 650–1,000 rpm and the muzzle velocity is 840m/s/2,755ft/s. The MAG is probably the most successful general-purpose machine gun in the world, having been used in one form or another by more than 75 countries. It is manufactured under licence in Argentina, Egypt, India, Singapore, the United States, and the UK.

GPMG hero

At 04.45 on 27 April 1965, in Plaman Mapu, Sarawak,a position held by 34 men from the British B Company HQ 2nd Battalion, the Parachute Regiment and a platoon of young soldiers fresh from the depot came under three attacks by a Javanese Para-Commando Regiment. Company Sergeant Major (CSM) Williams and other officers were with them, along with cooks, mortar crews and radio operators.

The Javanese gained a lodgement in the position. With the situation deteriorating, Williams grabbed a GPMG and clipped on two more belts to the one already on the gun. He recalls thinking, "this is it, this is the end of the story anyway, so I'll give them a bit of rapid fire". He stood firing from the hip as a corporal led a counterattack. Several Indonesian commandos charged straight at Williams, the nearest being killed only 2m/2.2yd from him.

When the second assault came in, Williams brought another GPMG up and mortar bombs fired by the Paras fell only 30m/33yd away. This broke up the second assault.

The third attack, just before dawn at about 05.45, was not pressed home with great vigour. When Williams took out a clearing patrol he found one Indonesian, whom he killed.

Old concepts, new designs

Originating from the MG42, the German MG3 machine gun can truly be called an old soldier in the world of small arms design. The Russian RPK-74 is in concept a 7.62mm RPK scaled down to 5.45mm ammunition. The American M60, however, was a machine gun that caused considerable problems and was therefore very unpopular with its users.

ABOVE The RPK-74 is similar in concept to the British light support weapon: an infantry rifle with a longer barrel and bipod to give a squad an automatic weapon for engaging targets at longer range.

The Maschinengewehr MG3

The MG3 is a modified version of the German MG42 belt-fed, air-cooled machine gun adapted to fire 7.62mm NATO M13 or DM 6 disintegrating link or German DM 1 continuous link. (When continuous link has been fired, the empty belt hangs off the gun for reloading later; disintegrating link unclips itself as it is fired.) It is in service in many countries including Chile, Denmark, Saudi Arabia, Norway, Austria and Portugal. The Sarac, an MG3 copy, is built in the former Yugoslavia, and the MG3 is made under licence in Greece, Iran, Italy, Pakistan, Spain , Sudan, Turkey and the United States. The MG3 began life as the MG42/59 in 1959, and after 1968 went into mass production as the MG3.

The MG3 fires from an open bolt and has a short recoil barrel with the bolt locking into the barrel extension via two rollers. Like the MG42, the MG3 has a quick change barrel. The normal drill is to replace it after a 150-round burst. However, in contact this rate can be increased to 200 to 250. As a GPMG the MG3 has a very high rate of fire – between 700 and 1,300 rpm.

The RPK-74

The Soviet Ruchnoi Pulemet Kalashnikova-74, or RPK-74, was developed along with the AK-74 assault rifle as a ten-man squad-level light-support weapon firing the new, small-calibre 5.45mm ammunition. The RPK-74 was adopted by the Soviet Army in the late 1970s and is still in use with the Russian Army today. The RPK-74 has a cyclic rate of 600–650 and a practical rate of 150 rpm. The maximum effective range is 460m/503yd.

LEFT Bundeswehr soldiers with the MG3. The gunner is using the trigger extension grip for the gun's sustained fire mount. The litter of empty cases shows that this post-war clone of the MG42 has a high rate of fire. Its quick-change barrel is replaced after 150 rounds.

Internally the RPK-74 is almost the same as the AK-74 rifle – a select-fire, gas-operated, rotating bolt-locked weapon – but it has a heavier and longer fixed barrel with a bipod, and redesigned buttstock. The RPK-74 can be fed from 45-round box magazines or standard AK-74 30-round magazines. Drum magazines holding 75 rounds similar in design to those of the RPK were also developed. They are much in demand with Russian troops in Chechnya.

Versions of the RPK-74 with a side-mount for the 1LH51 night-vision scopes are called RPK-74N. The first RPK-74s were manufactured with wooden pistol grips and fixed buttstocks, but current guns have polymer grips and side-folding polymer buttstocks.

M60 GPMG

Entering service in the late 1950s, the American M60 GPMG was designed towards the end of the 1940s. Its design drew on a number of German wartime developments including the MG42 machine gun and FG 42 automatic rifle. It had no gas regulator, which sometimes resulted in the gun jamming if fouled or, less usually, in a "runaway gun". This occurred when the working parts went back far enough to feed, chamber and fire a round but not far enough to be engaged by the sear, so that even if the pressure is taken off the trigger the gun keeps on firing. In these conditions the only option is to hold on to the belt to prevent it from feeding.

The M60 can be mounted as a sustained fire gun or on vehicles and has a quick-change barrel and integral bipod. Both the M60 and M60E3 have a cyclic rate of 550 rpm.

ABOVE A grizzled US soldier in Vietnam has belts of 7.62mm ammunition ready for use for his M60, draped over a tree trunk to ensure that they do not foul in the mud on the jungle floor.

The M60 – "The Pig"

The M60 machine gun was a weapon that seemed fine in theory but for soldiers in Vietnam terrible design defects were obvious. The bipod and the gas cylinder were permanently attached to the barrel, so quick barrel changes after firing bursts of 200 rounds proved extremely difficult during a contact. To handle the barrel, the Number 2 on the gun required a heat-protecting mitten, which was often lost on patrol or in a contact. Finally, key components in the operating group, such as the firing pin, were prone to fracturing.

Unsurprisingly, the gun came to be known by frustrated soldiers in Vietnam as "the Pig". A lighter version of the gun, designated the M60E3, was subsequently produced but it was actually no great improvement. It did have a non-removable gas cylinder supporting the bipod, and the new barrel had a carrying handle so barrel changes were quicker and easier. However, the new lightened gun was actually less reliable; the light barrel would burn out if 200 to 300 rounds were fired on fully automatic, so it had to be changed after 100 rounds in rapid fire.

New developments

While the Soviet PK machine gun and even the Belgian FN Minimi are significant improvements on the concept of a General-Purpose Machine Gun; the M134 and M61 look back to the Gatling concept.

ABOVE The first American female aerial gunner, photographed in 2002, appears in the door of an HH-60G Pave Hawk helicopter, equipped with a 7.62 M134 minigun.

M134 minigun

In Vietnam in the 1960s the US Army realized it was essential to arm its helicopters. It was necessary to deliver a heavy weight of fire over a short period of time, so designers at General Electric scaled down the proven M61 gun to enable it to fire 7.62 x 51mm NATO ammunition. The weapon designated the M134 Minigun had a phenomenal rate of fire of 4,000 rpm. It was normally mounted in chin turrets or wing pods on AH-1G Cobra attack helicopters. Usually, the AH-1G Cobra carried one or two miniguns in its chin turret, with 2,000–4,000 rounds of ammunition. The guns were also installed on door, pylon and pod mounts on UH-1 Huey helicopters, and on fixed-wing gunships such as the A/C-47 Dakota, nicknamed "Puff the Magic Dragon" after a children's television show.

PK machine gun

The development of a new 7.62mm General-Purpose Machine Gun (GPMG) for the Soviet Army began around 1953, and the lead was taken by the Nikitin-Sokolov (NS) machine gun. The Kalashnikov design bureau submitted a design in 1958, at the request of the Soviet Ministry of Defence, to provide a competitor for the NS gun. After extensive trials the Kalashnikov design was adopted as a new general-purpose machine gun, replacing the DPM light, RP-46 medium/company and SGM heavy machine guns in service. The PK fires from 100-, 200- or 250-round belts at a cyclic rate of 650 rpm.

A tank version that replaced the older SGMT was later developed by Kalashnikov with the designation PKT. Following user reports from the Soviet Army, a modified version of the PKM was adopted in 1969. It had an improved barrel and shorter flash hider, a stamped belt feed and was overall a lighter weapon. The sustained-fire PKMS had a new simple, lighter tripod. The PKM and its variants are still in production in Russia and it is in service in the Russian Army, former Warsaw Pact forces and many other forces worldwide. Copies – both licensed and pirated – have been made in Bulgaria, China, Poland, Romania, Ukraine and the former Yugoslavia.

Kalashnikov later developed a tank version, designated as PKT, which replaced in service older

ABOVE PK machine guns captured by US forces in Grenada in 1983. The gun has been exported throughout the world and copied by manufacturers in Europe and China. It is in widespread use in Iraq and Afghanistan.

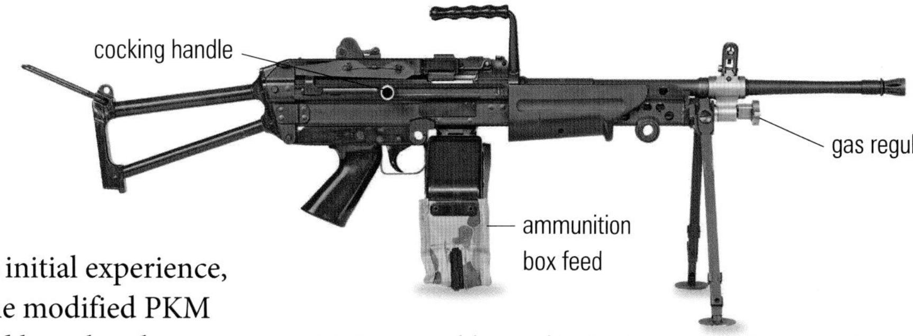

RIGHT The FN Minimi is a light weapon that is comfortable to fire and has proved popular with soldiers because its belt feed allows it to deliver a high volume of fire.

SGMT machine guns. Based on the initial experience, in 1969 the Soviet Army adopted the modified PKM machine gun, which had an updated barrel with shorter flash hider, stamped belt feed and a generally lightened construction. The PKMS (tripod-mounted) version also had a new, lighter tripod of simpler design. The PKM series of machine guns are still manufactured in Russia and are used by the Russian Army and armies of several other ex-USSR republics. In addition, PK/PKM copies are made in Bulgaria, China, Poland, Romania and Yugoslavia.

The FN Minimi

The Minimi light machine gun, designed by the Belgian Fabrique Nationale (FN), can fire, feeding from the left, either belted disintegrating link SS 109 NATO or US M193 5.5mm ammunition or it can fire from 30-round box magazines that are compatible with the American M16 and most NATO rifles.

A 200-round box of belted ammunition can be clipped directly to the Minimi, making it a formidable close-quarter battle (CQB) weapon. Gas operated, the Minimi is normally fired from its bipod, though a sustained fire tripod is available. The gun has a gas regulator with two settings: normal and adverse. The latter ensures a sufficient flow of gas against the piston to clear a malfunction. The adjustment can be made even with a hot barrel. It does not have the recoil forces of a full-size 7.62mm round and so consequently it can be fired with greater accuracy.

The Minimi has been adopted by the Australians as the F89, the US as the M249 Squad Automatic Weapon (SAW), and also by the Brazilian, Belgian, Canadian, Chilean, Dutch, Egyptian, Greek, Indonesian, Italian, Japanese, Norwegian, Portuguese, Swiss and Thai armed forces.

Back to the Gatling

By the early 1950s, the newly formed US Air Force realized that the speed of new jet fighters had made conventional gas or recoil-operated machine guns or cannon obsolete. The General Electric Company was approached to produce a new fast-firing gun under the project name "Vulcan". Multi-barrelled weapons seemed a promising research path, since between shots the barrels would have time to cool. In trials, 19th-century Gatlings were fitted with electrical drive instead of the manually operated crank. No longer reliant on muscle power, the gun had a staggering rate of fire of about 4,000 rounds per minute.

Further development resulted in some experimental, electrically driven, six barrelled .60-calibre machine guns, and in 1956, the six-barrelled 20mm T171 gun was officially adopted as the M61 aircraft gun capable of 4,000–6,000 rpm. M61 became the main aircraft gun for USAF fighters, and is also used by the US Army on the M161 and M163 Vulcan ground anti-aircraft gun mounts. The US Navy also returned to the Gatling with the Vulcan-Phalanx CIWS (Close-In Weapon System) designed to shred fast sea-skimming anti-ship missiles.

BELOW US soldiers on exercise in West Germany in the 1980s with a M161 Vulcan air defence system. The high rate of fire would be lethal against helicopters and low-flying ground attack aircraft.

KEY

1 Canada
2 United States
3 Mexico
4 Guatemala
5 Costa Rica
6 Cuba
7 Peru
8 Colombia
9 Chile
10 Dominican Rep.
11 Venezuela
12 Argentina
13 Paraguay
14 Brazil
15 Uruguay
16 Portugal
17 Spain
18 UK
19 France
20 Belgium
21 Netherlands
22 Switzerland
23 Germany
24 Italy
25 Norway
26 Denmark
27 Austria
28 Sweden
29 Czech Republic
30 Poland
31 Croatia
32 South Africa
33 Serbia
34 Hungary
35 Lithuania
36 Greece
37 Finland
38 Romania
39 Bulgaria
40 Ukraine
41 Russia
42 Egypt
43 Turkey
44 Israel
45 Ethiopia
46 S. Arabia
47 Iraq
48 Iran
49 Pakistan
50 India
51 China
52 Indonesia
53 Singapore
54 Australia
55 North Korea
56 South Korea
57 Japan
58 New Zealand

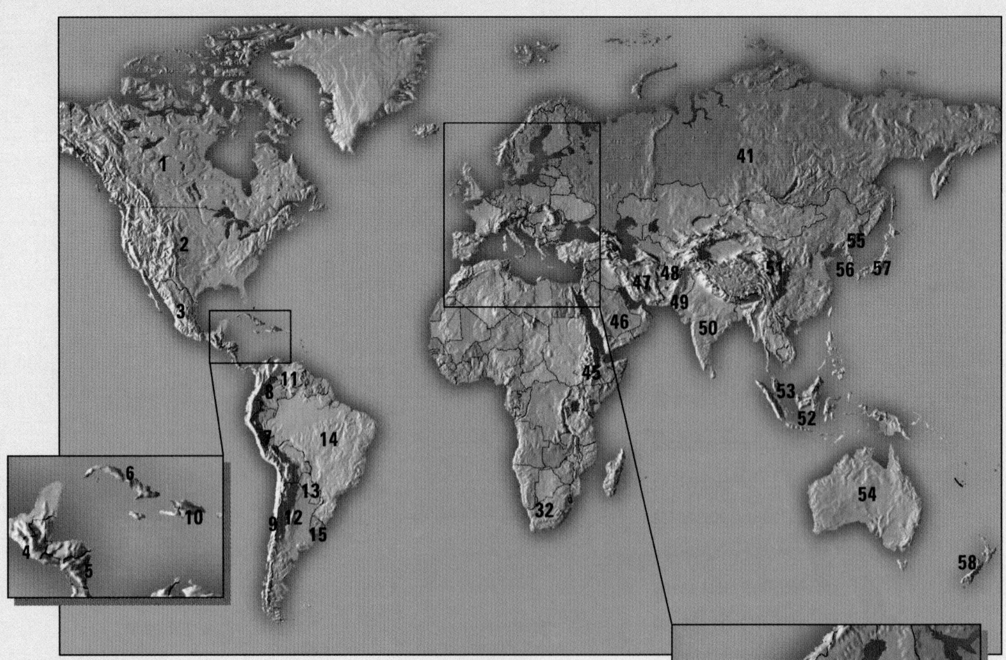

ABOVE The map indicates the countries of the world where rifles and carbines are featured in this section.

Note on specification boxes: Traditionally guns developed in the United States have been given their calibre in inches, while European countries have designated calibre in metric measurement. Guns have retained this designation in this book. Dimensions refer to the weapon shown, where illustrated. Weights and measurements may be approximate.

A directory of rifles and carbines from around the world

A variety of countries around the world produce and manufacture firearms. Some produce arms that are unique, while others produce or import versions of firearms from other countries under licence, sometimes with different fittings and specifications. Rifles are long guns, with rifled barrels, that can be fired from the standing, kneeling and prone position. Carbines are shorter, lighter and more portable than rifles. This directory is a cross-section of selected countries of the world – west to east – and some of the rifles and carbines that are available in those countries and their main features. Within each country guns are organized alphabetically by manufacturer except where its historical development is shown more clearly chronologically or a company changes its name. Each firearm has a description and a specification that lists its vital measurements, including its calibre and operating method.

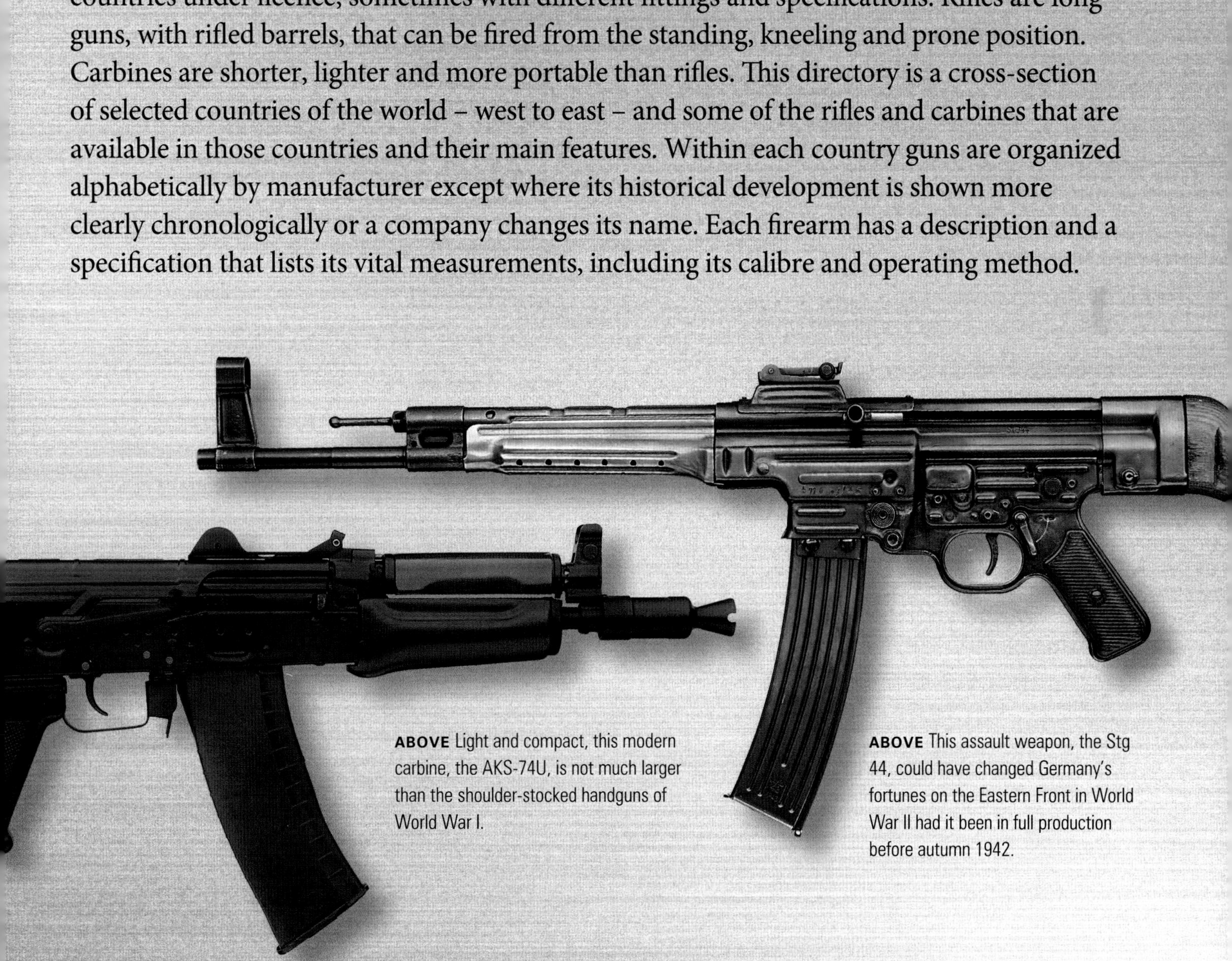

ABOVE Light and compact, this modern carbine, the AKS-74U, is not much larger than the shoulder-stocked handguns of World War I.

ABOVE This assault weapon, the Stg 44, could have changed Germany's fortunes on the Eastern Front in World War II had it been in full production before autumn 1942.

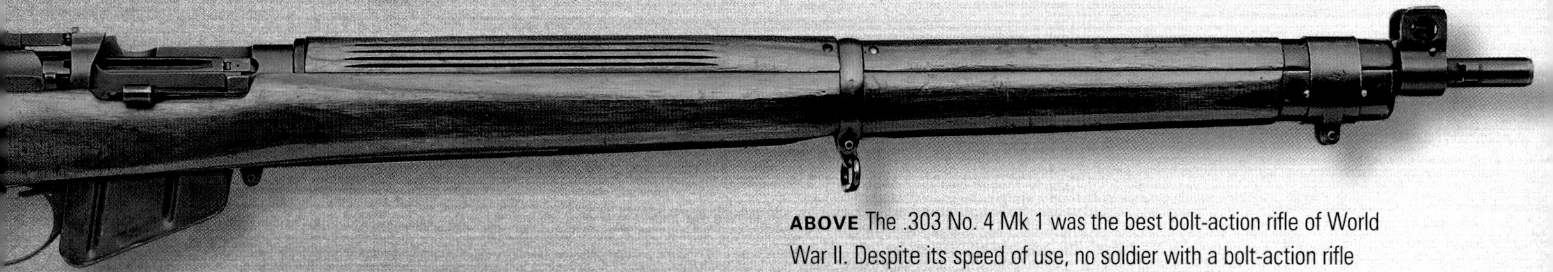

ABOVE The .303 No. 4 Mk 1 was the best bolt-action rifle of World War II. Despite its speed of use, no soldier with a bolt-action rifle could deliver as much firepower as with a semi-automatic.

Canada

Canada primarily used Commonwealth firearms, but also had numerous designers and manufacturing plants. In both World Wars Canada produced its own small arms. In 1903 it adopted the Canadian-designed Ross rifle. The failure of that rifle led to the use of SMLE Mark III* (Lee-Enfield) in 1916. Manufacture of military rifles in Canada re-started with the Long Branch Arsenal in Ontario making arms in 1940. After World War II Canada adopted the Fusil Automatique Léger (FAL), also made in Ontario.

Diemaco C7

The C7 was the Canadian version of the American M-16 rifle, the primary military rifle of the United States in the 1960s. When the United States upgraded the Colt M-16 to the M-16A2 in the late 1980s, it made sense for Canada to adopt a similar rifle. The C7 was an M-16 clone built by the Diemaco Corporation in Ontario. The barrel was upgraded and the lower receiver (which houses the operating parts of the gun) reinforced to prevent cracking at weak points. The M-16A1 sights were retained on the C7. The C7 was adopted in 1986 and is used to the present day.

SPECIFICATION

MANUFACTURER Diemaco Corporation
CALIBRE 5.56 x 45mm
MAGAZINE CAPACITY 20 or 30
ACTION Gas operated/rotating bolt
TOTAL LENGTH 1,016mm/40in
BARREL LENGTH 508mm/20in
WEIGHT UNLOADED 3.85kg/8.5lb

Diemaco C8A1

Along with the M-16A2, Canada adopted the American M4, an M-16 carbine. The M4 was intended to be a carbine for support troops, but it proved so successful that it was sought after by troops and units at all levels. As with the C7, the C8A1 was an improvement on the M4 rather than just a clone. The C8A1 uses a hammer-forged barrel, like the C7, for greater accuracy and longevity. However, like the M4, the C8A1 suffers from loss of velocity due to the barrel being shorter than the M-16. This is a common feature of all carbines, but a particular problem with the 5.56 x 45mm cartridge, which needs high bullet velocity to be effective. The Diemaco C8A1 was adopted immediately after Colt developed the M4 in 1995 and is still in use.

SPECIFICATION

MANUFACTURER Diemaco Corporation
CALIBRE 5.56 x 45mm
MAGAZINE CAPACITY 20 or 30
ACTION Gas operated/rotating bolt
TOTAL LENGTH 838mm/33in
BARREL LENGTH 370mm/14.5in
WEIGHT UNLOADED 2.52kg/5.55lb

FN C1A1

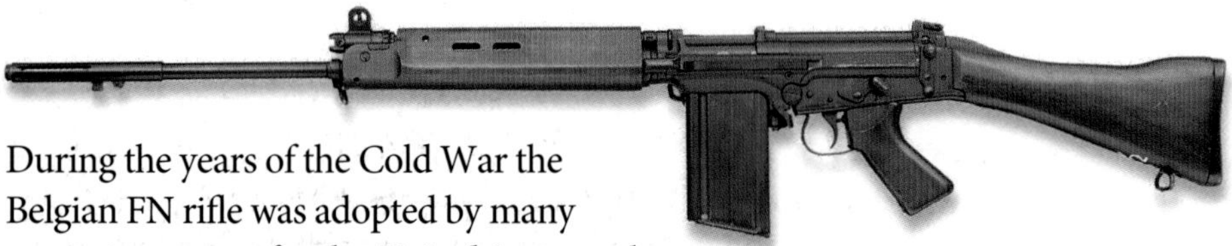

During the years of the Cold War the Belgian FN rifle was adopted by many countries, except for the United States and the countries of the Warsaw Pact. As Canada was a Commonwealth country, it made sense for her to adopt the rifle as well. Made in the Long Branch plant, the Canadian FN C1A1 rifles were finely fitted. The FN C1A1 was used from 1956 until replaced by the Diemaco C7 in the 1980s.

SPECIFICATION

MANUFACTURER Long Branch
CALIBRE 7.62 x 51mm
MAGAZINE CAPACITY 20
ACTION Gas operated/tilting lock
TOTAL LENGTH 1,136mm/44.75in
BARREL LENGTH 533mm/21in
WEIGHT UNLOADED 4.3kg/9.5lb

Ross Mark 3

SPECIFICATION	
MANUFACTURER	Ross Rifle Co.
CALIBRE	.303 British
MAGAZINE CAPACITY	5
ACTION	Straight-pull bolt action
TOTAL LENGTH	1,279mm/50.36in
BARREL LENGTH	768mm/30.25in
WEIGHT UNLOADED	4.47kg/9.85lb

Canadian Sir Charles Ross patented the Ross rifle at the turn of the 20th century. The Mark 3 Ross, developed a decade later, was fast and accurate. Yet the fine machining necessary for the design made it less than reliable when used in combat during World War I. When it was used in the mud, grit and ice of the trenches, the debris caught in the bolt bound the mechanism, and the Ross would quickly stop working. When the rumour spread that it could be reassembled incorrectly causing the bolt to blow out of the rifle, injuring the shooter, it quickly faded from use. The Ross Mark 3 was used from 1911 to 1914, when it was withdrawn from service except as a sniper rifle, and replaced with the SMLE Mark III* rifle.

Colt Canada C19

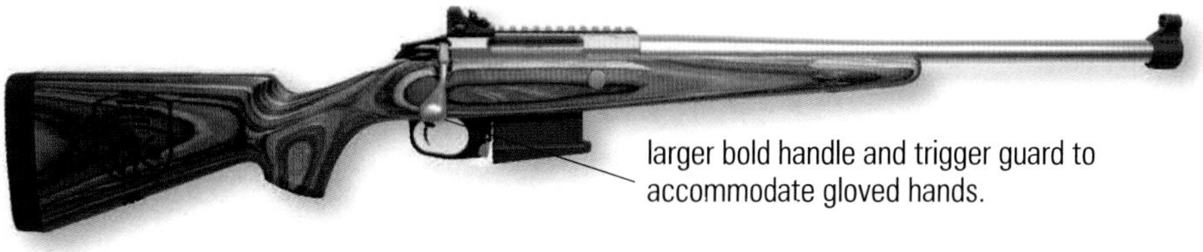

SPECIFICATION	
MANUFACTURER	Colt Canada
CALIBRE	7.62mm NATO
MAGAZINE CAPACITY	10
ACTION	Bolt action
TOTAL LENGTH	1,020mm/40in
BARREL LENGTH	510mm/20in
WEIGHT UNLOADED	4kg/9lb

An officially licensed version of the Finnish Tikka T3 CTR, the C19 was adopted in 2018 by the Canadian Rangers, a subcomponent of the Army that stations soldiers where it would otherwise be economically prohibitive. This bolt action rifle is used by the Rangers mainly as a defensive weapon against large animals, such as polar bears. It can fire standard 7.62mm NATO ammo as well as proprietary C180 hunting ammunition.

United States

Proud of the title "a nation of riflemen", the United States has a long history of making accurate and powerful rifles. Deciding on which one was best suited to the needs of the Army, however, has not always been easy and attempts to replace rifles such as the M-16 have often failed because of the costs involved.

M1 Carbine, commercial

SPECIFICATION	
MANUFACTURER	Alpine
CALIBRE	.30 carbine
MAGAZINE CAPACITY	5, 15 or 30
ACTION	Gas operated
TOTAL LENGTH	905mm/35.65in
BARREL LENGTH	457mm/18in
WEIGHT UNLOADED	2.44kg/5.4lb

The M1 military carbine was a compact and lightweight shoulder arm that was developed before World War II and issued to the US Army. Military production of the M1 had ceased by the 1960s. Although it took a while for surplus supplies to dwindle, the supply of military carbines was running low in the years after production stopped. This led to commercial manufacturers producing the carbine for civilian use. Most new manufacturers of the carbine were under-capitalized, however. As a result, shortcuts in manufacturing adversely affected quality of the production.

Armalite AR-50

The Armalite AR-50 is a single-shot long-range sniper rifle, first produced in the 1990s. It was designed for civilian use rather than for the military. It has unique octagonal receiver that is fixed into a stock of aluminium. Typically, a rifle loaded with .50 Browning Machine Gun (BMG) ammunition is light and easy to transport. Recoil (backward momentum) caused by firing is very mild because it is fitted with an excellent muzzle brake (designed to reduce recoil). This is essential, otherwise it could not be fired safely.

SPECIFICATION

MANUFACTURER Armalite
CALIBRE .50 BMG
MAGAZINE CAPACITY No magazine
ACTION Single shot
TOTAL LENGTH 1,499mm/59in
BARREL LENGTH 787mm/31in
WEIGHT UNLOADED 18.61kg/41lb

Barrett M82A1

The Barrett M82 is a semi-automatic rifle used by a marksman for long range sniper work. The M82A1 is the latest version, and represents the limit of portable rifle power. If it was any larger it would require either an entirely different recoil-control system, or become a low-velocity grenade launcher. Used in Iraq and Afghanistan, the Barrett has set new records for the range of successful sniper engagements. It has been in production since 1982.

SPECIFICATION

MANUFACTURER Barrett Manufacturing
CALIBRE 12.7 x 99mm
MAGAZINE CAPACITY 10
ACTION Recoil operated
TOTAL LENGTH 1,448mm/57in
BARREL LENGTH 737mm/29in
WEIGHT UNLOADED 12.9kg/28.4lb

Stoner 63

The 63 is the second of three rifle designs by Indiana-born military arms designer Eugene Stoner. It was produced between 1963 and 1969. The Stoner 63 differed from most other assault rifles in having "components". The basic receiver could be assembled by the user as a carbine, Light Machine Gun (LMG), belt-fed or sniper rifle. Although it was popular with the United States Navy Sea, Air and Land (SEAL) special forces in Vietnam, the model required more research and development. However it was in competition with the M16 which had been adopted by the US military in the 1960s.

SPECIFICATION

MANUFACTURER Cadillac Gage
CALIBRE 5.56 x 45mm
MAGAZINE CAPACITY 20, 30, belt-fed
ACTION Gas operated
TOTAL LENGTH 1,022mm/40.25in
BARREL LENGTH 508mm/20in
WEIGHT UNLOADED 4.37kg/9.65lb

Colt AR-15 Mod 08

The Colt AR-15 was produced between 1964 and 1966 as a survival rifle for pilots and helicopter crews. The simple tubular hand guard and plain butt plate make it lightweight, and the short pistol grip makes it very compact. However, today there is no advantage to this lightweight rifle over other firearms such as the XM-177 (a series of modified and shortened weapons) for pilots and crews. The full weight of a modern helicopter is so great that a rifle's weight is inconsequential to the craft's lift capacity.

SPECIFICATION

MANUFACTURER Colt
CALIBRE 5.56 x 45mm
MAGAZINE CAPACITY 20
ACTION Gas operated
TOTAL LENGTH 787mm/31in
BARREL LENGTH 330mm/13in
WEIGHT UNLOADED 2.67kg/5.9lb

XM-177E2

SPECIFICATION	
MANUFACTURER	Colt
CALIBRE	5.56 x 45mm
MAGAZINE CAPACITY	20 or 30
ACTION	Gas operated
TOTAL LENGTH	787mm/31in
BARREL LENGTH	342mm/13.5in
WEIGHT UNLOADED	2.76kg/6.1lb

As light and handy as the Colt M16 was in its earliest version, there was always a perceived requirement for something lighter and more compact. The XM-177 series went through several stock configurations, two barrel lengths and moderator designs. The moderator was designed to keep the short barrel from deafening the firer. However, conflicting regulatory definitions prevented Colt from exporting the moderator, and this meant that the model itself could not be sold abroad. As a result, Colt went on to perfect the M16 carbine in the form of the M4. The XM-177E2 was produced between 1966 and 1969.

AR-15 Heavy Barrel Mod 01

SPECIFICATION	
MANUFACTURER	Colt
CALIBRE	5.56 x 45mm
MAGAZINE CAPACITY	30
ACTION	Gas operated
TOTAL LENGTH	990mm/39in
BARREL LENGTH	508mm/20in
WEIGHT UNLOADED	3.40kg/7.5lb

Armalite sold the rights of the AR-15 to Colt. The AR-15 Mod 01 was an attempt to provide armed forces with a light machine gun based on the Colt M16 in the 1970s. Colt made their rifle with a heavy barrel and bipod, and fastened together three magazines side by side. However, this approach had its limitations. The AR15 was not popular and this was reflected in poor sales.

M16A2

SPECIFICATION	
MANUFACTURER	Colt, FNH-USA
CALIBRE	5.56 x 45mm
MAGAZINE CAPACITY	30
ACTION	Gas operated
TOTAL LENGTH	1,005mm/39.6in
BARREL LENGTH	508mm/20in
WEIGHT UNLOADED	3.85kg/8.5lb

The predecessor of the M16-A2 was the M16A1, a slightly-modified M16. However, it was not popular with the army and it was decided that it should be improved. The barrel was made heavier and with a faster twist to allow the use of heavier bullets. The plastic of the stock and forearms was strengthened. The sights were made click-adjustable. The result was a superb target rifle. The M16A2 was produced from 1985 to the present. However, it proved just too long and heavy for many types of combat.

M4

SPECIFICATION	
MANUFACTURER	Colt
CALIBRE	5.56 x 45mm
MAGAZINE CAPACITY	30
ACTION	Gas operated
TOTAL LENGTH	863mm/34in
BARREL LENGTH	368mm/14.5in
WEIGHT UNLOADED	3.4kg/7.5lb

The M4 carbine differs from the M16A2 rifle only by having a shorter barrel and a telescoped buttstock. However research and development by Colt led to significant improvements. The M4 has greatly increased reliability, durability and accuracy. This progress has made it very difficult for the Army to justify its desire to replace the M16. The short barrel length exists for one reason: it is the distance needed between the front sight housing and the muzzle to mount a bayonet. The M4 was produced from the 1990s to the present.

FN T48

The FN T48 (the Belgian FN FAL) was one of the competitors in the US Army rifle trials. These were held after World War II to find a replacement for the M1 Garand, the main rifle used by the United States since the 1930s. The T48 competed against the T44 rifle, a modified version of the M1 Garand. Testing proved them to be similar in performance, but the T44 was the winner. However, the FN T48 was the rifle that most other countries found to be most suitable.

SPECIFICATION

MANUFACTURER FN, Liège
CALIBRE 7.62mm T65
MAGAZINE CAPACITY 20
ACTION Gas operated
TOTAL LENGTH 1,089mm/42.9in
BARREL LENGTH 533mm/21in
WEIGHT UNLOADED 3.88kg/8.56lb

FN SCAR

In searching for a replacement rifle to the M16A2 and M4, the US Army Special Operations Command asked for a Special Operations Combat Rifle. The result was a polymer-shell encased, piston-driven M16 replacement. Two basic versions of SCAR system were produced – the SCAR-light (SCAR-L), and the SCAR-heavy (SCAR-H). The heavier model would be available in significantly more powerful chambering. Both models are easily adaptable in the field. They are designed to have the same control, handling and maintenance procedures. Intended to be quickly reconfigurable, and have barrels of various lengths, the SCAR is difficult to list in a "standard" configuration. Given the US Army's stringent testing procedures, the FN SCAR may never be used by the military. It was produced between 2000 and 2006.

SPECIFICATION

MANUFACTURER FNH-USA
CALIBRE 5.56 x 45mm (SCAR-light), 7.62mm NATO (SCAR-heavy)
MAGAZINE CAPACITY 30 (light), 20 (heavy)
ACTION Gas operated
TOTAL LENGTH 850 to 620mm/33.4 to 24.4in (light), 997 to 770mm/39.25 to 30in (heavy)
BARREL LENGTH 280 to 508mm/ 11 to 20in
WEIGHT UNLOADED 3.5kg/7.7lb (light), 3.68kg/8.11lb (heavy)

HK XM-8

Produced between 1999 and 2005, the US Army considered the XM-8 (a derivative of the Heckler & Koch G36) as a suitable replacement for the Colt M16. However, the changes they made to materials and mechanism of the rifle were not a sufficient improvement to make it viable. The costs of the war in Iraq consumed any budget for research and development that might have improved it further. The failure of the XM-8 has not changed the desire of the US army to find something "better".

SPECIFICATION

MANUFACTURER Heckler & Koch
CALIBRE 5.56 x 45mm
MAGAZINE CAPACITY 30
ACTION Gas operated
TOTAL LENGTH 838mm/33in
BARREL LENGTH 318mm/12.5in
WEIGHT UNLOADED 2.67kg/5.88lb

HK 416

Based on the AR-15 platform, the HK 416 uses a short stroke gas piston system that is proprietary and based on the company's G36 rifles. Designed for use by the US Army's Delta Force in close quarters combat, they adopted the rifle in 2005. In 2011, it was one of these firearms that was used in the US Navy SEAL Team Six raid that killed Osama bin Laden.

SPECIFICATION

MANUFACTURER Heckler & Koch
CALIBRE 5.56mm NATO
MAGAZINE CAPACITY 10, 20, 30 or 100
ACTION Gas operated
TOTAL LENGTH 709mm/28in
BARREL LENGTH 420mm/16in
WEIGHT UNLOADED 3.12kg/6.88lb

Armalite AR-18

Eugene Stoner was the designer of the AR-15 and its later competitor, the AR-18. Whereas the AR-15 uses a direct impingement gas system the AR-18 was designed to use the short piston gas system. The AR-15 was designed to use aluminium forgings, the AR-18 is fabricated by the use of sheet metal pressings. But by the time Stoner designed the rifle, the US government had settled, however reluctantly, on the AR-15/M16. The AR-15 ended up being made in three countries, but was not commercially successful. The AR-18 was manufactured from 1969 to 1978. It was resurrected by the Armalite company as the AR-180B in 2002.

SPECIFICATION

MANUFACTURER Howa, Sterling, Costa Mesa
CALIBRE 5.56 x 45mm
MAGAZINE CAPACITY 20 or 30
ACTION Gas operated
TOTAL LENGTH 965mm/38in
BARREL LENGTH 470mm/18.25in
WEIGHT UNLOADED 3.08kg/6.8lb

Johnson Model 1941

SPECIFICATION

MANUFACTURER Johnson
CALIBRE .30-06
MAGAZINE CAPACITY 10
ACTION Recoil operated
TOTAL LENGTH 1,155mm/45.5in
BARREL LENGTH 558mm/22in
WEIGHT UNLOADED 4.31kg/9.5lb

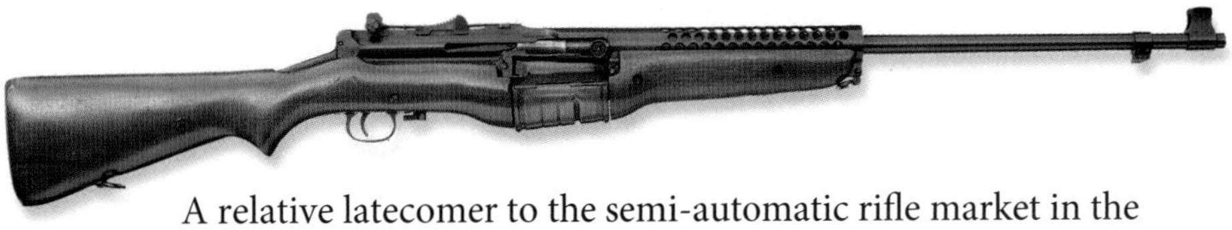

A relative latecomer to the semi-automatic rifle market in the 1930s, the Johnson had several unique features. Its internal, rotary magazine could be topped off at any time via stripper clips and the barrel could be removed for compact storage. However, it was not as robust as the Garand and found few buyers. Used by the US Marine Corps in 1941 and found wanting, it stayed in service due to wartime needs until 1945. It was declared surplus afterwards and sold off.

SPECIFICATION

MANUFACTURER Knight's Armament
CALIBRE 7.62mm NATO
MAGAZINE CAPACITY 20
ACTION Gas operated
TOTAL LENGTH 1,174mm/46.25in
BARREL LENGTH 508mm/20in
WEIGHT UNLOADED 4.42kg/9.75lb

Stoner SR-25 sniper

The desire for a medium- to long-range sniper rifle that was also a semi-automatic stemmed from the success of the M-21 sniper rifle used in the Vietnam war. The SR-25 is essentially an AR-10 rifle with the carry handle replaced by a slotted rail for scope attachment. The SR-25 is made by Knight's Armament, but there are a number of other manufacturers of AR-10-type rifles who also make a sniper rifle. The US Army and Marine Corps are currently purchasing the Knight's. It has been produced from the 1990s to the present.

McMillan M-87 sniper

SPECIFICATION

MANUFACTURER McMillan
CALIBRE .50 BMG
MAGAZINE CAPACITY 5
ACTION Bolt action
TOTAL LENGTH 1,448mm/57in
BARREL LENGTH 736mm/29in
WEIGHT UNLOADED 11.8kg/26.01lb

Where other long-range sniper rifles often look like a piece of industrial equipment, the McMillan looks like a sporting rifle. As with all .50 BMG rifles, the muzzle brake is a requirement, to reduce recoil. With proper ammunition and a good shooter, a McMillan can be expected to deliver its bullets within a 130mm/51in circle at 1,000m/3,200ft. It has been produced from the mid-1990s to the present.

M-40

Faced with the pressing need for a sniper rifle for use in the Vietnam War during the 1960s, the US Marine Corps rebuilt the sporting rifle Remington 700 and issued it as an accurate and durable military weapon. Unlike other services, the Marine Corps trains its own armourers, who build these rifles up from factory configuration. The result is a well designed sniper rifle that is still in use today. Some Vietnam-era M-40 rifles with new barrels, stocks and scopes are now called M-40A1. They are still in service. The M-40 has been produced from 1967 to the present.

SPECIFICATION

MANUFACTURER Remington Arms
CALIBRE 7.62mm NATO
MAGAZINE CAPACITY 5
ACTION Bolt action
TOTAL LENGTH 1,117mm/44in
BARREL LENGTH 660mm/26in
WEIGHT UNLOADED 6.57kg/14.5lb w/scope and mount

M24 Sniper Weapon System

Based on the Remington Model 700 commercial rifle, the M24 was adopted by the US Army in 1988. The rifle uses a long action bolt but fires a short action cartridge, which allows it to be reconfigured for longer cartridges if needed. Designed to be a complete weapon system, the rifle is issued with a scope and bipod.

SPECIFICATION

MANUFACTURER Remington Arms
CALIBRE 7.62mm NATO
MAGAZINE CAPACITY 5
ACTION Bolt action
TOTAL LENGTH 1,0592m/43in
BARREL LENGTH 610mm/24in
WEIGHT UNLOADED 5.4kg/11.8lb

Krag-Jorgensen 1898

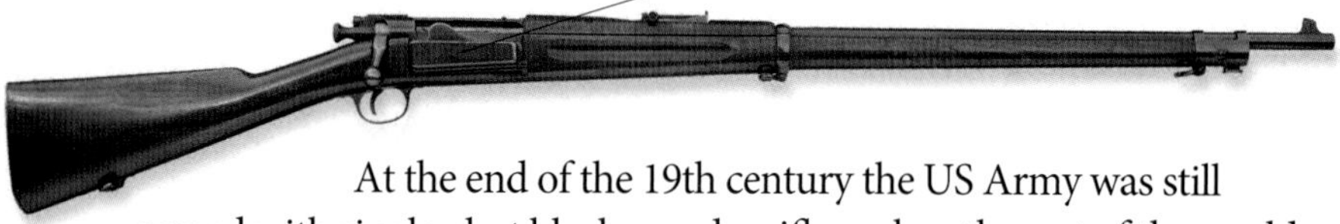

At the end of the 19th century the US Army was still armed with single-shot black powder rifles, when the rest of the world was transitioning to smokeless repeaters. Due to the mechanical limitations of the Krag (such as the inability to be recharged using stripper clips) it was soon replaced by the Springfield 1903. It was produced between 1898 and 1903. The new rifle was not common issue during the Spanish-American War. Many conflicts, such as that at San Juan Hill, Cuba had American troops with black powder single shots assaulting Spanish positions which were defended by Mauser rifles.

SPECIFICATION

MANUFACTURER Springfield
CALIBRE .30-40
MAGAZINE CAPACITY 5
ACTION Bolt action
TOTAL LENGTH 1,248mm/49.15in
BARREL LENGTH 762mm/30in
WEIGHT UNLOADED 4.08kg/9lb

Krag-Jorgensen 1898 carbine

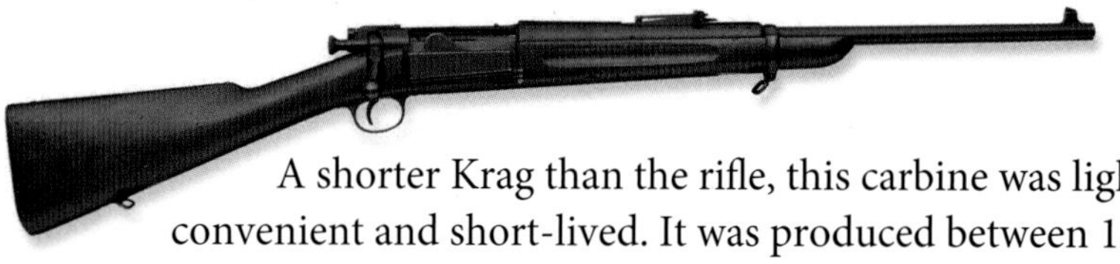

A shorter Krag than the rifle, this carbine was light, handy, convenient and short-lived. It was produced between 1898 and 1903. The 1898 carbines received the 1898 rifle sights. Then, they were recalled and rebuilt in the very early 1900s to receive improved 1899 pattern stocks and new sights. The carbine, along with the rifle, was replaced by the Springfield 1903, the "one size fits all" length rifle. The carbines were greatly prized by hunters in the first half of the 20th century, for being light, handy, accurate and powerful enough for American big game.

SPECIFICATION

MANUFACTURER Springfield
CALIBRE .30-40
MAGAZINE CAPACITY 5
ACTION Bolt action
TOTAL LENGTH 1,054mm/41.15in
BARREL LENGTH 559mm/22in
WEIGHT UNLOADED 3.51kg/7.75lb

Springfield M-1903

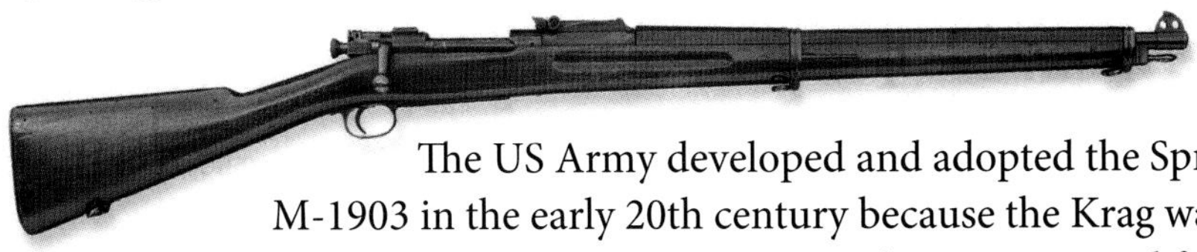

The US Army developed and adopted the Springfield M-1903 in the early 20th century because the Krag was not a powerful enough weapon. However, it used many patented features created by the German company Mauser. Mauser sued Springfield and won, collecting royalties until 1917. The M-1903 illustrated is the earliest model, with a rod bayonet beneath the barrel, where a cleaning rod is usually kept. President Theodore Roosevelt was so outraged by the rod bayonet he ordered it changed to a blade bayonet. It was in service through World War II.

SPECIFICATION

MANUFACTURER Springfield, Remington, Winchester
CALIBRE .30-06
MAGAZINE CAPACITY 5
ACTION Bolt action
TOTAL LENGTH 1,102mm/43.4in
BARREL LENGTH 615mm/24.2in
WEIGHT UNLOADED 3.85kg/8.5lb

Springfield M-1903 Mark 1

SPECIFICATION

MANUFACTURER Springfield
CALIBRE .30-06
MAGAZINE CAPACITY 5
ACTION Bolt action
TOTAL LENGTH 1,102mm/43.4in
BARREL LENGTH 615mm/24.2in
WEIGHT UNLOADED 3.85kg/8.5lb

The Mark 1 was the "solution" to the stalemate of trench warfare in World War I. With enough firepower, the Allies could keep the Germans in their trenches while covering the gap of no-man's land. The Mark 1 differed from the M-1903 in having an ejection port on the left side for the Pedersen Device (an optional attachment that allowed it to shoot a pistol-sized round in semi-automatic mode) cases to exit the rifle. It also had a slightly altered trigger mechanism. While production was underway the war ended. The rifles were simply used as regular bolt-action rifles, until they were replaced by the M1 Garand and M-14. They were then sold as surplus. It was produced in 1918.

Pedersen Device

The Pedersen Device was designed to convert the 1903 Springfield to a semi-automatic rifle for assaults across no-man's land. It replaced the bolt of a 1903 Springfield, and converted that rifle (the Mark 1) into a semi-automatic rifle firing a cartridge of submachine gun power. It was thought that the conversion was lighter, and avoided the need to issue two weapons. World War I ended before the futility of the approach could be demonstrated.

Springfield M1903A4 sniper

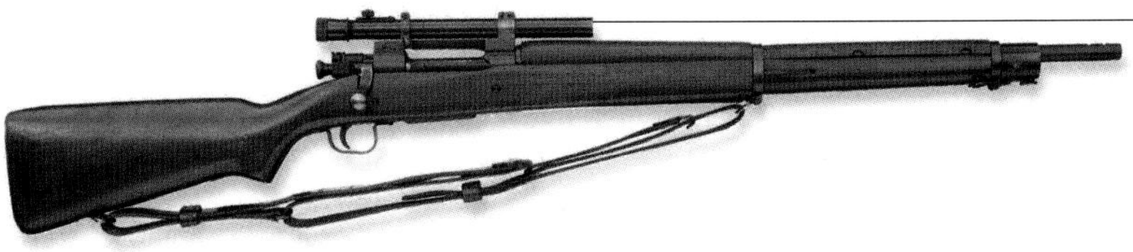

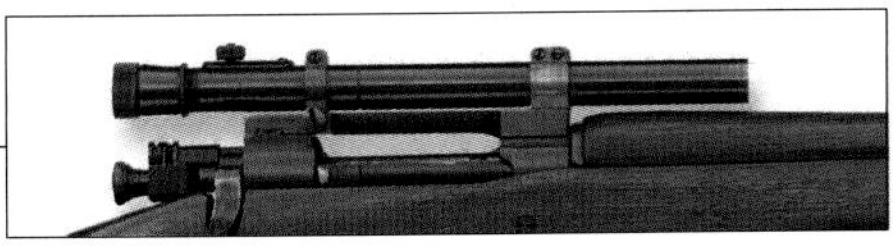

ABOVE A 3-power commerical hunting scope is attached to the Springfield M1903A4.

SPECIFICATION

MANUFACTURER Springfield
CALIBRE .30-06
MAGAZINE CAPACITY 5
ACTION Bolt action
TOTAL LENGTH 1,098mm/43.25in
BARREL LENGTH 609mm/24in
WEIGHT UNLOADED) 4.00kg/8.83lb

Faced with the need for more accurate fire in World War II, the US Army simply mounted commercial scopes in commercial bases on production 1903A3 rifles. The A4 designation simply means that the rifle never received iron sights at the factory, and always had a scope mount installed. Factory-produced A4 sniper rifles even had the receiver marking location moved, so they would be visible when the scope mount was attached. As a more accurate rifle in infantry use, it was good enough. But as a special-purpose sniper rifle it was not as effective as its Mauser counterparts. It was adopted in 1942 and, despite the development of the M1C and M1D Garand sniper variants, the Springfield remained in service through the Korean War.

T44E4

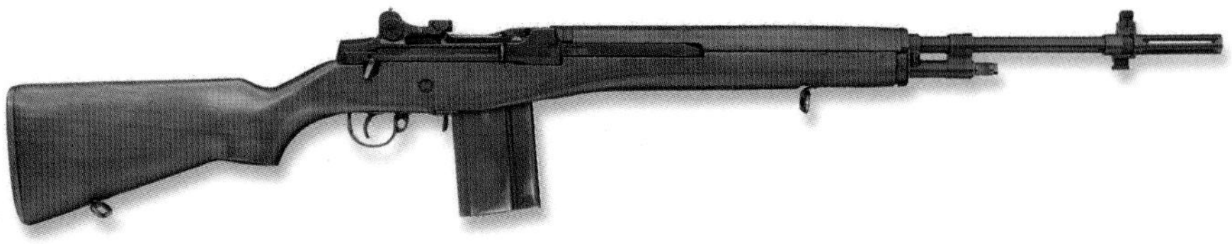

SPECIFICATION	
MANUFACTURER	Springfield
CALIBRE	7.62mm T65
MAGAZINE CAPACITY	20
ACTION	Gas operated
TOTAL LENGTH	1,117mm/44in
BARREL LENGTH	559mm/22in
WEIGHT UNLOADED	3.88kg/8.56lb

This Springfield rifle was one of the rifles that took part in the US trials between the wars. The US Army was so keen for their own design to be adopted that the tests were all but a sham. (The FAL was rejected in one phase for not passing a field combat test.) Every time the T44 series rifles failed a test, the test was rescheduled. The competing T48 (an FAL made by Harrington & Richardson) and FN-FAL from Liège never stood a chance. The T44E4 was produced in 1955 and went on to become the M-14.

M-14

SPECIFICATION	
MANUFACTURER	Springfield, H&R, TRW
CALIBRE	7.62mm NATO
MAGAZINE CAPACITY	20
ACTION	Gas operated
TOTAL LENGTH	1,117mm/44in
BARREL LENGTH	558mm/22in
WEIGHT UNLOADED	3.88kg/8.56lb

Based on World War II experience, the US Army needed more ammunition, increased firepower and greater adaptability. Unfortunately, the Americans spent twelve years and millions of dollars and ended up with a barely improved Garand. Worse still, they proposed to replace everything in inventory with one rifle: the M-14. It was supposed to replace the M1 Garand, the BAR and the M1 submachine gun. It was, however, too light to be a light machine gun (LMG), too large to be a submachine gun and not much improvement on the Garand. As a Designated Marksman Rifle (SDM-R), it saw a resurgence in Iraq. The M-14 was officially adopted in 1957 but production was slow at first as the Springfield Armoury alone (a government arsenal) was an insufficient production base for its requirements.

Ruger Mini-14

SPECIFICATION	
MANUFACTURER	Sturm, Ruger & Co.
CALIBRE	.223
MAGAZINE CAPACITY	5, 20 or 30
ACTION	Gas operated
TOTAL LENGTH	943mm/37.15in
BARREL LENGTH	470mm/18.5in
WEIGHT UNLOADED	3.06kg/6.75lb

Made in the 1970s as a sporting rifle to emulate the M-14 and M1 Garand, the Mini-14 proved to be useful as a semi-automatic rifle. Ruger originally marketed it as "The world's most expensive plinker". Plinking refers to shooting at chance targets, such as tin cans, using a .22 LR (Long Rifle) rifle or handgun. Despite using the much more expensive .223 ammunition, it sold very well. As a select-fire rifle for military or police use, the Ruger Mini-14 proved to be just a bit too lightly constructed, and not accurate enough.

Pedersen

SPECIFICATION	
MANUFACTURER	Vickers
CALIBRE	.276 Pedersen
MAGAZINE CAPACITY	10, en bloc clip
ACTION	Gas operated
TOTAL LENGTH	1,117mm/44in
BARREL LENGTH	558mm/22in
WEIGHT UNLOADED	4.12kg/9.1lb

This was another contender for the US Army semi-automatic research and testing between the wars. The Pedersen had a similar mechanism to the German Luger. The cartridges were coated with wax for easy extraction, although the wax could attract debris that would cause malfunctions. The .276 cartridge proved very effective in terminal ballistic testing, but the Army Chief of Staff, General Douglas MacArthur, vetoed any calibre change mainly due to conversion costs. The Pedersen was produced between 1932 and 1934.

M-1917 Enfield

SPECIFICATION

MANUFACTURER Winchester, Remington, Eddystone
CALIBRE .30-06
MAGAZINE CAPACITY 5
ACTION Bolt action
TOTAL LENGTH 1,176mm/46.3in
BARREL LENGTH 660mm/26in
WEIGHT UNLOADED 4.08kg/9lb

With Springfield and Rock Island Arsenals unable to increase production of the Model 1903 prior to World War I, the US Army had the British-designed and American-produced Enfield altered for their purposes. They were produced between 1917 and 1920 and their calibre was changed from .303 to .30-06. After World War I, the 1917s were put in storage while the more popular Springfield M-1903 was retained as the standard service rifle. Early in World War II, desperate for rifles, the British accepted many of the 1917s as part of an arrangement called the Lend-Lease Program. They had to be clearly marked as using non-standard .303 ammunition, with a large red stripe around the handguards, to avoid mistakes.

M2 Carbine

SPECIFICATION

MANUFACTURER Inland & Winchester
CALIBRE .30 carbine
MAGAZINE CAPACITY 15 or 30
ACTION Gas operated
TOTAL LENGTH 905mm/35.65in
BARREL LENGTH 457mm/18in
WEIGHT UNLOADED 2.45kg/5.42lb

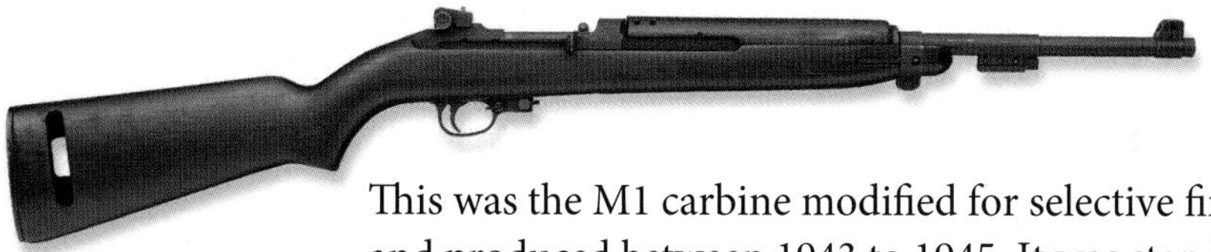

This was the M1 carbine modified for selective fire and produced between 1943 to 1945. It was standardized in October 1944, along with the 30-round magazine to go with it. The conversion kit designated T17 could be installed in any M1, and so produce a select-fire weapon. In wartime, many were converted in this way. Those made specifically as select-fire were marked "M2" on the receiver ring. Removing the select-fire parts from an M1 makes it a semi-automatic only rifle again, with no modifications to show it was ever a "machine gun".

M3 Carbine

SPECIFICATION

MANUFACTURER Winchester
CALIBRE .30 carbine
MAGAZINE CAPACITY 15 or 30
ACTION Gas operated
TOTAL LENGTH 905mm/35.65in
BARREL LENGTH 457mm/18in
WEIGHT UNLOADED 2.45kg/5.42lb

Sight, Night, M3 Carbine
This was an active scope, in that it projected a beam of infra-red light, so that the operator could then use the scope to see in the dark and fire. Modern electronics have made passive night vision equipment the new standard. Passive scopes, like the "Starlight", need no illumination but stars and moon, while Thermal Imaging detects the heat of the target against the background.

The M3 carbine was selected as the host weapon for the new infra-red sniper scope. Allowing the operator to see and aim in darkness, the scope was the future in hardware and promised to revolutionize warfare. The M3 was chosen as it was the lightest available rifle because the scope was very heavy and bulky. The M3 was produced from 1945 to the early 1950s.

M1 Garand

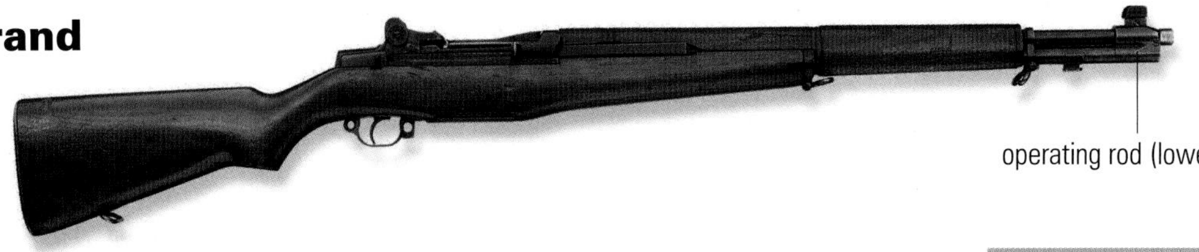

The product of almost twenty years of research and development, and controversial for almost all that time, the finished Garand was not much like the prototypes that preceded it. It uses an en bloc, Mannlicher-type clip, but the Garand clip is inserted from the top, and ejects out of the top when firing the last round. The "ping" of ejection was viewed as a problem by some, but few, if any, combat veterans had a problem with it between 1936 and 1957. The Garand was also used as a target rifle for many years, but the long, unsupported operating rod could cause problems for armourers as they tried to fit it without it degrading target accuracy.

SPECIFICATION

MANUFACTURER Various US
CALIBRE 7.62 x 63mm
MAGAZINE CAPACITY 8, en bloc clip
ACTION Gas operated/rotating bolt
TOTAL LENGTH 1,105mm/43.5in
BARREL LENGTH 609mm/24in
WEIGHT UNLOADED 4.31kg/9.5lb

Barrett MK22

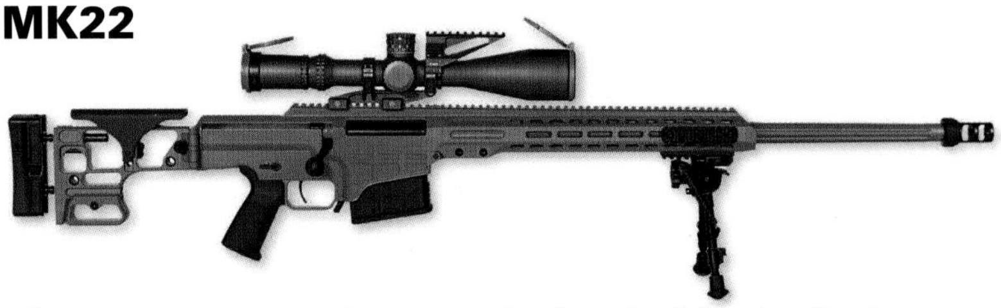

MK22 is the designation given to the Barrett Multi-role Adaptive Design (MRAD) sniper rifle. Designed in 2009 to meet specifications laid out by USSOCOM for a new precision sniper rifle, the MK22 is based on their 98B rifle. While the standard chambering is for 7.62mm NATO, the barrel can be swapped out in less than two minutes for alternate use in more than half a dozen other calibres.

SPECIFICATION

MANUFACTURER Barrett Firearms Manufacturing
CALIBRE 7.62mm NATO
MAGAZINE CAPACITY 10
ACTION Bolt action
TOTAL LENGTH 1,080mm/42.4in
BARREL LENGTH 510mm/20in
WEIGHT UNLOADED 6.3kg/13.9lb

Mexico

Before World War I, Mexico purchased rifles abroad. Between 1913 and the 1950s, it produced its own bolt-action Mauser rifles. In the late 1970s, Mexico obtained a licence from Heckler & Koch to produce the G3. It is now being replaced by the Mexican-designed and manufactured FX-05.

Mondragon M-1908

SPECIFICATION

MANUFACTURER SIG, Neuhausen
CALIBRE 7 x 57mm
MAGAZINE CAPACITY 8
ACTION Gas operated
TOTAL LENGTH 1,248mm/49.15in
BARREL LENGTH 620mm/24.4in
WEIGHT UNLOADED 4.74kg/10.45lb

The M-1908 was designed by a Mexican Army officer in the early 20th century. It was patented in the United States and built in Switzerland. The rifle was not only used in Mexico, but some were issued to the fledgling German air service, with drum (round) magazines, for air-to-air combat. The M-1908 was one of the first successful self-loading rifles. While it did not work particularly well, the fact that it worked at all in that period of time was a marvel. Some rifles went to Mexico in 1909; the leftovers were sold to Germany and served in the Luftwaffe (air force) to 1915. The Mondragon M-1908 was obsolete before World War I ended and is now found only in museums.

Mauser Model 1912

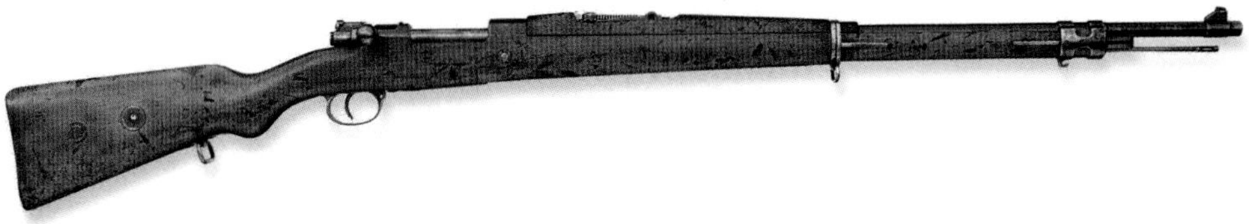

SPECIFICATION	
MANUFACTURER	Steyr
CALIBRE	7 x 57mm
MAGAZINE CAPACITY	5
ACTION	Bolt action
TOTAL LENGTH	1,242mm/48.9in
BARREL LENGTH	739mm/29.1in
WEIGHT UNLOADED	4.11kg/9.06lb

The Mexican Revolution of 1911 made the availability of rifles an important concern for the Mexican government. The supply of Mausers from Germany was not forthcoming, so Mexico turned to Steyr in Austria for Mauser rifles from 1911. Apart from being made in Austria, these models were no different from other Mauser bolt-action rifles. Unfortunately, they were in use on the losing side of the revolution.

FX-05 Xiuhcoatl

SPECIFICATION	
MANUFACTURER	Fabricas Militares
CALIBRE	5.56mm NATO
MAGAZINE CAPACITY	30
ACTION	Gas operated
TOTAL LENGTH	1,087mm/42.8in
BARREL LENGTH	480mm/18.9in
WEIGHT UNLOADED	3.8kg/8.6lb

The FX-05 was born out of the desire to replace foreign-made rifles with a more cost-effective rifle produced solely in Mexico. The FX-05 is capable of semi-automatic, three-round-bursts and fully-automatic fire and utilizes polygonal rifling instead of normal lands and grooves. Begun in 2005, financial issues plagued production and issuing of the rifle. By 2019, just 155,000 had been produced and issued to the Mexican Armed Forces.

Guatemala

Like many countries in Central America, Guatemala has suffered from civil war and unrest within its own borders. Internal strife, police duties and plantation protection all required arms. Lacking local manufacture, Guatemala has purchased and imported small arms from abroad.

Mauser CZ Model 1924

SPECIFICATION	
MANUFACTURER	CZ Brno
CALIBRE	7 x 57mm
MAGAZINE CAPACITY	5
ACTION	Bolt action
TOTAL LENGTH	1,100mm/43.3in
BARREL LENGTH	565mm/22.23in
WEIGHT UNLOADED	4.1kg/9.2lb

Between the World Wars, Guatemala chose to introduce a German Mauser rifle to its country. They settled on the 1924 short rifle, in 7mm. Made for Guatemala and so-marked, it has served from 1924 to the present day. While they were purchased for military and police use, almost all are probably in use guarding plantations, factories and other interests. The military and police have since moved to using assault rifles. The Mauser CZ was replaced in the Guatemalan Army by the Galil, purchased from Israel.

Costa Rica

Like many Caribbean islands, Costa Rica has few threats from outside its borders, and abolished its army in 1949. However, all countries need a defence force, and all governments in the Caribbean have to deal with smugglers, drug dealers and, despite relative stability, the possibility of internal strife.

Mauser Model 1910

Manufactured in Oberndorf, the Costa Rican Mauser was virtually identical to the Gew 98, a model made by Mauser through World War I. Unlike other buyers, Costa Rica ordered its rifles enough in advance of World War I to be sure of delivery. Deliveries took place from 1911 to 1914, and the rifles were in service until 1949. In the same year Costa Rica abolished its Army. All rifles either went to the police or were sold on the world surplus market.

SPECIFICATION

MANUFACTURER Mauser
CALIBRE 7 x 57mm
MAGAZINE CAPACITY 5
ACTION Bolt action
TOTAL LENGTH 1,239mm/48.8in
BARREL LENGTH 740mm/29.15in
WEIGHT UNLOADED 3.97kg/8.75lb

Cuba

For the last century Cuba has depended on a mélange of rifles from various sources. The Spanish 1896 Mauser, US Krags, Remington-Lee and even some Winchester 1895 lever-action rifles could all be found in various military and police units. The acquisition of FN-FAL rifles as the revolution was in progress was not perceived as a help to the government and, after the revolution, Soviet-pattern small arms were the order of the day. The fall of the Soviet Union has stopped the subsidies of material and money to the Cuban army.

FN FAL

This is a standard, select-fire Belgium FAL. The rifles were purchased from Fabrique Nationale (FN) in Belgium, shipped to Cuba and are probably used to this day. The reliable FAL was a prudent choice, as the cash-strapped Cuban economy could hardly afford spare parts and regular overhauls. The FAL seen on the shoulder of a Cuban policeman today probably has the same springs in it that it had when shipped from the manufacturers in Liège in 1958–9. It will have seen regular carry, if little firing, since then.

UIM Alejandro
Little is known about the Alejandro sniper rifle. Manufactured by UIM (Unión de Industrias Militares), it was designed in 2001 with production beginning in 2002. It uses 7.62x54R calibre cartridges and operates with a bolt action. The rifle takes its name from Fidel Castro's middle name.

SPECIFICATION

MANUFACTURER Fabrique Nationale, Liège
CALIBRE 7.62 x 51mm
MAGAZINE CAPACITY 20
ACTION Gas operated/tilting lock
TOTAL LENGTH 1,100mm/43.3in
BARREL LENGTH 533mm/24.3in
WEIGHT UNLOADED 4.45kg/9.81lb

Peru

Peru purchased Mauser rifles from many of the companies licensed to make Peter Paul Mauser's designs beginning in 1892. Those earlier purchases had to be rebuilt and brought up to a new standard each time Mauser unveiled an improvement. By the 1930s, the improvements had stopped coming and Peru could purchase rifles without need of further upgrades. After approaching the United States, France and Israel for arms without success, Peru contracted with the Soviet Union for armour in the 1970s. Today, small arms are purchased on the international market, products of the United States rather than Russia. Limited arms production is done in-country by the state-run Servios Industriales de la Marina S.A.

Fusil Automático Doble

SPECIFICATION

MANUFACTURER Servicios Industriales de la Marina S.A.
CALIBRE 5.56mm NATO
MAGAZINE CAPACITY 30
ACTION Blowback
TOTAL LENGTH 814mm/32in
BARREL LENGTH 450mm/17in
WEIGHT UNLOADED 3.6kg/7.9lb

In 2008, Peru was set to purchase more than a half million Russian AN-94 rifles, but they opted instead for the Fusil Automático Doble (FAD) instead due to costs. The FAD was designed in Peru and is made from polymer and stamped sheet metal, which keeps costs relatively low. Designed as a bullpup rifle, the trigger is located in front of the magazine, which keeps the overall length shorter. Spent cases are ejected from the bottom, making it ambidextrous to use without any modifications.

Colombia

The Colombian Army dates its inception to 1819, when the "Army of the Commoners" was formed to achieve independence from Spanish rule. To provide firearms for the armed forces, Colombia has negotiated foreign contracts with companies such as DMW, Loewe, Steyr, CZ and FN.

Mauser Steyr Model 1912

SPECIFICATION

MANUFACTURER OWG, Steyr
CALIBRE 7 x 57mm
MAGAZINE CAPACITY 5
ACTION Bolt action
TOTAL LENGTH 1,242mm/48.9in
BARREL LENGTH 739mm/29.1in
WEIGHT UNLOADED 4.11kg/9.06lb

National crest
Colombian rifles have the "Ejercito de Colombia" national crest on top of the chamber.

The Mauser Steyr Model 1912 was identical to the Mexican Model of 1912 except for its markings. The Mexicans had long had an excellent relationship with the German company Mauser. Their Mexican Model 1912 was an indigenous Mexican-built rifle based on the some of the earlier military rifles (such as the Model 1902) supplied by Germany and later by similar models from Austria-Hungary (such as the Model 1907). The Mexican and Colombian rifles were in the process of being manufactured by Steyr in Austria when World War I broke out. Once the war began, all outside contracts were suspended in Europe. Many of the German rifles were seized by the Austro-Hungarian government before they could be shipped to Mexico and Colombia and issued to Austro-Hungarian troops on the front line. When they appeared on the surplus market after the war, hunters and gunsmiths rapidly bought them up, as they were beautiful examples of pre-war craftsmanship. The Mauser Steyr Model 1912 was manufactured in 1913.

Chile

With Chile's long coastline, the navy has had a greater importance than the army. Chile has had only one conflict – war with Bolivia in 1884, which was won by Chile and long over before Chile started buying modern arms. Like so many other countries in South America, lacking an industrial base, Chile purchased modern small arms beginning with the adoption of repeating rifles, at the end of the 19th century.

Johnson M1941

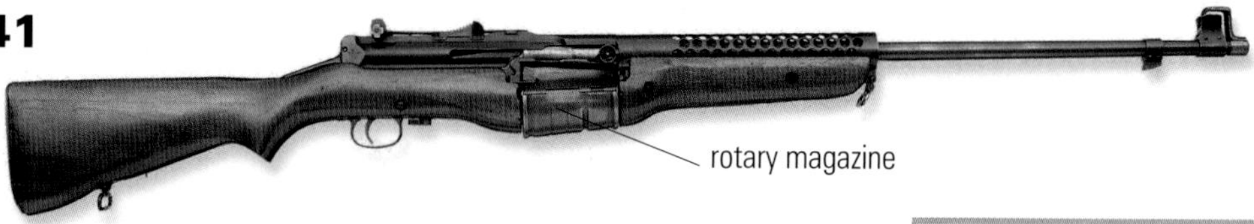

The M1941 rifle was designed by Melvin Johnson just before World War II. Despite heavy campaigning, the M1941 competed unsuccessfully with the US M1 Garand for adoption by the US Army. Yet production delays of the Garand gave the Johnson adherents time to argue their case. Early in World War II the need for rifles was so pressing that some Johnsons were used by the Marines on Guadalcanal in the Solomon Islands. Their experience and poor opinion put an end to the Johnson rifle, which did not work reliably with the attachment of a bayonet. The Johnson used the short recoil method instead of gas to work the action. The barrel moved a short distance, initiating the actions cycle, which meant that anything that interfered with the movement of the barrel could cause a malfunction. Chile bought a few hundred rifles, chambered in 7 x 57mm, during World War II. However, they were already obsolete by the time they were acquired in 1943.

SPECIFICATION

MANUFACTURER Johnson Arms
CALIBRE 7 x 57mm
MAGAZINE CAPACITY 10
ACTION Recoil operated/rotating bolt
TOTAL LENGTH 1,156mm/45.5in
BARREL LENGTH 559mm/22in
WEIGHT UNLOADED 4.31kg/9.5lb

CZ Mauser M1935

The M1935 was a carbine-sized rifle designed for the Chilean police forces. It proved easier for a policeman to carry around than the longer M1912. It was bought in 1935 and used until the adoption of the Sig 540 in 1986. The Chilean contract called for some minor design changes to the original Mauser model: the sling swivels (for carrying) were placed on the left side of the stock, the bolt handle was turned down and the stock relieved at the bolt handle to make it easier to grasp.

SPECIFICATION

MANUFACTURER Mauser-Werke AG
CALIBRE 7 x 57mm
MAGAZINE CAPACITY 5
ACTION Bolt action
TOTAL LENGTH 1,057mm/41.6in
BARREL LENGTH 545mm/21.45in
WEIGHT UNLOADED 3.63kg/8.0lb

Mauser Model 1912

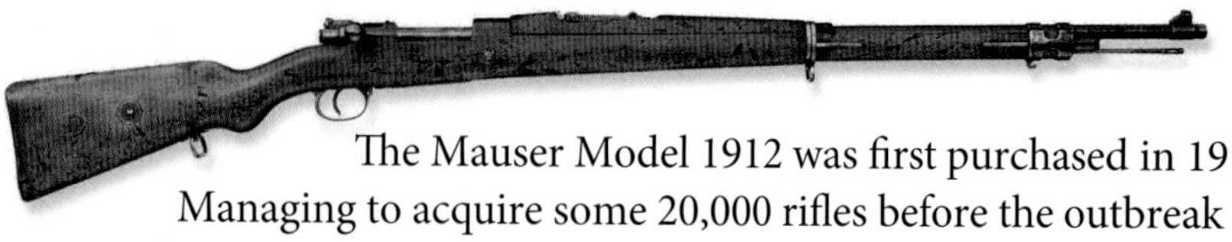

The Mauser Model 1912 was first purchased in 1912. Managing to acquire some 20,000 rifles before the outbreak of World War I, Chile used this rifle for military and police services. It was a standard Mauser rifle of the time in terms of its length, bolt handle and calibre. Chile, with a lengthy coast and few large cities, had little need of a compact arm for military and police work, so a full-size rifle worked well for it. The Mauser was officially dropped in 1986 when Chile adopted the Sig 540 as their issue rifle.

SPECIFICATION

MANUFACTURER Steyr
CALIBRE 7 x 57mm
MAGAZINE CAPACITY 5
ACTION Bolt action
TOTAL LENGTH 1,243mm/48.9in
BARREL LENGTH 735mm/28.95in
WEIGHT UNLOADED 4.11kg/9.06lb

Dominican Republic

The Dominican Republic is not normally associated with arms production. However, it started an arms manufacturing base in the 1940s at San Cristobal using the expertise of émigrés from Hungary and Italy. The first effort by Armeria San Cristobal small arms factory was a copy of the Italian Beretta M-1938 submachine gun. The company went on to produce a light semi-automatic rifle, the Christobal, that used the M1 carbine cartridge. The Christobal Model 2 was mainly used by the Dominican military and the rest exported to other countries in the Caribbean, including neighbouring Cuba.

Cristobal Model 2

SPECIFICATION	
MANUFACTURER	Armeria San Cristobal
CALIBRE	.30 carbine
MAGAZINE CAPACITY	30
ACTION	Delayed blowback
TOTAL LENGTH	945mm/37.2in
BARREL LENGTH	411mm/16.2in
WEIGHT UNLOADED	3.56kg/7.85lb

The Cristobal Model 2 was designed by a Hungarian exile, Pal Kiraly, who established the Cristobal company in 1948. Popular in Central and South America, this rifle sold in hundreds of thousands. Its popularity may have owed as much to buyers not wanting the American or Soviet strings attached to USA-supplied or Warsaw Pact-supplied small arms, as to the reliability of the Cristobal carbine. However, once Central America became flooded by US and Soviet weapons, it was no longer possible for competitors to sell other designs, and the Model 2 faded from production. Examples may still be seen in out-of-the-way police barracks. The Cristobal Model 2 was manufactured from the mid-1950s to the mid-1960s, remained in service long after, and is perhaps still used today.

Venezuela

On the north coast of the South American continent, Venezuela did not enjoy great economic significance until the discovery of large oil deposits in 1917. The Venezuelan army today mainly uses AK rifles, and the country has entered into production licensing with the Russian Federation.

SAFN M-49

SPECIFICATION	
MANUFACTURER	FN, Liège
CALIBRE	7 x 57mm
MAGAZINE CAPACITY	10
ACTION	Gas operated
TOTAL LENGTH	1,110mm/43.7in
BARREL LENGTH	589mm/23.2in
WEIGHT UNLOADED	4.30kg/9.48lb

This was simply the Belgian SAFN M-49 chambered in 7 x 57mm, and marked with the Venezuelan crest on the receiver ring. The SAFN M-49 (which was similar to a Russian Tokarev rifle) was produced by FN in Belgium in 1949 and used in many countries around the world including Brazil, Argentina, Colombia and Venezuela. The rifle had a short front-line service life, from 1951 to 1954. Within a few years after purchase the FAL became available, and Venezuela purchased many FALs in 7 x 49mm. Soon afterwards the FALs were converted to 7.62 x 51mm, as Venezuela updated small arms to recognize the near-universal shift to 7.62 x 51mm cartridges. As a result, the SAFN-M49 rifles were most likely to have gone to police units. Since then, some have occasionally surfaced in the surplus market.

Argentina

The State-owned Argentine ordnance factory is called Fabrica Militar de Armas Portatiles (FMAP). The factory produces and maintains the FAL rifles. A programme of conversion of 7.62mm rifles to 5.56mm was undertaken and work on the replacement design was abandoned.

FN SAFN M-1949

Manufactured in Liège in Belgium, the SAFN M-1949 was produced for Argentina in 7.62 x 63mm calibre. This calibre was dictated by the availability of surplus US ammunition after World War II. Most SAFN rifles were issued to the Navy. They were only in main-line service for a short while, from 1951 to 1959, and were then replaced by locally produced FN-FAL "metric" versions in 7.62mm NATO. The SAFN could be retro-fitted to use the magazine from the Browning Automatic Rifle (BAR), for a capacity of 20 rounds of .30-06 cartridges. The Argentinian SAFN is the result of that amalgam.

SPECIFICATION

MANUFACTURER FN, Liège
CALIBRE 7.62 x 63mm
MAGAZINE CAPACITY 10
ACTION Gas operated/tilting lock
TOTAL LENGTH 1,116mm/43.9in
BARREL LENGTH 590mm/23.2in
WEIGHT UNLOADED 4.31kg/9.5lb

Mauser Model 1891

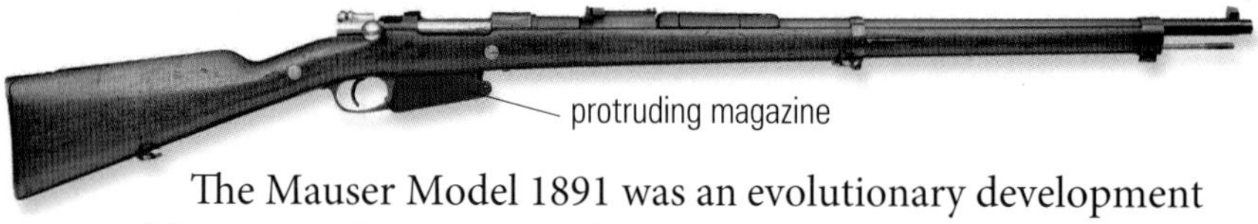

The Mauser Model 1891 was an evolutionary development of the 1889 rifle. Argentina bought some 180,000 Mauser Model 1891 rifles from Loewe, Berlin, in Germany. The 1891 model is distinctive, with its protruding single-stack magazine. While the design is entirely serviceable, the magazine is directly at the point of balance, making one-handed carry difficult. The 1891 model was used as a military rifle from 1891 until it was replaced by the 1909 Mauser. Once the army shifted to using the SAFN 49, all remaining 1891 Mausers were transferred to the police, who used them until the early 1950s.

SPECIFICATION

MANUFACTURER Ludwig Loewe, Berlin
CALIBRE 7.65mm Argentine
MAGAZINE CAPACITY 5
ACTION Bolt action
TOTAL LENGTH 1,234mm/48.6in
BARREL LENGTH 739mm/29.1in
WEIGHT UNLOADED 3.89kg/8.58lb

Mauser Model 1891 carbine

In the 1890s the flat grasslands of the Argentine Pampas was controlled by the cavalry. The standard rifle was too long for mounted use, so a shortened version of the 1891 was produced. Calibre remained the same, but the sights were re-calibrated for the shorter barrel and thus reduced muzzle velocity (the speed at which a bullet travels when it leaves the barrel of a weapon). The protruding magazine, with all rounds in a direct stack instead of staggered in the magazine, was less of a hindrance to cavalry than infantry. The carbines had an identical service life to the rifles. They were used by the military from 1891 to 1909, then became a police-issue rifle until the early 1950s.

SPECIFICATION

MANUFACTURER Ludwig Loewe, Berlin
CALIBRE 7.65mm Argentine
MAGAZINE CAPACITY 5
ACTION Bolt action
TOTAL LENGTH 940mm/37in
BARREL LENGTH 447mm/17.6in
WEIGHT UNLOADED 3.28kg/7.25lb

Paraguay

The German company Mauser succeeded in selling rifles to all sides in almost every South American conflict. They even sold rifles to peaceful countries such as Paraguay. Since a war lasting from 1865 to 1870, Paraguay has had internal security problems but has been at peace with her neighbours.

Mauser Model 1907

SPECIFICATION

MANUFACTURER DMW
CALIBRE 7.65 x 53mm
MAGAZINE CAPACITY 5
ACTION Bolt action
TOTAL LENGTH 1,247mm/49.1in
BARREL LENGTH 740mm/29.15in
WEIGHT UNLOADED 4.11kg/9.06lb

An almost exact copy of the standard German Army rifle of the time, the Mauser Model 1907 had minor differences in bands and nosecap. These modifications were something the manufacturer DMW could expect many customers to worry about. This model did not take the standard German cartridge. However, the different chambering was to be expected, and was just the standard Belgian cartridge in a South American contract rifle. Shipments began in 1907 and the service life of the rifle was well into the 1950s.

Brazil

Brazil imported mainly bolt-action rifles from the German company Mauser until 1945 when it set up its own arms industry. The rapid industrialization that took place after 1930 provided the infrastructure necessary for developing an arms industry. Today Brazil exports arms all over the world.

M954

SPECIFICATION

MANUFACTURER Fabrica de Armas de Itajuba
CALIBRE .30-06
MAGAZINE CAPACITY 5
ACTION Bolt action
TOTAL LENGTH 1,111mm/43.75in
BARREL LENGTH 599mm/23.6in
WEIGHT UNLOADED 4.17kg/9.2lb

The 08/34 was the first military rifle produced in Brazil. The M954 was an improved variant of this rifle, based on a German design, the G/K43. It differed in having a steel bolt installed in order to strengthen the buttstock and a threaded muzzle to attach a grenade launcher. Prototypes were made after World War II and the calibre was changed to use US ammunition (from 7 x 57mm to .30-06). Production began in 1954 and continued until the early 1960s, when it began to be replaced by the M964.

Imbel M964

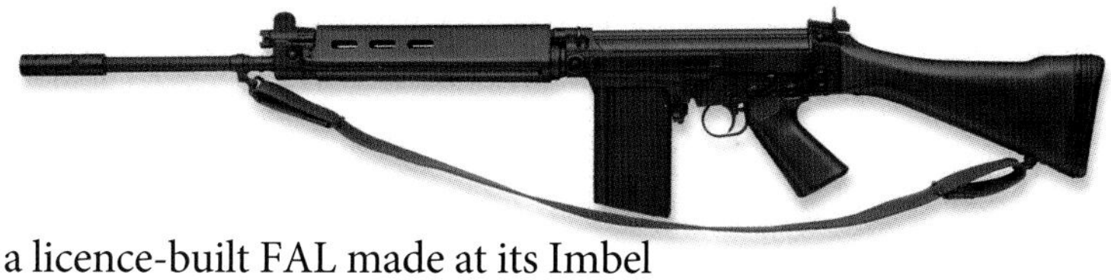

The Imbel M964 is a licence-built FAL made at its Imbel factory. The original FN FAL was produced in Belgium by FN from 1955–74. The design of the Imbel M964 is slightly stronger, and easier to machine than the Belgian FAL. The Imbel M964 uses a "type 3" receiver, designed by Imbel in 1964, which is well designed and well finished. As with all FAL designs not made in the Commonwealth, it is a "metric-pattern" and not an "inch-pattern" rifle and so the measurements were in metric. It was produced in high volume from 1964 to the mid-1990s, when it began to be replaced by the Imbel MD-2.

SPECIFICATION

MANUFACTURER Imbel
CALIBRE 7.62mm NATO
MAGAZINE CAPACITY 20
ACTION Gas operated/tilting lock
TOTAL LENGTH 1,100mm/43.3in
BARREL LENGTH 533mm/21in
WEIGHT UNLOADED 4.45kg/9.8lb

Imbel MD-2

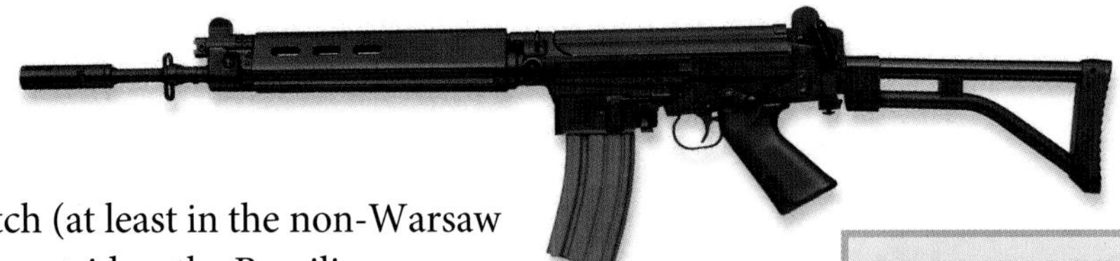

Faced with the worldwide switch (at least in the non-Warsaw Pact countries) to the 5.56mm cartridge, the Brazilian arms industry could not let market share slip away. The MD-1 and then MD-2 were scaled-down FAL rifles in 5.56 x 45mm. Like the Belgian company FN, Imbel first tried a tilting-bolt design. The tilting-bolt design of the FAL proved to be unreliable in extracting fired cases of the 5.56mm cartridge, so the MD-2 was changed from the tilting block of the FAL (in the MD-1) to a rotating bolt like the M16. In addition to the M16 type bolt, the MD-2 uses M16 magazines. This was the same step taken by FN when they changed from the CAL to the FNC. Production began in 1985 and continues to the present.

SPECIFICATION

MANUFACTURER Imbel
CALIBRE 5.56 x 45mm
MAGAZINE CAPACITY 20 or 30
ACTION Gas operated/rotating bolt
TOTAL LENGTH 1,010mm/39.7in
BARREL LENGTH 453mm/17.8in
WEIGHT UNLOADED 4.4kg/9.7lb

Imbel IA2

Designed and manufactured in Brazil, the IMBEL IA2 was created to replace foreign-made rifles. First adopted in 2012, the IA2's design borrows heavily on existing firearms. For example, the 5.56 variant uses standard STANG magazines and the 7.62 variant uses FAL magazines. The 7.63 variant also uses the FAL's tilting breech block. The charging handle is also the same as the FAL in both calibres. Because of the numerous borrowed FAL design integrations, many have criticized the design for not going far enough to advance beyond the shortcomings of the existing design.

SPECIFICATION

MANUFACTURER Imbel
CALIBRE 5.56mm NATO or 7.62mm NATO
MAGAZINE CAPACITY 20 or 30
ACTION Gas operated
TOTAL LENGTH 740mm/29in
BARREL LENGTH 510mm/20in
WEIGHT UNLOADED 3.2 or 3.7kg/7.1 or 8.2lb

Uruguay

The South American country of Uruguay is not a world military power. It currently fields a mix of American, European and Soviet armoured vehicles, and is still using FN-FAL rifles, many decades after most other armies have switched to another assault rifle in 5.56mm calibre.

Daudeteau carbine

The Mauser M71 single shot rifle was cutting-edge when first made in Germany in 1871. By the time the rifles were sold to Uruguay in 1887 – where they were known as the Daudeteau carbine – they were already obsolete. The carbines were sent to the French Armoury at St Denis for conversion to the 6.5mm Daudeteau cartridge, and may have acted as an emergency stop-gap rifle. They remained in service until 1895, and Uruguay purchased 10,000 M1895 carbines less than ten years later.

SPECIFICATION

MANUFACTURER OWG-Steyr
CALIBRE 6.5 x 53mm Daudeteau
MAGAZINE CAPACITY Single shot
ACTION Bolt action
TOTAL LENGTH 994mm/39.15in
BARREL LENGTH 505mm/19.9in
WEIGHT UNLOADED 3.42kg/7.54lb

Portugal

Leaving it a little late in upgrading its rifles, Portugal adopted a single shot Guedes in 1885. It immediately abandoned the Guedes, and then the Kropatschek in 1886, a tube-magazine rifle that was obsolete almost as soon as it was fielded. Finally, Portugal settled on a bolt-action magazine repeater, the Mauser-Verguiero, in 1904. That rifle was then produced in Portugal under licence.

Mauser-Verguiero 1904

SPECIFICATION

MANUFACTURER DMW
CALIBRE 6.5 x 58mm
MAGAZINE CAPACITY 5
ACTION Bolt action
TOTAL LENGTH 1,223mm/48.15in
BARREL LENGTH 738mm/29.05in
WEIGHT UNLOADED 3.79kg/8.37lb

Mannlicher-Schoenauer rifles and carbines were first manufactured by Steyr in Austria in 1903. However, the Mannlicher-Schoenauer was rejected by Portugal as too expensive for an issue rifle. A Portuguese officer, Verguiero, designed a rifle with a collection of features, using the split bridge (where the bolt handle is in front of the rear bridge) of the Mannlicher-Schoenauer, a dual half-cocking action (half on opening, half on closing) and a Mauser magazine. However, Portugal found it could not manufacture the rifle itself, so it was made in Germany. The Mauser-Verguiero was produced from 1904 to 1909 and used through the 1950s.

G3

SPECIFICATION

MANUFACTURER Fabrica de Braco de Porta
CALIBRE 7.62mm NATO
MAGAZINE CAPACITY 20
ACTION Roller-delayed blowback
TOTAL LENGTH 1,021mm/40.2in
BARREL LENGTH 450mm/17.7in
WEIGHT UNLOADED 4.49kg/9.9lb

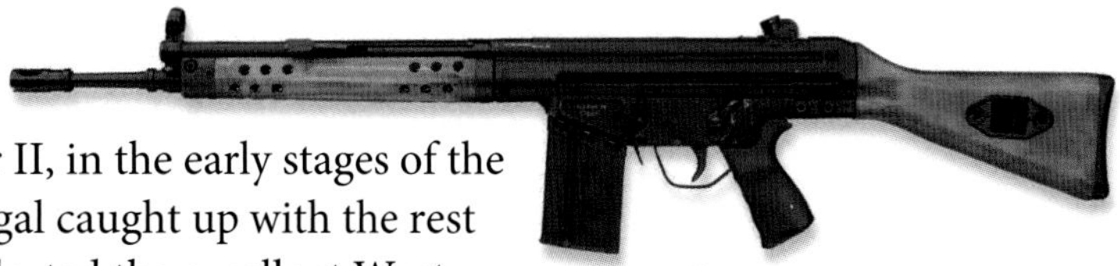

After World War II, in the early stages of the Cold War, Portugal caught up with the rest of Europe and selected the excellent West German Heckler & Koch rifle as their issue rifle. Made under licence in Portugal, it is identical to the West German G3, which in its day competed with rifles such as the FAL. Production commenced in the early 1960s and the rifles are in use to the present day. The G3 was the standard infantry weapon of the German Bundeswehr until 1997, and is still being used by several armed forces around the world. Portuguese troops on peacekeeping missions can be seen with licenced G3 rifles.

Guedes M-1885

SPECIFICATION

MANUFACTURER Steyr
CALIBRE 8 x 60R
MAGAZINE CAPACITY Single shot
ACTION Tilting block
TOTAL LENGTH 1,218mm/47.9in
BARREL LENGTH 845mm/33.25in
WEIGHT UNLOADED 4.10kg/9.04lb

The Guedes was an Portuguese single-shot rifle, developed by Portuguese Lieutenant (later General) Luis Guedes Dias. The M-1885 was an example of how not to go about acquiring a rifle: the rifle was designed in Portugal, and a few tool room samples were made in 11mm calibre. However, Portugal was unable to mass-produce the rifles so Austrian manufacturer Steyr was asked to make them. Even before production could begin, smokeless powder and smaller cartridges were adopted in firearms across Europe. Portugal requested Steyr to change the calibre rifle from 11mm to 8mm. By the time they were finally made in 1885–6, single-shots were obsolete, so they were put in storage while the Kropatschek was being developed. This rifle was built for Portugal by Steyr in lieu of the short-lived Guedes M-1885.

Kropatschek M-1886

Having become obsolete in 1885, the Guedes was replaced with the Kropatscheck, a blend of the French Mle. 1878 and the German Gew 71/84 with an improved cartridge lifter. While the Guedes was obsolete before it was adopted, the Kropatschek had just over 20 years of use before it became obsolete. It was in service from 1886 to 1904.

SPECIFICATION	
MANUFACTURER	Steyr
CALIBRE	8 x 60R
MAGAZINE CAPACITY	8-round tube
ACTION	Bolt action
TOTAL LENGTH	1,319mm/51.95in
BARREL LENGTH	801mm/31.55in
WEIGHT UNLOADED	4.88kg/10.07lb

Mannlicher-Schoenauer, Trials pattern

Austrian manufacturer Steyr pushed the Mannlicher-Schoenauer on to the market, but found few buyers. It was made only in 1901 for the Portuguese Trials, and never adopted by the country as it was too expensive. Portugal decided to choose the Vergueiro instead.

SPECIFICATION	
MANUFACTURER	Steyr
CALIBRE	6.5 M-S
MAGAZINE CAPACITY	5
ACTION	Bolt action
TOTAL LENGTH	1,225mm/48.25in
BARREL LENGTH	725mm/28.55in
WEIGHT UNLOADED	3.76kg/8.31lb

Spain

Spain suffered internal military strife in the 20th century, during the Civil War (1936–9) that saw the overthrow of the monarchy and the establishment of the Republic. After World War II, German engineers emigrated to Spain, and brought with them their ideas, leading to CETME and the rifles that followed.

Destroyer carbine

The original Destroyer carbines were simple to the point of being crude, where the bolt handle was the only locking lug of the bolt to the receiver. However, that was strong enough for the handgun cartridge it was chambered in (the 9mm Largo). It was made from 1920 until the Civil War in 1936. After the Republic was established, the police force of Spain was reorganized. They also turned in their Winchester M-92 lever-action rifles for a new police carbine. The new Destroyer was a bolt-action carbine much like a scaled-down Mauser. The magazine was detachable, and held five rounds, although a good gunsmith could no doubt have fabricated one of greater capacity. For a police officer, armed with even lesser weapons, it was sufficient. And if stolen or turned against the government, it would prove less useful than a modern rifle. First issued in the mid-1930s, the carbines continued to be used until they were replaced by Star submachine guns in the late 1960s.

SPECIFICATION	
MANUFACTURER	Ayra Duria, Eibar
CALIBRE	9mm Largo
MAGAZINE CAPACITY	5
ACTION	Bolt action
TOTAL LENGTH	1,003mm/39.5in
BARREL LENGTH	495mm/19.5in
WEIGHT UNLOADED	2.72kg/6lb

Police weapons

With rare exceptions, police officers need a firearm only as a badge of office. A bolt-action rifle using pistol ammunition was adequate until the late 20th century.

CETME Model A

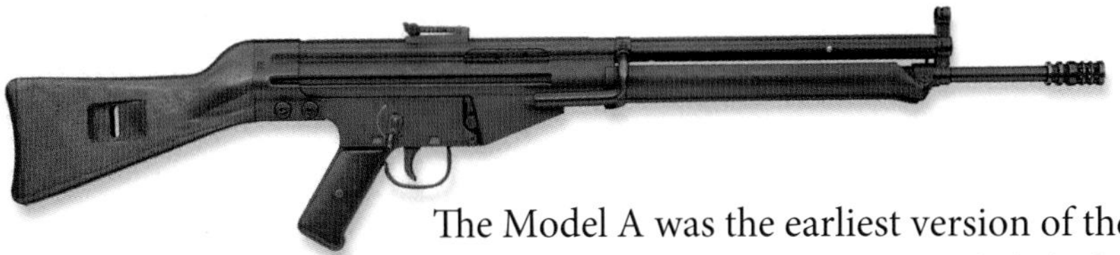

SPECIFICATION

- **MANUFACTURER** CETME
- **CALIBRE** 7.62 x 51mm
- **MAGAZINE CAPACITY** 20
- **ACTION** Roller-delayed blowback
- **TOTAL LENGTH** 1,015mm/39.95in
- **BARREL LENGTH** 450mm/17.7in
- **WEIGHT UNLOADED** 4.48kg/9.88lb

The Model A was the earliest version of the CETME (Centro de Estudios Técnicos de Materiales Especiales), before German manufacturers Heckler & Koch became involved in the design and production of a blueprint version of the CETME, the G3. The Model A fired from an open bolt in fully automatic fire, and a closed bolt in semi-automatic fire. The CETME Model A was built in 1955 and remained in service for only a short time. The initial models of the CETME used an under-powered dimensionally identical version of the 7.62mm NATO cartridge.

CETME Model C

SPECIFICATION

- **MANUFACTURER** CETME
- **CALIBRE** 7.62mm NATO
- **MAGAZINE CAPACITY** 20
- **ACTION** Roller-delayed blowback
- **TOTAL LENGTH** 1,015mm/39.95in
- **BARREL LENGTH** 450mm/17.7in
- **WEIGHT UNLOADED** 4.58kg/10.1lb

The CETME Model C was strengthened to accept the full-power 7.62mm NATO instead of the lower-powered 7.62mm Spanish cartridge that used the same case. Heckler & Koch were involved and the CETME and the G3 were in parallel development. It was made in the late 1950s, as part of the final development process towards the G3/G33 and CETME production rifles.

CETME Model L

SPECIFICATION

- **MANUFACTURER** CETME
- **CALIBRE** 5.56 x 45mm
- **MAGAZINE CAPACITY** 30
- **ACTION** Roller-delayed blowback
- **TOTAL LENGTH** 925mm/36.42in
- **BARREL LENGTH** 400mm/15.75in
- **WEIGHT UNLOADED** 3.4kg/7.50lb

This was the final derivation of the CETME. It was built to use the widely accepted 5.56mm cartridge fed from near-ubiquitous M16 magazines. It differed cosmetically from the Heckler & Koch G3/G33 series, but the design was the same even if parts did not interchange. It was replaced in Spanish service by the Heckler & Koch G36 because it was too heavy to use a 5.56mm cartridge. It was also showing its age, especially in comparison with the new G36. The Model L was in service from 1984 to 1999.

Mauser Model 1943

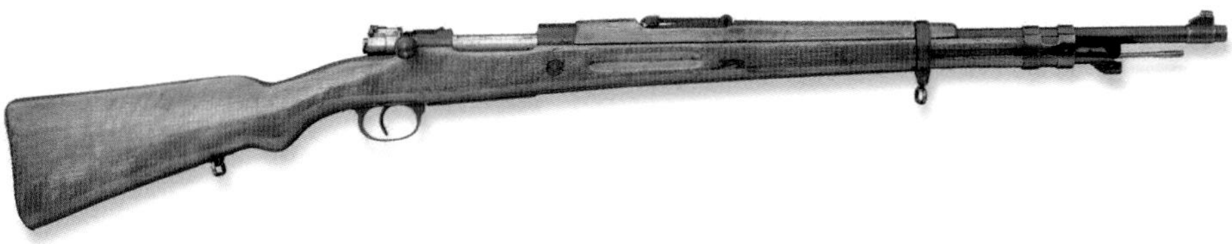

SPECIFICATION

- **MANUFACTURER** La Coruña
- **CALIBRE** 7.92 x 57mm
- **MAGAZINE CAPACITY** 5
- **ACTION** Bolt action
- **TOTAL LENGTH** 1,105mm/43.5in
- **BARREL LENGTH** 599mm/23.6in
- **WEIGHT UNLOADED** 3.90kg/8.62lb

A standard Mauser action, this rifle was built in Spain for local use. The rifle calibre was changed to 7.92 x 57mm from the earlier 7 x 57mm to allow for easier supply, as most machine guns had also been changed to this calibre. When sold as surplus, a rifle manufactured by La Coruña was highly desired by custom gunsmiths, as a base on which to build hunting rifles. Thousands were stripped down to bolt and receiver, the rest of the parts discarded. The Mauser Model 1943 remained in use until the mid-1950s.

FR-8

The FR-8 was made by converting M-1896 Mauser rifles already in Spanish armouries. This bolt-action rifle was re-barrelled to 7.62mm, gained an aperture rear sight, a flash hider (a device to reduce muzzle flash), grenade launcher, and used the CETME/G3 bayonet. The idea was to build it into a reserve rifle that would use G3 ammunition, grenades and bayonets, but not cost as much as new G3 rifles. It was converted, put into storage, then sold as surplus decades later. The conversion work lasted from the mid 1950s to the early 1960s. The FR-8s were sold off at the beginning of the 1980s.

SPECIFICATION

MANUFACTURER La Coruña
CALIBRE 7.62mm NATO
MAGAZINE CAPACITY 5
ACTION Bolt action
TOTAL LENGTH 989mm/38.95in
BARREL LENGTH 470mm/18.5in
WEIGHT UNLOADED 3.75kg/8.27lb

Remington Rolling Block Model 1871 carbine

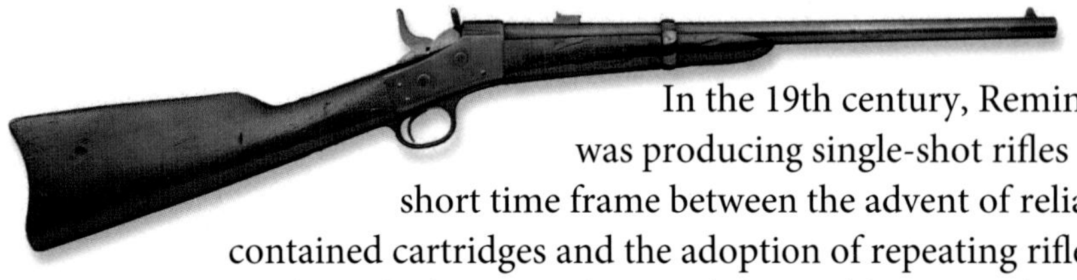

In the 19th century, Remington was producing single-shot rifles in the short time frame between the advent of reliable contained cartridges and the adoption of repeating rifles. The Remington Rolling Block was used around the world. It was adaptable to just about any rifle cartridge, for a price, and could be custom made to order. Spain bought the Remington Rolling Block in 1871 and it was in action until 1885 before becoming obsolete.

SPECIFICATION

MANUFACTURER Remington
CALIBRE 11 x 58R
MAGAZINE CAPACITY Single shot
ACTION Single shot
TOTAL LENGTH 962mm/37.9in
BARREL LENGTH 588mm/23.15in
WEIGHT UNLOADED 3.27kg/7.23lb

United Kingdom

Historically a dominant military power, Britain has a long history of weapons design, manufacturing and export. Britain was unique in the "sealed pattern" method of fixing dimensions and features. Once a firearm was finalized, a single sample would be selected and "sealed", or marked, as the definitive sample against which all others would be compared or measured. British rifle designs have always been driven by the needs of the army rather by the export market, as exemplified by Mauser.

Accuracy International suppressed

In the early 1980s the L42 sniper rifle was showing its age and so the British Army embarked on a search for a replacement. The Accuracy International (AI) design has a bedding block. (Bedding is the fitting of the metal parts of the barrel and receiver to the wood stock.) The receiver is bolted to the bedding block and the two halves of the stock are bolted to the block from the sides. Although heavy, the design eliminates loss of accuracy through stock warping. Accuracy of sniper and target rifles are usually measured by the "minute of angle" (MOA) which is approximately a 60th part of a degree (or an inch of group size at 100yd). The AI delivers sub-MOA accuracy (i.e. below the minute of an angle). It has been in service since 1986.

SPECIFICATION

MANUFACTURER Accuracy International
CALIBRE 7.62mm NATO, 7mm Rem Mag, .300 Win mag, .338 Lapua
MAGAZINE CAPACITY 5
ACTION Bolt action
TOTAL LENGTH 1,270mm/50in w/o suppressor
BARREL LENGTH 686mm/27in
WEIGHT UNLOADED 6.8kg/15lb w/o scope

EM 2

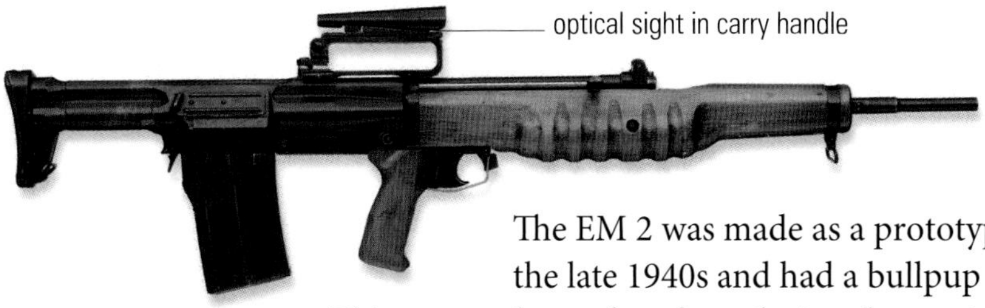

SPECIFICATION

MANUFACTURER Chambons Tool Co., Enfield, BSA, Long Branch
CALIBRE .280/30
MAGAZINE CAPACITY 20
ACTION Gas operated/pivoting flaps
TOTAL LENGTH 884mm/34.8in
BARREL LENGTH 609mm/24.6in
WEIGHT UNLOADED 3.65kg/8.06lb

The EM 2 was made as a prototype in the late 1940s and had a bullpup design. This means that rather than placing the receiver and magazine in front of the grip and trigger, they were placed behind them. This design was not new, but all the other features of the EM 2 were. The sights were in the carry handle, high over the bore, and the bore was directly in line with the stock. The calibre was the low-recoil .280/30. The US Army insisted on a cartridge no less powerful than the .30-06. The EM 2 could not compete with the Belgian FN FAL and languished both as a design and a concept.

Martini-Metford carbine

SPECIFICATION

MANUFACTURER Enfield
CALIBRE .303 British
MAGAZINE CAPACITY None
ACTION Single shot/tilting block
TOTAL LENGTH 947mm/37.3in
BARREL LENGTH 543mm/21.4in
WEIGHT UNLOADED 2.97kg/6.56lb

With old rifles on hand, the new .303 cartridge in production and many troops to equip, it made sense to rebuild old rifles in the late 19th century. The Martini was strong enough to take the new cartridge, and plentiful enough to be widely distributed. From front-line use to colonial, the boy scouts and drill rifles, the Martini could be found at every gun club and many armouries. Some even came out of storage for issue to the Home Guard during World War II. Unfortunately, this carbine was obsolete even when brand new in 1885.

Martini-Enfield Mark 1

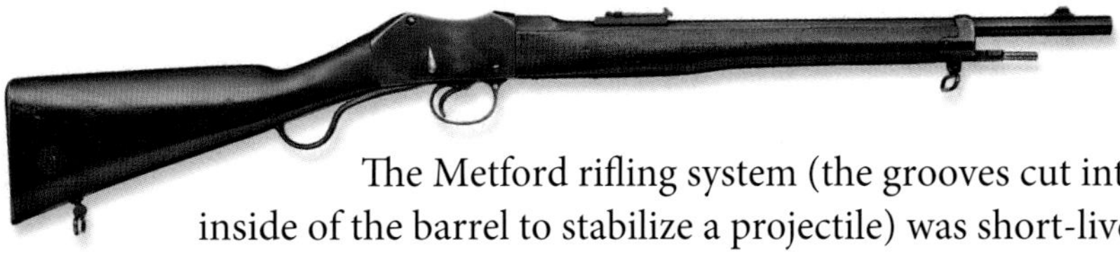

SPECIFICATION

MANUFACTURER Enfield
CALIBRE .303 British
MAGAZINE CAPACITY None
ACTION Single shot/tilting block
TOTAL LENGTH 1,181mm/46.5in
BARREL LENGTH 767mm/30.2in
WEIGHT UNLOADED 3.77kg/8.31lb

The Metford rifling system (the grooves cut into the inside of the barrel to stabilize a projectile) was short-lived due to erosion caused to the inside of the barrel by new cordite gunpowder. The Enfield rifling proved to have a longer service life and was used when rebuilding Martini rifles. The manufacture of Enfield-rifled barrels would provide plenty of jobs at the Enfield factory. The rifle was very suitable for issue to indigenous troops in the colonies – it was durable, single-shot and with a fine bayonet mount. It was never used apart from in the colonies.

Lee-Metford Mark 1

SPECIFICATION

MANUFACTURER Enfield
CALIBRE .303 British, black powder load
MAGAZINE CAPACITY 8
ACTION Bolt action
TOTAL LENGTH 1,266mm/49.285in
BARREL LENGTH 767mm/30.19in
WEIGHT UNLOADED 4.73kg/10.43lb

Adopted in 1888, the Lee-Metford first fired .303 British cartridges loaded with compressed charges of black powder. The extreme length of the Lee-Metford reflects 19th century tactical use. The lack of a clip-charging guide until later would prove a problem when facing Boers in South Africa. While the Lee-Metford was only in service a short time in the late 1880s and early 1890s, long rifles, and the bayonets mounted on them, would later be found wanting in the trenches of World War I.

Lee-Speed carbine

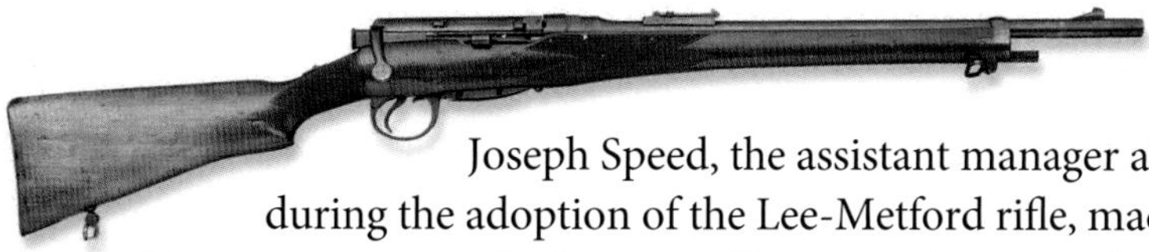

Joseph Speed, the assistant manager at Enfield during the adoption of the Lee-Metford rifle, made a number of improvements to the Lee, as well as patenting some features. These improvements included the wooden handguard above the barrel, the magazine cut-off and the patented magazine attachment to the receiver. Previously, barrels had often been left bare, and could burn the user after rapid firing. The radical magazine cut-off kept ammunition in reserve, a key concern for almost every military establishment in the world in the late 19th century. Continued updating of the Lee-Enfield makes this 1890 Speed carbine quite rare.

SPECIFICATION	
MANUFACTURER	Enfield
CALIBRE	.303 British
MAGAZINE CAPACITY	10
ACTION	Bolt action
TOTAL LENGTH	1,013mm/39.9in
BARREL LENGTH	527mm/20.75in
WEIGHT UNLOADED	3.47kg/7.65lb

Lee-Enfield Mark 1*

The Lee action was certainly fast and accurate enough for the British Army at the beginning of the 20th century. It had been proved that the rifling eroded in the earlier Lee-Metfords, so the Enfield-pattern rifling was immediately adopted. The Lee-Enfield Mark 1* had a long way to go before it became the standard pattern – for example, it needed a charging guide, so the magazine could be quickly reloaded with clips of ammunition. The Mark 1* was only current for a few years in the 1890s, being replaced by newer marks.

SPECIFICATION	
MANUFACTURER	Enfield
CALIBRE	.303 British
MAGAZINE CAPACITY	10
ACTION	Bolt action
TOTAL LENGTH	1,257mm/49.5in
BARREL LENGTH	767mm/30.19in
WEIGHT UNLOADED	4.19kg/9.25lb

Lee-Enfield Cavalry Mark 1

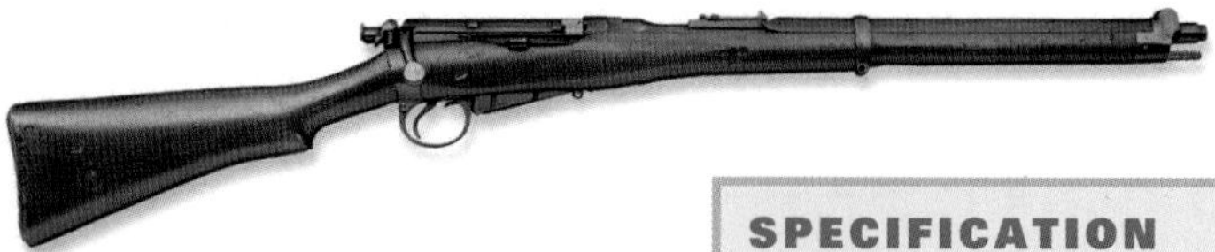

The Lee-Metford carbine lasted two years, and was replaced by the Lee-Enfield Cavalry Mark 1 carbine in 1896. The only changes from Metford to Enfield were the rifling pattern and the elimination of the sling bar on the right side of the buttstock. The sling bar was an attachment point for a hook so the cavalry rider stayed attached to the carbine even if he let go to handle the reins. It was replaced by a scabbard which moved the weight of the rifle from the trooper to the mount and also protected the rifle from the elements. In a little less than twenty years the cavalry unit to which this rifle was issued would become obsolete.

SPECIFICATION	
MANUFACTURER	Enfield
CALIBRE	.303 British
MAGAZINE CAPACITY	6
ACTION	Bolt action
TOTAL LENGTH	988mm/39.3in
BARREL LENGTH	527mm/20.75in
WEIGHT UNLOADED	3.37kg/7.44lb

Lee-Enfield RIC

This rifle was made from the Lee-Enfield carbine specifically for the Royal Irish Constabulary (RIC) from the 1890s to the 1920s. The nosecap was modified to take the pattern 88 bayonet. At this time handguns were the weapons of military officers, and police constables, if they needed arms, used rifles or carbines. As the police rarely needed weapons, they spent more time in racks at the station than out with the constables. The RIC is as compact as other bolt-action rifles, but by today's standards is it not compact enough to be a carbine. After World War I, standard-issue rifles would be as compact.

SPECIFICATION	
MANUFACTURER	Enfield
CALIBRE	.303 British
MAGAZINE CAPACITY	6
ACTION	Bolt action
TOTAL LENGTH	1,016mm/40in
BARREL LENGTH	527mm/20.75in
WEIGHT UNLOADED	3.37kg/7.43lb

No. 1 SMLE Mark III

SPECIFICATION

MANUFACTURER Enfield
CALIBRE .303 British
MAGAZINE CAPACITY 10
ACTION Bolt action
TOTAL LENGTH 1,130mm/44.5in
BARREL LENGTH 640mm/25.19in
WEIGHT UNLOADED 3.91kg/8.62lb

Adopted in 1907, the Mark III was the issue rifle when Great Britain entered World War I. Beautifully built by the best craftsmen and armourers of the time, it was smooth in function, balanced, accurate and suitable for combat. It was, however, too costly to make in wartime volume, and hand-fitting by trained craftsmen slowed production. The demands of wartime production diminished the rifle's surface appearance but not its performance. It was made from 1907 to 1915, when it was replaced with the Mark III*.

No. 1 SMLE Mark III*

SPECIFICATION

MANUFACTURER Enfield, BSA, Nottingham
CALIBRE .303 British
MAGAZINE CAPACITY 10
ACTION Bolt action
TOTAL LENGTH 1,130mm/44.5in
BARREL LENGTH 640mm/25.19in
WEIGHT UNLOADED 3.91kg/8.62lb

Manufacture of the Mark III* lasted from 1915 to 1918. In gaining its star (*), the Mark III* lost the long-range sight on the side of the rifle, the magazine cut-off, and less attention was given to polishing out tool marks. Despite the changes, the new Mark III* was rugged, durable and accurate enough for trench warfare. It was made in the millions and is still in use around the world. The durability of the design and the quality of manufacture means many are still standing in rifle racks today, as reliable as the day they were made.

No. 4 Mark 1

SPECIFICATION

MANUFACTURER Enfield, Long Branch (Canada), Stevens Arms (USA)
CALIBRE .303 British
MAGAZINE CAPACITY 10
ACTION Bolt action
TOTAL LENGTH 1,130mm/44.5in
BARREL LENGTH 640mm/25.2in
WEIGHT UNLOADED 3.99kg/8.8lb

The No. 1 Mark III* served heroically through World War I, but it had some shortcomings. It was time-consuming to machine the receiver and the sights were only adequate at best. The re-design and testing process continued until adoption of the No. 4 Mark 1 in 1931. The No. 4 was designed with mass-production in mind, and incorporated a better sighting system as well as a heavier barrel. The receiver was altered to allow for manufacturing with fewer machine operations, lowering production costs. When World War II made even greater demands; the design was simplified further for mass production and became the No. 4 Mark 1*, made in Britain, Canada and the United States. The No. 4 action was strong enough to survive the adoption of the 7.62mm NATO cartridge, and has been built by some custom gunsmiths for even larger cartridges. Many No. 4s were still in use in the late 1950s, especially in former countries of the Empire.

Sniper No. 4 Mark 1 (T)

SPECIFICATION

MANUFACTURER Enfield, Holland & Holland, London
CALIBRE .303 British
MAGAZINE CAPACITY 10
ACTION Bolt action
TOTAL LENGTH 1,130mm/44.5in
BARREL LENGTH 640mm/25.2in
WEIGHT UNLOADED 4.62kg/10.2lb

Like many armies between the wars, Britain dropped sniper rifles from inventories and removed sniper training from schedules. The new aircraft and tanks were thought to be the future. The needs of World War II changed that outlook, and the result was the No. 4 Mark 1. Each was a standard rifle with a telescopic sight affixed and a cheekpiece on the stock to make aiming more comfortable. The production and quality of sniper rifles quickly improved. When Britain changed to the 7.62mm NATO, the No. 4 Mark 1 (T) rifles that had served since 1942 were retired, and new 7.62mm versions built.

No. 5 Mark 1

For all of its strengths, the No. 4 Mark 1 was too long and heavy for use in the jungle and by support troops. The No. 5 used a shorter and lighter barrel and had lightening cuts made to the receiver. The foresight assembly incorporated a flash hider. However, it suffered accuracy problems, maybe as a result of the cuts. To dampen the recoil of a lighter rifle using the .303 cartridge, the No. 5 was made with a rubber recoil pad. After a few years, the pads were usually rock-hard and did little to dampen felt recoil. However, the No. 5 was well thought of by those who used it. The No. 5 Mark 1 was a late-war introduction in 1944, kept in service to the end of the 1950s.

SPECIFICATION

MANUFACTURER Enfield
CALIBRE .303 British
MAGAZINE CAPACITY 10
ACTION Bolt action
TOTAL LENGTH 1,003mm/39.5in
BARREL LENGTH 475mm/18.7in
WEIGHT UNLOADED 3.24kg/7.15lb

DeLisle silent carbine

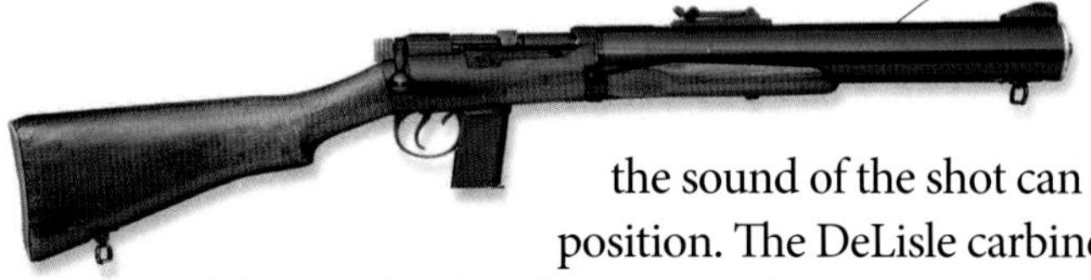

Despite camouflage, the sound of the shot can give away a sniper's position. The DeLisle carbines (designed by William DeLisle) were fitted with an integral suppressor. The suppressor dampens the sound of the shot, even at close range. As a .45 ACP "rifle", however, it was not intended for long-range shooting, being more of a sentry removal or commando weapon. The initial order of 500–600 was reduced to just over 100, making it quite rare. As a close-range quiet weapon, it was state-of-the-art in World War II, and used from 1942 to 1945. By the 1960s it was almost quaint.

SPECIFICATION

MANUFACTURER Enfield
CALIBRE .45 ACP
MAGAZINE CAPACITY 7 (using M-1911 magazines)
ACTION Bolt action
TOTAL LENGTH 895mm/35.25in
BARREL LENGTH 184mm/7.25in
SUPPRESSOR LENGTH 267mm/10.5in
WEIGHT UNLOADED 3.74kg/8.25lb

L1A1

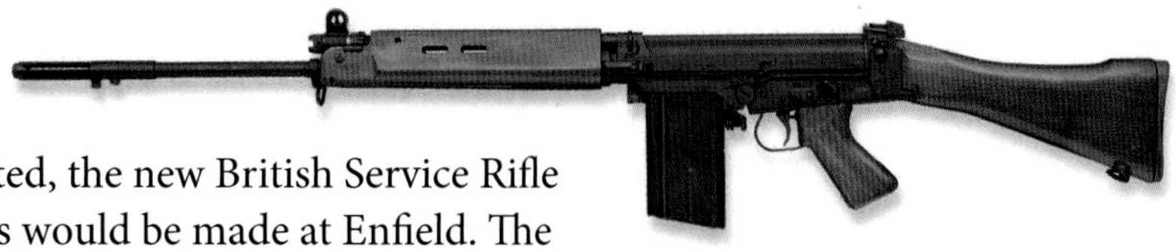

Once adopted, the new British Service Rifle of the 1950s would be made at Enfield. The result was a licensed version of the Belgian FAL rifle, rugged enough to serve around the world for over 30 years. The Commonwealth FALs are known as "inch pattern" rifles, as the dimensions were in imperial rather than metric. British magazines also differed in the attachment blocks on the tube, making them unusable in metric rifles, but metric magazines were usable in British rifles. The L1A1 remained in service from adoption in 1956 until replaced by the dismal SA80 in 1985.

SPECIFICATION

MANUFACTURER Enfield
CALIBRE 7.62mm NATO
MAGAZINE CAPACITY 20
ACTION Gas operated/tilting bolt
TOTAL LENGTH 1,054mm/45in
BARREL LENGTH 533mm/21in
WEIGHT UNLOADED 4.33kg/9.56lb

No. 4 Enfield Target

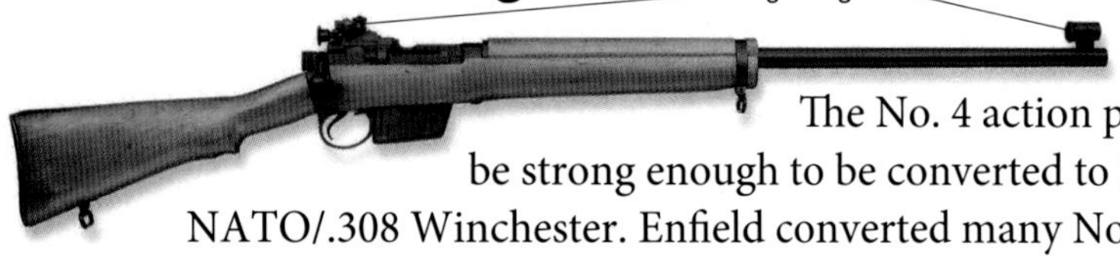

The No. 4 action proved to be strong enough to be converted to 7.62mm NATO/.308 Winchester. Enfield converted many No. 4 rifles by replacing the extractor, barrel and magazine. A few smaller parts needed modification or replacement, and the end result was an accurate rifle for target shooting. With a heavier barrel, the same conversions were used by the British Army as the L42A1 sniper rifle. The No. 4 Enfield was used as a target rifle from the 1950s to the end of firearms ownership in England in the 1990s.

SPECIFICATION

MANUFACTURER Enfield
CALIBRE 7.62mm NATO/.308 Winchester
MAGAZINE CAPACITY 10
ACTION Bolt action
TOTAL LENGTH 1,181mm/46.5in
BARREL LENGTH 698mm/27.5in
WEIGHT UNLOADED 4.42kg/9.75lb

LSW prototype

SPECIFICATION

MANUFACTURER Enfield
CALIBRE 5.56 x 45mm
MAGAZINE CAPACITY 30
ACTION Gas operated/rotating bolt
TOTAL LENGTH 899mm/35.4in
BARREL LENGTH 645mm/25.4in
WEIGHT UNLOADED 5.28kg/11.65lb

The Squad Automatic Weapon (SAW) was tested using the 4.85mm cartridge system, developed by British designers in the mid-1970s searching for ideal small bore ammunition. The Light Support Weapon (LSW) had a long and heavy barrel, a bipod and was issued with a 30-round magazine. It lacked a quick-change barrel, leaving it prone to overheating in extended use. It did, however, evolve into the L85/86 series of SAWs using the American 5.56mm NATO cartridge. The LSW was made in the late 1970s only as a prototype.

EWS Experimental

SPECIFICATION

MANUFACTURER Enfield
CALIBRE 4.85mm
MAGAZINE CAPACITY 20 or 30
ACTION Gas operated/rotating bolt
TOTAL LENGTH 769mm/30.3in
BARREL LENGTH 518mm/20.4in
WEIGHT UNLOADED 4.13kg/9.1lb

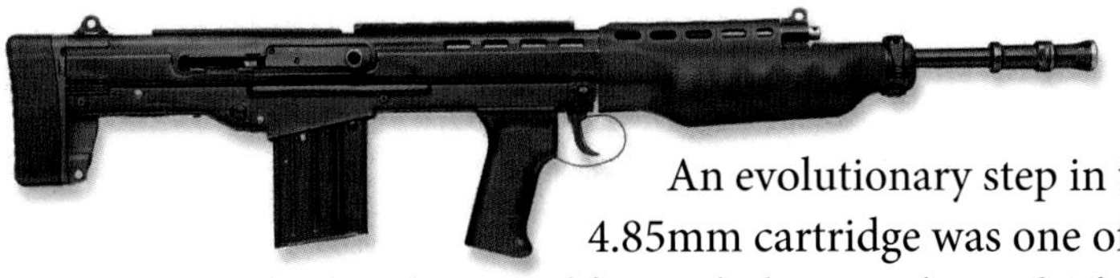

An evolutionary step in the L85, the small 4.85mm cartridge was one of the attempts at producing high volumes of fire with decreased recoil. The idea was that a soldier could fire much faster and with greater accuracy than with larger calibres. This was perhaps correct, but it failed against the 5.56mm NATO cartridge and ended up as the L85A1 in 5.56 x 45mm. Given the half-century of wrangling over the performance of the 5.56mm cartridge, anything smaller in calibre would have caused a storm of controversy. The Enfield Weapon System (EWS) was made as a prototype in the late 1970s.

L85A1

In 1967, the British Army began a programme to find a new rifle to replace the L1A1. Initially tested with a new compromise cartridge, the 6.25 x 43mm, the rifle evolved from that through the 4.85mm cartridge and finally, in 1976, was adopted in the near-ubiquitous 5.56mm chambering. Initially known as the SA80, unlike the earlier EN 2, the L85 used the Stoner rotating bolt. It had, however, several major design flaws, and suffered from manufacturing problems. Apparently, bits and pieces fell off the rifle in hard use. It has since been overhauled by Heckler & Koch, to no avail. While some insist it is good enough, many users want a different weapon. The L85A1 was fielded in 1980 and is still in use.

SPECIFICATION

MANUFACTURER Enfield, Nottingham
CALIBRE 5.56 x 45mm
MAGAZINE CAPACITY 30
ACTION Gas operated/rotating bolt
TOTAL LENGTH 785mm/30.9in
BARREL LENGTH 518mm/20.4in
WEIGHT UNLOADED 4.13kg/9.1lb

L85A2, Heckler & Koch Models

SPECIFICATION

MANUFACTURER Enfield
CALIBRE 5.56 x 45mm
MAGAZINE CAPACITY 30
ACTION Gas operated/rotating bolt
TOTAL LENGTH 780mm/30.7in
BARREL LENGTH 518mm/20.4in
WEIGHT UNLOADED 4.13kg/9.1lb

After years of improvement, modifications, adjustments and upgrades, the SA80 was still not reliable. Heckler & Koch was given the contract to rebuild all SA80 rifles and improve their reliability. Some 200,000 of the 320,000 in inventory were serviced. The serviced weapons were tested, and approved. The Afghanistan campaign of 2002 proved that the efforts had not been successful. Some units were insisting on being issued other weapons instead of the L85. The rifles suffered from numerous malfunctions, and accuracy was often poor. They were issued first in 1985 and are still used today.

FN FAL Prototype

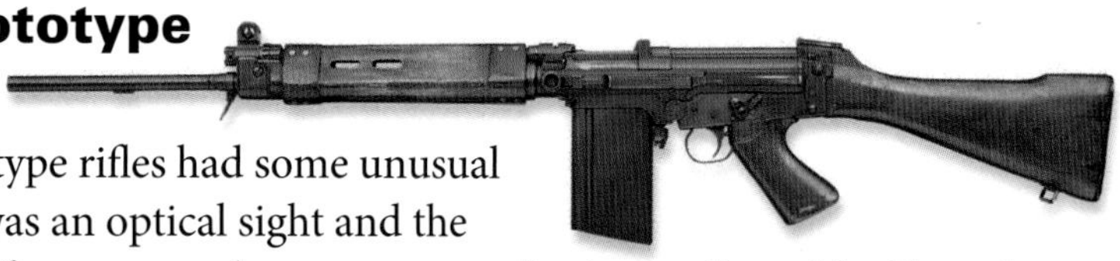

The initial prototype rifles had some unusual features. There was an optical sight and the top cover in one form or another was a type of stripper clip guide. They also had grenade launchers fitted during the consideration phase. The idea of an optical sight was radical in the early 1950s, as optics were rightly deemed as being too fragile for general issue. It was some time, however, before designers gave up on rifle-launched grenades as more than an emergency tool. The prototypes were made in the very early 1950s, and tested by the British Army.

SPECIFICATION

MANUFACTURER FN, Liège
CALIBRE 7.62 x 51mm T65
MAGAZINE CAPACITY 20
ACTION Gas operated/tilting bolt
TOTAL LENGTH 1,054mm/41.5in
BARREL LENGTH 533mm/21in
WEIGHT UNLOADED 4.13kg/9.12lb

FN FAL Trials Model

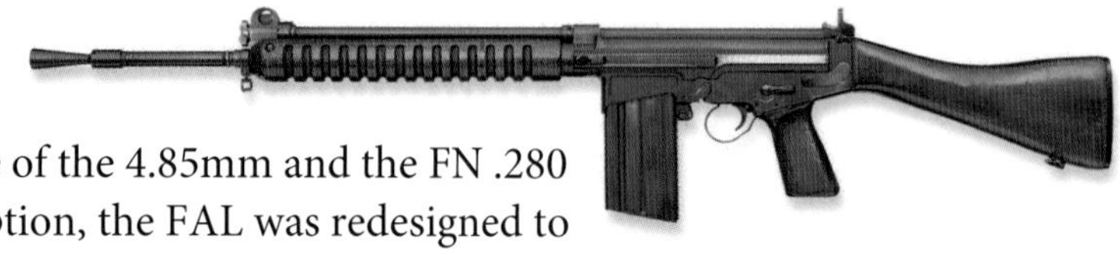

After the failure of the 4.85mm and the FN .280 for NATO adoption, the FAL was redesigned to use the US 7.62 x 5mm cartridge, as the T65. The trials model eliminated the grenade launcher and optical sight of the prototypes and incorporated sand cuts to increase reliability in desert conditions. The sand cuts were locations in the action rails where sand, mud or dirt could collect and not interfere with the rifle's operation. While the US Army rejected the FAL, it went on to be widely used. Curiously, the shortcomings the US Army found were not noted by other testers. The Trials models were made in 1954.

SPECIFICATION

MANUFACTURER FN, Liège
CALIBRE 7.62 x 51mm T65
MAGAZINE CAPACITY 20
ACTION Gas operated/tilting bolt
TOTAL LENGTH 1,054mm/41.5in
BARREL LENGTH 533mm/21in
WEIGHT UNLOADED 4.03kg/8.9lb

P-14 Mark 1*

Before World War I, Britain set out to improve or replace the Lee Enfield with an accurate long-range rifle. The P-13 did away with the two-piece stock of the Lee-Enfield, and featured a greatly improved rear sight. Chambered in a new 7mm cartridge, it was undergoing testing when World War I broke out. Rather than have two calibres in the supply system, Britain contracted with American firms to make the P-13 in .303 British. Called the P-14, or Enfield, it proved robust, accurate and reliable. When the United States entered World War I, they simply ordered it re-chambered in .30-06 and had millions more made. Used from 1914 through 1918, they went into storage after the war.

SPECIFICATION

MANUFACTURER Remington, Winchester, Eddystone
CALIBRE .303 British
MAGAZINE CAPACITY 5
ACTION Bolt action
TOTAL LENGTH 1,174mm/46.25in
BARREL LENGTH 660mm/26in
WEIGHT UNLOADED 4.35kg/9.6lb

M-1903 Springfield conversion prototype

Faced again with a critical shortage of small arms at the outset of World War II, Britain sought to have the American company of Remington Arms re-tool the US M-1903 Springfield rifle for the .303 cartridge (which were much larger than those of the .30-06 and unlikely even to accommodate five rounds.) For the amount of work the task would have involved, the fact that more than one prototype was made is amazing. With existing designs better suited to the .303 cartridge already in production, the idea was abandoned. The .303 Springfield was manufactured in 1940, only as a prototype.

SPECIFICATION

MANUFACTURER Remington
CALIBRE .303 British
MAGAZINE CAPACITY 5
ACTION Bolt action
TOTAL LENGTH 1,097mm/43.2in
BARREL LENGTH 609mm/24in
WEIGHT UNLOADED 3.94kg/8.69lb

Armalite AR-18

After Armalite sold the rights to the AR-15 to Colt, Eugene Stoner designed several new rifles. The AR-18 differed from his earlier AR-15 in several respects. Instead of aluminium forgings the AR-18 used steel pressings. The gas system of the AR-18 was basically that of the AK-47 and the stock could be designed and made as a folding unit as the recoil springs were not in the buttstock. The AR-18 did not achieve military acceptance (due partly to the United States giving free M16s to any country that asked and partly to the AR-18 not passing any military tests) and had a limited commercial production. It was made in three countries: United Kingdom, United States and Japan. Shooters and collectors still argue over which was the better made of the three, but all are extremely reliable and sought after by collectors. Production lasted from 1967 to 1979, occasionally in two of the three locations at the same time. The shorter barrel seen here is a non-factory modification to make the AR-18 more compact when the stock is folded.

SPECIFICATION

MANUFACTURER Sterling, Costa Mesa, Howa
CALIBRE 5.56 x 45mm
MAGAZINE CAPACITY 20 or 30
ACTION Gas operated/rotating bolt
TOTAL LENGTH 965mm/38in
BARREL LENGTH 470mm/18.25in
WEIGHT UNLOADED 3.26kg/7.18lb

Sterling Mark 6 Semi-automatic

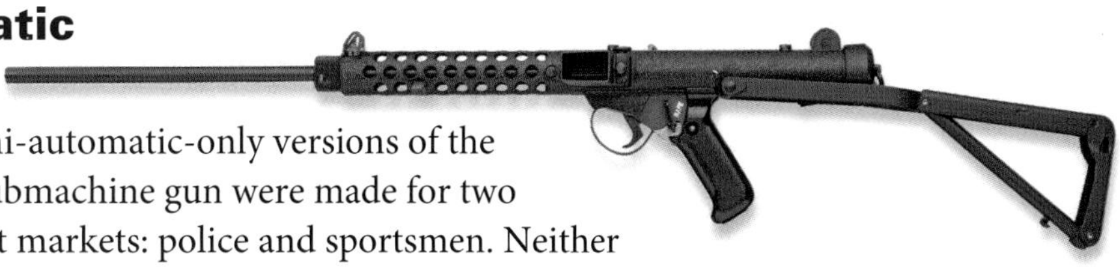

The semi-automatic-only versions of the L2A1 submachine gun were made for two different markets: police and sportsmen. Neither version accepts the internal parts of the submachine gun, while both accept the L2A1 magazines. As heavy as the Sterling carbine is, the recoil of the 9mm Parabellum is almost inconsequential. The submachine gun fires from an open bolt, while the semi-automatic version fires from a closed bolt. As an inexpensive practice rifle, or one for use indoors, the Sterling Mark 6 is fine. As a military or police weapon, the lack of full-automatic fire is something of a hindrance. The Sterling Mark 6 was made for a short time in the 1980s, and has been in service since then.

SPECIFICATION

MANUFACTURER Sterling
CALIBRE 9mm Parabellum
MAGAZINE CAPACITY 34
ACTION Blowback
TOTAL LENGTH 914mm/36in (711mm/28in police version)
BARREL LENGTH 406mm/16in (203mm/8in police version)
WEIGHT UNLOADED 2.95kg/6.5lb

Pedersen Vickers

The search for a viable self-loading rifle was quite vigorous between the World Wars. John Pedersen designed a rifle in his proprietary cartridge, the .276 Pedersen that used 10-shot en bloc clips. The action is basically a gas-operated version of the toggle lock of the German Luger. One concern of testers was that the toggle, breaking open and pivoting up, might strike the hat brim or helmet of a shooter. As good as the design was, it needed waxed cartridges to work. Any rifle or machine gun needing extra lubrication for its cartridges is simply not robust enough for combat. The .276 Pedersen cartridge preceded, by a decade, other attempts at a controllable assault weapon and cartridge, even though the Pedersen was meant as a battle rifle. Prototypes and a few production runs were made between 1930 and 1935, as Vickers vigorously promoted it.

SPECIFICATION

MANUFACTURER Vickers
CALIBRE .276 Pedersen
MAGAZINE CAPACITY 10
ACTION Gas operated/toggle lock
TOTAL LENGTH 1,148mm/45.2in
BARREL LENGTH 520mm/20.5in
WEIGHT UNLOADED 4.13kg/9.1lb

France

With the development of Poudre B in around 1885, the first useful smokeless powder, France made all existing military rifles in their own, and all other armouries, obsolete. Combined with the new repeating rifles the change swept all military organizations. The last two decades of the 19th century saw all existing rifle designs continuously replaced, owing to the French policy of retaining and reworking existing designs rather than adopting new and improved ones.

Lebel Model 1886 M93

The Model 1886 M93, with its tubular magazine, was found to be more durable than the M-1916 when used in the rifle-grenade launching role. As a result, it was retained for that service even after World War I. The combination of pointed bullets and a tubular magazine required an odd rim design on the Lebel cartridge, with a groove machined in it to catch the bullet tip. Otherwise recoil might initiate a chain-fire in the magazine. The M93 was in service with France from 1886 to the 1930s.

SPECIFICATION

MANUFACTURER St Etienne and others
CALIBRE 8mm Lebel
MAGAZINE CAPACITY 10
ACTION Bolt action
TOTAL LENGTH 1,303mm/51.3in
BARREL LENGTH 798mm/31.4in
WEIGHT UNLOADED 4.24kg/9.35lb

Lebel Mannlicher-Berthier Model 1890 Cuirassier

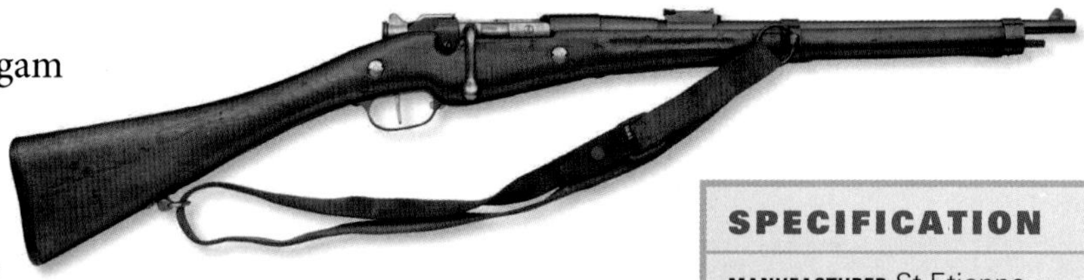

The Mannlicher-Berthier is the amalgam of the Berthier bolt action and the Mannlicher magazine feed. The Mannlicher clip drops free when empty, and thus requires an opening in the magazine bottom plate. Most other Mannlicher-magazine rifles had a five-shot capacity, but the large rim of the Lebel cartridge made more than three difficult. The 1890 Cuirassier model has a buttstock shaped for use by heavy cavalry when wearing their steel back and breastplate. The incongruity of cavalry and repeating rifles had not yet become apparent in 1890. The rifle was in service from 1890 to 1914, when cavalry (and breastplates) became obsolete.

SPECIFICATION

MANUFACTURER St Etienne
CALIBRE 8mm Lebel
MAGAZINE CAPACITY 3
ACTION Bolt action
TOTAL LENGTH 945mm/37.2in
BARREL LENGTH 454mm/17.85in
WEIGHT UNLOADED 3.02kg/6.66lb

Mannlicher-Berthier Model 1916

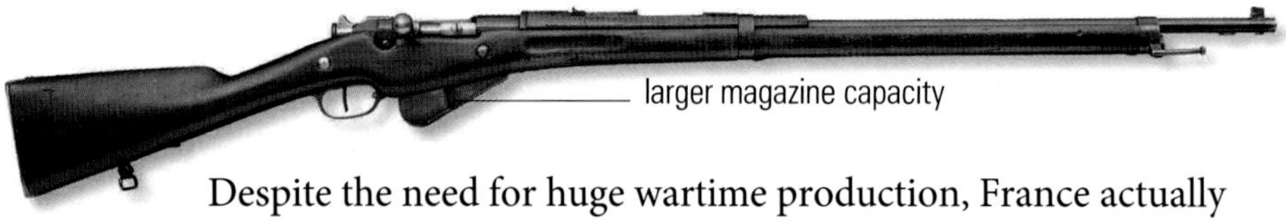

Despite the need for huge wartime production, France actually improved the basic Model 1907/15 design in 1916, based on operational experience. The magazine capacity of the Mannlicher clips was raised to five (although what having two different Mannlicher clips in the supply system did can only be imagined) and the ejection port for the expended clips was given a hinged cover. The Model 1916 was still in service in 1939, even though the planned upgrades (sights and handguards) in the 1920s and early 1930s had not all been done.

SPECIFICATION

MANUFACTURER St Etienne
CALIBRE 8mm Lebel
MAGAZINE CAPACITY 5
ACTION Bolt action
TOTAL LENGTH 1,305mm/51.4in
BARREL LENGTH 802mm/31.6in
WEIGHT UNLOADED 4.27kg/9.24lb

Mannlicher-Berthier M16 Artillery

SPECIFICATION

MANUFACTURER St Etienne and others
CALIBRE 8mm Lebel
MAGAZINE CAPACITY 5
ACTION Bolt action
TOTAL LENGTH 945mm/37.2in
BARREL LENGTH 453mm/17.85in
WEIGHT UNLOADED 3.24kg/7.16lb

A modified M92, using the M1916 Mannlicher clip for greater capacity, this was issued to artillery, as well as mounted and motorized infantry machine gun crews and bicycle troops. The sling hardware was moved to the side of the rifle for greater ease of carry. It was used in military service until 1939 and used by gendarmerie, customs and prison guards into the 1960s.

MAS Model 1936

SPECIFICATION

MANUFACTURER St Etienne
CALIBRE 7.5 x 54mm
MAGAZINE CAPACITY 5
ACTION Bolt action
TOTAL LENGTH 1,022mm/40.25in
BARREL LENGTH 575mm/22.65in
WEIGHT UNLOADED 3.75kg/8.27lb

Decades after the Mauser design had proven superior, France designed a new bolt-action rifle. The action was compact, with the locking lugs at the rear of the bolt. That necessitated angling the bolt handle forward to avoid striking the firer's hand during recoil. At least it was chambered for the M1929 short cartridge, and not the 8mm Lebel of earlier French bolt-action rifles. The rifle was obsolete the moment it was unveiled. It was manufactured from 1937 to 1940, and again from 1945 to 1953.

MAS Model 49

SPECIFICATION

MANUFACTURER St Etienne
CALIBRE 7.5 x 54mm
MAGAZINE CAPACITY 10
ACTION Gas operated/direct impingement
TOTAL LENGTH 1,075mm/42.35in
BARREL LENGTH 580mm/22.85in
WEIGHT UNLOADED 4.06kg/8.97lb

When the St Etienne region of France was liberated after World War II, the French introduced the MAS Model 44. The MAS Model 49 was an improved auto-loading rifle. While experimental models were made in .30-06, the Model 49 was designed in the standard French calibre, with improved gas system, and it dispensed with the Model 36 bayonet. It was rather awkward in handling, but reasonably reliable in function. The magazine catch, unique to the French, is on the side of the magazine, not the front and rear as other designs use. The MAS Model 49 was in service from 1949 to the early 1970s.

FR-F2

SPECIFICATION

MANUFACTURER GIAT Industries
CALIBRE 7.62mm NATO
MAGAZINE CAPACITY 10
ACTION Bolt action
TOTAL LENGTH 1,138mm/44.8in
BARREL LENGTH 600mm/24in
WEIGHT UNLOADED 5kg/11lb

Used by French military and police, the FR-F2 was a redesigned, upgraded version of the French MAS 36 rifle, chambered in 7.62mm NATO. The free-floating, tapered, three-groove barrel is guarded by a polymer heat shield along most of its length, and is designed to engage targets up to 800 metres. Unlike most rifles where the bipod is mounted near the muzzle, the FR-F2's is located at the front of the receiver. In 2018, the French announced plans to replace the FR-F2, which has been in service as their standard sniper rifle since 1986. At the time of writing, the rifle is still being used and a complete replacement of the FR-F2 has not yet occurred.

Famas F1

Known as *le clarion*, or the bugle, by the troops, this bullpup design is unmistakable owing to the extended carry handle. The Fusil Assault MAS (FAMAS) distinctive handle is on top, inside the carry handle, as in the earliest Armalite designs. The top-mount charging handle therefore avoids the biggest problem left-handed shooters have with bullpups. The carry handle is also the mounting point for the integral bipod. By reversing the bolt head and ejection port cover/ cheekpiece, the rifle can be converted from right- to left-hand use. While the delayed blowback system is barely strong enough for the brisk 5.56 x 45mm cartridge, and extraction and ejection problems are not rare, the Famas F1 remains in service, although only with the French forces; it has not been adopted outside of the French Army or French Foreign Legion. The FAMAS F1 was introduced in 1976 to replace the Model 49, and is in service to the present.

SPECIFICATION

MANUFACTURER MAS
CALIBRE 5.56 x 45mm
MAGAZINE CAPACITY 20 or 30
ACTION Delayed blowback
TOTAL LENGTH 757mm/29.8in
BARREL LENGTH 487mm/19.2in
WEIGHT UNLOADED 3.93kg/8.66lb

Hecate II

When snipers require a long range, and precision rifle fire is used to deal with dangerous situations, the .50 BMG cartridge is finding more and more favour. PGM Precision makes their Ultima Ratio bolt action in .50 BMG for long-range precision shooting, and for engaging harder targets. The muzzle brake is essential in order to enable snipers to shoot it more than once or twice. The blast is quite impressive, and it has served France well (quite often in formations of the Foreign Legion) from 1989 to the present.

SPECIFICATION

MANUFACTURER PGM Precision
CALIBRE 12.7 x 99, .50 BMG
MAGAZINE CAPACITY 7
ACTION Bolt action
TOTAL LENGTH 1,380mm/54.3in
BARREL LENGTH 700mm/27.55in
WEIGHT UNLOADED 13.8kg/30.42lb

Belgium

Belgium had no national arms source until the formation of FN (Fabrique Nationale) in 1889. It quickly became a powerhouse in the arms market. When German weapons manufacturer Peter Paul Mauser introduced his improved repeating rifle designs at the end of the 19th century, FN procured licensing to produce this rifle, first for themselves, then for the world market.

M-1889

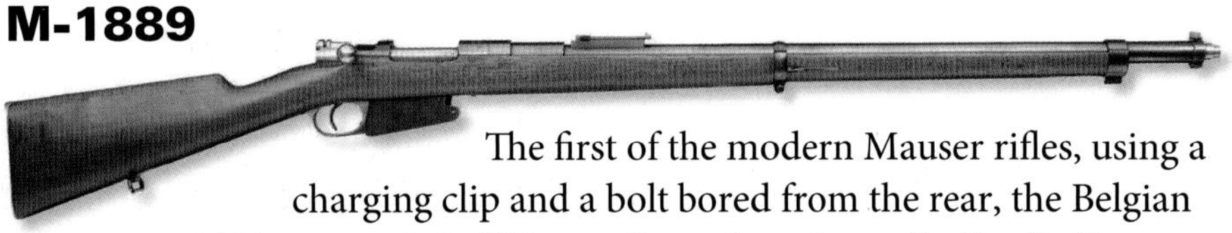

The first of the modern Mauser rifles, using a charging clip and a bolt bored from the rear, the Belgian 1889 was made in FN as well as other plants. Earlier (before Mauser) bolt-action rifle designs lacked clip-charging, and some were made with detachable bolt heads, like the Lee-Metford. The M-1889 was modern when unveiled, but soon fell behind due to Mauser's own design advances. The sheet metal cover on the barrel, designed for protection, was itself susceptible to denting and quickly allowed moisture to rust the barrel underneath. It also did nothing to protect the firer from the hot barrel. The M-1889 was used from 1889 to 1905, when many were upgraded and rebuilt.

SPECIFICATION

MANUFACTURER FN, Liège
CALIBRE 7.65mm Mauser
MAGAZINE CAPACITY 5
ACTION Bolt action
TOTAL LENGTH 1,273mm/50.13in
BARREL LENGTH 780mm/30.69in
WEIGHT UNLOADED 4.03kg/8.88lb

M-1889 carbine

SPECIFICATION

MANUFACTURER FN, Liège
CALIBRE 7.65mm Mauser
MAGAZINE CAPACITY 5
ACTION Bolt action
TOTAL LENGTH 1,045mm/41.16in
BARREL LENGTH 550mm/21.65in
WEIGHT UNLOADED 3.51kg/7.75lb

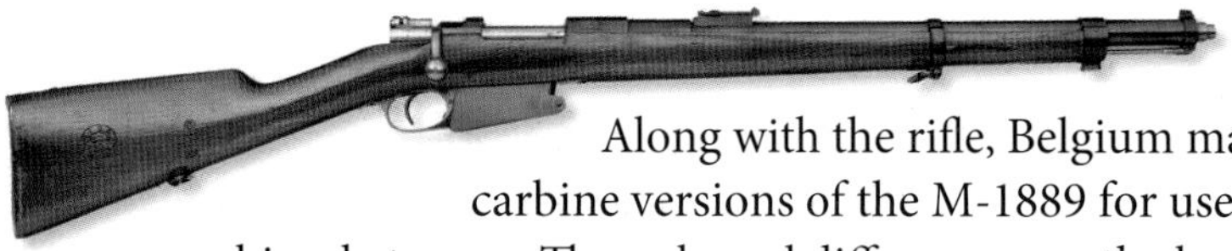

Along with the rifle, Belgium manufactured carbine versions of the M-1889 for use by cavalry and bicycle troops. The only real difference was the barrel and overall length. While the protruding magazine of the 1889 looks very much like that of rifles with a Mannlicher-type magazine, the 1889 did not use enbloc clips. The cartridges were stripped off the charger into the rifle's internal magazine by the user. Thus, unlike the Mannlicher, the bottom of the M-1889 magazine was sealed against the elements. As with the rifles, the M-1889 carbine was used from 1889 until 1905.

Mauser FN M-1924

SPECIFICATION

MANUFACTURER FN, Liège
CALIBRE 7.92mm Mauser
MAGAZINE CAPACITY 5
ACTION Bolt action
TOTAL LENGTH 1,099mm/43.3in
BARREL LENGTH 589mm/23.2in
WEIGHT UNLOADED 3.85kg/8.5lb

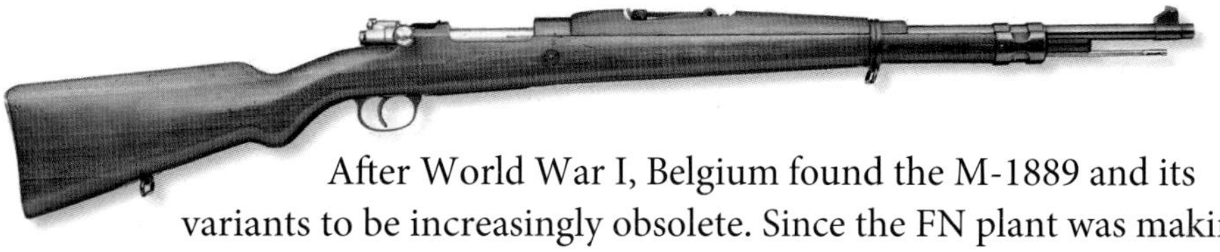

After World War I, Belgium found the M-1889 and its variants to be increasingly obsolete. Since the FN plant was making Mauser 1898-type rifles for over 20 clients, it was easy to make more for the Belgian Army. The refined Mauser M-1924 became the essential military rifle for much of the world between the wars. Compared to previous models, the M-1924 was compact and handy, and still very reliable. FN not only equipped the Belgian Army with it, but sold great numbers around the world in a number of calibres, but mostly in 7.92mm. The M-1924 was made for Belgian and export use until 1940 and used by the German Army until the end of 1944.

Mauser FN M-1935

SPECIFICATION

MANUFACTURER FN, Liège
CALIBRE 7.65mm Mauser
MAGAZINE CAPACITY 5
ACTION Bolt action
TOTAL LENGTH 1,099mm/43.3in
BARREL LENGTH 589mm/23.2in
WEIGHT UNLOADED 3.85kg/8.5lb

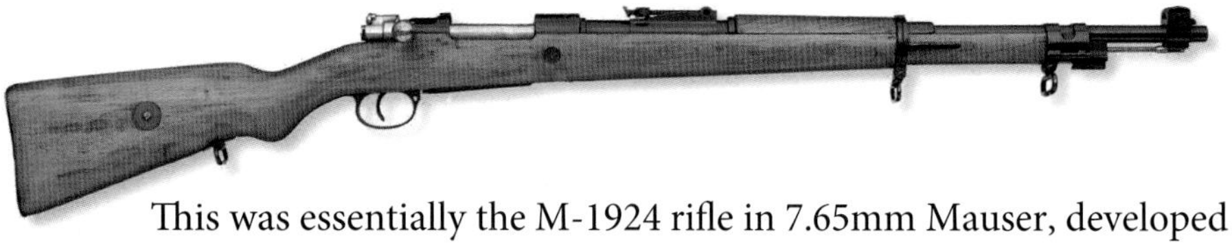

This was essentially the M-1924 rifle in 7.65mm Mauser, developed in the 1930s in order to use up existing stocks of 7.65mm ammunition, which could not simply be discarded. After the 7.65mm ammunition supply was exhausted, the plan was to re-barrel rifles to the new standard 7.92 x 57mm calibre. The programme began in 1935 and was still going along slowly in 1940 when work stopped due to the invasion by Germany in World War II.

M-1936

SPECIFICATION

MANUFACTURER FN, Liège
CALIBRE 7.65mm Mauser
MAGAZINE CAPACITY 5
ACTION Bolt action
TOTAL LENGTH 1,099mm/43.3in
BARREL LENGTH 601mm/23.7in
WEIGHT UNLOADED 3.94kg/8.7lb

In the middle of the worldwide depression of the 1930s, Belgium sought to upgrade its arms, but not go to the full cost of new rifles. The M-1936 rifles were simply M-1889 rifles with the steel tube removed, re-stocked and with cocking pieces similar to the Mauser 1898 installed. The result was a rifle that looked and worked much like the M-1935 but which still used the ample supplies of 7.65mm ammunition stacked in warehouses. As with the M-1935, work began in 1936 and proceeded slowly until 1940.

FN SAFN M-1949

The experience of World War II made it clear that the days of the bolt-action rifle as a combat arm were over. As the first European-made self-loading rifle after the war, the M-1949 reflected designs from before the war. For a brief time after World War II, FN and Belgium sought to arm the world with M-1949 rifles. The basic design of the 1949 tilt-bolt action can be found in the FAL, the rifle FN developed and sold world-wide. The FAL replaced the M-1949, so sales were limited in volume and production of the M-1949 ceased in the late 1950s.

SPECIFICATION	
MANUFACTURER	FN, Liège
CALIBRE	.30-06
MAGAZINE CAPACITY	10
ACTION	Gas operated/tilting bolt
TOTAL LENGTH	1,109mm/43.7in
BARREL LENGTH	589mm/23.2in
WEIGHT UNLOADED	4.30kg/9.48lb

FN .280 prototype

Between 1949–53 FN addressed the wider need for short- to medium-range firepower for the infantry with the .280 prototypes. They did not have the full power of the .30-06, 7.92mm Mauser or .303 British, but no one except the US Army felt the need for a rifle that could kill at 914m/1,000yd. In the end the US Army won, and the .280 was relegated to museums. In less than 20 years, the US army would switch to the 5.56mm, and thus prove the wisdom of the FN approach. Had the US Army Ordnance experts not had their way, one of the FN .280 prototypes would probably be in service today.

SPECIFICATION	
MANUFACTURER	FN, Liège
CALIBRE	7 x 43mm
MAGAZINE CAPACITY	20
ACTION	Gas operated/tilting bolt
TOTAL LENGTH	1,000mm/39.3in
BARREL LENGTH	500mm/19.68in
WEIGHT UNLOADED	4.3kg/9.47lb

FAL

During World War II many observers noted that the long range of a conventional rifle cartridge was not needed. More often, a high volume of fire at close to medium distances, large capacity and mild recoil were more useful. The FAL was originally conceived to fill that need. American insistence on the 7.62mm x 51 cartridge compelled other NATO countries to follow, and the FAL was scaled up to accept the 7.62mm. By modern standards the FAL fulfilled requirements for quite a long time. Starting with the required adoption of the T65 cartridge in 1953, the FAL was made as late as the 1980s.

SPECIFICATION	
MANUFACTURER	FN, Liège
CALIBRE	7.62mm NATO
MAGAZINE CAPACITY	20
ACTION	Gas operated/tilting block
TOTAL LENGTH	1,090mm/42.9in
BARREL LENGTH	533mm/21in
WEIGHT UNLOADED	4.11kg/9.06lb

FAL-Para

By the middle of the 20th century airborne troops were the new elite. They required rifles that were both shorter and lighter. The FAL-Para features a folding stock, making it 245mm shorter than the standard weapon. It is not, however, much lighter unless the lower receiver is made of aluminium alloys. The FAL cannot be made much lighter as machined forgings are used in its upper receiver, the load-bearing part of the rifle. The Para version had a parallel service life to that of the standard FAL: 1958 to late 1980s. The aluminium-alloy version was half a kilo (one pound) lighter.

SPECIFICATION	
MANUFACTURER	FN, Liège
CALIBRE	7.62mm NATO
MAGAZINE CAPACITY	20
ACTION	Gas operated/tilting block
TOTAL LENGTH	845mm/42.9in
BARREL LENGTH	533mm/21in
WEIGHT UNLOADED	4.11kg/9.06lb

FN CAL

SPECIFICATION
MANUFACTURER FN, Liège
CALIBRE 5.56 x 45mm
MAGAZINE CAPACITY 20 or 30
ACTION Gas operated/rotating bolt
TOTAL LENGTH 980mm/38.6in
BARREL LENGTH 467mm/18.4in
WEIGHT UNLOADED 3.31kg/7.3lb

The decision by the US army to adopt the 5.56mm cartridge prompted FN to develop and build the Carabine Automatique Légère (CAL) in the 1960s to replace the FAL. The CAL started as a tilting-bolt rifle, but extraction problems forced the designers to change to a rotating-bolt design. It was produced from 1966 to the early 1970s, and never adopted. Belgium found it too expensive to justify manufacture, and too unreliable to trust in combat. Plagued with problems, and with no apparent customers, FN eventually dropped the CAL. It was resurrected to some extent in the FNC, rushed to the market to compete in American rifle trials, but it differs markedly from the CAL.

FN P-90

SPECIFICATION
MANUFACTURER FN, Liège
CALIBRE 5.7 x 28mm
MAGAZINE CAPACITY 50
ACTION Blowback
TOTAL LENGTH 500mm/19.64in
BARREL LENGTH 263mm/10.35in
WEIGHT UNLOADED 2.54kg/5.6lb

In the late 1980s NATO expressed a need for a Personal Defence Weapon (PDW). The PDW was to be more than a handgun, but much handier than a rifle or carbine. Intended for use by support troops, the PDW is a new name for an old idea. The FN P-90 also introduced a new cartridge, the 5.7 x 28mm, which is vigorous enough to penetrate body armour. The P-90 comes with an optical sighting system as standard equipment. The P-90 was slowly adopted after 1990 and is presently in use, mostly in the law enforcement area.

FN SPR

SPECIFICATION
MANUFACTURER FN, Liège
CALIBRE 7.62mm NATO, .30 WSM
MAGAZINE CAPACITY 5 (7.62mm) 3 (WSM)
ACTION Bolt action
TOTAL LENGTH 1,118mm/44in
BARREL LENGTH 609mm/24in
WEIGHT UNLOADED 5.62kg/12.4lb w/o scope

The FN SPR (Special Purpose/Police rifle) is a long-range precision rifle (or sniper) built on a "blueprinted" (machined to the exact dimensions of the drawings) Winchester M-70 action. The result is a rifle of great accuracy and durability. While the standard is 7.62mm NATO, those needing longer range (but losing two rounds in the magazine) can opt for the .300 Winchester Short Magnum, a cartridge no longer than the 7.62mm NATO which delivers performance of the much longer .300 Winchester Magnum. The FN SPR is a dual project by Winchester and FN, manufactured from 1998 to the present.

F2000

SPECIFICATION
MANUFACTURER FN, Liège
CALIBRE 5.56 x 45mm
MAGAZINE CAPACITY 20 or 30
ACTION Gas operated/rotating bolt
TOTAL LENGTH 694mm/27.32in
BARREL LENGTH 400mm/15.74in
WEIGHT UNLOADED 3.6kg/7.9lb

The FN bullpup solves the one glaring problem that all other bullpup rifles have – ejection of empty brass. Most are one-side-only rifles, as few can be reassembled to offer left-side ejection. The F2000 (introduced in the year 2000) ejects the empty brass forward through a tube. The shooter thus need not worry about empty brass being ejected into the face, nor an operating handle cycling on one side or the other. The mechanism of the F2000 is enclosed in a polymer shell, and can have optical sights mounted on the top rail. The forearm can be removed and replaced with a grenade launcher. A new design and product, it has already been purchased by Slovenia for military/police use.

Netherlands

The early Dutch rifles were entirely serviceable until the advent of self-loading rifles after World War II. By then, there were good ones to choose from, and more on the way. Except for the brief run of AR-10 rifles, the Netherlands has always purchased small arms as needed.

Armalite AR-10

Once the US company Armalite had perfected the AR-10 in the 1950s, they sought manufacturers. (Armalite was only a design, research and development company, not a manufacturing one.) Armalite granted manufacturing rights to Artillerie-Inrichtigen in the Netherlands in the hope that once there was a Dutch contract, other orders would follow, but this never came about. There was a brief interest around the world and Sudan and Portugal bought some rifles for their military, but then the US Army turned down the AR-10. The brief production period of 1959 to 1962 was enough to create a legend that weapons cognoscenti would not let go of for decades afterwards. Indeed, to this day the 7.62mm Armalite is still being offered by one company or another. But the Armalite of that time had a brief moment of interest, but little return for the investment placed in it.

SPECIFICATION

MANUFACTURER Artillerie-Inrichtigen, Zaandam
CALIBRE 7.62 x 51mm
MAGAZINE CAPACITY 20
ACTION Gas operated/rotating bolt
TOTAL LENGTH 1,049mm/41.3in
BARREL LENGTH 508mm/20in
WEIGHT UNLOADED 3.11kg/6.85lb

Mannlicher Model 1895

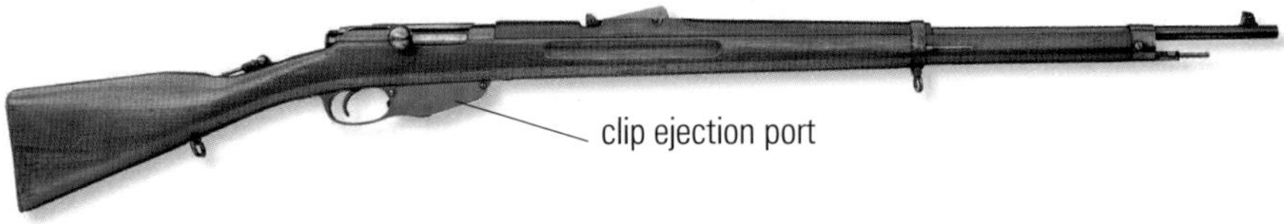

Essentially the same as the Romanian M-1893 Mannlicher, the Dutch used the same style Mannlicher magazine, where the clip fell out when the last round in it was chambered. To reload the rifle, a new clip with cartridges had to be inserted, which was a simple and quick operation. While the 6.5mm Dutch cartridge is no powerhouse, it was good enough to serve as an infantry cartridge. The rifles served from 1895 to 1920.

SPECIFICATION

MANUFACTURER Steyr
CALIBRE 6.5 x 53R
MAGAZINE CAPACITY 5
ACTION Bolt action
TOTAL LENGTH 1,295mm/51in
BARREL LENGTH 790mm/31.1in
WEIGHT UNLOADED 4.30kg/9.48lb

Model 1895 carbine (Old Model)

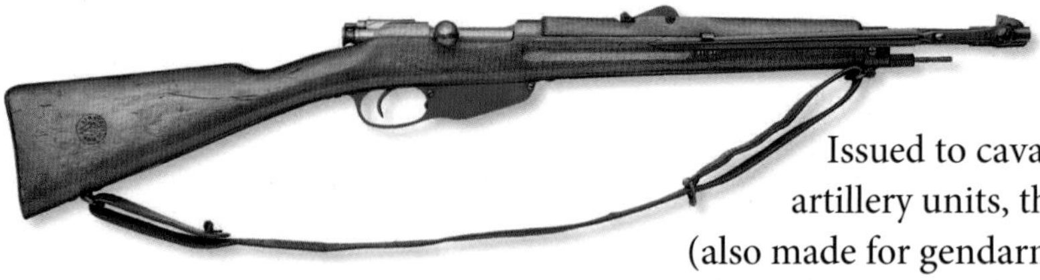

Issued to cavalry and artillery units, the carbine (also made for gendarmerie) came in a host of variants. The Old Model did not have the wooden fairing pinned on to the stock to preclude the magazine abrading uniforms. In a peacetime army, and with gendarmerie, the look of a uniform is very important. Despite the wear to uniforms, the carbine served well, from 1897 to 1920.

SPECIFICATION

MANUFACTURER Steyr, Artillerie-Inrichtigen
CALIBRE 6.5 x 53R
MAGAZINE CAPACITY 5
ACTION Bolt action
TOTAL LENGTH 952mm/37.5in
BARREL LENGTH 450mm/17.7in
WEIGHT UNLOADED 3.11kg/6.85lb

Switzerland

Independent, neutral, and fiercely protective of her borders, Switzerland has a citizen army. All adults go through a period of active service and then remain in the Reserves all their lives. Annual rifle qualification is a requirement. While ready for action, the Swiss have avoided being in a war for centuries.

SPECIFICATION

MANUFACTURER EW, Bern
CALIBRE 7.5 x 53.5mm
MAGAZINE CAPACITY 12
ACTION Straight-pull bolt action
TOTAL LENGTH 1,323mm/52.1in
BARREL LENGTH 780mm/30.7in
WEIGHT UNLOADED 4.5kg/9.94lb

Schmidt-Rubin 1889 Experimental

The original 1889 rifle was good when it was designed, but that period was one of intense rifle and cartridge development. The original 7.5mm cartridge could not be improved unless the 1889 rifle was improved, so Eidenossische Waffenfabrik (EW) in Bern strengthened the 1889 rifle. EW went on to make further improvements to the design, culminating in the M-1931. The experimental models were made only for a short time, between 1888 and 1897.

SPECIFICATION

MANUFACTURER EW, Bern
CALIBRE 7.5 x 55mm
MAGAZINE CAPACITY 6
ACTION Gas operated
TOTAL LENGTH 1,103mm/43.45in
BARREL LENGTH 592mm/23.3in
WEIGHT UNLOADED 3.92kg/8.65lb

Schmidt-Rubin M-1911 carbine

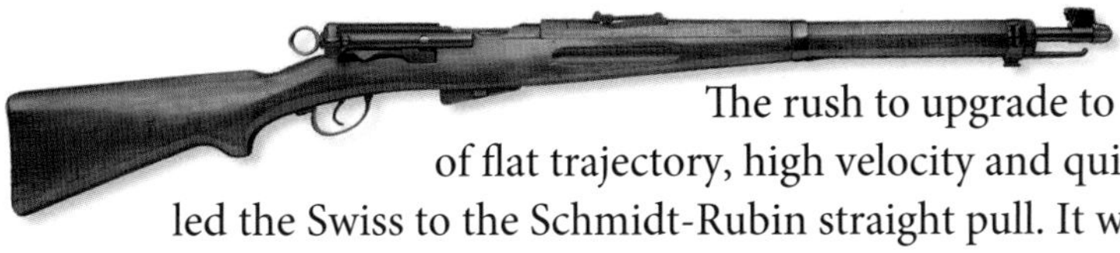

The rush to upgrade to repeating rifles of flat trajectory, high velocity and quick reloading led the Swiss to the Schmidt-Rubin straight pull. It was not quite as robust as a turnbolt in the mud of trench warfare, but this was unlikely to be required. It was also introduced in 1911 and served until the last upgrade of the Schmidt-Rubin, in 1931. Many simply went into the home rifle racks of the reservists to whom they were issued, and could be called on today.

SPECIFICATION

MANUFACTURER EW, Bern
CALIBRE 7.5 x 55mm
MAGAZINE CAPACITY 6
ACTION Straight-pull bolt action
TOTAL LENGTH 1107mm/43.6in
BARREL LENGTH 651mm/25.65in
WEIGHT UNLOADED 4.01kg/8.85lb

Schmidt-Rubin M-1931

This rifle had a stronger lockup, shorter action and thus better accuracy. The improved action was shorter and stronger than the 1911 action. Note that the 1931 rifle was much the same size as the earlier carbine. Switzerland, along with many other countries, went to a shorter rifle as the standard for all units, and the few carbines manufactured were very compact. The M-1931 served until the mid 1950s, when they began to be replaced by the Stgw 57 in 1957.

SPECIFICATION

MANUFACTURER EW, Bern
CALIBRE 6.45 x 48mm
MAGAZINE CAPACITY 20
ACTION Gas operated
TOTAL LENGTH 1,001mm/39.4in
BARREL LENGTH 528mm/20.8in
WEIGHT UNLOADED 4.1kg/9.04lb

BEW+F Mod SG E22

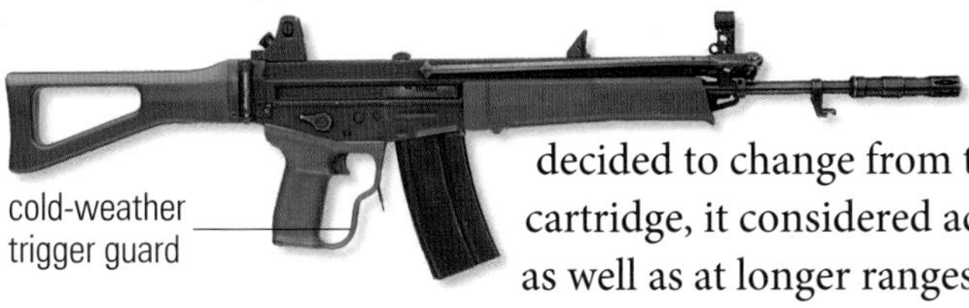

When the Swiss Army decided to change from the 7.5mm to a smaller cartridge, it considered accuracy at 300m/984ft as well as at longer ranges. One cartridge tested used a shortened and necked-down 7.62mm NATO case: the 6.5 x 48mm, but the accuracy of heavier-bullet 5.56mm ammunition made the intermediate cartridge unnecessary. The Mod SG E22 was prototyped in the late 1970s.

Mannlicher Model 1893 carbine

The 1889 Schmidt action was too long to be turned into a carbine, so Switzerland, after trials, adopted the straight-pull design from Mannlicher as their carbine. The main problem with turning the 1889 Schmidt action into a carbine was the length of the bolt and action. In order to make the whole rifle compact enough, the barrel would have to have been shortened below a usable length. The Mannlicher only lasted a short time, and was in regular service from 1898 to 1905. The improved Schmidt-Rubin action could be made in carbine length.

SPECIFICATION	
MANUFACTURER	SIG, Neuhausen
CALIBRE	7.5 x 53.5R
MAGAZINE CAPACITY	6
ACTION	Straight-pull bolt action
TOTAL LENGTH	1,016mm/40in
BARREL LENGTH	550mm/21.65in
WEIGHT UNLOADED	3.08kg/6.8lb

Mondragon Model 1908

The Mondragon 1908 was built for Mexico, with only part of the order (400 rifles) delivered before the Mexican revolution of 1911. However, it was not until the 1930s that self-loading rifle designs became truly reliable enough for combat. Had the Mexican government not lost the war, SIG may well have continued development of the design. Left with the rest of the production run, SIG fitted Model 1908s with drum magazines and sold the rifles to Germany early in World War I. They were manufactured in 1911, and had all been shipped to Germany by 1915.

SPECIFICATION	
MANUFACTURER	SIG, Neuhausen
CALIBRE	7 x 57mm
MAGAZINE CAPACITY	8
ACTION	Gas operated
TOTAL LENGTH	1,239mm/48.8in
BARREL LENGTH	620mm/24.4in
WEIGHT UNLOADED	4.42kg/9.75lb

Mondragon German Air Service

Produced in 1915, the Mondragon was bought by the German Air Service for air-to-air combat before machine guns became common. Using a drum magazine, it was marginally more useful than a bolt-action rifle or a handgun. As soon as it became possible (and common) to mount machine guns on aircraft, the Mondragons went into storage.

SPECIFICATION	
MANUFACTURER	SIG, Neuhausen
CALIBRE	7 x 57mm
MAGAZINE CAPACITY	20
ACTION	Gas operated
TOTAL LENGTH	1,239mm/48.8in
BARREL LENGTH	620mm/24.4in
WEIGHT UNLOADED	4.58kg/10.1lb

SIG SG551-2

Called by some "the best-made AK-47 in existence", the Sig 551 uses an AK gas system, with a 5.56mm cartridge and proprietary magazines. The Special Weapons And Tactics (SWAT) version has a cheekpiece on the buttstock and an optics rail. The magazines are manufactured of polymer and have nubs and sockets on them that allow them to be snapped together side-by-side. They are not compatible with M16 magazines, as the Swiss felt the aluminium M16 magazines were far too flimsy for their use. Manufacturing began in 1986 and the 551 still stands as the issue rifle to Swiss forces.

SPECIFICATION	
MANUFACTURER	SIG, Neuhausen
CALIBRE	5.56 x 45mm
MAGAZINE CAPACITY	30
ACTION	Gas operated
TOTAL LENGTH	843mm/33.2in
BARREL LENGTH	358mm/14.1in
WEIGHT UNLOADED	4.1kg/9.04lb

Germany

Driven by the demands of two World Wars, German small arms inventiveness seems to have had no limits. Very few German designs can be said to be fragile or unreliable. However, the penalty for robust designs quite often seems to be weight. Some designs, although certain of action, are somewhat portly. During World War II, the German small arms procurement system was not very centralized. The Luftwaffe, navy and Waffen-SS all procured their own weapons. Since the parachute units were part of the Luftwaffe, this added more confusion. Today, Germany's Heckler & Koch is one of the most well-known arms companies in the world.

HK-CETME Prototype

curved 7.62 x 39mm magazine

SPECIFICATION

- **MANUFACTURER** CETME
- **CALIBRE** 7.62 x 39mm
- **MAGAZINE CAPACITY** 20
- **ACTION** Roller-delayed blowback
- **TOTAL LENGTH** 939mm/37.4in
- **BARREL LENGTH** 431mm/17in
- **WEIGHT UNLOADED** 4.76kg/10.5lb

Derived from the Stg45(M) using the Vorgrimmler roller-delayed blowback action, the original CETME rifles were not designed for the full-power NATO cartridge. Early prototypes used the 7.92 x 33mm, 7.92 x 40mm and a lightly loaded 7.62 x 51mm cartridge. The lack of initial extraction (that is, no rotating bolt) means the CETME and all derivatives must use a fluted chamber to prevent case adhesion in the chamber and case breakage which leads to malfunctions. The refined design saw limited production in the late 1940s to mid 1950s.

Commission Model 1888

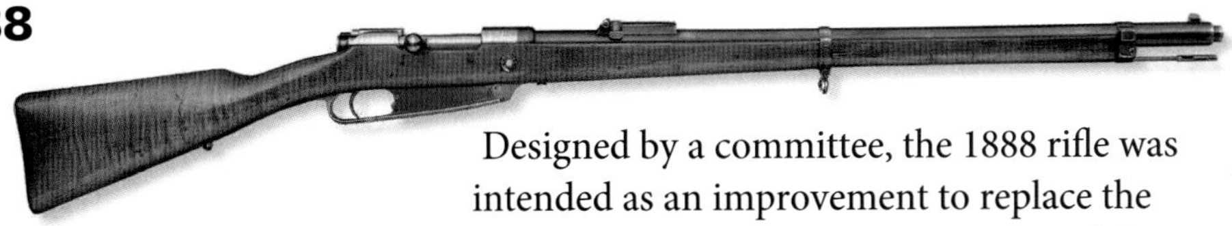

SPECIFICATION

- **MANUFACTURER** Danzig, Erfurt, Spandau
- **CALIBRE** 7.92 x 57mm
- **MAGAZINE CAPACITY** 5
- **ACTION** Bolt action
- **TOTAL LENGTH** 1,244mm/49in
- **BARREL LENGTH** 740mm/29.15in
- **WEIGHT UNLOADED** 3.9kg/8.6lb

Designed by a committee, the 1888 rifle was intended as an improvement to replace the already obsolete Gew 71/84 rifles in service. The committee did not consult Peter Paul Mauser, nor was his firm awarded any contracts to build the new rifles. Some speculate that this oversight or slight drove him to design and refine his own rifle which ended up as the 1898. The 1888 rifle fired a 7.92 x 57mm cartridge using a .318 diameter round-nosed bullet. When the German military cartridge was updated to use a spitzer bullet, the diameter was increased to .323. It is generally unsafe to fire the later ammunition in earlier rifles. Production began in 1888 but by 1898 it was obsolete.

Cavalry Carbine, Commission Model 1888

SPECIFICATION

- **MANUFACTURER** Danzig, Erfurt, Spandau
- **CALIBRE** 7.92 x 57mm
- **MAGAZINE CAPACITY** 5
- **ACTION** Bolt action
- **TOTAL LENGTH** 952mm/37.5in
- **BARREL LENGTH** 435mm/17.15in
- **WEIGHT UNLOADED** 3.08kg/6.8lb

The committee-designed M-1888 rifle was modified for cavalry service by shortening the barrel and bending the bolt handle down. As with the rifle, the carbine used the Mannlicher magazine system. Using the same 7.92 x 57mm cartridge with a .318 diameter round-nosed bullet as the rifle, the felt recoil of the much lighter carbine had to be quite stout. Likewise with the rifle, it is generally unsafe to fire the later ammunition (with its larger-diameter 8mm bullet) in these earlier-model carbines. Production began in 1890 but by 1898 it was obsolete and replaced by cavalry-version Model 1898 Mauser designs.

Kar 98 Cavalry

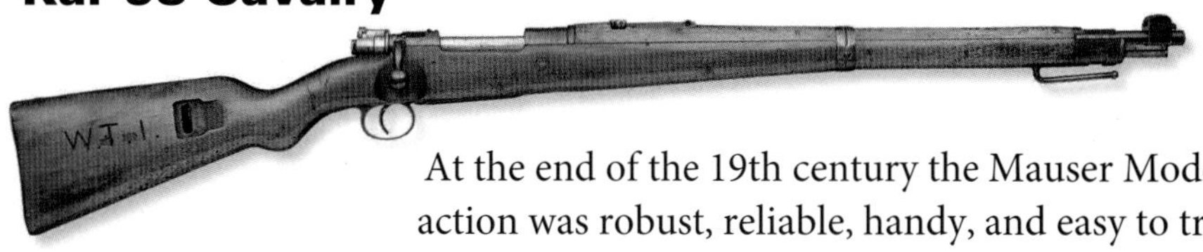

At the end of the 19th century the Mauser Model 98 action was robust, reliable, handy, and easy to train troops in its use. The cavalry, however, had not yet been replaced. Thus a short rifle for mounted use was designed, tested, and began issue in 1909. By the spring of 1915, there was no more need for cavalry, and short rifles went to artillery crews and machine gunners. After the war, rifles got shorter still, to the point of being almost as compact as pre-war carbines had been. The Kar 98 Cavalry was in service from 1909 to 1918.

SPECIFICATION

MANUFACTURER Danzig, Erfurt, Amberg
CALIBRE 7.92 x 57mm
MAGAZINE CAPACITY 5
ACTION Bolt action
TOTAL LENGTH 1,079mm/42.9in
BARREL LENGTH 589mm/23.2in
WEIGHT UNLOADED 3.71kg/8.18lb

Luger Model 1902

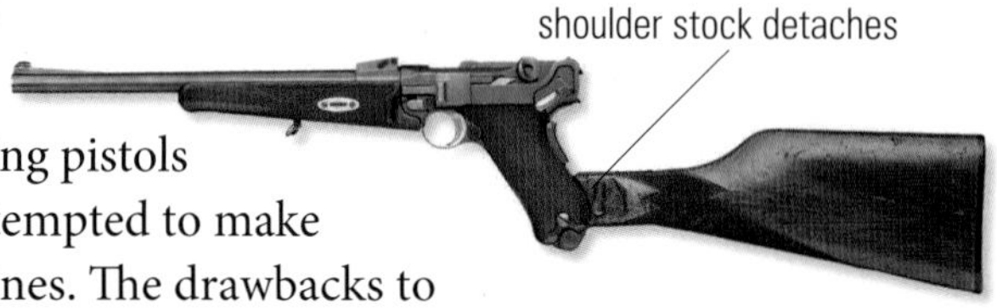

Almost as soon as self-loading pistols were invented, designers attempted to make them into self-loading carbines. The drawbacks to the handy (for a carbine) size were lack of power and range, and decreased durability. For close-in work, especially in the trenches, however, a shoulder-stocked Luger carbine had a number of advantages. During World War I all Lugers were made to accept, and many fitted with stocks, which were issued to machine gun and artillery crews. After the war, with many submachine gun designs being developed, shoulder-stocked pistols fell out of favour. The Luger Model 1902 was popular from 1902 to 1918.

SPECIFICATION

MANUFACTURER DMW
CALIBRE 7.65 x 21mm
MAGAZINE CAPACITY 8, 32 round "snail" drum
ACTION Recoil operated/toggle lock
TOTAL LENGTH 222mm/8.75in (longer with longer barrels)
BARREL LENGTH 101mm/4in (6, 8in also)
WEIGHT UNLOADED 0.875kg/1.93lb (stock adds 0.68kg/1.5lb)

FN FAL G1 sniper

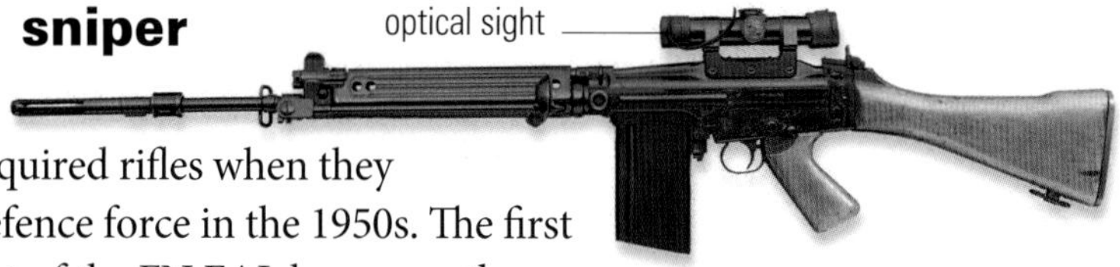

The Germans required rifles when they reorganized a defence force in the 1950s. The first rifle was a variant of the FN FAL known as the G1. The differences from the Belgian version were minor, with the sights on a slightly lower sighting plane, a sheet-metal handguard and integral bipod. The sniper version features optics for precise aim at longer ranges. Their request to build future G1 rifles themselves was brusquely turned down by FN. Their next rifle was the G3. Sniper variants are a standard model, once regular rifles have been provided in volume. It was produced from the late 1950s to early 1960s.

SPECIFICATION

MANUFACTURER FN, Liège
CALIBRE 7.62mm NATO
MAGAZINE CAPACITY 20
ACTION Gas operated
TOTAL LENGTH 1,100mm/43.3in
BARREL LENGTH 533mm/20.98in
WEIGHT UNLOADED 4.45kg/9.81lb

Volksturm VG1-5

At the end of World War II, with central control crumbling, many local designs showed up. The *Volksturm* ("People's Force") needed weapons, and with no central supply, they manufactured what they needed whenever possible. The VG 1-5 uses the Stg44 magazines and ammunition, but the gas ports under the handguards bleed gas to delay the blowback action rather than initiate it. Crude but effective, it was far too little and too late to make any difference. The VG1-5 was made only in the spring of 1945 and could prove hazardous to fire.

SPECIFICATION

MANUFACTURER Gustloffwerke am Suhl
CALIBRE 7.92 x 33mm
MAGAZINE CAPACITY 30
ACTION Gas-retarded blowback
TOTAL LENGTH 889mm/35in
BARREL LENGTH 374mm/14.75in
WEIGHT UNLOADED 4.61kg/10.18lb

Haenel MKb42(H)

SPECIFICATION

- **MANUFACTURER** Haenel
- **CALIBRE** 7.92 x 33mm
- **MAGAZINE CAPACITY** 30
- **ACTION** Gas operated
- **TOTAL LENGTH** 939mm/37in
- **BARREL LENGTH** 365mm/14.37in
- **WEIGHT UNLOADED** 5.0kg/11.06lb

By the mid-1930s the German Army had finally concluded that the standard 7.92mm cartridge was too powerful, and settled on a new cartridge: the 7.92 x 33mm. Both Haenel and Walther were given contracts to develop carbines using this round. The Haenel design proved superior and, after extensive use on the Eastern Front, the design was refined and production increased. The project was kept from Hitler, who thought only full-power rifles were suitable for combat. When he found out about it, only personal intervention by Eastern Front combat veterans convinced him the new carbines were useful for combat. The Haenel MKb42(H) was made in 1942, and, once tested and improved, manufactured as the MP-43.

MP-43/1

SPECIFICATION

- **MANUFACTURER** Haenel, Mauser, Erma
- **CALIBRE** 7.92 x 33mm
- **MAGAZINE CAPACITY** 30
- **ACTION** Gas operated
- **TOTAL LENGTH** 939mm/37in
- **BARREL LENGTH** 419mm/16.5in
- **WEIGHT UNLOADED** 5.21kg/11.5lb

The MP-43 series were the first assault rifles fielded in combat. The stamped-steel construction made manufacture fast and easy and the medium-powered cartridge made volume fire effective. Long-range rifle fire was no longer needed, and it was popular on the Eastern Front. At first, its issue was hidden from Hitler, who felt the only real rifle a soldier needed was a 98k. Only the incessant bombing of production facilities and rail lines prevented Germany from fielding this series in huge numbers. It was used from 1943–5.

HK G3

SPECIFICATION

- **MANUFACTURER** Heckler & Koch
- **CALIBRE** 7.62mm NATO
- **MAGAZINE CAPACITY** 20
- **ACTION** Roller-delayed blowback
- **TOTAL LENGTH** 1,021mm/40.2in
- **BARREL LENGTH** 450mm/17.7in
- **WEIGHT UNLOADED** 4.5kg/9.9lb

Developed from the CETME, the G3 came about from FN's refusal to allow German production of the G1, the FAL in German service. To make the CETME work with the 7.62mm NATO cartridge, and give it the durability required, it ended up being heavy. (The officially-stated weight is less than any example weighed so far.) The roller-delayed blowback action requires a fluted chamber to be sure of certain extraction, and the resultant ejection is quite vigorous. In the past 50 years, more than 50 countries have issued the G3 to their armed forces including Greece, Turkey, Saudi Arabia, Iran, Pakistan and Ethiopia.

HK G36

This was the replacement for the G3. While Heckler & Koch made a variant of the G3 in 5.56mm, it was not particularly popular and it was also quite heavy for a 5.56mm rifle. The G36 is lighter than the G3 and has a folding stock and built-in optical sight. With the collapse of Communism, and the G11 project no longer needed, the Bundeswehr was left with the G3. The G36 was the immediately available replacement as the German service rifle, produced from the mid-1990s to the present.

SPECIFICATION

- **MANUFACTURER** Heckler & Koch
- **CALIBRE** 5.56 x 45mm
- **MAGAZINE CAPACITY** 30
- **ACTION** Gas operated
- **TOTAL LENGTH** 998mm/39.24in
- **BARREL LENGTH** 480mm/18.8in
- **WEIGHT UNLOADED** 3.6kg/7.93lb

HK G41

This was the last in the line of roller-delayed blowback Heckler & Koch weapons. The G41 was planned as the Reservist weapon, backing up the G11. Using standard 5.56 x 45mm ammunition, and M16 magazines, and working exactly like the familiar G3, it would be a cost-effective reserve weapon to the more expensive G11. The lower receiver was made of polymer and moulded, to reduce weight and cost. Where the regular Army would be using G11s, the Reservists (who had mostly trained on G3s) would be using the G41. The collapse of Communism threw all those plans into disarray. It was produced in the mid-1980s, never fielded, was not successful as an export weapon. Today it is found only in museums.

SPECIFICATION

MANUFACTURER Heckler & Koch
CALIBRE 5.56 x 45mm
MAGAZINE CAPACITY 30, NATO standard
ACTION Roller-delayed blowback
TOTAL LENGTH 997mm/39.2in
BARREL LENGTH 450mm/17.7in
WEIGHT UNLOADED 4.1kg/9.03lb

Heckler & Koch G11 prototype

Desiring a leap past the American M16, Germany spent a great deal of time (through Heckler & Koch) developing a radical new rifle that used caseless ammunition. The magazine is above the bore and parallel to it. The rounds are positioned nose-down and the bolt rotates ninety degrees to cycle a round from the magazine. The bolt is also the chamber. In full-auto fire the cyclic rate is 600 rpm, but in three-shot burst mode the three shots are fired at a cyclic rate of 2,000 rpm. The idea is for all three shots to be on target, and gone from the muzzle before the weapon can move in recoil. The largest technical obstacle with caseless ammunition is heat: the ejected brass of conventional cartridges takes a large amount of heat with it. Caseless ammunition does not have that heat-loss option, and the propellant had to be specially formulated to avoid cook-offs. (If an over-heated weapon has a round left in the chamber, the heat can cause combustion of the propellant, known as a cook-off.) When Communism collapsed, the requirement and the funding disappeared. Germany suddenly no longer needed them. The Heckler & Koch G11 was made in limited numbers in the 1980s as test models, but never fielded.

SPECIFICATION

MANUFACTURER Heckler & Koch
CALIBRE 4.7mm
MAGAZINE CAPACITY 50
ACTION Recoil
TOTAL LENGTH 750mm/29.52in
BARREL LENGTH 540mm/21.25in
WEIGHT UNLOADED 3.6kg/7.93lb

The design
The futuristic design sealed the mechanism from the elements and reduced malfunctions.

Mauser M96

SPECIFICATION

MANUFACTURER Mauser
CALIBRE 7.65 x 25mm
MAGAZINE CAPACITY 10
ACTION Recoil operated
TOTAL LENGTH 508mm/20in w/stock installed
BARREL LENGTH 133mm/5.25in
WEIGHT UNLOADED 1.25kg/2.75lb

The Mauser System, as the M96 was called, was more than just an autoloading pistol. The holster/stock also allowed its user to press it into service with aimed fire as a short-range carbine, or to deliver a great deal of firepower in a short time at close range. The internal magazine is reloaded using stripper clips, or chargers. Some models used external, or box, magazines which could be exchanged like any other pistol when more ammunition was needed. Manufacture began in 1896, and the M96 remained in use through the 1930s. Some were issued to motorcycle troops in Germany during World War II.

G-41

SPECIFICATION

MANUFACTURER Mauser
CALIBRE 7.92 x 57mm
MAGAZINE CAPACITY 10
ACTION Gas operated
TOTAL LENGTH 1,175mm/46.25in
BARREL LENGTH 552mm/21.75in
WEIGHT UNLOADED 5.10kg/11.25lb

The G-41 was an early attempt at a full-power self-loading rifle. Not very successful, the G-41 suffered from excessive size and weight, poor reliability and clumsy operation. For example, the charging handle worked very much like that of a bolt on a bolt-action rifle but did not reciprocate when fired. It was used solely to chamber the first round of a magazine. Field-testing proved its faults, and it was quickly replaced by improved designs such as the G-43. It was produced between 1941 and 1942.

FG 42

SPECIFICATION

MANUFACTURER Rheinmettal-Borsig
CALIBRE 7.92 x 57mm
MAGAZINE CAPACITY 20
ACTION Gas operated
TOTAL LENGTH 940mm/37in
BARREL LENGTH 501mm/19.75in
WEIGHT UNLOADED 4.5kg/9.93lb

The German parachute units needed more firepower, but machine guns were too large and heavy for the limited Luftwaffe transport capacity to have as many as needed. The Luftwaffe sought self-loading rifles for their use. The two variants of the FG 42 were both select-fire box magazine fed rifles in the full power 7.92mm cartridge. Made of heavy-gauge steel stampings, they proved useful but not entirely satisfactory. As semi-auto rifles they worked fine, but when pressed into service as automatic weapons they recoiled quite briskly and overheated quickly. The FG 42 was in service from 1942 to 1945.

Walther G43

SPECIFICATION

MANUFACTURER Walther
CALIBRE 7.92 x 57mm
MAGAZINE CAPACITY 10
ACTION Gas operated
TOTAL LENGTH 1,117mm/44in
BARREL LENGTH 549mm/21.62in
WEIGHT UNLOADED 4.3kg/9.5lb

This was the relatively perfected full-power semi-auto rifle in German service during World War II. Using the bolt of the G41(W) and a gas system similar to the Tokarev M-1940, it was produced in large numbers. A quarter of a million semi-auto rifles in a war with millions of combatants, however, was not nearly enough. Typically it was issued with a low-power optical sight, mounted on the dovetail rail built into the right side of the receiver. The rifle was reliable and accurate, and saw service for a short time after the war in the Czech armed forces. It was in service in Germany from 1943 to 1945.

Wa 2000 Sniper

This rifle was developed around the .300 Winchester Magnum cartridge, and was meant to be a long range sniper rifle of extreme accuracy. The bullpup design allowed for a high-performance cartridge in a relatively compact package. It was ultimately a failure, and whether this was due to high cost or continued mechanical problems is unknown. The Wa 2000 was built and offered for sale from 1982 to 1988.

SPECIFICATION

MANUFACTURER Walther
CALIBRE 7.5 x 55mm, 7.62mm NATO, .300 Winchester Magnum
MAGAZINE CAPACITY 6
ACTION Gas operated
TOTAL LENGTH 905mm/35.65in
BARREL LENGTH 650mm/25.6in
WEIGHT UNLOADED 7.95kg/17.54lb

Gew 98

Adopted in April of 1898 to replace the Commission 1888 rifles, the new Mauser was a revelation. It was strong, fast, almost impossible to use incorrectly, and durable. It also reflected the idea of the time for infantry rifles: long, and suitable for a long bayonet. It was the rifle with which Germany entered World War I and it served her well in that conflict. In one form or another it is still in production today. In the depicted version, it served from 1898 to 1918, but was replaced after the war by shorter rifles. Some Gew 98 rifles were still in use by police officers when Allied troops entered Germany in 1944.

SPECIFICATION

MANUFACTURER Various
CALIBRE 7.92 x 57mm
MAGAZINE CAPACITY 5
ACTION Bolt action
TOTAL LENGTH 1,249mm/49.2in
BARREL LENGTH 740mm/29.15in
WEIGHT UNLOADED 4.09kg/9.02lb

Gew 98 sniper

Germany appreciated earlier than other combatants the usefulness of snipers in trench warfare. It was some time before the British realized that the "random" deaths due to head wounds were in fact deliberate. By today's standards the Gew 98 is quite rough as a sniper rifle but it was certainly good enough to give its users a significant edge on the Western Front for some time. While Germany maintained some sniper training and equipment between the wars, even they were surprised at the large number of Soviet snipers, and had to revamp their programme significantly. The Gew 98 was in use from 1915 to 1918.

SPECIFICATION

MANUFACTURER Various
CALIBRE 7.92 x 57mm
MAGAZINE CAPACITY 5
ACTION Bolt action
TOTAL LENGTH 1,249mm/49.2in
BARREL LENGTH 739mm/29.1in
WEIGHT UNLOADED 4.62kg/10.2lb

98k

After World War I, Germany realized that the best rifle was what had been considered a cavalry carbine before the war – namely something shorter, lighter and handier. The 98k was just such a rifle. The bolt handle was turned down to get it out of the way, and the sword bayonet was abandoned for a design half as long. In slow design changes from post-World War I, the 98k reached its final form in 1935 and was in service until 1945.

SPECIFICATION

MANUFACTURER Various
CALIBRE 7.92 x 57mm
MAGAZINE CAPACITY 5
ACTION Bolt action
TOTAL LENGTH 1,109mm/43.7in
BARREL LENGTH 599mm/23.6in
WEIGHT UNLOADED 3.91kg/8.64lb

Stg 44

SPECIFICATION

MANUFACTURER Various
CALIBRE 7.62 x 33mm
MAGAZINE CAPACITY 30
ACTION Gas operated/tilting bolt
TOTAL LENGTH 940mm/37in
BARREL LENGTH 419mm/16.5in
WEIGHT UNLOADED 5.21kg/11.5lb

Made only in 1944 and 1945, this was the refined and battle-tested "storm rifle". With large magazine capacity, select fire, moderate recoil and greater range and accuracy than any submachine gun, it proved a highly effective weapon among the swarms of Soviet soldiers on the Eastern Front. The Stg 44 is a further product-improved MP-43, with production shortcuts intended to speed factory output. It came, however, too late to make much difference. Had the German trials boards in the 1930s reports been acted on, Germany could have had the whole army equipped with the MP-43/Stg 44 for the duration of the war. However, they were ignored until it was too late.

Volksturm VG1

SPECIFICATION	
MANUFACTURER	Various
CALIBRE	7.92 x 57mm
MAGAZINE CAPACITY	VG1: 10, VK-1; 5, some single shots
ACTION	Bolt action
TOTAL LENGTH	1,092mm/43in
BARREL LENGTH	589mm/23.2in
WEIGHT UNLOADED	3.76kg/8.3lb

This was another stopgap weapon made in the days of World War II. The VG1 used the magazine of the G43 semi-automatic rifle, with a Mauser action. A similar weapon was the VK98, a Mauser stripped to its simplest form: a board/stock with a bolt action rifle screwed or bolted to it, lacking even a magazine. On both weapons every possible machining operation that could be left undone was avoided. Parts were sub-contracted to any small shop that could make them. The rifle would not accept a bayonet. It did, however, fire the full-power 7.92mm cartridge, and would shoot for as long as its owners cared to use it. Produced in the spring of 1945 alone, the VG1 was probably unsafe to fire.

MPi-KM (AK-47)

SPECIFICATION	
MANUFACTURER	Various
CALIBRE	7.62 x 39mm
MAGAZINE CAPACITY	30
ACTION	Gas operated/rotating bolt
TOTAL LENGTH	867mm/34.2in
BARREL LENGTH	414mm/16.3in
WEIGHT UNLOADED	4.3kg/9.48lb

As a Soviet satellite, East Germany was expected to provide troops and build weapons for the Soviets. The East-German AK is noted by the pebble texture of the synthetic furniture, in the pistol grip and buttstock. When Germany re-unified, they were of no use at all, and were either destroyed or their parts sold as surplus. The MPi-KM was made from the late 1950s to the late 1970s, when replaced by AK-74 variants. Many of the AK variants seen in news photos from Iraq are ex-East-German MPi-KM rifles.

MPi-KMS74

SPECIFICATION	
MANUFACTURER	Various
CALIBRE	5.45 x 39mm
MAGAZINE CAPACITY	30
ACTION	Gas operated/rotating bolt
TOTAL LENGTH	956mm/37.65in
BARREL LENGTH	415mm/16.35in
WEIGHT UNLOADED	4.85kg/10.7lb

Production of the MPi-KMS74, the East-German variant of the AK-74, had barely begun to replace existing 7.62mm weapons when the Berlin Wall fell in 1989, and Germany became one country again. The East-German rifles had no place in the new, unified Germany because all service rifles had to be 5.56mm in calibre. As with the AK variants, the MPi-KMS74 was scrapped or its parts were sold as surplus. It was in service for only a brief time from 1983 to 1989.

HK G95A1

SPECIFICATION	
MANUFACTURER	Heckler & Koch
CALIBRE	5.56mm NATO
MAGAZINE CAPACITY	30
ACTION	Gas operated
TOTAL LENGTH	1,030mm/40.6in
BARREL LENGTH	420mm/16.5in
WEIGHT UNLOADED	3.8kg/8.4lb

In December 2022, Germany announced plans to adopt the HK 416A8 under the G95A1 name. The "System Sturmgewehr Bundeswehr" or System Assault Rifle Bundeswehr will reportedly be made up of two variants of the HK416 – the G95A1, likely to have a 16.5 inch barrel, and the G95KA1 carbine variant which will have a 14 inch barrel. As with all rifles in the HK416 family the rifles use a short-stroke gas piston system and a rotating bolt head locking mechanism. It will replace the G36 rifles.

Italy

Rather than simply adopt the Mauser that was sweeping the world in the late 19th century, Italy elected to go with an amalgamation of local features. The Carcano rifles used a Mauser-type bolt, but the receiver bridge was split, so the bolt handle could pass through the slot in the receiver. Without Mannlicher clips in the magazine, the rifle was a single-shot. Unlike the M1 Garand clips, the Carcano clips were quite flimsy and easily damaged. The 7.35mm cartridge was introduced in 1938 after Italian troops found themselves out-ranged in Ethiopia, against troops armed with Mausers in 7.92mm. The 7.35mm was dropped two years later when Italy entered World War II.

Vetterli Model 1934

The Swiss-designed Vetterli rifle originated as a tube-magazine repeating rifle shooting a black powder 10mm cartridge. It was also made in Italy as a tube-fed then later as a magazine-fed rifle. In the 1930s, Italy had the 10mm barrels lined to accept the 6.5mm Carcano cartridge, altered the box magazine, and issued the Vetterli as training rifles. They were used from 1934 to 1940.

SPECIFICATION

MANUFACTURER Beretta
CALIBRE 6.5 x 52mm
MAGAZINE CAPACITY 5
ACTION Bolt action
TOTAL LENGTH 919mm/36.2in
BARREL LENGTH 450mm/17.7in
WEIGHT UNLOADED 3.12kg/6.9lb

Garand

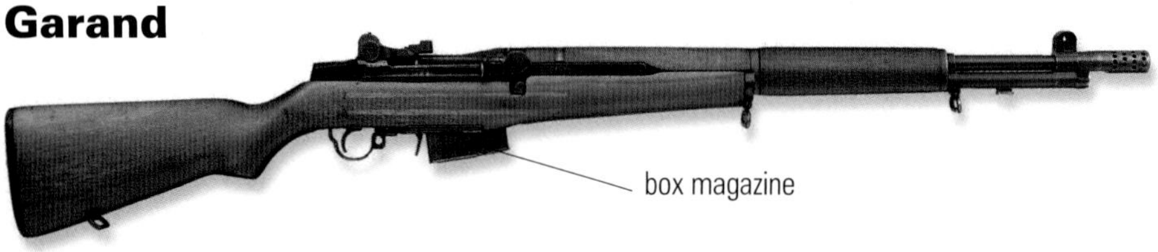

After World War II, Italy adopted the Garand, and Beretta started to produce it. Identical to the US-made Garand, it lasted only a short time in Italian service (1952–9) before being replaced by the BM-series of rifles. This transitional Garand had a box magazine rather than an en bloc clip.

SPECIFICATION

MANUFACTURER Beretta
CALIBRE .30-06
MAGAZINE CAPACITY 8, en bloc clip
ACTION Gas operated/rotating bolt
TOTAL LENGTH 1,103mm/43.4in
BARREL LENGTH 610mm/24in
WEIGHT UNLOADED 4.32kg/9.52lb

BM59

With Beretta set up to make Garands, and the United States switching to the M14, Italy decided to make the Garand into an M14. It perhaps cost Italy as much to convert every Garand on hand into their BM59 (and make more) as it cost the US to develop and test the M14. The BM59 magazine, however, was not the same as the magazine of the M14, and the magazines were not interchangeable. Quarter-masters had to be aware of this issue when North Atlantic Treaty Organization (NATO) forces were stationed in Italy during the 1950s and 1960s. All the Italian efforts were negated in less than ten years when the US switched again to the M16. The BM59 was issued at the beginning of 1959 and the rifles continued in service until the mid-1970s.

SPECIFICATION

MANUFACTURER Beretta
CALIBRE 7.62mm NATO
MAGAZINE CAPACITY 20
ACTION Gas-operated/rotating bolt
TOTAL LENGTH 945mm/37.2in
BARREL LENGTH 450mm/17.7in
WEIGHT UNLOADED 3.69kg/8.15lb

Beretta BM62

SPECIFICATION

MANUFACTURER Beretta
CALIBRE 7.62mm NATO
MAGAZINE CAPACITY 20
ACTION Gas operated/rotating bolt
TOTAL LENGTH 977mm/38.5in
BARREL LENGTH 447mm/17.6in
WEIGHT UNLOADED 3.96kg/8.75lb

This was an export version of the BM59 rifle. After only a short time in development, the BM59 rifle had gained a new and improved gas system and been offered in nearly a dozen versions. The BM62 was slightly shorter, with a new flash hider but without the built-in bipod of the BM59. It was produced as a semi-auto-only rifle from 1962 to the early 1980s. Large numbers were bought by the United States. The Italian version had a quick-detach muzzle brake to make it more compact for paratroopers.

M70

SPECIFICATION

MANUFACTURER Beretta
CALIBRE 5.56 x 45mm
MAGAZINE CAPACITY 30
ACTION Gas operated/rotating bolt
TOTAL LENGTH 955mm/37.6in
BARREL LENGTH 451mm/17.8in
WEIGHT UNLOADED 3.85kg/8.5lb

While the United States had switched to the M16, and other manufacturers were looking to get into the 5.56mm market, Beretta designed and produced the M70. Unlike the M16, the M70 does not use the Stoner gas system. The long-stroke piston above the barrel is a cross between the AK and the AR-18. The M70 was a contender in the Swedish rifle trials, but lost to the Fabrique Nationale Carbine (FNC) from FN. Continued development has changed some features, as Beretta keeps the design current and relevant. Production ran from 1972 to 1983, with improved models since then with different model numbers.

Model 1957 carbine

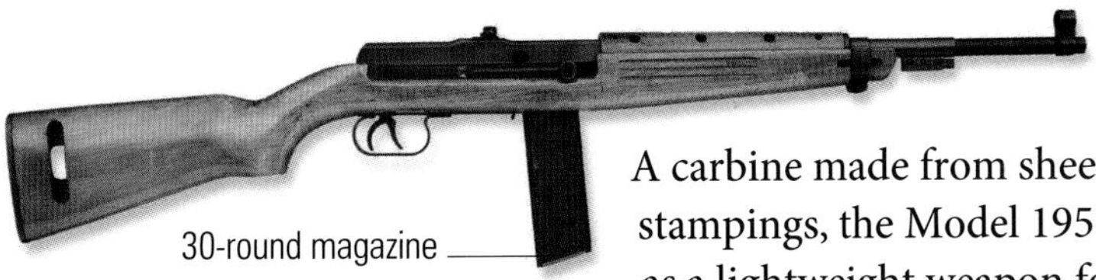

SPECIFICATION

MANUFACTURER Luigi Franchi
CALIBRE .30 US carbine
MAGAZINE CAPACITY 15 or 30
ACTION Gas operated
TOTAL LENGTH 925mm/36.4in
BARREL LENGTH 429mm/16.9in
WEIGHT UNLOADED 3.40kg/7.5lb

A carbine made from sheet metal stampings, the Model 1957 was intended as a lightweight weapon for use by non-combat personnel. An interesting attempt at a compact, reasonably powerful close and medium-range weapon, it came too late, as the AK was already in production and the AR-15 was soon to arrive. The carbine was an early effort at a Personal Defence Weapon. Probably due to the US M1 carbines that were already widespread, it found no buyers and had only a short production life, between 1957 and 1958.

Model 1891

SPECIFICATION

MANUFACTURER Terni
CALIBRE 6.5 x 52mm
MAGAZINE CAPACITY 5
ACTION Bolt action
TOTAL LENGTH 1,290mm/50.8in
BARREL LENGTH 780mm/30.7in
WEIGHT UNLOADED 3.90kg/8.6lb

A typical late-19th-century bullet-launching bayonet mount, the Model 1891 was reasonably well designed for its time. Although long, it was not excessively heavy, and the recoil of the 6.5mm cartridge was moderate enough to make the rifle easy to shoot. By the beginning of World War I, however, it was dated. It would have been a relatively easy task to update it, and change the Mannlicher magazine for a Mauser type. Yet Italy did not take this route and instead stuck with it. First fielded in 1891, the Model 1891 was still in service in 1945.

Mannlicher-Carcano Ballila

This training rifle for the Opera Nazionale Balilla, the Youth Fascist Organization, was neither intended for nor mechanically suited for use with standard ammunition. As a lightweight and compact rifle, it was suitable for teaching marksmanship basics at Mussolini's fascist youth camps. It was supplied with an attached, but hinged, bayonet, similar to the standard Model 91 carbines. It was used from the 1920s to 1945.

SPECIFICATION

MANUFACTURER Terni
CALIBRE 6mm
MAGAZINE CAPACITY N/A
ACTION Gas operated/tilting lock
TOTAL LENGTH 711mm/28in
BARREL LENGTH 366mm/14.43in
WEIGHT UNLOADED 2.04kg/4.5lb

Model 91/38 TS

A carbine version of the Model 1891, the TS uses a knife-type bayonet instead of the permanently attached bayonet of the 1891 carbine, which pivoted into place. A detachable bayonet was a useful tool. Production began in 1938 and service lasted until 1945. The 91/38 was the rifle Italy should have had from the early 1920s. When the rest of Europe was changing to the carbine-size Model 1924, Italy retained a long rifle until 1938.

SPECIFICATION

MANUFACTURER Terni
CALIBRE 6.5 x 52mm
MAGAZINE CAPACITY 5
ACTION Bolt action
TOTAL LENGTH 919mm/36.2in
BARREL LENGTH 450mm/17.7in
WEIGHT UNLOADED 3.12kg/6.9lb

Model 1941

This was a new rifle, in the old calibre, for use in World War II. It was slightly shorter, but not otherwise markedly different from the Model 1891. Taking 100mm/4in off the excessive length of the 1891 did not make it much easier to handle or reduce the weight significantly. Model 1941s were, however, solidly made and reliable. Introduced in 1941, few were made before Italy changed sides in 1943 and dropped production.

SPECIFICATION

MANUFACTURER Terni
CALIBRE 6.5 x 52mm
MAGAZINE CAPACITY 5
ACTION Bolt action
TOTAL LENGTH 1,171mm/46.1in
BARREL LENGTH 691mm/27.2in
WEIGHT UNLOADED 3.72kg/8.21lb

Norway

Once a province of Sweden, and later a sovereign country invaded by the Germans in World War II, Norway has a long history of weapons manufacture. Reliable function in extreme cold, deep snow and the rains of coastal areas are important considerations when selecting a rifle for use in Norway.

1912/18 carbine

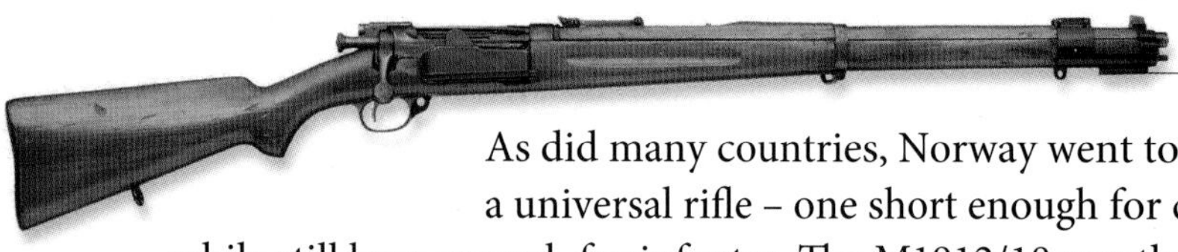

As did many countries, Norway went towards a universal rifle – one short enough for cavalry while still long enough for infantry. The M1912/18 was their pre-war attempt at a one-size-fits-all rifle. Field use uncovered a stock weakness, so after 1916 rifles were made with a new nose cap with strengthening collar. The rifle was in service from 1912 to the 1950s.

SPECIFICATION

MANUFACTURER Kongsberg
CALIBRE 6.5 x 55mm
MAGAZINE CAPACITY 5
ACTION Bolt action
TOTAL LENGTH 1,106mm/43.55in
BARREL LENGTH 610mm/24in
WEIGHT UNLOADED 4.01kg/8.86lb

Krag-Jorgensen Model 1925

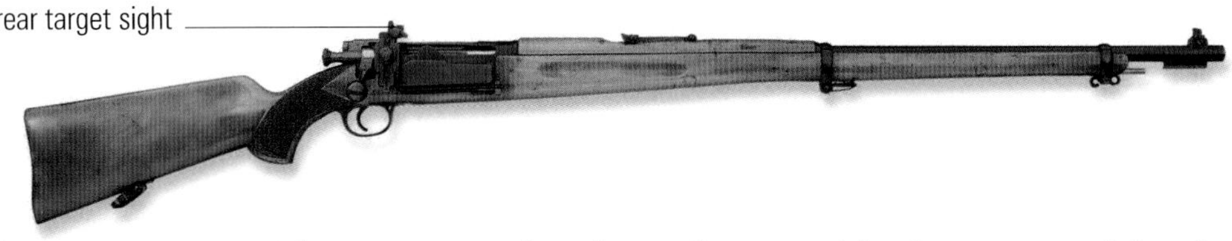

SPECIFICATION

MANUFACTURER Kongsberg
CALIBRE 6.5 x 55mm
MAGAZINE CAPACITY 5
ACTION Bolt action
TOTAL LENGTH 1,260mm/49.6in
BARREL LENGTH 759mm/29.9in
WEIGHT UNLOADED 4.05kg/8.93lb

The Krag action has design features with advantages and drawbacks. The bolt has only one locking lug, which limits the strength of the cartridges it can use. But the action as a result is very smooth and fast to cycle. When all rifles were bolt-action rifles, a fast-working bolt action was an asset to any army. The magazine cover hinges open (down, on the Norwegian Krag) and can be easily topped off with single rounds. However, the Krag cannot be quickly reloaded with chargers or stripper clips, which is a drawback. The M1925 is an iron-sighted sniper or target model, with aperture rear sight, heavy barrel and protected front sight. It was a service rifle from 1925 to 1940 and used as a target rifle into the 1950s.

Krag-Jorgensen Model 1925 carbine

SPECIFICATION

MANUFACTURER Kongsberg
CALIBRE 6.5 x 55mm
MAGAZINE CAPACITY 5
ACTION Bolt action
TOTAL LENGTH 1,107mm/43.6in
BARREL LENGTH 610mm/24in
WEIGHT UNLOADED 3.99kg/8.8lb

For every rifle, there has to be a carbine. The M1925 carbine is simply a shortened Krag with a shortened version of the heavy barrel of the rifle. It was issued first in 1925 and lasted on the target ranges to the 1950s.

Krag experimental model

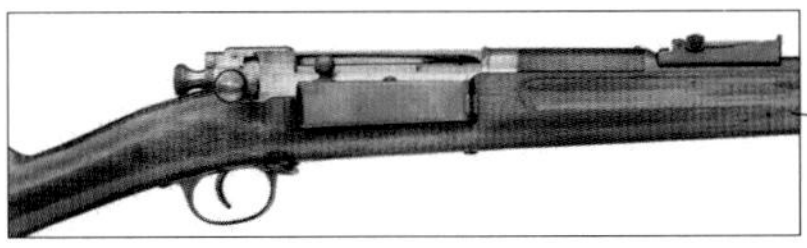

ABOVE The Krag magazine hinges open downwards for loading and unloading. It cannot take chargers for fast reloading.

SPECIFICATION

MANUFACTURER Kongsberg
CALIBRE 7.92 x 57mm
MAGAZINE CAPACITY 5
ACTION Bolt action
TOTAL LENGTH 1,106mm/43.55in
BARREL LENGTH 610mm/24in
WEIGHT UNLOADED 4.01kg/8.86lb

After World War II, with large quantities of 98k rifles and 7.92 x 57mm ammunition on hand, Norway put together M1912 carbine actions with surplus Colt 8mm machine-gun barrels. The Krag action, when made from the right alloys, had just enough strength to contain the 7.92 x 57mm cartridge. As a means of using up a surplus supply of non-standard ammunition and barrels, the process was a good one. It was not, however, meant for use as a military arm. The Krag experimental was sold commercially in Norway for target shooting from 1948 to 1951, and used in target competition for years afterwards.

Denmark

Denmark had an army complete with cavalry and artillery units by the 19th century. Some service rifles in the late 19th and first half of the 20th century were made in Denmark while others were acquired from the original manufacturers. A forward-looking country, Denmark adopted the Madsen M1896 rifle and was the first country to adopt a semi-automatic service rifle for general issue, but it did not last long.

Krag-Jorgensen Model 1889

Denmark was the first country to adopt the Norwegian rifle designed by Krag and Jorgensen in the late 19th century. The rifle was modified in Denmark for its later adoption by the United States and Norway. The magazine box on the Danish Krag opens horizontally, hinging towards the muzzle, while the US and Norwegian Krags have the box pivoting down. They all suffered from the same shortcoming of the Krag magazine: it could not be recharged via stripper clips. Rounds had to be individually handled and dropped into the open magazine well while the rifle was tilted to the left. The complexity of manufacturing this magazine was probably why many countries did not adopt the Krag-Jorgensen. Manufacture ran from 1889 to 1921.

SPECIFICATION

MANUFACTURER KT, Copenhagen
CALIBRE 8 x 58R
MAGAZINE CAPACITY 5
ACTION Bolt action/single-locking lug
TOTAL LENGTH 1,328mm/52.3in
BARREL LENGTH 950mm/37.4in
WEIGHT UNLOADED 4.58kg/10.1lb

Model 1889 Cavalry

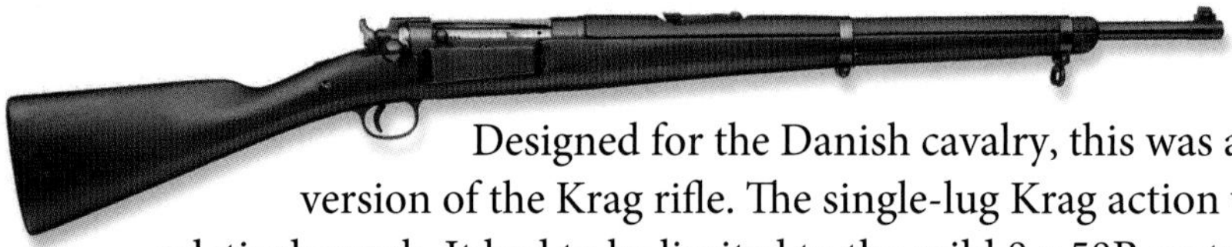

Designed for the Danish cavalry, this was a shorter version of the Krag rifle. The single-lug Krag action was relatively weak. It had to be limited to the mild 8 x 58R cartridge. The mild cartridge did not lose as much velocity when fired in a carbine as more powerful cartridges would. The Model 8 x 58R Cavalry was manufactured from 1912 to 13 and was still in service when Germany invaded in 1940.

SPECIFICATION

MANUFACTURER KT, Copenhagen
CALIBRE 8 x 58R
MAGAZINE CAPACITY 5
ACTION Bolt action/single-locking lug
TOTAL LENGTH 1,100mm/43.3in
BARREL LENGTH 599mm/23.6in
WEIGHT UNLOADED 4.03kg/8.9lb

Bang Model 1927

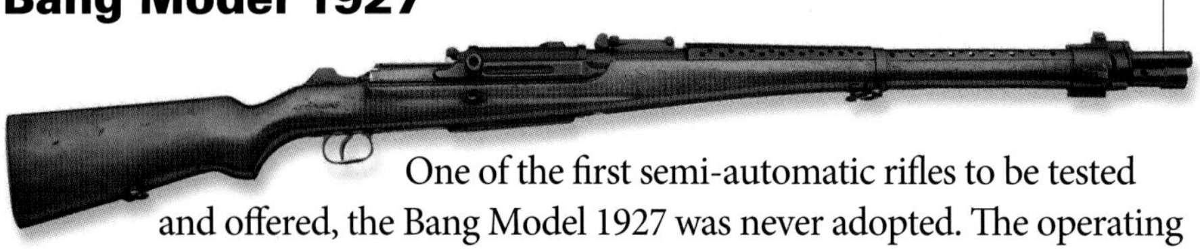

One of the first semi-automatic rifles to be tested and offered, the Bang Model 1927 was never adopted. The operating system used a cup around the muzzle to capture gases and power the action. The method was sensitive to powder-burn rates and charge weights, and the corrosive primers of the time prevented the system from working effectively. Heavy corrosion from the priming compound fouled the cup and operating system, leading to malfunctions. The Bang system was used later in the German Gew 41 and caused the same problem. While mechanically interesting, it was not reliable enough for military use, and was not adopted, even by the Danes. Development began in 1911 and continued until 1929 when the project was abandoned.

SPECIFICATION

MANUFACTURER Dansk Industri Syndikat
CALIBRE .256, .276 Pedersen, .30-06
MAGAZINE CAPACITY 6
ACTION Gas operated
TOTAL LENGTH 1,118mm/44in
BARREL LENGTH 508mm/20in
WEIGHT UNLOADED 4.08kg/9lb

Ljungman

SPECIFICATION	
MANUFACTURER Dansk Industri Syndikat	
CALIBRE 7 x 57mm, 7.92 x 57mm	
MAGAZINE CAPACITY 10	
ACTION Gas operated/tilting bolt	
TOTAL LENGTH 1,205mm/47.45in	
BARREL LENGTH 622mm/24.5in	
WEIGHT UNLOADED 4.64kg/10.25lb	

The Ljungman rifle is capable of causing significant injury to the user who does not know its peculiarities. The gas system functions by direct impingement: the gas is fed through a tube directly back to the bolt carrier. The pressure of the gas launches the carrier back, taking the bolt with it. The action requires a strong recoil spring to work reliably. The uncovered bolt and feedway allow unwary users to get their fingers in the bolt path while manipulating the action, and injury can result. Built as development for a Danish service rifle, with licensing from Sweden, the Madsen-Ljungman project began in 1946 and dragged on for a number of years before being abandoned in the early 1950s.

SPECIFICATION	
MANUFACTURER Dansk Industri Syndikat	
CALIBRE 7 x 57mm, 7.65 x 53mm, .30-06, 7.92 x 57mm	
MAGAZINE CAPACITY 5	
ACTION Bolt action	
TOTAL LENGTH 1,100mm/43.3in	
BARREL LENGTH 596mm/23.45in	
WEIGHT UNLOADED 3.85kg/8.5lb	

Madsen M47

Built as an export item, the Madsen 47 was designed for the smaller military force. In a world awash with surplus arms from World War II, the Madsen bolt-action rifle found few buyers. The receiver had the rear bridge split, and the bolt handle passed through it as the bolt was worked. On closing, the bolt handle acted as a safety lug. Offered in a variety of calibres, the only large contract was to Colombia, for rifles chambered in .30-06. When manufactured in 1947, it was immediately obsolete. The largest of the world's armies had begun to re-equip with semi-auto rifles.

SPECIFICATION	
MANUFACTURER Dansk Industri Syndikat	
CALIBRE 7.62mm NATO	
MAGAZINE CAPACITY 20	
ACTION Gas operated/rotating bolt	
TOTAL LENGTH 1,100mm/43.3in	
BARREL LENGTH 523mm/20.6in	
WEIGHT UNLOADED 4.64kg/10.23lb	

LAR

Initially developed as an assault rifle for the Finnish trial of 1958, the Light Automatic Rifle (LAR) began as a rifle chambered in 7.62 x 39mm. As it evolved it grew to encompass the 7.62 x 51mm cartridge and adopted an alloy receiver, a free-floating barrel and chromium-plated operating parts. However, the LAR could not compete on the world market with products from Belgium, Germany, the United States and the Soviet Union. It was abandoned in 1965, just before Denmark adopted the G-3 as the new service rifle.

SPECIFICATION	
MANUFACTURER Various US	
CALIBRE 7.62 x 63mm	
MAGAZINE CAPACITY 8, en-bloc clip	
ACTION Gas operated/rotating bolt	
TOTAL LENGTH 1,105mm/43.5in	
BARREL LENGTH 609mm/24in	
WEIGHT UNLOADED 4.31kg/9.5lb	

Gavaer Model 1950

After World War II, the Danish armed forces wisely elected to use American M1 Garands as their service rifle. Although they were never manufactured in Denmark, Danish armouries rebuilt and overhauled them as needed. They manufactured small parts, stocks and handguards, but kept the barrelled receivers of the original rifles in service. The M1 Garand went into service in Denmark as the Gevaer Model 1950. It was retained until the adoption of the M/66 (G3) in 1966.

Austria

Austria and Austro-Hungary, positioned in the middle of Western Europe, spent many centuries struggling against their neighbours. They consequently have a long tradition of arms-making and armouries, as well as weapons design. Many of the armouries continued manufacture under the flag of their new countries.

Mannlicher 1888

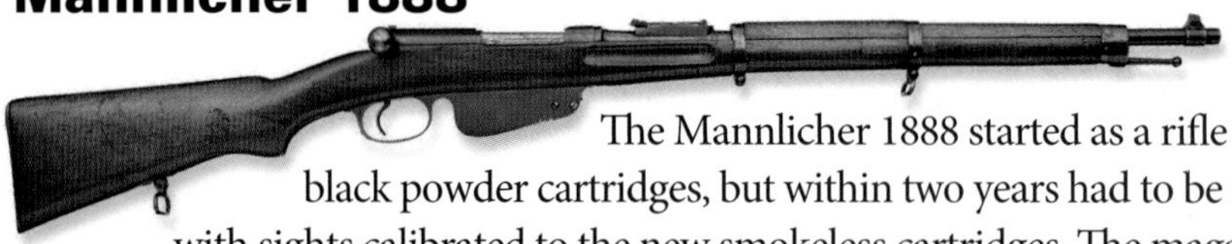

The Mannlicher 1888 started as a rifle using black powder cartridges, but within two years had to be rebuilt with sights calibrated to the new smokeless cartridges. The magazine was a marvel of the time: each five-round clip was self-contained. The user simply opened the bolt, pressed in a new loaded clip and, once it locked in place, closed the bolt. The fast reload was a desirable feature. However, the bottom of the magazine housing had to be open for the clip to fall free when empty, and the opening allowed dirt, dust and mud to enter. Introduced in 1888, the Mannlicher 1888 was obsolete in ten years but was nevertheless still issued as late as 1918.

SPECIFICATION

MANUFACTURER Steyr
CALIBRE 8 x 50 M-88 black powder
MAGAZINE CAPACITY 5
ACTION Straight-pull bolt action
TOTAL LENGTH 1,279mm/50.38in
BARREL LENGTH 765mm/30.14 in
WEIGHT UNLOADED 4.40kg/9.7lb

Mannlicher M1895

The Mannlicher M1895 was Austro-Hungary's principle arm during World War I. A bolt action of straight-pull design (the bolt handle was simply pulled back, instead of being turned up before retracting), it was easy and quick to manipulate. The disadvantage of this design was its poor performance in combat, particularly trench warfare. Mud bound the spiral grooves machined in the bolt, which stopped the rifle. As with all Mannlicher rifles, it needed a sheet-metal clip holding five rounds, or could be used as a single-shot rifle. The clip dropped out of the bottom of the rifle when the last round was chambered. Issued from 1895 to 1918, after World War I it was used by other countries formed from Austro-Hungary.

SPECIFICATION

MANUFACTURER Steyr
CALIBRE 8 x 50R
MAGAZINE CAPACITY 5
ACTION Straight-pull bolt action
TOTAL LENGTH 1,270mm/50in
BARREL LENGTH 765mm/30.12in
WEIGHT UNLOADED 3.76kg/8.31lb

Mannlicher M1895 carbine

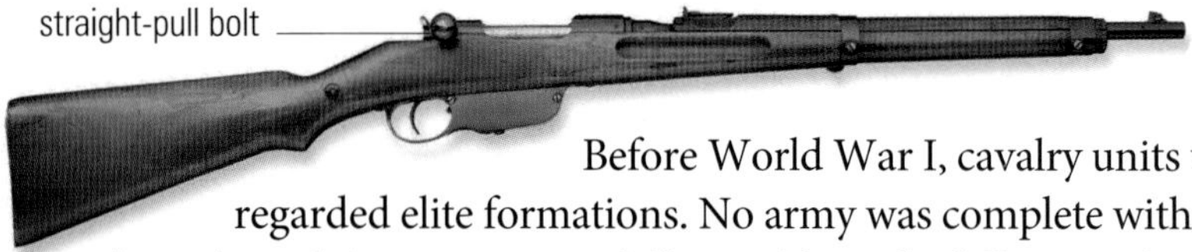

Before World War I, cavalry units were highly regarded elite formations. No army was complete without a cavalry branch, and Austria was no different. The only differences between the carbine and M1895 rifle issued to the Austrian cavalry from 1895 to 1918 were overall length, barrel length and weight. In the cavalry, the problem of mud was less crucial than in the infantry, but by the spring of 1915 all Austrian cavalry units were relegated to an infantry role. Horses had no place in trench warfare, and the 1895 carbine was too short for bayonet combat. After the war, many carbines ended up as police weapons, due to their convenient size. They were rapidly made obsolete by the flood of Mauser rifles in the 1920s and 1930s.

SPECIFICATION

MANUFACTURER Steyr
CALIBRE 8 x 50R
MAGAZINE CAPACITY 5
ACTION Straight-pull bolt action
TOTAL LENGTH 1,003mm/39.5in
BARREL LENGTH 500mm/19.65in
WEIGHT UNLOADED 3.17kg/7.0lb

Steyr SSG 69

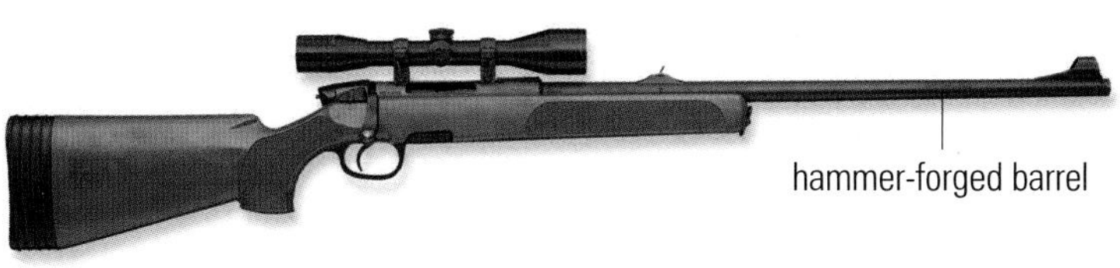

SPECIFICATION	
MANUFACTURER	Steyr
CALIBRE	7.62mm NATO
MAGAZINE CAPACITY	5, 10 or 20
ACTION	Bolt action
TOTAL LENGTH	1,143mm/45in
BARREL LENGTH	650mm/25.6in
WEIGHT UNLOADED	4.64kg/10.25lb

The bolt-action Steyr Scharf Shutzen Gewehrifle (SSG 69) was introduced in 1969. It has a smooth bolt movement, partly because of the locking lugs at the rear of the bolt. The lugs are cammed into and out of the bolt body as the bolt rotates, unlike other bolt actions where the locking lugs are fixed to the bolt body. Steyr hammer-forged barrels are accurate and durable. Within the range limitations of the 7.62mm NATO cartridge, the SSG 69 is a superb sniper rifle. The detachable box magazines allow different natures of ammunition. The SSG 04 was adopted in 2004 as a complement to the SSG 69, rather than a replacement.

Steyr SSG 08

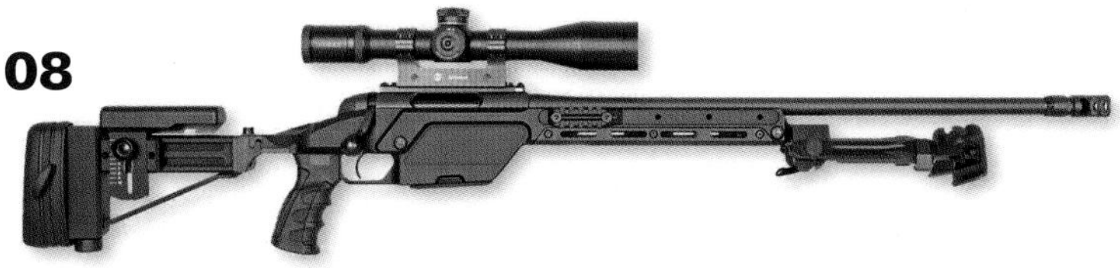

SPECIFICATION	
MANUFACTURER	Steyr Mannlicher
CALIBRE	7.62mm NATO
MAGAZINE CAPACITY	10
ACTION	Bolt action
TOTAL LENGTH	1,270mm/50.1in
BARREL LENGTH	690mm/26.2in
WEIGHT UNLOADED	5.5kg/12.1lb

Just four years later, in 2008, the SSG 08 was also adopted to complement the SSG 04. Improvements to the design include a folding buttstock, adjustable cheekpiece, aluminum alloy stock, customizable pistol grip, and a muzzle brake that allows for the easy attachment of a suppressor. The SSG 08 is advertised as capable of sub-MOA accuracy with proper ammunition.

Steyr AUG

SPECIFICATION	
MANUFACTURER	Steyr
CALIBRE	5.56 x 45mm
MAGAZINE CAPACITY	30 (M-16 magazines)
ACTION	Gas operated/rotating bolt
TOTAL LENGTH	805mm/31.7in
BARREL LENGTH	508mm/20in
WEIGHT UNLOADED	3.8kg/8.4lb

The Steyr Armee Universal Gewehr (AUG) solved the problem left-handed shooters have with the bullpup design – the ejection port is usually right where their face would be, when firing. The bolt in the Steyr AUG can be switched from right- to left-ejection. The first polymer-constructed rifle, the AUG is also unique in other regards: the barrels are quickly exchanged, and the firing selector is incorporated in the trigger system. A clean press delivers a single shot. Clutch the trigger back briskly and the mechanism automatically goes to full-auto fire until released.

Steyr AUG Police

SPECIFICATION	
MANUFACTURER	Steyr
CALIBRE	9 x 19mm
MAGAZINE CAPACITY	32
ACTION	Blowback
TOTAL LENGTH	533mm/21in
BARREL LENGTH	256mm/10in
WEIGHT UNLOADED	3.3kg/7.27lb

This is a 9mm Parabellum version of the Steyr Armee Universal Gewehr (AUG) for police and auxiliary unit use. It is also known as the "Para" version. The AUG can be converted between 5.56mm and 9mm in ten minutes. Since the AUG is already compact, changing it to 9mm to make it more compact is only useful for training rather than for tactical utility. Many indoor ranges cannot take the 5.56mm cartridge with safety because of its destructive power. The AUG Police was introduced in 1989 and is still in use today.

Sweden

Sweden has always sought reliable and durable rifles. From the Mauser bolt actions to semi-automatic rifles of several origins, Sweden quickly transformed from purchaser to manufacturer. The country's century-long reputation for producing superb steel greatly assisted this transformation.

Mauser Model 1894 carbine

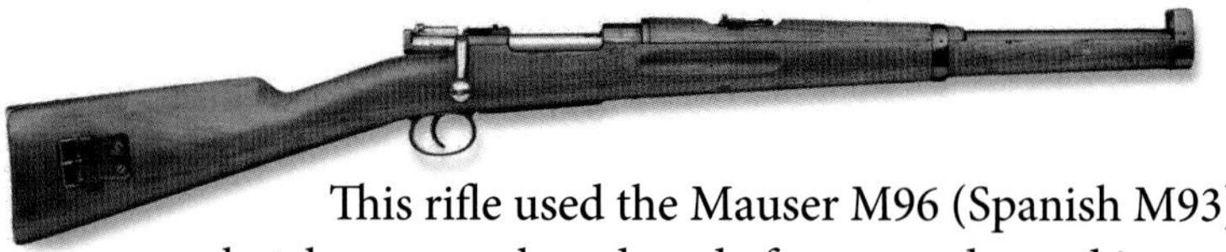

This rifle used the Mauser M96 (Spanish M93) action. The first batch was purchased, and after upgrades and improvements was adopted in 1899. Production began in Sweden in 1900. It was used as a rifle in the reserves, and as a hunting rifle, long after it was dropped as the issue rifle of the Swedish Army. While in service from 1894 to the 1940s, it hung on in the reserves until the 1950s. As with many carbines, rapid fire can heat the forearm to a noticeable degree.

SPECIFICATION	
MANUFACTURER	Mauser, Oberndorf/ Carl Gustaf
CALIBRE	6.5 x 55mm
MAGAZINE CAPACITY	5
ACTION	Bolt action
TOTAL LENGTH	949mm/37.4in
BARREL LENGTH	439mm/17.3in
WEIGHT UNLOADED	3.31kg/7.3lb

Mauser Model 41 sniper

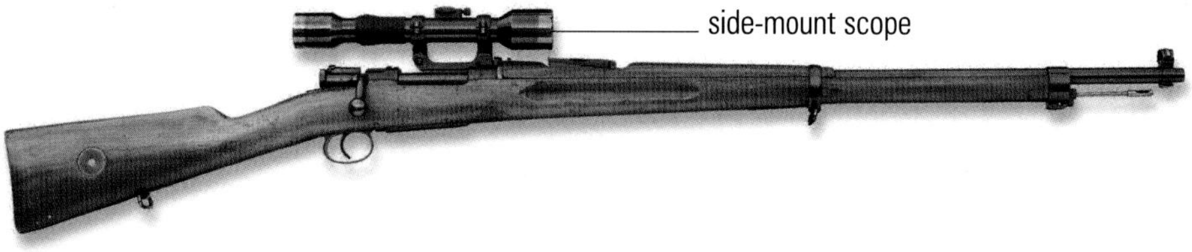

This was a converted Model 1896 rifle. A sidemount with a mounting dovetail was fitted on to the receiver. With a scope installed, it was issued for sniper use. Even after self-loading rifles were introduced the Model 41 sniper was kept in service until a new sniper variant of the AK4 could be fielded. It was first issued in 1941 and was still in regular service until the early 1960s.

SPECIFICATION	
MANUFACTURER	Carl Gustaf
CALIBRE	6.5 x 55mm
MAGAZINE CAPACITY	5
ACTION	Bolt action
TOTAL LENGTH	1,256mm/49.45in
BARREL LENGTH	739mm/29.1in
WEIGHT UNLOADED	4.37kg/9.65lb

Carl Gustaf M/42 AT

In service during 1942–4, this weapon had a single-shot early recoilless design and was intended as an anti-tank weapon for the infantry. The M/42 used a 20mm solid projectile. The huge case had a blowout vent in the base, and gas venting to the rear combined with the muzzle brake to reduce recoil. A tolerable level of recoil was gained at the expense of a large backblast caused by firing a solid projectile. The backblast was a hazard to the assistant gunner and potentially lethal to anyone to the rear of the weapon. The weapon was outclassed in less than two years. However, the manufacturing and cartridge design experience lead Carl Gustaf to the recoilless 84mm calibre rifle, introduced in 1946 and still in use today.

SPECIFICATION	
MANUFACTURER	Carl Gustaf
CALIBRE	20 x 180R
MAGAZINE CAPACITY	Single shot
ACTION	Semi-recoilless
TOTAL LENGTH	1400mm/55.11in
BARREL LENGTH	1050mm/41.33in
WEIGHT UNLOADED	11.2kg/24.69lb

Carl Gustaf M63 sniper

SPECIFICATION	
MANUFACTURER	Carl Gustaf
CALIBRE	7.62 x 51mm
MAGAZINE CAPACITY	5
ACTION	Bolt action
TOTAL LENGTH	1,028mm/40.5in
BARREL LENGTH	510mm/20.1in
WEIGHT UNLOADED	4.19kg/9.25lb

The commercial variant of the M1896 rifle was the M63, fielded in the late 1950s. Many rifles were converted to sporting use, and some were built up as sniper rifles. The action, made of excellent Swedish steel, was strong enough to use the 7.62mm NATO cartridge, so early efforts at developing a sniper rifle in 7.62mm were focused on the Krag rifles at hand, and the Carl Gustaf M63 sniper was produced. Carl Gustaf was amalgamated with Husqvarna Waffenfabrik just before Sweden adopted the AK4, and once enough sniper-variant AK4s were on hand, Sweden dropped the M63 and earlier rifles. The Model 63 was in service from the late 1950s until the early to mid 1960s.

AK4

SPECIFICATION	
MANUFACTURER	Husqvarna, Carl Gustaf
CALIBRE	7.62mm NATO
MAGAZINE CAPACITY	20
ACTION	Roller delayed blowback
TOTAL LENGTH	1,020mm/40.15in
BARREL LENGTH	450mm/17.7in
WEIGHT UNLOADED	4.39kg/9.68lb

The Automatkarbin 4 (AK4) was the Swedish version of the Heckler & Koch G3, built under licence in Sweden. Adopted when 7.62mm rifles were still in their ascendancy, they were replaced twenty years later by 5.56mm rifles. However, all useable AK4 rifles were overhauled and rebuilt, gaining rails for optical sights and placed in storage for Home Guard use in an emergency. The AK4 was in service from 1965 to 1985 with the regular army, and was then replaced by the Automatkarbin 5 (AK5). It has been maintained as a reserve rifle.

Ljungman AG42B

SPECIFICATION	
MANUFACTURER	Husqvarna
CALIBRE	6.5 x 55mm
MAGAZINE CAPACITY	10
ACTION	Gas operated
TOTAL LENGTH	1,205mm/47.45in
BARREL LENGTH	622mm/24.5in
WEIGHT UNLOADED	4.64kg/10.25lb

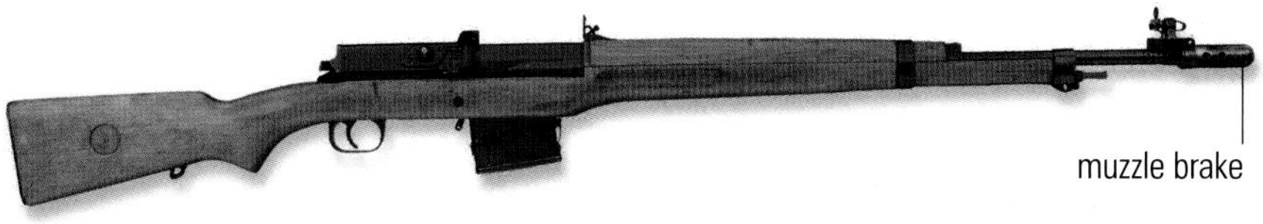

Production of the Ljungman was undertaken at the Husqvarna factory to avoid interfering with current-issue rifle production during World War II. The Ljungman uses a direct-impingement gas system, doing away with a piston or operating rod. It can be hazardous to the untrained. If the bolt is locked back, the feedway is open to finger access. If a user trips the bolt catch with a finger in the bolt path, a serious injury can occur. During the war the Ljungman was issued to rifle squads to increase firepower. The tooling was sold to Egypt in 1954. Despite being out of production and replaced in line units by the AK4, the Ljungman remained in Swedish reserves until the early 1970s.

AK5

SPECIFICATION	
MANUFACTURER	FFV
CALIBRE	5.56 x 45mm
MAGAZINE CAPACITY	30
ACTION	Gas operated
TOTAL LENGTH	1,007mm/39.65in
BARREL LENGTH	460mm/18.1in
WEIGHT UNLOADED	3.90kg/8.6lb

When the AK4 began to show its age, and Sweden faced the shift to 5.56mm calibre, rifle trials were instituted in order to find a new rifle. The winner was the FN FNC, which Sweden modified. The trigger guard and cocking handle were made larger, to accommodate mittens, and the fore end was given cross-hatched grooves. As with the AK4, Sweden acquired licensing to build the rifles itself. Production and issue began in 1985, and the AK5 is the present standard-issue rifle of the Swedish Defence Forces.

Czech Republic

After World War I, the new country of Czechoslovakia made and sold Mausers. After invading in 1939, Germany took over arms production. When World War II ended in 1945, the country became a Soviet ally and the Czech firearms industry mostly produced clones of the various Kalashnikovs.

Mauser VZ24

The Mauser VZ24 is basically a Kar 98k, but with slightly different fittings and furniture. The standard infantry rifle of Czechoslovakia, it was also an export item, competing successfully with FN for the world market. Upon their arrival in the spring of 1939, German supervisors simply changed the acceptance stamps and continued production to the end of the war. The Mauser VZ24 was produced between 1924 and 1945.

SPECIFICATION	
MANUFACTURER	CZ Brno
CALIBRE	7.92 x 57mm
MAGAZINE CAPACITY	5
ACTION	Bolt action
TOTAL LENGTH	1,100mm/43.3in
BARREL LENGTH	589mm/23.2in
WEIGHT UNLOADED	4.07kg/8.98lb

Mauser G33/40

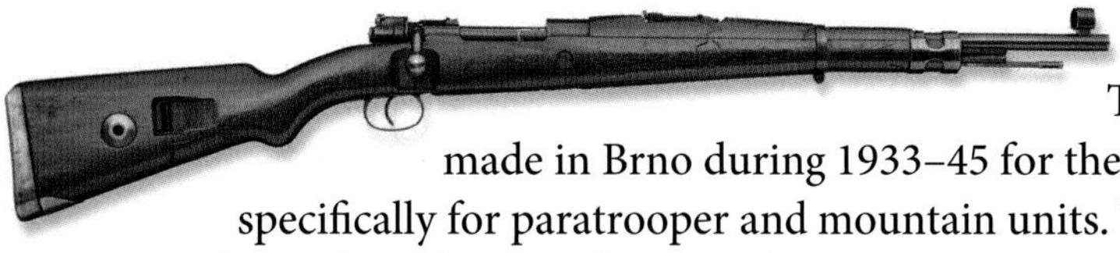

The G33/40 was made in Brno during 1933–45 for the German Army, specifically for paratrooper and mountain units. The receiver was extensively machined in an effort to reduce weight, the lightness somewhat offset by the steel reinforcing plate bolted to the buttstock. The idea was to produce as light and compact a rifle as possible without giving up durability. After the war, hunters stripped them down to build custom rifles for hunting.

SPECIFICATION	
MANUFACTURER	CZ Brno
CALIBRE	7.92 x 57mm
MAGAZINE CAPACITY	5
ACTION	Bolt action
TOTAL LENGTH	993mm/39.1in
BARREL LENGTH	490mm/19.29in
WEIGHT UNLOADED	3.58kg/7.9lb

Mauser 98k

Called a carbine when first developed (because it was shorter than the then-standard Gew98 rifle by nearly 200mm/8in), the Mauser 98k was built in all German-occupied countries that had a factory set up to build Mauser-type rifles. Germany aimed to produce as many recognizable Mauser rifles as possible for use in the war. During 1939–45, CZ Brno took part in this project. After the war, no army wanted bolt-action rifles, and Brno turned to the hunting rifle market, to which the 98k action was well-suited.

SPECIFICATION	
MANUFACTURER	CZ Brno
CALIBRE	7.92 x 57mm
MAGAZINE CAPACITY	5
ACTION	Bolt action
TOTAL LENGTH	1,107mm/43.6in
BARREL LENGTH	599mm/23.6in
WEIGHT UNLOADED	3.62kg/8.6lb

VZ52

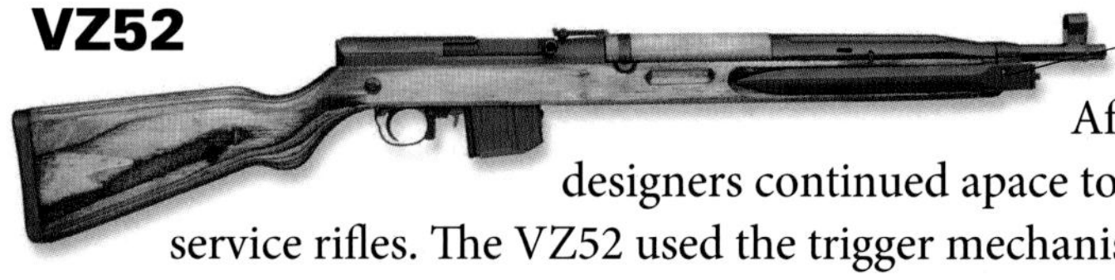

After World War II, designers continued apace to produce semi-auto service rifles. The VZ52 used the trigger mechanism of the Garand, the gas system of the Mkb42W and a box magazine designed in Czechoslovakia but similar to the German K43. Production of the VZ52 began in 1952 and continued to the early 1960s until AK production was great enough to replace it. The VZ52/57 was the same rifle chambered in the Soviet M43; large numbers were exported to aid "liberation fronts" around the world.

SPECIFICATION	
MANUFACTURER	CZ Brno
CALIBRE	7.62 x 45mm
MAGAZINE CAPACITY	10
ACTION	Gas operated/tilting bolt
TOTAL LENGTH	1,000mm/39.37in
BARREL LENGTH	525mm/20.66in
WEIGHT UNLOADED	4.44kg/9.8lb

VZ58

SPECIFICATION
MANUFACTURER CZ Brno
CALIBRE 7.62 x 39mm
MAGAZINE CAPACITY 30
ACTION Gas operated/pivoting latch
TOTAL LENGTH 838mm/33in
BARREL LENGTH 401mm/15.8in
WEIGHT UNLOADED 3.31kg/7.3lb

At first glance the VZ58 appears to be an AK clone. Internally it is quite different, as the firing pin is a striker, not a hammer-struck pin. The VZ58 uses a pivoting locking block, attached to the bolt, to lock the action when fired. After the calibre was changed to that of the Soviet Union, the Czech-produced VZ58 was chambered in the Soviet M43, 7.62 x 39mm cartridge. Around a half kilo (1lb) lighter than most AKs, the recoil of the VZ58 must have been considerable in full-auto fire. Production began in 1958 and continued to the mid-1970s.

ZH29

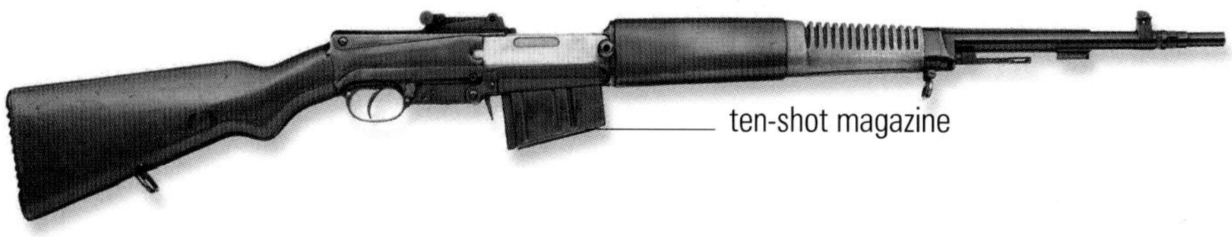

SPECIFICATION
MANUFACTURER Zbrojovka Brno, s.r.o
CALIBRE 7.92 x 57mm
MAGAZINE CAPACITY 5, 10 or 25-round magazines
ACTION Gas operated/tilting bolt
TOTAL LENGTH 1,156mm/45.5in
BARREL LENGTH 546mm/21.5in
WEIGHT UNLOADED 4.53kg/10lb

Not to be left behind by the most advanced armies, Czechoslovakia designed and experimented with semi-automatic rifles. Designed by Emmanuel Holek, the ZH29 was not only a successful semi-automatic rifle, but also used box magazines. The design found limited interest, but was tested by the USA at the Aberdeen Proving Ground in .276 Pedersen calibre. The worldwide Depression and World War II turned it into a museum piece. Manufactured only as a prototype and trial rifle and never adopted for service use, it was made from the mid-1920s to the early 1930s. Although its appearance seemed odd, before the Depression the ZH29 was the epitome of a modern rifle. Had it been accepted in any number, the ZH29 might well have been the first general-issue semi-automatic rifle, beating the Garand by a decade.

CZ 805 BREN

SPECIFICATION
MANUFACTURER Zbrojovka Brno, s.r.o
CALIBRE 5.56mm NATO or 7.62x39mm
MAGAZINE CAPACITY 30
ACTION Gas operated
TOTAL LENGTH 930mm/36.6in
BARREL LENGTH 360mm/14in
WEIGHT UNLOADED 3.6kg/7.9lb

The 805 BREN was designed as a modular piston-operated selective-fire rifle. It is specifically built to switch between calibres and magazine systems quickly and easily. The barrel/piston system can be swapped out with just six screws. Drive out one pin to change the bolt face and the rifle can shoot a range of different cartridges. Pop two pins and you can switch between CZ's proprietary magazines and STANAG magazines.

Poland

After World War I, newly independent Poland began production for its own needs right away. Production continued under German and then Soviet control. Production under Germany consisted of the speeded-up manufacture of Mauser rifles. Under the Soviets the emphasis was on manufacturing AKs.

Maroszek WZ35 A/T

SPECIFICATION	
MANUFACTURER	Panstwowa Fabryka
CALIBRE	7.92 x 107mm
MAGAZINE CAPACITY	4
ACTION	Bolt action
TOTAL LENGTH	1,760mm/69.29in
BARREL LENGTH	1,200mm/47.24in
WEIGHT UNLOADED	9.5kg/20.94lb

Using a high-velocity hard-cored bullet, this anti-tank rifle could penetrate the light armour found on tanks at the beginning of World War II – at 100m/s/328ft/s it could penetrate about 30mm/1in of armour. The high pressure and velocity put great stress on the rifle, which had a frequent maintenance/ barrel replacement schedule of less than a thousand rounds. The Maroszek was used from 1935 until Poland was invaded in 1939. Soon after, armour development left all such rifles useless against armoured vehicles.

Mauser G98A/40

The G98A/40 was produced from 1930 to 1939 for Poland, and from 1939 to 1944 for the Germans. It was built as a copy of the short rifles many countries adopted at the time, such as the VZ-Brno 24, on Mauser-type receivers. The G98A/40 was similar to the VZ24 but designed and produced independently. Once Germany invaded in 1939, production continued for German use. When the Soviets arrived, production stopped.

SPECIFICATION	
MANUFACTURER	FB Radom
CALIBRE	7.92 x 57mm
MAGAZINE CAPACITY	5
ACTION	Bolt action
TOTAL LENGTH	1,102mm/43.4in
BARREL LENGTH	599mm/23.6in
WEIGHT UNLOADED	4.09kg/9.02lb

PMK-MS

The PMK-MS is simply the updated Soviet AK, with a sheet-metal receiver and under-folding stock instead of the fixed stock and forged receiver of the original. It was made in volume for use by Polish infantry and motorized infantry units that were to follow the East German and Soviet armoured divisions on an anticipated invasion of Western Europe. The PMK-MS was made from the early 1960s until the AK-74 variants came on line in the 1970s, and used as reserve weapons until the mid-1980s.

SPECIFICATION	
MANUFACTURER	FB Radom
CALIBRE	7.62 x 39mm
MAGAZINE CAPACITY	30
ACTION	Gas operated/rotating bolt
TOTAL LENGTH	870mm/34.25in
BARREL LENGTH	415mm/16.33in
WEIGHT UNLOADED	3.14kg/6.92lb

KA wz/88 Tantal

The KA wz/88 Tantal was a Polish-designed improvement of the AK-74S, with a three-shot burst setting and a side-folding stock of the East German heavy-gauge wire design. It was meant both as a Polish Army

SPECIFICATION	
MANUFACTURER	FB Radom
CALIBRE	5.45 x 39mm, 5.56 x 45mm
MAGAZINE CAPACITY	30
ACTION	Gas operated/rotating bolt
TOTAL LENGTH	943mm/37.1in
BARREL LENGTH	423mm/16.65in
WEIGHT UNLOADED	3.4kg/7.49lb

rifle and as an export item. While similar, the two cartridges in which it is available are not a close enough match to use the same magazines, and the receivers are not identical either. The selector is on the left side (convenient for a right-handed user's thumb), and the sights have tritium night-sight inserts, which glow in the dark. The KA wz/88 Tantal was produced between 1988 and 1997, when it was replaced by an improved model called the Beryl.

Wz/96 Beryl

Upon joining NATO, Poland needed a rifle that would use NATO ammunition; the wz/96 could take both SS109 and M193 ammunition. The Radom arsenal updated the Tantal/Onyks line with a new stock, new furniture, an optical sight rail and a new grenade launcher. It was also made in a short-barrel variant. Accurate and reliable, the rifle was made to endure tough environmental conditions. Production of the Beryl began in 1997 and continues to the present day.

SPECIFICATION	
MANUFACTURER	FB Radom
CALIBRE	5.56 x 45mm
MAGAZINE CAPACITY	30
ACTION	Gas operated/rotating bolt
TOTAL LENGTH	943mm/37.1in
BARREL LENGTH	457mm/18in
WEIGHT UNLOADED	3.89kg/8.59lb

FB MSBS Grot C

This new rifle takes its name from the Modular Firearm System "Spearhead" (MSBS) and Home Army commander, General Stefan "Grot" Rowecki. The modularity of this rifle allows parts to be easily swapped between rifles and light machine guns. Barrel changes are also a big plus, allowing the user to swap between lengths to allow use as either a carbine or a designated marksman rifle. It is fully ambidextrous, uses STANAG magazines, and is Poland's first rifle that is completely compliant with NATO standards.

SPECIFICATION	
MANUFACTURER	FB Radom
CALIBRE	5.56mm NATO
MAGAZINE CAPACITY	30
ACTION	Gas operated
TOTAL LENGTH	980mm/39in
BARREL LENGTH	508mm/20in
WEIGHT UNLOADED	3.7kg/8.2lb

Croatia

Croatia became a nation after the break-up of Yugoslavia. With great experience in arms manufacture and a need for defence owing to the tensions in the Balkans, Croatia makes small arms for its own use and for export. Croatia is now the third largest exporter of firearms to the United States.

APS 95

SPECIFICATION	
MANUFACTURER	RH-Alan
CALIBRE	5.56 x 45mm
MAGAZINE CAPACITY	35
ACTION	Gas operated/rotating bolt
TOTAL LENGTH	980mm/38.5in
BARREL LENGTH	450mm/17.7in
WEIGHT UNLOADED	3.8kg/8.37lb

The APS 95 was developed to replace the ageing Yugoslavian-made M70 rifles. It is a mechanical if not cosmetic licensed copy of the Israeli Galil but with an optical sight of 1.5x incorporated into the carrying handle. The carrying handle is almost as large as that of the French FAMAS, extending from the rear of the receiver cover to the receiver over the chamber. Although the basic AK system is old, the APS 95 has remained in production since 1995 and is unlikely to be replaced in the near future.

HS Produkt VHS

SPECIFICATION

MANUFACTURER HS Produkt
CALIBRE 5.56mm NATO
MAGAZINE CAPACITY 30
ACTION Gas operated
TOTAL LENGTH 765mm/30.1in
BARREL LENGTH 500mm/19.7in
WEIGHT UNLOADED 3.4kg/7.5lb

Designed to meet NATO standards, the VHS entered Croatian service in 2008. The rifle's body is made of high-impact polymer in a monoblock design and a bullpup configuration, which locates the magazine behind the trigger for a shorter overall rifle. Initially designed to accept STANAG magazines, this was quickly changed to G36 magazines because Croatia had more of those on hand. Slight design changes were made in 2013 that included a different selector switch, adjustable buttstock, and an ambidextrous ejection system.

South Africa

As both a Dutch and British colony, and as an independent nation, South Africa has experienced many conflicts throughout its history. Given the wide open spaces and the need for rifles for hunting and defence, South Africans have a well-earned reputation as top marksmen.

R4

SPECIFICATION

MANUFACTURER Lyttelton Eng Co.
CALIBRE 5.56 x 45mm
MAGAZINE CAPACITY 35
ACTION Gas operated
TOTAL LENGTH 979mm/38.55in
BARREL LENGTH 460mm/18.1in
WEIGHT UNLOADED 4.20kg/9.26lb

Basically a Galil with minor changes owing to South African manufacturing necessities, the R4 was reliable, if heavy for its power. However, police and military units sometimes found the 5.56mm cartridge to be lacking, especially when attempting to penetrate the tough bush of South Africa. They therefore kept many FALs in reserve for the extra power the 7.62mm cartridge provided. Manufacture of the R4 began in 1982 and continues to the present day.

Mauser Model 1896

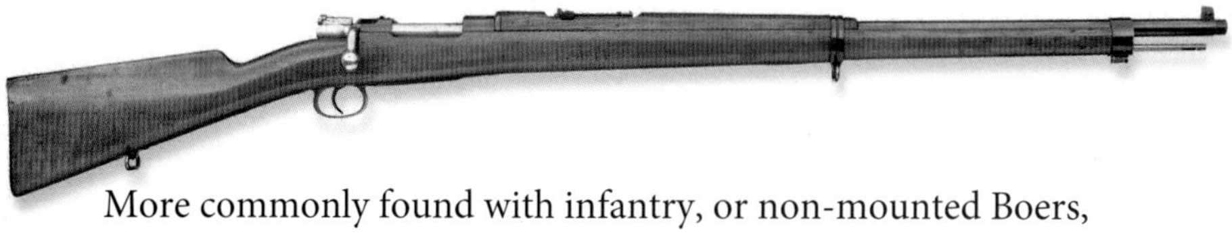

SPECIFICATION

MANUFACTURER Mauser, Oberndorf
CALIBRE 7 x 57mm
MAGAZINE CAPACITY 5
ACTION Bolt action
TOTAL LENGTH 1,250mm/49.2in
BARREL LENGTH 740mm/29.15in
WEIGHT UNLOADED 3.62kg/8lb

More commonly found with infantry, or non-mounted Boers, the Mauser Mod 1898 was handy and very accurate. The 7 x 57mm cartridge was relatively mild in recoil, accurate, and a suitable hunting cartridge for all but the largest game. During the Boer War (1899–1902), British troops found out just how useful the clip-charging feature of the Mauser could be. With Boer marksmen firing at high rates of speed, the British often found themselves at a severe disadvantage. The rifle was in service from 1896 to the mid-20th century.

Mauser Mod 1896 carbine

Commonly smuggled into South Africa during the Boer War, the Mauser Mod 1896 carbine was a constant companion to the mounted Boer and served until the middle of the 20th century. It was the same as the rifle but had a shorter 51cm/20in barrel. Typically, carbines had sling swivels on the side of the stock as well as a saddle loop on the rear sling swivel plate. The rifle could be carried by the trooper on his back or in a saddle loop hung off the saddlehorn.

SPECIFICATION

MANUFACTURER Mauser, Oberndorf
CALIBRE 7 x 57mm
MAGAZINE CAPACITY 5
ACTION Bolt action
TOTAL LENGTH 944mm/37.2in
BARREL LENGTH 434mm/17.1in
WEIGHT UNLOADED 3.28kg/7.25lb

Serbia

The Balkans have been a flashpoint and source of conflict for centuries. Serbia was once part of the Austro-Hungarian Empire and for a while part of Yugoslavia. Starting with basic Mauser bolt actions and Kalashnikovs, the Yugoslavian arms industry produced an array of military and sporting products. It also extended the Kalashnikov action to include calibres its designer would not have thought of.

Mauser Koka Model 1884

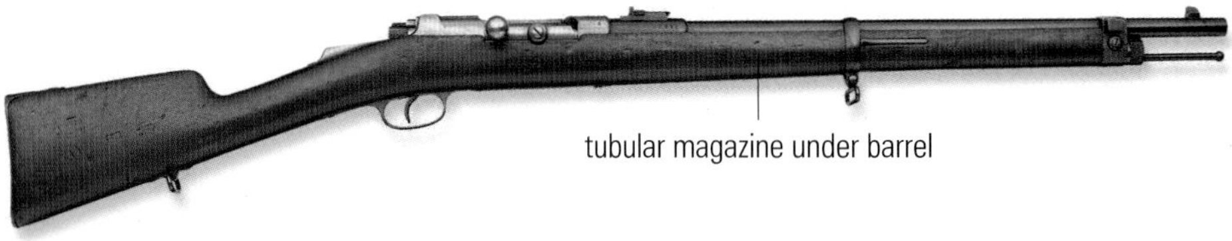

Basically a Gew 71/84 built for Serbia, the Koka had a tubular magazine similar to the German Kropatschek model, all in keeping with a transitional cavalry rifle/carbine of the late 19th century. Within a few years all such designs would be obsolete. Following advances in bullet construction and shape, smokeless powder and stronger actions, any country wishing to remain at the forefront of weapons development found it necessary to adopt these new technologies. The Koka was in service in the Serbian armed forces from 1884 to 1899.

SPECIFICATION

MANUFACTURER Mauser, Oberndorf
CALIBRE 10.15mm x 63R
MAGAZINE CAPACITY 5
ACTION Bolt action
TOTAL LENGTH 955mm/37.6in
BARREL LENGTH 465mm/18.3in
WEIGHT UNLOADED 3.75kg/8.27lb

Cavalry issue
The Koka is generally considered a cavalry-issue carbine, as there is no provision for mounting a bayonet, while the artillery carbines can take a bayonet.

Mauser Model 1910

With the purchase of the MM 1910, Serbia was as modern as anyone in Europe, and had a rifle fully capable of serving in any future war the Empire might call them up for. The calibre was also state-of-the-art for the time and popular around the world for good reason. That it was the standard export model of Mauser did not detract from its excellence. Within a few years the rifles and soldiers would be called up and sent off to the front. It was in service from 1910 to 1918. After that, there was no Austro-Hungarian Empire and Serbia was pretty much on its own.

SPECIFICATION

MANUFACTURER Mauser, Oberndorf
CALIBRE 7 x 57mm
MAGAZINE CAPACITY 5
ACTION Bolt action
TOTAL LENGTH 1,238mm/48.75in
BARREL LENGTH 740mm/29.15in
WEIGHT UNLOADED 4.11kg/9.06lb

Mauser Model 1924

SPECIFICATION

MANUFACTURER FN & CZ Brno
CALIBRE 7.92 x 57mm
MAGAZINE CAPACITY 5
ACTION Bolt action
TOTAL LENGTH 1,098mm/43.25in
BARREL LENGTH 590mm/23.25in
WEIGHT UNLOADED 4.14kg/9.13lb

The Mauser Model 1924 was the standard export model of Mauser design between the wars. The "short" rifle was universally popular. Yugoslavia purchased large numbers to replace the miscellaneous collection of rifles it possessed as a legacy of the Austro-Hungarian Empire and World War I. The Model 1924 was purchased in the late 1920s and remained in service to 1945. It was used in resistance to German occupation 1941–1945.

M59/66

SPECIFICATION

MANUFACTURER Zastava
CALIBRE 7.62 x 39mm
MAGAZINE CAPACITY 10
ACTION Gas operated
TOTAL LENGTH 1,120mm/44.1in
BARREL LENGTH 519mm/20.45in
WEIGHT UNLOADED 4.01kg/8.85lb

The M59/66 was the SKS (a Russian carbine) with a twist, as the flash hider was also a grenade launcher. It was made as a reserve carbine, semi-automatic only, for the emergency inventory. Since there was no emergency, it became common on the surplus market. Manufacture began in 1959, and the rifles were updated with new barrels and grenade launchers from 1966. It remained in service until the late 1970s.

M70AB2

SPECIFICATION

MANUFACTURER Zastava
CALIBRE 7.62 x 39mm
MAGAZINE CAPACITY 30
ACTION Gas operated
TOTAL LENGTH 877mm/34.55in
BARREL LENGTH 415mm/16.35in
WEIGHT UNLOADED 3.58kg/7.9lb

The M70AB2 was the modernized AK, the AKM, with a sheet-metal receiver and folding stock. It was manufactured both for use in the Yugoslavian Army and as an export item, of which a number in semi-automatic only form ended up in the United States. It was manufactured from the early 1960s to 1990s. The parts were supplied to Iraq for assembly there as the Iraqi issue rifle.

M77B1

SPECIFICATION

MANUFACTURER Zastava
CALIBRE 7.62mm NATO
MAGAZINE CAPACITY 10
ACTION Gas operated
TOTAL LENGTH 1,135mm/44.7in
BARREL LENGTH 550mm/21.65in
WEIGHT UNLOADED 4.25kg/9.37lb

The M77B1 was a Kalashnikov extended to take the .308/7.62mm NATO cartridge. It was also made in 7.92 x 57mm where the calibre would sell better. The AK action is at its limit of cartridge size and durability when stretched to take the high-pressure 7.62mm NATO round, and recoil is heavy even given the rifle's weight. Produced between 1976 and the 1990s, it sold badly; buyers preferred rifles tailored to the NATO round.

M21

SPECIFICATION

MANUFACTURER Zastava Arms
CALIBRE 5.56mm NATO
MAGAZINE CAPACITY 30
ACTION Gas operated
TOTAL LENGTH 1,000mm/39in
BARREL LENGTH 460mm/18in
WEIGHT UNLOADED 4.1kg/9.1lb

Based on the Kalashnikov design, the Zastava M21 has a stamped metal receiver and was designed to be a modular weapon that could be configured for different tasks. Equipped with conventional iron sights, the M21 is available with the standard Kalashnikov-style side mount for optics or the more versatile option of Picatinny rail. A 40mm underbarrel grenade launcher can also be attached to the M21.

SPECIFICATION

MANUFACTURER Zastava Arms
CALIBRE 6.5 Grendel or 7.62x39mm
MAGAZINE CAPACITY 20, 25 or 30
ACTION Gas operated
TOTAL LENGTH 910mm/35.8in
BARREL LENGTH 415mm/16.3in
WEIGHT UNLOADED 3.8kg/8.3lb

M19

Adopted in 2022, the M19 is also a modular weapon similar to the M21. One of the biggest differences between the two is that the M19 has a cross-latch on the receiver that allows the user to easily switch barrels between those chambered in 6.5 Grendel and 7.62x39mm without the need for tools or disassembly. This allows the user to have one firearm that is capable of fulfilling multiple roles without the hassle of needing more than one rifle.

Hungary

From part of the Austro-Hungarian Empire to an independent country, to an ally of Germany and then the USSR, Hungary is now charting its own course once again. During much of its history, Hungary had little choice in what it made or fielded. The cost of a modern army and the need for NATO interoperability have severely restricted Hungarian choices in small arms design and issue in the current era.

Model 35

A Mannlicher-magazined bolt-action rifle, chambered for the rimmed 8mm Hungarian cartridge, the Model 35 had a short service life. It was designed and built in Hungary for use by the Hungarian Army. While sturdy and reliable, its production was questionable since Europe and most of the rest of the world was awash in Mauser rifles in the 1930s. After Germany occupied Hungary in 1944, the Model 35 was redesigned and the designation changed to G98/40. It was then issued as an alternate German rifle. The Model 35 was in production only from 1935 to 1942 but was used by Hungarian units until 1945.

SPECIFICATION

MANUFACTURER Danuvia Arms Works
CALIBRE 8 x 56mm M31
MAGAZINE CAPACITY 5
ACTION Bolt action
TOTAL LENGTH 1,107mm/43.6in
BARREL LENGTH 599mm/23.6in
WEIGHT UNLOADED 4.03kg/8.9lb

Mannlicher G98/40

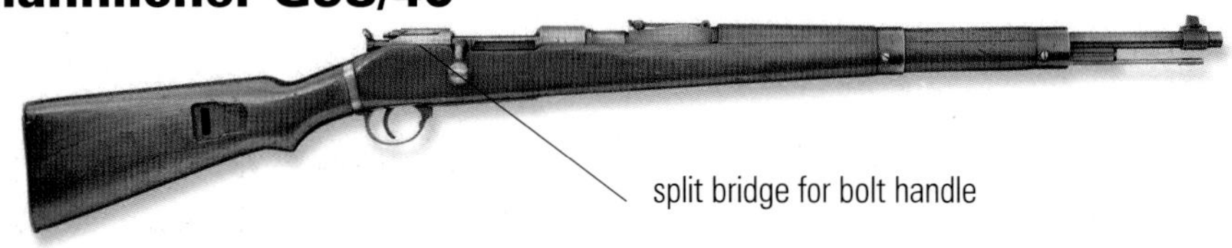

The Mannlicher G98/40 was known as the Model 43 in Hungarian service. From a Mannlicher-magazine bolt action, the rifle was modified to take a Mauser-style magazine, and the calibre changed from 8 x 56 to 7.92 x 57mm. These modifications enabled it to be issued as an alternative rifle in German units during World War II. While not handsome, the action was strong enough for the task. Production of the new rifle lasted from 1943 to 1945.

SPECIFICATION

MANUFACTURER Danuvia Arms Works
CALIBRE 7.92 x 57mm
MAGAZINE CAPACITY 5
ACTION Bolt action
TOTAL LENGTH 1,107mm/43.6in
BARREL LENGTH 599mm/23.6in
WEIGHT UNLOADED 4.03kg/8.9lb

AMD-65

The distinctive sheet-metal hand guard and forward-angled front grip of the Automata Módosított Deszant (AMD-65) make it stand out in any photo of troops in the field. The intention was to keep the firer's hand away from the heat from the barrel, created by extensive shooting. This was a common problem in all AK-47 rifles. Made both with wooden and steel wire folding stock, the mild recoil of the M43 cartridge, combined with the control the front grip provides, makes the flimsy wire stock sufficient to the task. It was introduced in 1965 and remained in use until the early 1990s.

SPECIFICATION

MANUFACTURER Fégyver es Gépgyár (FEG)
CALIBRE 7.62 x 39mm
MAGAZINE CAPACITY 30
ACTION Gas operated/rotating bolt
TOTAL LENGTH 870mm/34.25in
BARREL LENGTH 415mm/16.34in
WEIGHT UNLOADED 4.85kg/10.7lb

AMM

AMM is the local designation given to the AK-63 in military use in Hungary. Visually very similar to the AMD-65, the main differences are in the heat shield and the forward grip. The Hungarian Defense Ministry requested FEG come up with a new AKM-style design, and the AMM was adopted in 1977 because it was less expensive to build than the AMD-65.

SPECIFICATION

MANUFACTURER Fegyver és Gépgyár (FEG)
CALIBRE 7.62 x 39mm
MAGAZINE CAPACITY 10, 20, 30, 40, 75 or 100
ACTION Gas operated
TOTAL LENGTH 880mm/34.6in
BARREL LENGTH 415mm/16.3in
WEIGHT UNLOADED 3.6kg/7.9lb

AMP-69, Grenade-launching

SPECIFICATION

MANUFACTURER FEG
CALIBRE 7.62 x 39mm
MAGAZINE CAPACITY 5 or 30
ACTION Gas operated/rotating bolt
TOTAL LENGTH 914mm/36in
BARREL LENGTH 444mm/17.5in
WEIGHT UNLOADED 5.44kg/12lb

Fitted with a grenade-launching muzzle device, and with an adjustable sight for ranging and aiming, the AMP-69 was designed for launching grenades. Given the proliferation of the RPG and its much more effective (and further-ranging) warhead, its use was somewhat limited. It could, however, use standard M43 service ammunition, so an assigned grenadier could contribute to the firepower of a small unit. The AMP-69 was first issued in 1969, and although it was gradually replaced by the AK-74 from the early 1980s, it remained in reserve service until the early 1990s.

Lithuania

Achieving independence in 1918, Lithuania struggled between the wars to remain free from both the USSR and Poland. Occupied again in 1939, first by the USSR, then Germany, and again by the USSR, Lithuania did not regain independence until 1990. Since then, Lithuania has become a member of NATO and produces high-quality ammunition that is NATO-accepted.

Mauser FN 1924

SPECIFICATION

MANUFACTURER FN, Liège
CALIBRE 7.92 x 57mm
MAGAZINE CAPACITY 5
ACTION Bolt action
TOTAL LENGTH 1,089mm/42.9in
BARREL LENGTH 591mm/23.25in
WEIGHT UNLOADED 3.80kg/8.4lb

The Mauser FN 1924 was the standard FN export short rifle that achieved huge sales in the 1920s and 1930s. Other than the Lithuanian crest and inspectors' marks, it was like any other 1924 short rifle. The FN 1924 was purchased first in 1924 and used until the initial occupation by Germany in 1939.

Lithuanian funded rifles

Many FN 1924 rifles are marked "Ginklu Fondas" on the receiver, which indicates they were purchased with funds donated by the Lithuanian people in 1937 to equip the army.

AKM

SPECIFICATION

MANUFACTURER Unk
CALIBRE 7.62 x 39mm
MAGAZINE CAPACITY 30
ACTION Gas-operated/rotating bolt
TOTAL LENGTH 877mm/34.55in
BARREL LENGTH 415mm/16.35in
WEIGHT UNLOADED 3.82kg/8.42lb

As a Soviet republic from 1944 to 1991, Lithuania produced the standard Soviet weapon, the Automat Kalashnikova Modernized (AKM) with sheet-metal receiver; indistinguishable from Soviet-produced rifles except for the inspectors' marks. When Lithuania became independent in 1991 and joined NATO and the EU, it began manufacturing new 5.56mm variants of its AK rifles, designated the AK-4MT. While building a NATO-compatible force, Lithuania is purchasing new equipment, although it also produces its own submachine gun as well as NATO-accepted 5.56mm and 7.62 x 51mm ammunition.

HK G36

SPECIFICATION

MANUFACTURER Heckler & Koch
CALIBRE 5.56 x 45mm
MAGAZINE CAPACITY 30
ACTION Gas-operated
TOTAL LENGTH 998mm/39.2in
BARREL LENGTH 480mm/18.8in
WEIGHT UNLOADED 3.6kg/7.93lb

The G36 was adopted by Lithuania's armed forces in 2017 as their standard service rifle. It is also used by their Special Operations Forces. The G36 is lighter than the G3 and uses a variant of the short-stroke gas system of the Armalite AR-18. To date, the country has spent at least 40 million US dollars in acquiring these rifles, with the latest batch slated for issue to the Lithuanian Riflemen's Union.

Greece

Independent from the Ottoman Empire since 1831, Greece spent much of the 19th century struggling with its neighbours. The Balkans, then as now, were a source of international friction. At the dawn of the 20th century, Greece needed modern rifles with which to equip its army. Lacking an industrial base, Greece set out to purchase rifles from foreign manufacturers. Its first choices were perhaps more expensive than they should have been, but later models were more in line with contemporary designs and cost.

FN M1930

The new short rifle, wisely selected and purchased by Greece, was a carbine by pre-World War I standards. The M1930 was the rifle all the world was adopting: the Mauser/FN/98k Model of 1924. Greece simply purchased standard FN Model 1924 rifles, which were marked for the use of the Greek forces and renamed them the M1930. The rifle was in use from 1930 to the early 1950s, when it was replaced by the M1 Garand, which had served the Americans through World War II.

SPECIFICATION	
MANUFACTURER	FN, Liège
CALIBRE	7.92 x 57mm
MAGAZINE CAPACITY	5
ACTION	Bolt action
TOTAL LENGTH	1,099mm/43.3in
BARREL LENGTH	589mm/23.2in
WEIGHT UNLOADED	3.85kg/8.5lb

Mannlicher-Shoenauer Model

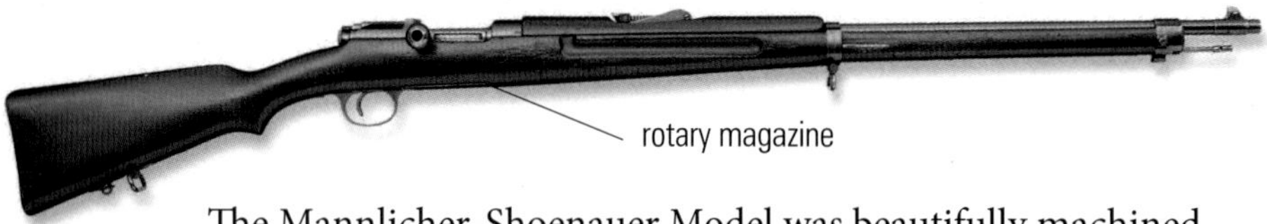

The Mannlicher-Shoenauer Model was beautifully machined, very smooth and costly as a military weapon. The rotary magazine of the Mannlicher-Shoenauer action functioned so well that shooters and hunters sought it out for building expensive rifles. Greece bought M-S models as a combat arm, a role for which they were not well suited. Many were given up as war reparations after World War I and replaced by a miscellaneous collection of Austrian Mannlichers and Turkish Mausers. Purchased in 1903, this rifle remained in service until 1918.

SPECIFICATION	
MANUFACTURER	Steyr
CALIBRE	6.5 x 54mm
MAGAZINE CAPACITY	5
ACTION	Bolt action
TOTAL LENGTH	1,227mm/48.3in
BARREL LENGTH	724mm/28.5in
WEIGHT UNLOADED	3.76kg/8.31lb

Mannlicher-Shoenauer M1903 carbine

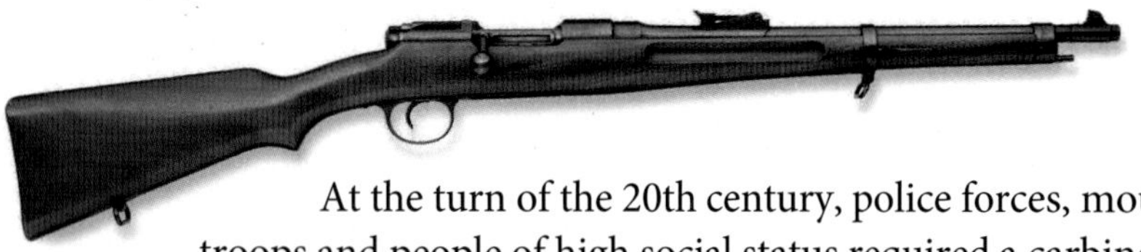

At the turn of the 20th century, police forces, mounted troops and people of high social status required a carbine. The police and mounted troops needed carbines for their short length and lighter weight than a rifle. Civilians seeking to enhance their status acquired carbines because they were less common than the rifle. Thus Greece purchased Mannlicher-Shoenauer (M-S) carbines as well as the rifles. The only difference between M-S rifles and carbines was the barrel and stock (forearm) length. The M-S M1903, like the M-S rifle, was in service from 1903 to 1918. It cost at least twice as much as any Mauser rifle Greece could have purchased.

SPECIFICATION	
MANUFACTURER	Steyr
CALIBRE	6.5 x 54mm
MAGAZINE CAPACITY	5
ACTION	Bolt action
TOTAL LENGTH	1023mm/40.3in
BARREL LENGTH	520mm/20.5in
WEIGHT UNLOADED	3.62kg/8lb

Final Mannilicher
The 1903 was the final design by Ferdinand Ritter von Mannlicher.

Finland

Having fought for independence from Russia at the time of the 1917 Revolution, Finland naturally used Russian-pattern small arms. The Finns then began to produce their own weapons. Finnish-built and overhauled small arms tended to be better-fitted and finished than their Soviet counterparts.

SPECIFICATION

MANUFACTURER Lithgow
CALIBRE 5.56 x 45mm
MAGAZINE CAPACITY 30
ACTION Gas operated/tilting lock
TOTAL LENGTH 710mm/27.95in
BARREL LENGTH 420mm/16.5in
WEIGHT UNLOADED 3.3kg/7.27lb

Valmet M-82

The Valmet M-82 was an M-76 in a bullpup polymer shell, with the sights elevated to line up with the shooter's eye. It was an export item with almost no sales, and suffered from all the problems of an AK design in a bullpup shell: the stock is removed and the buttplate located on the rear of the receiver. The pistol grip goes in front of the magazine. However, the AK safety on a bullpup is out of sight and almost unreachable for the shooter. The M82 had a short production period, from 1978 to 1986.

SPECIFICATION

MANUFACTURER Sako
CALIBRE 7.62 x 54R
MAGAZINE CAPACITY 5
ACTION Bolt action
TOTAL LENGTH 1,185mm/46.65in
BARREL LENGTH 685mm/26.95in
WEIGHT UNLOADED 4.35kg/9.61lb

Mosin-Nagant 28-30 Civil Guard

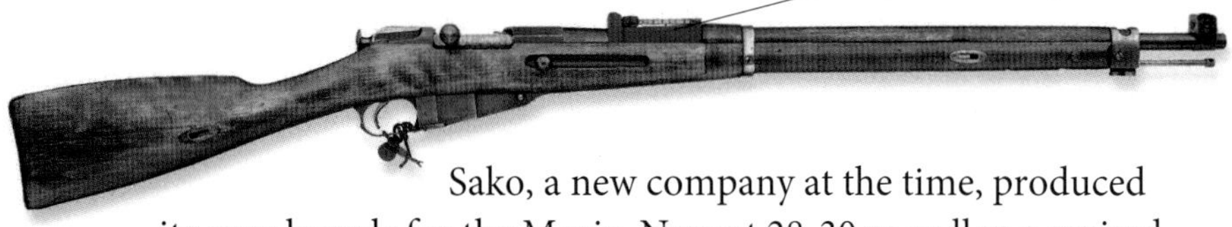

Sako, a new company at the time, produced its own barrels for the Mosin-Nagant 28-30 as well as a revised magazine and improved rear sight. Otherwise, the 28-30 was a standard Mosin-Nagant bolt-action rifle, of which Finland would need many during World War II. It was produced from 1931 to 1940.

SPECIFICATION

MANUFACTURER Sako
CALIBRE .338 Lapua magnum
MAGAZINE CAPACITY 5
ACTION Bolt action
TOTAL LENGTH 1,200mm/47.24in
BARREL LENGTH 690mm/27.16in
WEIGHT UNLOADED 5.1kg/11.24lb

Sako TRG

As infantry units get ever more powerful weapons, snipers need larger cartridges and rifles to reach their targets from further distances. The Sako TRG is available in the 22 and 42 models. The 22 is a standard 7.62 x 51mm chambering, but the 42 is available in the exemplary .338 Lapua magnum. A trained sniper can easily strike a point target 1,500m/1,640yd away, or a vehicle or radar array at 2,000m/2,187yd. As with all sniper rifles, scope selection can affect weight. Production began in 1995 and continues today.

SPECIFICATION

MANUFACTURER Tikka
CALIBRE 7.62 x 51mm
MAGAZINE CAPACITY 5
ACTION Bolt action
TOTAL LENGTH 1,070mm/42.15in
BARREL LENGTH 570mm/22.45in
WEIGHT UNLOADED 3.65kg/8.05lb

Tikka Finlander M-68 sniper, silent

An improved and refined Mauser action, the Tikka sniper rifle is also a hunting rifle modified for sniper use. More accurate than the Mosin-Nagant sniper rifles in the Finnish Defence Forces inventory, the Tikka also can use a suppressor, a feature the Mosin-Nagant is unable to use. Production began in 1968 and has continued until the present day.

Valmet M-62

An improved M-60 rifle, the M-62 lasted for 40 years as the standard Finnish Defence Force rifle. Attempts to replace it with the M-76 were unsuccessful, as the sheet-metal receiver of the M-76 was not as durable as the milled M-62 receiver. A little less weight did not count as much as continued function in arctic warfare. Despite its durability, the ageing M-62 required replacement, and the low cost of imports made it possible to purchase Chinese-made AKs in the late 1990s. The Valmet M-62 was in service from 1962 to the late 1990s, and probably can still be found in an armoury or police station in Finland today.

SPECIFICATION	
MANUFACTURER	Valmet
CALIBRE	7.62 x 39mm
MAGAZINE CAPACITY	30
ACTION	Gas operated/rotating bolt
TOTAL LENGTH	914mm/36in
BARREL LENGTH	420mm/16.55in
WEIGHT UNLOADED	4.09kg/9.02lb

Valmet M-76

This "improved" M-62 used a stamped steel receiver like that of the AKM, and was offered in both Soviet and American chamberings. Also, the buttstock was synthetic instead of the steel tube of the M-62. Finland found the stamped-steel receiver to be less durable than desired, something other countries have not. It was offered as an export item as well, but the cost of a Finnish-made rifle could not compete with those made in developing countries on the international arms market. The Valmet M-76 was manufactured from 1977 to 1990.

SPECIFICATION	
MANUFACTURER	Valmet
CALIBRE	7.62 x 39mm & 5.56 x 45mm
MAGAZINE CAPACITY	30
ACTION	Gas operated/rotating bolt
TOTAL LENGTH	913mm/35.95in
BARREL LENGTH	420mm/16.55in
WEIGHT UNLOADED	3.66kg/8.09lb

Mosin-Nagant 1927 cavalry

This was a short rifle rather than a carbine, but still better suited to mounted use than the full-sized rifle. In the harsh winter climate of Finland, durability was more important than light weight or quick handling. As a previous province of Russia, Russian-pattern small arms such as the Mosin-Nagant were well-known, and Finns were trained in using them. The Mosin-Nagant was used from 1927 to 1939.

SPECIFICATION	
MANUFACTURER	VKT
CALIBRE	7.62 x 54R
MAGAZINE CAPACITY	5
ACTION	Bolt action
TOTAL LENGTH	1,110mm/43.7in
BARREL LENGTH	607mm/23.9in
WEIGHT UNLOADED	3.97kg/8.77lb

Mosin-Nagant M-39 sniper

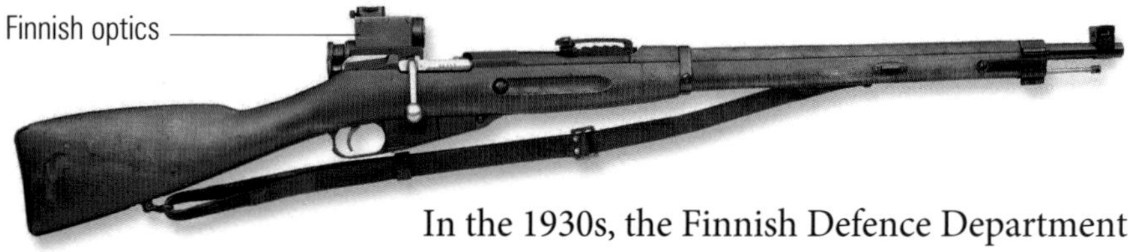

In the 1930s, the Finnish Defence Department undertook a programme to consolidate all Mosin-Nagant production into a single, improved design. The resulting M39 was issued in 1939. It had a more robust stock – with re-contoured buttstock and pistol grip – and a heavier handguard, made from Arctic birch, which was resistant to warping in the extreme cold. It had higher-quality barrels than the standard Soviet version. The M-39 was regularly overhauled and rebuilt, and used into the 1990s.

SPECIFICATION	
MANUFACTURER	VKT
CALIBRE	7.62 x 54R
MAGAZINE CAPACITY	5
ACTION	Bolt action
TOTAL LENGTH	1,232mm/48.5in
BARREL LENGTH	729mm/28.7in
WEIGHT UNLOADED	5.12kg/11.3lb

Romania

The Romanians found themselves between Germany and Russia in both World War I and World War II. As with so many central European countries in World War II, they received the worst of both: **siding with Germany, only to suffer great losses on the Eastern Front (reported as high as 200,000 at Stalingrad alone) and then occupation for decades as a satellite state of the Soviet Union.**

FPK

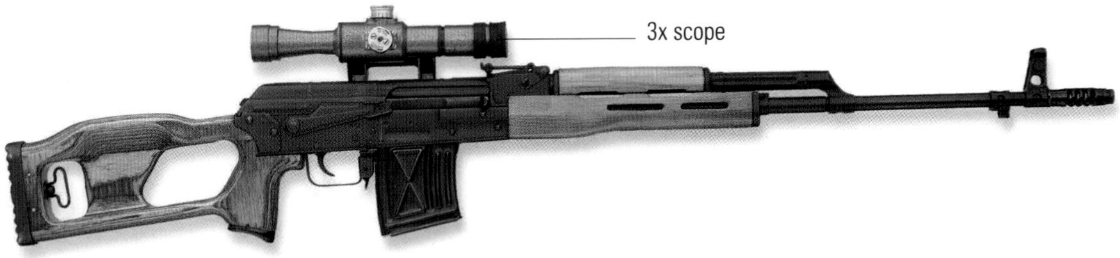

SPECIFICATION	
MANUFACTURER	State armoury
CALIBRE	7.62 x 54R
MAGAZINE CAPACITY	10
ACTION	Gas operated
TOTAL LENGTH	1,225mm/48.22in
BARREL LENGTH	620mm/24.4in
WEIGHT UNLOADED	4.31kg/9.50lb

The FPK (as it is sometimes known) was a Romanian-produced rifle resembling the Dragunov and, like all the other versions, was meant not so much as a sniper rifle (for long-range precision shooting) as a squad Designated Marksman Rifle (DMR). The former fires on high-value targets at extreme range, while the DMR rifleman fires on close to medium-range targets in order to solve the immediate problems of his field commander. The FPK, like the Dragunov, is a solid and serviceable weapon that is quite dangerous to opponents when in capable hands. Manufacture began in the 1960s and the rifles are in service today.

AKM

SPECIFICATION	
MANUFACTURER	State armoury
CALIBRE	7.62 x 39mm
MAGAZINE CAPACITY	30
ACTION	Gas operated/rotating bolt
TOTAL LENGTH	870mm/34.25in
BARREL LENGTH	415mm/16.33in
WEIGHT UNLOADED	3.14kg/6.92lb

The Romanian AKM (an improved Kalashnikov with a sheet-metal receiver) is instantly recognizable by the foregrip. The forearm of the Romanian rifle has a vertical grip that is angled towards the muzzle. The AK, in sustained fire, makes the firer's forearm very hot. The foregrip, besides being more ergonomic, and allowing for greater control in full-auto fire, keeps the firer's hand further from the heat. Soon after manufacture commenced in Russia, client states such as Romania were making the new version, replacing the receiver of forged steel with a metal pressing. Production lasted from the early 1960s to the late 1970s, but the 7.62mm rifles remained in use for years afterwards.

Puşcã Automatã Model 1986

SPECIFICATION	
MANUFACTURER	ROMARM
CALIBRE	5.45 x 39mm
MAGAZINE CAPACITY	30
ACTION	Gas operated
TOTAL LENGTH	943mm/17.1in
BARREL LENGTH	432mm/17in
WEIGHT UNLOADED	3.6kg/8.1lb

While many Warsaw Pact countries followed suit when the Soviet Union switched from the AKM to the AK-74, Romania resisted. Their new rifle, while chambered in 5.45x39mm, was not a clone of the AK-74 and has a blend of features from both. For example, the gas block design is at 45 degrees, but the vent is 90 degrees. This double-angle gas port makes it harder to clean. An AG-40 grenade launcher can be mounted if the normal lower handguard is removed.

AKS74

This was the improved (sheet-metal receiver) AK in the new Soviet cartridge. The "S" denotes the folding stock version. As the USSR found its military aspirations harder to achieve, it required its client states to assist. Some, such as Romania, made small arms for export to Soviet allies. This was a Romanian-produced clone of the standard Soviet assault rifle, fielded in the early 1980s to the present day.

SPECIFICATION	
MANUFACTURER	State Armoury
CALIBRE	5.45 x 39mm
MAGAZINE CAPACITY	30
ACTION	Gas operated
TOTAL LENGTH	943mm/37.12in
BARREL LENGTH	415mm/16.33in
WEIGHT UNLOADED	3.43kg/7.56lb

Mannlicher Model 1893 carbine

Differing in minor details, but essentially the Dutch 1895 Mannlicher, the Romanian 1893 Mannlicher carbine was a serviceable rifle for the trench warfare of World War I. Made for cavalry use, the carbine was particularly useful. After the war it was replaced with the VZ24 rifle, although undoubtedly many 1893 carbines remained in storage in 1939. The Model 1893 was in service in the Austro-Hungarian Empire from 1893 to the 1920s.

SPECIFICATION	
MANUFACTURER	Steyr
CALIBRE	6.5 x 53R
MAGAZINE CAPACITY	5
ACTION	Gas operated
TOTAL LENGTH	952mm/37.5in
BARREL LENGTH	450mm/17.7in
WEIGHT UNLOADED	3.30kg/7.25lb

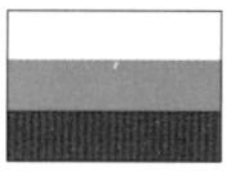

Bulgaria

Before World War I, Bulgaria manufactured rifles for the Austro-Hungarian empire of which it was part. During World War II, Bulgaria was forced to supply Germany with war material. Post-war, as a member of the Warsaw Pact, Bulgaria manufactured Soviet-pattern rifles.

AK-47

As with all Soviet client states, Bulgaria adopted the AK-47 for its own use. Early-issue AK-47s for the Bulgarian Army came from Poland; Bulgarian manufacture began in 1965. The Bulgarian AK-47 is of excellent quality, enabling Bulgaria to compete with small arms sales from the Russian Federation after the break-up of the USSR in 1991. The rifle remained in service from 1965 until the early 1980s.

SPECIFICATION	
MANUFACTURER	FÉG, Budapest
CALIBRE	7.62 x 39mm
MAGAZINE CAPACITY	30
ACTION	Gas operated/rotating bolt
TOTAL LENGTH	877mm/34.55in
BARREL LENGTH	415mm/16.35in
WEIGHT UNLOADED	3.82kg/8.42lb

AK-74

This modernized AK was essentially a clone of the Soviet AK-74 in a smaller calibre. Most Bulgarian AK-74 rifles were demilitarized – declared surplus and sold for parts. When Bulgaria joined the EU, it had to change to NATO-compliant small arms. It was easier to make new AK-74s in 5.56mm than to rebuild the old ones to the new calibre. The AK-74 was manufactured from the early 1980s to the mid-1990s.

SPECIFICATION	
MANUFACTURER	FÉG, Budapest
CALIBRE	5.45 x 39mm
MAGAZINE CAPACITY	30
ACTION	Gas operated/rotating bolt
TOTAL LENGTH	956mm/37.65in
BARREL LENGTH	415mm/16.35in
WEIGHT UNLOADED	4.85kg/10.7lb

AKS-74S

SPECIFICATION	
MANUFACTURER	FÉG, Budapest
CALIBRE	5.45 x 39mm
MAGAZINE CAPACITY	30
ACTION	Gas operated/rotating bolt
TOTAL LENGTH	643mm/26.55in (421mm/16.6in w/stock folded)
BARREL LENGTH	225mm/8.85in
WEIGHT UNLOADED	3.08kg/6.8lb

This was the short-barrelled variant of the standard AK-74. A flash hider/gas booster was required for reliable function. The shortened barrel, without the special flash hider, would not supply enough gas to the action for reliable function. Typically, short-barrelled rifles not equipped like this fail to eject the empty case. The allure and apparent exclusivity of short rifles keeps them in service even when the compact design is not needed, but the loss of down-range performance is a real shortcoming. The 74S went the same path as the 74 when Bulgaria changed calibres; the 74S declared surplus, disassembled and the rifles and parts (with rare exception) are now all exported from Bulgaria.

AR-M1

SPECIFICATION	
MANUFACTURER	Arsenal AD
CALIBRE	5.56mm NATO or 7.62x39mm
MAGAZINE CAPACITY	30
ACTION	Gas operated
TOTAL LENGTH	930mm/36.6in
BARREL LENGTH	415mm/16.3lb
WEIGHT UNLOADED	3.6kg/7.93lb

In the 1950s, Bulgaria's military had used Kalashnikov rifles imported from the Soviet Union. By the 1960s, they wanted to produce a licensed version in their own country at a state-run factory. Today, that gun is known as the AR-M1 and is made by Arsenal AD. It is currently exported and used in 20 other countries besides Bulgaria.

Ukraine

Absorbed into Russia under the Tsars, Ukraine was independent from 1917 to 1921. Then it was divided between the new Poland and the Soviet Union. After the fall of the Soviet Union, Ukraine became an independent country which needed to modernize and make its own arms without subsidies from Russia. Since February 2022, Ukraine has seen a tremendous influx of foreign small arms in varying numbers from countries all over the world to help in its fight against the 2022 Russian invasion.

Vepr

SPECIFICATION	
MANUFACTURER	MOLOT
CALIBRE	5.45 x 39mm
MAGAZINE CAPACITY	30
ACTION	Gas operated
TOTAL LENGTH	702mm/27.66in
BARREL LENGTH	415mm/16.35in
WEIGHT UNLOADED	3.45kg/lb

An upgraded AK, and manufactured since 2003, the Vepr is an AK-74 in bullpup configuration. Offered with an optional grenade launcher and built-in optical sight rail, the charging handle has been moved from the right side of the receiver to the left handguard, but the safety remains in the Kalashnikov location. While possibly a major improvement over the AK-74, it has all the faults of a bullpup: the safety lever is hard to reach, the magazine is difficult to exchange, and the trigger mechanism now incorporates a bar to reach from the new pistol grip location back to the receiver. The bar makes the AK trigger pull (which was always poor) worse.

Z-15

SPECIFICATION

MANUFACTURER Zbroyar
CALIBRE 5.56mm NATO
MAGAZINE CAPACITY 30
ACTION Gas operated
TOTAL LENGTH 800mm/31.5in
BARREL LENGTH 365.7mm/14.4in
WEIGHT UNLOADED 3.2kg/7.2lb

The Z-15 is very similar to the AR pattern firearms originally made in the United States. Overall, it is a carbine length firearm with a carbine length gas system, free floating match-grade barrel made from chrome-moly 4140 steel, and has a chrome-lined chamber. The handguard is made from aircraft-grade aluminum.

Russia

With an army of millions, Russia needed plenty of rifles. In both world wars, initial losses and rapid expansion of the army entailed a frantic search for a sufficient volume to resupply the army. With many arsenals and designers available, there was often plenty of choice. Despite efforts to replace the elderly Mosin-Nagant rifle, the Soviet Army stuck with it, as all potential replacements had operational problems of one sort or another. After World War II, the army was completely resupplied with AK-47s.

Degtyarev PTRD41

An anti-tank rifle using the larger of the Soviet heavy machine-gun cartridges, the Degtyarev is unique: it is a self-activating single-shot bolt-action rifle. The recoil-reduction system is simple: the entire receiver recoils rearwards over the stock frame, similar to the Boys A/T rifle, but unlike the Boys, the PTRD includes opening the bolt and ejecting the empty case in its cycle. The advent of better armour enabled its use as a bunker-buster for infantry. Issued first in the 1930s, it served to the end of the war in 1945. All anti-tank rifles became obsolete when armour became thicker.

SPECIFICATION

MANUFACTURER Degtyarev
CALIBRE 14.5mm
MAGAZINE CAPACITY Single-shot bolt action
ACTION Gas operated
TOTAL LENGTH 2,000mm/78.74in
BARREL LENGTH 1,350mm/53.15in
WEIGHT UNLOADED 17.42kg/38.40lb

SKS 45

Having been type-defined in 1943, the Samozaryadniy Karabin sistemi Simonova (SKS) was finalized in 1945 but not put into mass production until 1949. It used the 7.62 x 39mm cartridge. The fixed magazine can be loaded with single rounds or via stripper clips of ten rounds. Many models made outside Russia are crude, but the SKS works with great reliability. China made several variants, mostly for export, that used detachable magazines. The SKS was made from 1949 to the late 1960s, and is presently still in use around the world. It was made obsolete in Soviet service as soon as there were enough AK-47s for all the armed forces.

SPECIFICATION

MANUFACTURER Izhevsk, others
CALIBRE 7.62 x 39mm
MAGAZINE CAPACITY 10
ACTION Gas operated
TOTAL LENGTH 1,121mm/44.15in
BARREL LENGTH 519mm/20.45in
WEIGHT UNLOADED 3.86kg/8.5lb

AK-47 1st Model

The initial production AKs were made with a receiver of a sheet steel pressing, in a "U" channel, with the front and rear trunnions rivetted to it. (The trunnions are steel castings used to secure the barrel in front and the stock in the rear to the receiver.) Sheet-metal stampings in Russia in 1949 were not up to the task, so production was shifted to a forged and machined receiver from 1951 to 1959, while the Soviets continued to study the sheet-metal pressing technologies they had obtained from Germany. The forged receiver added more than a pound of weight to the original design. The AK was produced between 1949 and 1975, in one form or another.

SPECIFICATION

MANUFACTURER Izhevsk, Tula, others
CALIBRE 7.62 x 39mm
MAGAZINE CAPACITY 30
ACTION Gas operated
TOTAL LENGTH 868.68mm/34.2in
BARREL LENGTH 414mm/16.3in
WEIGHT UNLOADED 4.3kg/9.48lb

AKM

This was an improved version of the Kalashnikov. Initially, the sheet-metal pressing receiver was not successful. Soviet technology was not up to the task of producing a rugged metal-pressing receiver, and the sheet-metal pressing machines were needed for higher-priority aircraft production. Once the problem was sorted out, the AKM was produced in large quantities. The AKM also introduced the "rate reducer", which is actually an anti-bounce device. It adds a few more parts to a simple and sturdy design, but not at any great cost in weight, complexity, reliability or manufacturing. The AKM was introduced in 1959 and remained in service to the late 1970s, when it was replaced by the AK-74.

SPECIFICATION

MANUFACTURER Izhevsk
CALIBRE 7.62 x 39mm
MAGAZINE CAPACITY 30
ACTION Gas operated
TOTAL LENGTH 878mm/34.55in
BARREL LENGTH 415mm/16.34in
WEIGHT UNLOADED 3.38kg/7.45lb

SVD

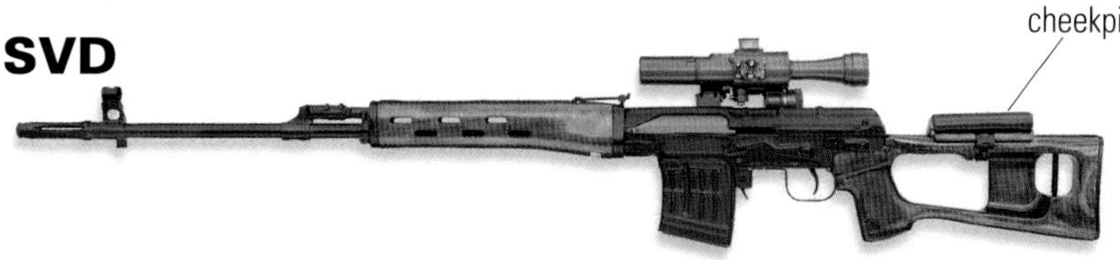

More a Designated Marksman Rifle (DMK) than a sniper rifle, the Snayperskaya Vintovka Dragunova (SVD) is a solid, if unspectacular, short-to-medium-range sniping rifle that is effective up to 500–600m/1,600–2,000ft. The cutaway buttstock, pistol grip and long barrel make it impossible to mistake the SVD for any other rifle on the battlefield. The rimmed Russian cartridge must have made designing a reliable magazine particularly problematic.

SPECIFICATION

MANUFACTURER Izhevsk
CALIBRE 7.62 x 54R
MAGAZINE CAPACITY 10
ACTION Gas operated
TOTAL LENGTH 1,226mm/48.25in
BARREL LENGTH 549mm/21.45in
WEIGHT UNLOADED 4.76kg/10.5lb

Federov Model 1916

The Federov Model 1916 was the first small arm that could be called an assault weapon. It was initially designed around a proprietary 6.5mm cartridge, but then changed to use the readily available 6.5 x 50mm Japanese cartridge. With a detachable magazine, selective fire and a vertical foregrip, it was far ahead of any other contender. The rifle was made in numbers large enough to see some action during World War I, and no doubt the 1917 Russian Revolution as well. Introduced in 1916, it remained in service until 1925.

SPECIFICATION

MANUFACTURER Sestroretsk
CALIBRE 6.5mm Arisaka
MAGAZINE CAPACITY 25
ACTION Short recoil
TOTAL LENGTH 975mm/38.4in
BARREL LENGTH 519mm/20.45in
WEIGHT UNLOADED 4.45kg/9.8lb

Mosin-Nagant M-1891

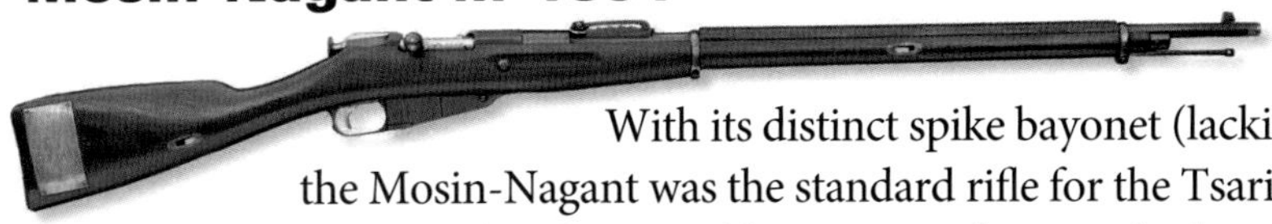

With its distinct spike bayonet (lacking a sheath), the Mosin-Nagant was the standard rifle for the Tsarist, and later Soviet, armies. Rugged and reasonably accurate, the army had enough on hand until war broke out. With the mobilized army several million men greater than the supply of rifles, the Tsar had to order additional rifles made in France and the United States. The Mosin-Nagant was in service from 1891 to 1945. Despite its length, it is well balanced and handy, although the balance comes at the expense of barrel weight. Also, with sustained fire of 20 rounds in two–three minutes, the barrel and hand guards became too hot to handle.

SPECIFICATION

MANUFACTURER Russian & French arsenals, American arms companies
CALIBRE 7.62 x 54R
MAGAZINE CAPACITY 5
ACTION Bolt action
TOTAL LENGTH 1,318mm/51.9in
BARREL LENGTH 820mm/32.3in
WEIGHT UNLOADED 4.06kg/8.95lb

Mosin-Nagant Mod 1891/30 sniper

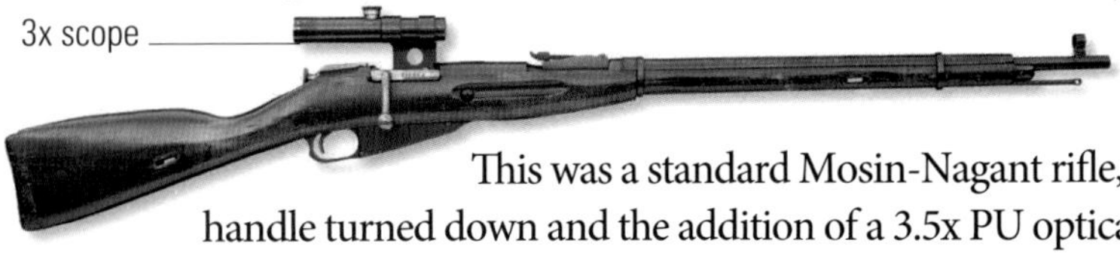

This was a standard Mosin-Nagant rifle, with the bolt handle turned down and the addition of a 3.5x PU optical sight, installed via a sidemount. The 3.5 power scope did not allow for effective long-range sniping, but on the Eastern Front there were plenty of opportunities to locate German officers or machine-gun crews at close to medium range. The rifle was developed in 1930 and served in the Red Army until 1945. During the war, the Tokarev M1938 was to be issued with optics and replace all Mosin sniper rifles. However, the Tokarev was not accurate and so Mosin sniper rifles went back into production.

SPECIFICATION

MANUFACTURER Tula, Izhevsk, others
CALIBRE 7.62 x 54R
MAGAZINE CAPACITY 5
ACTION Bolt action
TOTAL LENGTH 1,231mm/48.45in
BARREL LENGTH 730mm/28.75in
WEIGHT UNLOADED 4.4kg/9.7lb

Mosin-Nagant Carbine M-1907

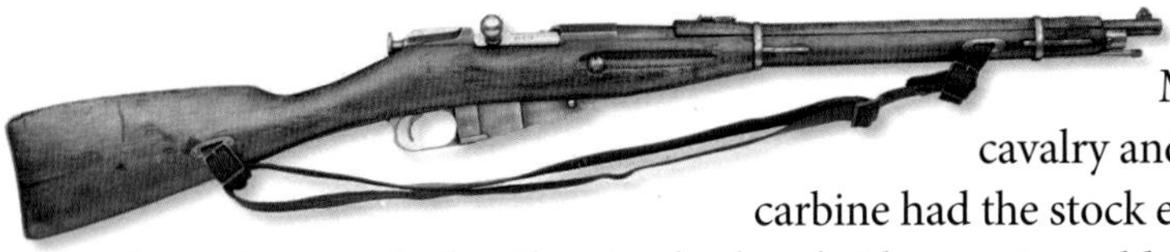

Made for Tsarist cavalry and artillery, the first carbine had the stock extended so closely to the muzzle that the standard socket bayonet would not fit. When the 7.62 x 54R cartridge was upgraded in 1908, the sights on all Mosin-Nagant rifles and carbines had to be changed. While the Mosin-Nagant has an undeserved reputation as being rather awkward, the 1907 carbine is handy and well-balanced. It served from 1907 to 1918, and until all the models were used up.

SPECIFICATION

MANUFACTURER Tula
CALIBRE 7.62 x 54R
MAGAZINE CAPACITY 5
ACTION Bolt action
TOTAL LENGTH 1,020mm/40.15in
BARREL LENGTH 509mm/20.05in
WEIGHT UNLOADED 3.41kg/7.51lb

Tokarev Model 1938

SPECIFICATION

MANUFACTURER Tula, Izhevsk
CALIBRE 7.62 x 54R
MAGAZINE CAPACITY 20
ACTION Gas operated
TOTAL LENGTH 1,220mm/48.05in
BARREL LENGTH 635mm/25in
WEIGHT UNLOADED 3.95kg/8.7lb

The winner of the semi-auto rifle trials of the 1930s, the Tokarev Model 1938 was an entirely acceptable battle rifle. But the situation changed during World War II, when entire Russian units were armed with submachine guns. After the war, assault rifles like the AK-47 became the standard-issue weapon. The Tokarev has a very effective muzzle brake. However, while the firer experiences reduced recoil, anyone standing near him is blasted by high-pressure gases. The Model 1938 is a solid wartime weapon and served from 1938 to 1945. It was subsequently withdrawn from service.

Tokarev SVT 40

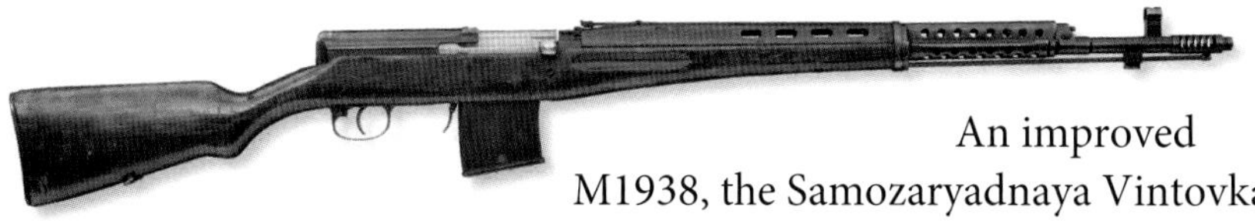

SPECIFICATION	
MANUFACTURER	Tula, Izhevsk
CALIBRE	7.62 x 54R
MAGAZINE CAPACITY	20
ACTION	Gas operated
TOTAL LENGTH	1,220mm/48.05in
BARREL LENGTH	636mm/25in
WEIGHT UNLOADED	3.9kg/8.6lb

An improved M1938, the Samozaryadnaya Vintovka Tokareva (SVT) 40 replaced the fragile two-piece stock with a more durable single-piece stock. The cleaning rod was moved back to the traditional location under the barrel. It also incorporated design changes to make manufacturing less expensive and faster. Despite the improvements, it was still far more costly to manufacture than other rifles, and the decreased quality of wartime ammunition made it less reliable. The SVT 40s were so commonly captured that the German Army produced ammunition (which worked better than the Soviet type) and training manuals for it. Made and issued from 1940, production dwindled until in 1945 it ceased entirely.

Mosin-Nagant M44 carbine

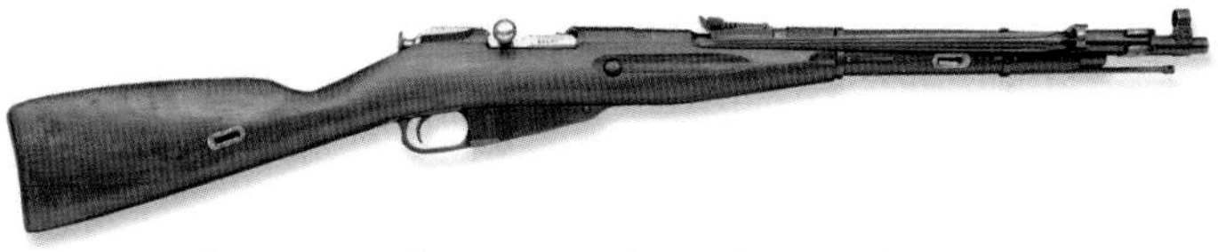

SPECIFICATION	
MANUFACTURER	Tula, others
CALIBRE	7.62 x 54R
MAGAZINE CAPACITY	5
ACTION	Bolt action
TOTAL LENGTH	1,020mm/40.15in
BARREL LENGTH	509mm/20.05in
WEIGHT UNLOADED	4.04kg/8.9lb

Modern warfare required shorter weapons with greater firepower than the Mod 1891/30 Mosin-Nagant, but the realities of production meant keeping that bolt-action rifle in full production. The M44 is merely a shortened rifle, the stock and metal furniture not even modified on the remaining length. After testing a number of bayonet designs, the USSR settled on a side-folding spike. Although relatively compact, the M44 carbine was as heavy as many other rifles. Entering service in 1944, it remained as a military rifle to the early 1950s, but was produced into the 1960s in some Communist bloc countries.

AKS-74U

SPECIFICATION	
MANUFACTURER	Tula
CALIBRE	5.45 x 39mm
MAGAZINE CAPACITY	30
ACTION	Gas operated
TOTAL LENGTH	730mm/28.74in
BARREL LENGTH	210mm/8.27in
WEIGHT UNLOADED	2.71kg/5.97lb

A short-barrelled assault rifle, the AKS-74U has a side-folding stock that reduces it to a compact package. The length of the barrel and the sight radius reduce power and accuracy, but this is thought to be an acceptable trade-off for the compactness of the weapon. It was made from the mid-1970s to the mid-1990s.

OC-14 Groza

This is a bullpup version of the modern Kalashnikov, with several additions or modifications, including a detachable grenade launcher. It can also be made in a special large-bore cartridge optimized for use with a suppressor. It can sometimes be difficult to insert magazines on AK bullpups. The AK magazine seats in place by catching the front lip in the receiver, then pivoting the rear back until it locks. Many bullpup designs have the pistol grip located in front of the magazine well, in the path of the tipped magazine. This rifle was produced in the late 1980s and remains in use today with the Russian Internal Affairs ministry.

SPECIFICATION	
MANUFACTURER	Tula
CALIBRE	7.62 x 39mm, 9 x 39mm
MAGAZINE CAPACITY	30
ACTION	Gas operated
TOTAL LENGTH	700mm/27.56in
BARREL LENGTH	415mm/16.34in
WEIGHT UNLOADED	3.2kg/7.05lb

Winchester 1895

Unable to find or make enough Mosin-Nagant rifles in World War I, Russia contracted Winchester to provide its lever-action 1895 in the Russian calibre. Complete with stripper-clip guides and bayonet mounts, the Winchester was certainly up to the task of warfare. The fortunes of World War I went against the Tsar, and deliveries, which started in 1915, stopped in 1917. Out of 426,000 manufactured by Winchester over 300,000 were shipped to the Russian Army.

SPECIFICATION	
MANUFACTURER	Winchester
CALIBRE	7.62 x 54R
MAGAZINE CAPACITY	5
ACTION	Lever action
TOTAL LENGTH	1,160mm/45.65in
BARREL LENGTH	712mm/28.05in
WEIGHT UNLOADED	4.1kg/9.04lb

Egypt

Egyptian firearms manufacture began with the production of Remington rolling-block rifles for the army in the late 19th century. Later, King Farouk (1936–52) upgraded the small arms inventory by purchasing from FN. After his overthrow, Egypt alternated between purchasing Soviet small arms and producing Soviet and other designs in-country, causing difficulties for the supply staff.

SAFN Model 1949

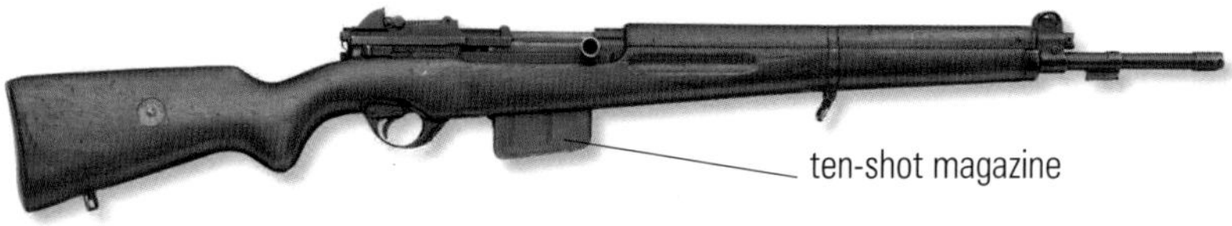

Produced for Egypt by FN, the SAFN Model 49 was certainly durable and reliable enough to cope with the climate and dust of the desert region. The 7.92 x 5mm cartridge had the range necessary for open-desert combat. Egyptian rifles can be recognized by the royal cipher of King Farouk above the chamber, and the Arabic numerals on the rear sight. The SAFN Model 1949 was purchased from 1950 to 1956, and continued in use for decades after. As a general-issue weapon it was replaced by the AK, which was produced in large quantities in Egypt. There may well be SAFNs still in use today, somewhere in the region.

SPECIFICATION	
MANUFACTURER	FN, Liège
CALIBRE	7.92 x 57mm
MAGAZINE CAPACITY	10
ACTION	Gas operated/tilting lock
TOTAL LENGTH	1,110mm/43.7in
BARREL LENGTH	589mm/23.2in
WEIGHT UNLOADED	4.30kg/9.48lb

Remington Rolling Block

SPECIFICATION	
MANUFACTURER	Remington Arms
CALIBRE	11.43 x 50R
MAGAZINE CAPACITY	Single shot
ACTION	Pivoting breechblock
TOTAL LENGTH	1,278mm/50.3in
BARREL LENGTH	889mm/35in
WEIGHT UNLOADED	4.15kg/9.15lb

At the time Egypt purchased it, the Remington Rolling Block was a sensible choice of rifle, and certainly as good as any other single-shot breech-loading model. Within ten years, repeaters using smokeless powder were being manufactured and issued, but Egypt retained the Remington for a long time. At the time, many defence duties were undertaken by British Army units, which made armaments expenditure less pressing. The Remington Rolling Block was first obtained in 1876 and used well into the early 20th century.

Ljungman-Hakim

SPECIFICATION	
MANUFACTURER	State Factory 54
CALIBRE	7.92 x 57mm
MAGAZINE CAPACITY	10
ACTION	Gas operated/tilting lock
TOTAL LENGTH	1,209mm/47.6in
BARREL LENGTH	590mm/23.25in
WEIGHT UNLOADED	4.82kg/10.63lb

In July 1952, revolution erupted in Egypt and King Farouk, who had reigned since 1936, was forced to abdicate from the throne in favour of his son. The SAFN 49 was deemed unsuited for desert use, and the new rifle had to be of local manufacture. Husqvarna sold the tooling for the Ljungman-Hakim (LH) to Egypt. State Factory 54, in Port Said, was tasked with building the rifles. Longer and heavier than the SAFN Model 49, the Ljungman action was entirely unsuited to the combination of desert sand and dust and imperfect maintenance routines. The muzzle brake was difficult to fire when prone in the desert, and the resultant cloud of dust would have given away the firer's position. The LH was made from the mid-1950s to mid-1960s and sold as surplus in the 1980s.

Rasheed

SPECIFICATION	
MANUFACTURER	State Factory 54
CALIBRE	7.62 x 39mm
MAGAZINE CAPACITY	10
ACTION	Gas operated/tilting lock
TOTAL LENGTH	1,077mm/42.4in
BARREL LENGTH	570mm/22.45in
WEIGHT UNLOADED	3.74kg/8.25lb

Derived from the Ljungman designed by Erik Eklund, a Swedish engineer, the Rasheed was essentially a scaled-down and improved Hakim, without the muzzle brake and chambered for the Soviet M43 cartridge. In appearance a combination of the Hakim and the Soviet SKS, it is not clear why it was deemed necessary to design a different weapon. The Rasheed may have been manufactured to equip reserves or the police force. The local production of AK-47 rifles had already started when the Rasheed was being built; the Rasheed may have been produced to provide a weapon that would fire Soviet ammunition until AK production was sufficient to meet Egypt's needs. Only about 8,000 of the rifles were ever produced. The Rasheed was made between 1959 and 1960 and immediately became obsolete.

AK-47

Also known as the Maadi, the Egyptian AK-47 is made with Russian-supplied tooling and machinery. It is an example of the AKM as built in the Soviet Union from the late 1950s until the 1970s. While neither being as accurate as the SAFN Model 1949 nor as powerful as any of the rifles chambered in 7.92 x 57mm, the Maadi was more reliable in desert conditions than the Hakim. Manufacture began in the late 1950s and continues today. The Maadi was the first semi-auto-only AK made for export to the USA.

SPECIFICATION	
MANUFACTURER	State Factory 54
CALIBRE	7.62 x 39mm
MAGAZINE CAPACITY	30
ACTION	Gas operated/rotating bolt
TOTAL LENGTH	870mm/34.25in
BARREL LENGTH	415mm/16.35in
WEIGHT UNLOADED	4.44kg/9.8lb

Turkey

Before World War I the Ottoman Empire was on good terms with Germany and purchased many small arms from German firms. Once in Turkey, the local arsenals made modifications as needed. Often, the resulting rifle, while still named by its original designation, bore little resemblance to the factory blueprints. Today, some small arms are made in Turkey by MKEK.

Mauser Model 1905 carbine

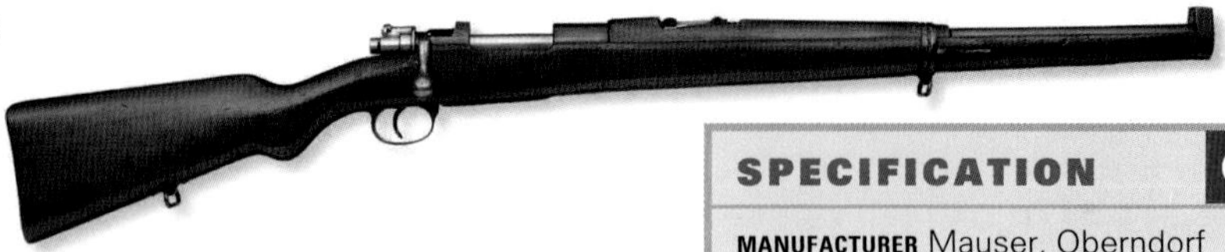

The Mauser Model 1905 was an 1898 Mauser action in 7.65mm calibre, made for mounted troop and artillery unit use. Turkey was quite aggressive in requesting improved versions of the rifles it purchased, moving swiftly from the Gewehr 88 to M93 to 96 to 98 versions. With the collapse of the Ottoman Empire and the start of Kemal Atatürk's rule (1922–38), Turkey began converting many older rifles in 7.65mm to 7.92 x 57mm, for which they had a large supply of ammunition. The Mauser Model 1905 carbine was purchased in 1905 and served in the original or later calibre until the 1950s.

SPECIFICATION

MANUFACTURER Mauser, Oberndorf
CALIBRE 7.65 x 53mm
MAGAZINE CAPACITY 5
ACTION Bolt action
TOTAL LENGTH 1,045mm/41.15in
BARREL LENGTH 550mm/21.65in
WEIGHT UNLOADED 3.92kg/8.25lb

MKEK MPT-76

In 2014, the MPT-76 was introduced to replace the MKEK G3, licensed from Germany, and which had been in use since 1966 but not made since 1983. The design was based on the AR-15, but some of the design has been influenced by the HK417. The first batch of rifles were delivered to the Turkish Armed Forces in 2017 with more than 400,000 having been made to date.

SPECIFICATION

MANUFACTURER Makina ve Kimya Endüstrisi Kurumu
CALIBRE 7.62mm NATO
MAGAZINE CAPACITY 20 or 30
ACTION Gas operated/rotating bolt
TOTAL LENGTH 920mm/36in
BARREL LENGTH 406mm/16in
WEIGHT UNLOADED 4.2kg/9.3lb

Israel

Until it achieved independence in 1948, Israel had to make the best of whatever rifles were at hand. Afterwards, it bought and later produced its own arms. Israel's experience and reputation allowed it to enter the export market and sell small arms – and designs – to other countries.

NATO FN-FAL

The FN-FAL was issued from the early 1960s to 1990. The earliest rifles were FN-made, but later rifles were assembled in Israel using FN receivers and locally made parts. While robust and reliable, the FN-FAL was over 1m/3ft long and heavy. Much Israeli combat was urban, and the length of the rifle proved awkward. The IDF is a citizen force, and when the citizens complained about the weight of the issue weapon, a lighter model had to be found. The FN-FAL was standard issue until M16 rifles became common after 1973.

SPECIFICATION

MANUFACTURER FN, Liège
CALIBRE 7.62mm NATO
MAGAZINE CAPACITY 20
ACTION Gas operated/tilting lock
TOTAL LENGTH 1,016mm/40in
BARREL LENGTH 533mm/21in
WEIGHT UNLOADED 4.10kg/9.06lb

Galil

SPECIFICATION

MANUFACTURER IMI
CALIBRE 5.56 x 45mm, 7.62mm NATO
MAGAZINE CAPACITY 35 (5.56) or 25 (7.62)
ACTION Gas operated/rotating bolt
TOTAL LENGTH 970mm/38.2in
BARREL LENGTH 460mm/18.1in
WEIGHT UNLOADED 4.4kg/9.7lb

Limitations
The Galil was a better version of the AK but was costly and heavy. The IDF limited issue to artillery and headquarters units, issuing M16s to all others.

An improved AK, the Galil features some updates to the basic Kalashnikov design. The rear sight is on the dust cover for a longer sighting radius, and is an aperture sight for more precise aiming. The safety/selector has a lever on the left side of the receiver, to be pushed by the thumb. The bipod incorporates a wire cutter. The folding stock is more solid and easier to fire with than the under folder of most AK-47s, and more durable than the side folder of the AK-74. The 7.62mm Galil was planned to replace the FAL and heavy-barrel FAL. However, the Galil turned out to be too heavy compared to the M16 and too expensive to manufacture. The Galil was first fielded in the early 1970s and has been in continued but diminished use to the present. Nowadays, it is found in only a few units of the IDF.

TAR-21

SPECIFICATION

MANUFACTURER IMI
CALIBRE 5.56 x 45mm
MAGAZINE CAPACITY 30
ACTION Gas operated/rotating bolt
TOTAL LENGTH 720mm/28.34in
BARREL LENGTH 460mm/18.11in
WEIGHT UNLOADED 2.8kg/6.17lb

The Tavor Assault Rifle (TAR-21) is the newest Israeli assault rifle, gradually being introduced to replace the M16 and all other rifles in service, including the AK and Galil. Basically an AK action in 5.56mm in a polymer bullpup shell, it is more compact, lighter and more durable than existing rifles. By 2007, it was still unclear whether the basic problems of the bullpup design would be solved by the TAR-21. (Bullpups are difficult and hazardous for left-handed shooters to use, and right-hand building corners are always a problem). Manufacture of the TAR-21 began in 1998 and continues to the present day.

X95

SPECIFICATION

MANUFACTURER Israel Weapon Industries
CALIBRE 5.56mm NATO
MAGAZINE CAPACITY 30
ACTION Gas operated
TOTAL LENGTH 714mm/28.1in
BARREL LENGTH 419mm/16.5in
WEIGHT UNLOADED 3.61kg/8lb

In November 2009, the Israel Defense Force announced that the X95 would become the standard infantry weapon of the IDF, with the addition of an integrated grenade-launcher. With a conversion kit, the X95 can be converted from a 5.56mm assault rifle to a 9mm submachine gun. A suppressor can also be attached as part of the 9mm conversion kit, or as part of a replacement handguard which integrates the muzzle brake, suppressor, and handguard.

Ethiopia

Ordering rifles from FN, Ethiopia (then Abyssinia) took delivery just before Italy invaded in October 1935. Although armed with the best rifles of the time, Ethiopian troops could not successfully resist the Italian Army. While Mussolini easily conquered the African state, he did not learn from this experience that his army was woefully equipped and trained, and his troops suffered in World War II as a result.

Mauser FN Model 1924 carbine

This was a standard export carbine of the mid-1930, in the standard calibre. The receiver bore the royal cipher of Emperor Haile Selassie (officially Emperor of Ethiopia from 1930 to 1974). It was purchased from 1933 to 1935 and used for decades afterwards. Using the standard 7.92mm Mauser cartridge, Ethiopia could acquire ammunition for rifles and light machine guns from any manufacturer in Europe, Britain or the United States. It made sense in a poor country for all rifles and machine guns to use a common calibre.

SPECIFICATION	
MANUFACTURER	FN, Liège
CALIBRE	7.92 x 57mm
MAGAZINE CAPACITY	5
ACTION	Bolt action
TOTAL LENGTH	996mm/39.2in
BARREL LENGTH	493mm/19.4in
WEIGHT UNLOADED	3.67kg/8.1lb

Mauser Model 1933

The Mauser Model 1933 was the standard model short rifle as produced by FN in the mid-1930s. Except for the royal cipher and Lion of Juda markings, it would have been similar to any other country's Mauser-pattern rifle of the time. As with the carbine, the Mauser Model 1933 was purchased between 1933 and 1935 and in use for decades afterwards.

SPECIFICATION	
MANUFACTURER	FN, Liège
CALIBRE	7.92. x 57mm
MAGAZINE CAPACITY	5
ACTION	Bolt action
TOTAL LENGTH	1,107mm/43.6in
BARREL LENGTH	600mm/23.62in
WEIGHT UNLOADED	3.99kg/8.8lb

Saudi Arabia

With no natural resources besides people and oil, Saudi Arabia initially purchased its small arms. With oil revenues after World War II, it began to invest in its own manufacturing. Saudi Arabia ranks among the world's most heavily armed nations, and it has plans to further upgrade its arsenal.

G3

Initially purchased from Hecker & Koch, Saudi Arabia bought manufacturing rights and began making its own G3s, which could be distinguished from West German G3s only by the markings. Once the 7.62mm NATO cartridge was replaced, the Saudis purchased the Steyr AUG. The G3 was produced from 1968 to the early 1980s. Since it is not practical to march through the desert, much of the patrolling by Saudi units would be vehicular, thus the weight of the G3 did not present a problem.

SPECIFICATION	
MANUFACTURER	H&K, al-Khardj Arsenal
CALIBRE	7.62mm NATO
MAGAZINE CAPACITY	20
ACTION	Roller-delayed blowback
TOTAL LENGTH	1,021mm/40.2in
BARREL LENGTH	450mm/17.7in
WEIGHT UNLOADED	4.49kg/9.9lb

Iraq

From a miscellaneous collection of British arms, Iraq went mostly for Soviet-pattern rifles during the later stages of the Cold War. Given the dusty desert conditions in Iraq, the durability of the AK and its variants were an asset. France, China, Egypt and the United States have all supplied arms to Iraq.

SPECIFICATION	
MANUFACTURER	Zastava/Iraq
CALIBRE	7.62 x 39mm
MAGAZINE CAPACITY	30
ACTION	Gas operated/rotating bolt
TOTAL LENGTH	869mm/34.25in
BARREL LENGTH	415mm/16.34in
WEIGHT UNLOADED	4.02kg/8.87lb

Tabuk M70

The Tabuk M70 was assembled in Iraq using the M70 Zastava AKM rifles as a pattern, and in many cases using Yugoslavian-manufactured parts such as the gas block. Other parts, such as the wood furniture, pins and springs, were locally made. Except for minor dimensional details, the Yugo/Iraqi AK is the same as any other sheet-metal receivered AK and works identically. It is made in both wood-stock and folding-stock versions. The M70 was assembled in Iraq from the early 1970s until 2003.

SPECIFICATION	
MANUFACTURER	Various
CALIBRE	5.56mm NATO
MAGAZINE CAPACITY	30
ACTION	Gas operated
TOTAL LENGTH	1,007mm/39.6in
BARREL LENGTH	508mm/20in
WEIGHT UNLOADED	3.4kg/7.5lb

M16

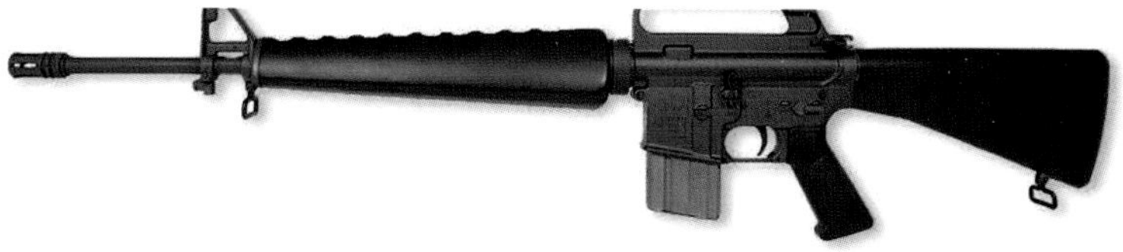

Both M16A1 and M16A2 rifles have been seen in use in Iraq. As full-length rifles, they have 20-inch barrels and fixed buttstocks. Made from alloys and polymers, the M16 is much lighter than the M14 in 7.62mm NATO that it replaced. Many of these rifles were either provided by or captured from United States forces. The M4 is the smaller carbine version of the larger M16 rifle.

Iran/Persia

Iran became significant to the world economy after oil was discovered there in the early 20th century. After the price of oil increased in the early 1970s, Iran's export earnings increased, and the government was able to update much of its military equipment, including small arms. After the Iranian Revolution of 1979, Iran fought a war with Iraq (1980–90). Iran now has its own manufacturing base for small arms.

SPECIFICATION	
MANUFACTURER	CZ Brno/Iran
CALIBRE	7.92 x 57mm
MAGAZINE CAPACITY	5
ACTION	Bolt action
TOTAL LENGTH	1,250mm/49.2in
BARREL LENGTH	740mm/29.13in
WEIGHT UNLOADED	4.12kg/9.1lb

VZ 98/29

The standard VZ export rifle of 1930, the Persian 98/29 was at first made in Brno, Czechoslovakia. Production was increased in Iran once World War II began and supplies from the Czechs stopped. With VZ tooling on-site, the VZ 98/29 did not differ at all from the standard VZ/Mauser rifle, except for Iranian markings on the left rail in Farsi. Purchased rifles were issued in 1930, and local production began in Iran within a couple of years, lasting to the late 1960s. Iranian-produced rifles showed more alterations as time went on.

G3

SPECIFICATION	
MANUFACTURER	H&K, Mosalsalasi
CALIBRE	7.62 x 51mm
MAGAZINE CAPACITY	20
ACTION	Roller-delayed blowback
TOTAL LENGTH	1,021mm/40.2in
BARREL LENGTH	450mm/17.7in
WEIGHT UNLOADED	4.16kg/9.9lb

The G3 was provided at first by Hecker & Koch in the early 1970s, then built in Iran at the State Arms Factory at Mosalsalasi. Given the German attention to detail, the only difference between HK-produced and Iranian-produced rifles would have been the markings. Slightly modified and called the G3A6, it continued in production even after the Iranian Revolution. Purchased and locally manufactured rifles were first issued in the early 1970s and continue to serve to the present.

Model 49 carbine

The Model 49 was a carbine designed and produced only in Iran for Iranian use. It differed from the CZ-provided carbines in barrel band and sling-swivel configuration. The sling-swivel design was modified for local preferences and produced on Iranian designed and fabricated tooling and patterns, alongside the CZ tooling. Production of the new model began in 1949 and the rifles are no doubt in use somewhere to this day.

SPECIFICATION	
MANUFACTURER	Iran
CALIBRE	7.92 x 57mm
MAGAZINE CAPACITY	5
ACTION	Bolt action
TOTAL LENGTH	965mm/38in
BARREL LENGTH	454mm/17.91in
WEIGHT UNLOADED	3.8kg/8.4lb

Pakistan

As part of the former British colony of India, it was natural for Pakistan to start with British-pattern rifles upon achieving independence in 1979. Pakistan then began its own arms industry. The long border with Afghanistan and the Soviet influence there brought extensive exposure to the AK system. Yet AKs have been phased out of service in Pakistan in favour of locally produced G3 rifles. Although many countries have switched to the 5.56mm or 5.45mm calibres, Pakistan sticks with the 7.62mm NATO and the G3.

SMLE No. 4 Mark 2

The Mark 2 of the ubiquitous No. 4 SMLE had the trigger mounted to the underside of the receiver instead of on the frame around the magazine opening. This produced a more consistent trigger pull. Made at the end of World War II, it it was kept longer in service in Pakistan solely due to a pressing need for rifles. It was first fielded in 1947 and was kept in service until the late 1960s.

SPECIFICATION	
MANUFACTURER	Enfield
CALIBRE	.303 British
MAGAZINE CAPACITY	10
ACTION	Bolt action
TOTAL LENGTH	1,129mm/44.45in
BARREL LENGTH	640mm/25.2in
WEIGHT UNLOADED	4.11kg/9.06lb

AKMS

Given the border with Afghanistan, war-torn since the Soviet invasion of 1979, the presence of Kalashnikovs in Pakistan is not surprising. The AKMS has been in use in Pakistan since the 1960s. A gas-operated assault rifle, chambered to fire 7.62 x 39mm ammunition, it is built on a sheet-metal receiver, not milled from a forged billet. First produced in the USSR, Pakistani industry is fully geared up to the task of making the AKMS, even in small machine shops.

SPECIFICATION

MANUFACTURER Unk
CALIBRE 7.62 x 39mm
MAGAZINE CAPACITY 30
ACTION Gas operated/rotating bolt
TOTAL LENGTH 877mm/34.55in
BARREL LENGTH 415mm/16.35in
WEIGHT UNLOADED 3.81kg/8.42lb

G3

SPECIFICATION

MANUFACTURER Wah
CALIBRE 7.62mm NATO
MAGAZINE CAPACITY 20
ACTION Roller-delayed blowback
TOTAL LENGTH 1,020mm/40.15in
BARREL LENGTH 450mm/17.7in
WEIGHT UNLOADED 4.08kg/9.68lb

A locally produced G3, made under licence from Heckler & Koch, the G3 has been the standard Pakistani Army rifle since its introduction there in 1967. The earliest rifles were purchased, but within a short time Pakistan was making its own. Except for the markings, this was a direct and exact copy of the G3, and equally unbreakable. Production began in 1967, and the rifles are still in regular use.

India

While India was a British colony, it was far enough away from Britain, and important enough, to warrant having its own armouries. Once independent after 1947, India continued making its own small arms. The Indian Army can count on more than 40 active armories and weapons manufacturers.

SMLE No.1 Mark III*

SPECIFICATION

MANUFACTURER Ishapore
CALIBRE .303 British
MAGAZINE CAPACITY 10
ACTION Bolt action
TOTAL LENGTH 1,130mm/44.5in
BARREL LENGTH 640mm/25.19in
WEIGHT UNLOADED 3.91kg/8.62lb

Produced in-country for local use, the Indian SMLE rifle was considered rough by some users but entirely serviceable. Many were produced during World War II. It was simply an Indian-made No.1 Mark III*. Production began at the Ishapore plant in 1907, and continued until 1955. After 1947 the imperial marking on the SMLE was replaced with the Indian Ashoka.

SMLE Mod2A1

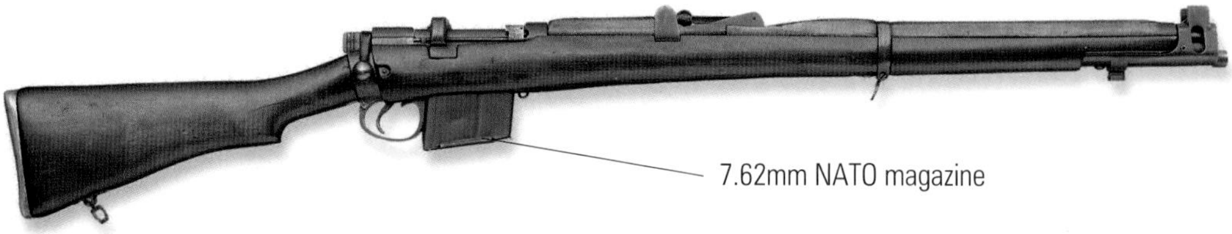

Collectors' rifle
The Mod2A1 is popular with collectors.

SPECIFICATION	
MANUFACTURER	Ishapore
CALIBRE	7.62 x 51mm
MAGAZINE CAPACITY	10
ACTION	Bolt action
TOTAL LENGTH	1,130mm/44.5in
BARREL LENGTH	640mm/25.19in
WEIGHT UNLOADED	3.91kg/8.62lb

India did not switch to the No. 4 action as Britain did in the 1940s. Therefore, in 1955, when it was necessary to convert rifles to the 7.62 x 51mm cartridge, it had none suitable for conversion. Instead, India used the No. 1 action blueprint to make new receivers out of a much tougher alloy, with better heat-treating. The new rifle, the SMLE Mod2A1, was deemed strong enough for the new cartridge. With an army of nearly 1.5 million men, a large number of rifles was required. The Mod2A1 was intended as an interim arm until the new FAL-derived rifle was made, but owing to the slow progress of the FAL project, was kept in service far longer than anticipated. The Mod2A1 is distinguished from the No. 1 by its square-profile magazine (the SMLE magazine is tapered). Manufacture began in the mid-1950s, and the rifles were in service until the mid-1980s.

FN 1A

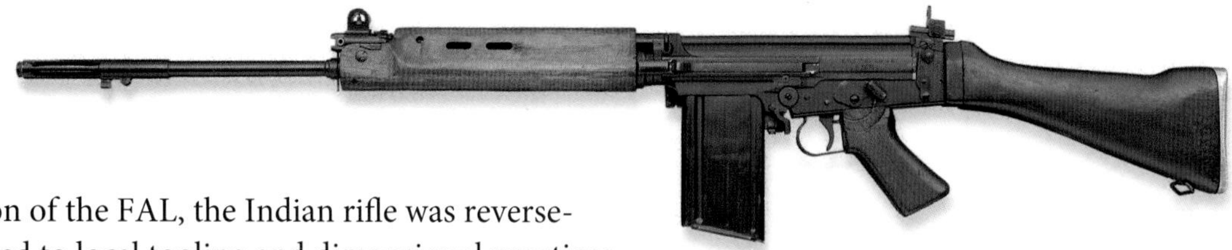

A non-licensed version of the FAL, the Indian rifle was reverse-engineered and adapted to local tooling and dimensional practices, so parts did not easily interchange with any other FAL. Without the FN licensing and support, initial production was small, and the rifle was rough at first. However, the basic design was solid. After a few years, Indian FN 1As were solid, reliable, and coming off the production lines in sufficient numbers for domestic use. By the mid-1980s the FN 1A was showing its age, and India started the Indian Small Arms System (INSAS) programme. Delays in production led to the continued use of ageing FN 1A rifles and the interim purchase of AKM rifles from various ex-Warsaw Pact countries. Introduced in Indian service in 1963, the FN 1A did not replace the 2A1 for a number of years. It lasted in regular service to the mid-1990s until replaced by the INSAS, but probably remains in police service in distant provinces.

SPECIFICATION	
MANUFACTURER	Ishapore
CALIBRE	7.62 x 51mm
MAGAZINE CAPACITY	20
ACTION	Gas operated/tilting lock
TOTAL LENGTH	1,089mm/42.9in
BARREL LENGTH	533mm/21in
WEIGHT UNLOADED	3.90kg/8.6lb

INSAS

An amalgam of three different rifles, built in India for use by its armed forces, the Indian National Small Arms System (INSAS) has the gas system and general layout of the AK, the gas regulator of the FAL, and a cocking handle on the upper left side like that of the Heckler & Koch G3. Adopted to replace the ageing stock of FAL rifles, it is a recent introduction and one intended for the usual triumvirate: rifle, carbine and squad automatic weapon. Production began in the late 1990s and the INSAS is the present issue weapon.

SPECIFICATION	
MANUFACTURER	Ishapore
CALIBRE	5.56 x 45mm
MAGAZINE CAPACITY	30
ACTION	Gas operated/rotating bolt
TOTAL LENGTH	945mm/37.2in
BARREL LENGTH	464mm/18.26in
WEIGHT UNLOADED	3.2kg/7.05lb

China

Before the Communist Revolution of 1949, a variety of rifles were found in China, including imports and locally produced guns. After 1949 China settled on Soviet designs, principally the AK and Simonov rifles. China began to manufacture large numbers of both Soviet and Western designs for export. In recent years it has begun working on its own assault weapons system.

Kalashnikov Type 56

An early convert to the AK-47, China initially made forged-receiver Type 56 rifles. It switched to the stamped, AKM style in the mid-1960s. Chinese AKs have attached bayonets that are pivoted to deploy. Select-fire models are for military production. Via the Norinco Company, China has manufactured tens of thousands of semi-auto fire-only AKs for the United States market. Once production began in the late 1950s for Chinese needs, production did not slacken off for almost three decades. It picked up again to supply the US market, starting in the 1980s.

SPECIFICATION

MANUFACTURER Factory 66, Norinco
CALIBRE 7.62 x 39mm
MAGAZINE CAPACITY 30
ACTION Gas operated/rotating bolt
TOTAL LENGTH 870mm/34.25in
BARREL LENGTH 415mm/16.35in
WEIGHT UNLOADED 4.4kg/9.81lb

Model 311 (M16A1 copy)

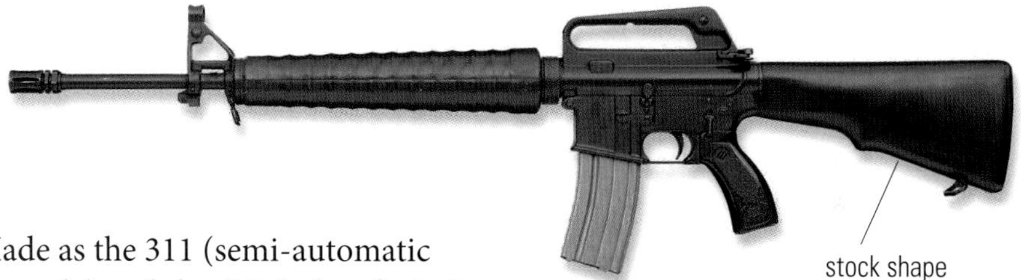

SPECIFICATION

MANUFACTURER Norinco
CALIBRE 5.56 x 45mm
MAGAZINE CAPACITY 20, 30
ACTION Gas operated/rotating bolt
TOTAL LENGTH 990mm/39in
BARREL LENGTH 508mm/20in
WEIGHT UNLOADED 2.85kg/6.31lb

Made as the 311 (semi-automatic fire only) and the CQ (select fire), the Norinco-made rifle is similar to an M16A1. Yet the pistol grip, handguards and stock are shaped differently and are made from a different formula plastic than US-made rifles. The rifling twist of the 311 is the old A1 rate (one turn in twelve inches), so it will not stabilize the newer SS-109 cartridge. As a result, firing SS-109 ammunition in a Model 311 is not advised. The Model 311 was produced from the early to late 1980s, for export sales only.

SPECIFICATION

MANUFACTURER Norinco
CALIBRE 7.62 x 51mm
MAGAZINE CAPACITY 20
ACTION Gas operated/rotating bolt
TOTAL LENGTH 1,117mm/44in
BARREL LENGTH 559mm/22in
WEIGHT UNLOADED 3.8kg/8.56lb

Model 305 (M14)

When the US Army dropped the M14 as a service rifle, target and sports shooters sought replacements. Curiously, China was in a position to make semi-auto only (the original M14 is select fire; semi and fully automatic) rifles for it. The US clients complained occasionally that the bolts were made of soft alloys and that the receivers had not been heat treated, but the shipments were nevertheless rapidly purchased. It was produced throughout the 1990s.

QBZ-95

SPECIFICATION
MANUFACTURER Unk
CALIBRE 5.8 x 42mm
MAGAZINE CAPACITY 20
ACTION Gas operated/rotating bolt
TOTAL LENGTH 760mm/29.9in
BARREL LENGTH 520mm/20.47in
WEIGHT UNLOADED 3.4kg/7.49lb

China approached the question of a new assault rifle by first designing a new cartridge for it, the 5.8 x 42mm. Then, the type 95 rifle, a bullpup design, could be built around the cartridge. It was intended as part of a family of weapons, to include a compact version, a Squad Automatic Weapon (SAW) and a sniper rifle. China also makes the QBZ-97 variant, chambered in 5.56 x 45mm, for export. Production of the QBZ-95 began in 1995 and continues to the present. The QBZ-95 and its ammunition are so closely guarded that no rifles, and only a few dozen rounds of ammunition, are known to exist outside China.

Mosin-Nagant Type 53

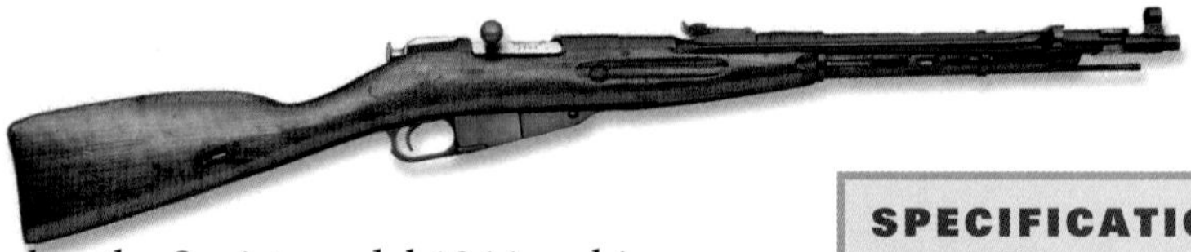

The Mosin-Nagant Type 53 is identical to the Soviet model 1944 carbine, except for the Chinese armoury markings. The bayonet is attached to the rifle and pivots from alongside the handguard. A spike rather than a blade, the bayonet is more useful as a tent peg than as a cutting tool. However, by attaching the bayonet directly to the rifle, it could not be lost, so troops armed with the carbine were still armed even if they did not have ammunition. Production commenced in 1953 and continued until the early 1960s, when there were enough SKS carbines to replace them.

SPECIFICATION
MANUFACTURER Various
CALIBRE 7.62 x 54R
MAGAZINE CAPACITY 5
ACTION Bolt action
TOTAL LENGTH 1,020mm/40.15in
BARREL LENGTH 509mm/20.05in
WEIGHT UNLOADED 3.9kg/8.6lb

Simonov Type 56

Also known as the SKS, the Simonov carbine has a fixed magazine with a hinged floorplate for unloading. The magazine can be charged via stripper clips of ten rounds, or with individual rounds with the bolt locked back. It is semi-automatic only. Compact and handy, if somewhat heavy for a carbine, the SKS is rugged and reliable. Sturdy through design rather than materials, some Simonov carbines were made with steel that was not heat-treated yet still functioned properly. The Simonov could be repaired by blacksmiths if necessary. The Simonov Type 56 was produced from 1956 until the supply of AK-47s was sufficient for Chinese needs in the 1960s.

SPECIFICATION
MANUFACTURER Various
CALIBRE 7.62 x 39mm
MAGAZINE CAPACITY 10
ACTION Gas operated/tilting lock
TOTAL LENGTH 1,121mm/44.15in
BARREL LENGTH 519mm/20.45in
WEIGHT UNLOADED 3.8kg/8.5lb

Type 68

The Type 68 has a blend of features from the SKS Simonov Type 56 carbine and the AK-47 Kalashnikov Type 56. Externally the Type 68 appears to be an SKS with an AK magazine in place of the ten-shot SKS magazine. Internally, it uses a bolt similar to that of the AK instead of the tilting bolt of the Simonov. Additionally, the Type 68 has an adjustable gas regulator. It was built as an adjunct to AK production. First made in 1968, production of the Type 68 continued until the late 1980s.

SPECIFICATION
MANUFACTURER Various
CALIBRE 7.62 x 39mm
MAGAZINE CAPACITY 20 & 30
ACTION Gas operated/rotating bolt
TOTAL LENGTH 1,029mm/40.5in
BARREL LENGTH 520mm/20.5in
WEIGHT UNLOADED 3.5kg/7.7lb

Dragunov Type 85

The Dragunov Type 85 was an improved model of the Type 79 and a copy of the Dragunov sniper rifle. Soviet (and probably Chinese) sniper tactics are less concerned with long-range hits than short-to-medium range use to increase the effectiveness of the infantry in attack or defence. A self-loading rifle increases the sniper's rate of fire, and allows more targets of opportunity to be engaged. In Western military units, that niche is now filled by 5.56mm rifles, referred to as Designated Marksman Rifles. The Chinese Dragunov presents an equally serious a threat at 600m/1,969ft as the Soviet model. Production has run since 1985, and no viable replacements have yet emerged.

SPECIFICATION

MANUFACTURER Various
CALIBRE 7.62 x 54R
MAGAZINE CAPACITY 10
ACTION Gas operated/rotating bolt
TOTAL LENGTH 1,220mm/48.0in
BARREL LENGTH 620mm/24.4in
WEIGHT UNLOADED 4.4kg/9.7lb

Indonesia

The Netherlands ruled Indonesia as a colony primarily for its rich oil fields and rubber plantations. It was then occupied by Japan during World War II. Indonesia gained independence in 1945. From the 1970s, the country purchased large numbers of M16s from the United States.

Arisaka Type 38

SPECIFICATION

MANUFACTURER Koishikawa, Tokyo
CALIBRE 6.5 x 50mm
MAGAZINE CAPACITY 5
ACTION Bolt action
TOTAL LENGTH 1,021mm/50.2in
BARREL LENGTH 799mm/31.45in
WEIGHT UNLOADED 4.11kg/9.08lb

After World War II, many Japanese rifles were left behind by the former occupation forces. In Indonesia during the struggle for independence from Japan, and as an independent country afterwards, the Type 38 was common. Other than cleaning them up, Indonesia did nothing to alter them from the original issue, even keeping the calibre. With large stocks of ammunition on hand, there was no reason to alter them. The Arisaka Type 38 was in regular use from 1940 to 1949.

SS2

SPECIFICATION

MANUFACTURER Pindad
CALIBRE 5.6mm NATO
MAGAZINE CAPACITY 30
ACTION Gas operated
TOTAL LENGTH 985mm/38.8in
BARREL LENGTH 403mm/15.8in
WEIGHT UNLOADED 3.8kg/8.4lb

The SS2 is a licensed version of the FN FNC, but with some differences. The flash suppressor is the birdcage style from the M16A2 and the front sight is from a Kalashnikov style rifle. Slow to be developed, the SS2 was first ordered in 2002 but not delivered until 2006. Since then, Pindad builds approximately 40,000 per year. Many non-state users have expressed interest in adopting the SS2, but nothing has been firmly established.

Singapore

One of the very few city-states left in the modern world, Singapore has the economic muscle to make its own way in the Asian market. After occupation during World War II, Singapore joined briefly with the Federation of Malaya in 1963 to form Malaysia. It is now independent and builds its own small arms.

CIS Armalite M-16S1

SPECIFICATION

MANUFACTURER Chartered Industries of Singapore (CIS)
CALIBRE 5.56 x 45mm
MAGAZINE CAPACITY 30
ACTION Gas operated
TOTAL LENGTH 1,006mm/39.6in
BARREL LENGTH 508mm/20in
WEIGHT UNLOADED 3.7kg/8.15lb

This is a licensed copy of the Colt rifle, produced by the CIS for local use and export sales. Except for the markings, it is a Colt rifle, with all parts interchangeable. By establishing an offshore manufacturing presence, Colt could derive income from sales to entities the US State Department might otherwise deny them. CIS could earn cash for Singapore and supply the Singapore Defence Forces with small arms. The CIS Armalite was manufactured from 1970 to the early 1980s and was the standard rifle of the Singapore Defence Forces.

CIS SAR-80

Based on the US-designed Armalite AR-18 with improvements, the CIS produced the Singapore Assault Rifle (SAR)-80 for local use and export. It is a gas-operated, selective-fire rifle, which uses a short-stroke gas piston to push the large bolt carrier with a rotating bolt. The piston system allows the SAR-80 to be fitted with a folding stock. Used by the Singapore Army and exported to clients including Croatia, Sri Lanka and Somalia, there was stiff competition to the SAR-80 on the world market. It was manufactured from 1981 to the early 1990s.

SPECIFICATION

MANUFACTURER CIS
CALIBRE 5.56 x 45mm
MAGAZINE CAPACITY 30
ACTION Gas operated
TOTAL LENGTH 970mm/38.18in
BARREL LENGTH 459mm/18.0in
WEIGHT UNLOADED 3.7kg/8.15lb

SAR 21

The SAR 21 is an acronym for Singapore Assault Rifle – 21st Century. Adopted in 1999, it became the replacement for their licensed copy of the M16A1. A bullpup design, the rifle has some interesting features built into it such as a 1.5x scope that is integral to the carry handle as well as a laser aiming device. Safety features include a Kevlar cheekpiece and a high pressure vent in case of a chamber explosion.

SPECIFICATION

MANUFACTURER ST Kinetics
CALIBRE 5.56mm NATO
MAGAZINE CAPACITY 30
ACTION Gas operated
TOTAL LENGTH 805mm/31.7in
BARREL LENGTH 508mm/20in
WEIGHT UNLOADED 4kg/8.8lb

BR18

SPECIFICATION

MANUFACTURER ST Kinetics
CALIBRE 5.56mm NATO
MAGAZINE CAPACITY 10, 20 or 30
ACTION Gas operated
TOTAL LENGTH 645mm/25.3in
BARREL LENGTH 370mm/14.5in
WEIGHT UNLOADED 2.9kg/9.3lb

The BR18 is meant to replace the SAR 21, which has been in service for more than 20 years. The rifle is very similar to the SAR 21, but it was designed to be ambidextrous, with spent casings being ejected forward and to the right. Additionally, the trigger guard can be flipped out to accommodate use with gloved hands.

Australia

Australia did not have its own government rifle factory until the establishment of the Lithgow Arsenal in 1912. Between the world wars, rather than switch to the No. 4 design, as Britain did, Australia produced the No. 1 Mark III*, which remained in production until 1955.

SMLE No. 1 Mark III*

Manufactured in Lithgow, as all subsequent Australian service rifles have been, the No. 1 began production in 1912. Once the volume of rifles needed for combat in World War I became apparent, all Australian rifles, save an essential reserve, were shipped to Britain until the end of the war. Production for Australian needs continued until after the Korean War (1950–53). Lithgow looked into a short "jungle carbine" conversion and a conversion of the Mark III* to 7.62mm NATO, but neither plan went ahead. The SMLE No. 1 was the standard Australian military rifle from 1912 until replaced by the Australian-made inch pattern FAL, the L1A1.

SPECIFICATION

MANUFACTURER Lithgow
CALIBRE .303 British
MAGAZINE CAPACITY 10
ACTION Bolt action
TOTAL LENGTH 1,130mm/44.5in
BARREL LENGTH 640mm/25.2in
WEIGHT UNLOADED 3.92kg/8.65lb

L1A1

SPECIFICATION

MANUFACTURER Lithgow
CALIBRE 7.62 x 51mm
MAGAZINE CAPACITY 20
ACTION Gas operated/tilting lock
TOTAL LENGTH 1,136mm/45in
BARREL LENGTH 533mm/24.3in
WEIGHT UNLOADED 4.77kg/10.5lb

Manufactured by Lithgow, the L1A1 was an inch-pattern copy of the FAL, made under licence. The weight proved something of a hindrance in jungle fighting in the Vietnam War (1954–75). As a result it was not unusual for Australian Special Air Service to be seen with the lighter M16s. As with all inch-pattern FAL rifles, the L1A1 could be fitted with metric-pattern magazines in an emergency. The inch-pattern magazines use a large front block as an attachment point; the metric uses a small one. The rifle was produced and issued from 1955 to 1992, when the Australian Defence Force switched the Steyr AUG.

F88

ejection can be changed from right to left

SPECIFICATION

MANUFACTURER Lithgow
CALIBRE 5.56 x 45mm
MAGAZINE CAPACITY 30
ACTION Gas operated/rotating bolt
TOTAL LENGTH 790mm/31in
BARREL LENGTH 508mm/20in
WEIGHT UNLOADED 3.6kg/7.9lb

In the early 1990s Australia adopted the 5.56mm cartridge, as used in the Austrian AUG. The F88 was manufactured under licence by Lithgow. Offered in the basic AUG form as the F88, it was also produced with a shorter barrel as a carbine, and as a model with an integral rail for mounting optics. When the army changed from the L1A1 to the F88, the decreased recoil and increased accuracy of the F88 produced high range-qualification scores, and the ratings had to be recalculated. It has been produced since 1992 and has been used by Australian forces in East Timor, Iraq and Afghanistan.

F88 materials
Many of the major components of the F88 are made from non-corroding polymers.

North Korea

North Korea, with assistance from the Chinese, has spent the last half-century manufacturing rifles and machine guns of the Soviet model for its 1.2 million-man army. While perhaps deficient in electronics, North Korea does not lack factories for producing small arms and ammunition.

AK-47

The AK-47 was a thoroughly standard AKM although it lacked the rate-reducer/anti-bounce mechanism. The bolt and carrier of the AK bounce when closing. This is an unavoidable result of the steel-on-steel impact of the carrier striking the front of the receiver when the bolt closes. Occasionally, in full-auto fire, an AK built without the anti-bounce feature will misfire. The cause is due to the hammer striking the bolt just as it has bounced away from the front of the receiver. It is not known why North Korea builds AKs lacking the anti-bounce parts, since they are not difficult to manufacture or to install. The AK-47 was produced and fielded from the 1950s to 1990s.

SPECIFICATION

MANUFACTURER N. Korea Arsenal
CALIBRE 7.62 x 39mm
MAGAZINE CAPACITY 30
ACTION Gas operated/rotating bolt
TOTAL LENGTH 877mm/34.55in
BARREL LENGTH 415mm/16.35in
WEIGHT UNLOADED 3.81kg/8.42lb

South Korea

After the Korean War (1950–53), South Korea built up a modern economy. While depending on the United States for support in defending against a potential North Korean attack, South Korea has developed its own arms manufacture. As well as rifles, South Korea produces ammunition.

Daewoo K2

Basically an M16 with the gas system of an AK-47 instead of the direct gas impingement system, the Daewoo K2 allows the user to have a folding polymer or a telescoping wire stock. The rifle uses standard M16 magazines, and the AK gas system avoids the gas fouling that causes problems in the Stoner system. Also, the Daewoo lacks the carry handle of the M16, and the charging handle of the Daewoo is on the right side, attached to the bolt carrier. While manufacture began in the early 1980s and the K2 remains in South Korean service to the present time, it has not been accepted as a service rifle outside of Korea.

SPECIFICATION

MANUFACTURER Daewoo
CALIBRE 5.56 x 45mm
MAGAZINE CAPACITY 30
ACTION Gas operated
TOTAL LENGTH 980mm/38.58in
BARREL LENGTH 465mm/18.30in
WEIGHT UNLOADED 3.26kg/7.19lb

Daewoo in the West
In the early 1990s the K2 was available in North America, but its simple sights and basic finish ensured that it was never popular with shooters.

Japan

When the Japanese economy first opened up to the West in 1868, it was centuries behind the industrial economies. Starting with no industrial base or tradition of arms design and production, Japan adopted existing ideas. Later Japanese designs proved to be quite idiosyncratic, and in some cases were unreliable in the field. Compounding the design and production problems, during World War II, each Japanese Defence branch organized its own design, production and distribution of arms. Post-war Japan was forbidden from creating a defence force and so had no need of small arms. When a new force was established in the 1950s, Japan designed and produced its own small arms weapons.

Type 64

SPECIFICATION

MANUFACTURER Howa
CALIBRE 7.62 x 51mm
MAGAZINE CAPACITY 20
ACTION Gas operated/tilting lock
TOTAL LENGTH 989mm/38.95in
BARREL LENGTH 450mm/17.7in
WEIGHT UNLOADED 4.40kg/9.72lb

After 1957, when the post-war restrictions on Japanese military production were lifted, Japan started to design its own rifles. The first was the Type 64, produced from 1964 until 1985. With its gas regulator, the Type 64 could fire either reduced-power 7.62mm ammunition or full-power 7.62mm NATO. While a 7.62 battle rifle in 1964 made a lot of sense, by the 1980s even the low-recoil ammunition was perceived to have too many shortcomings. There was still too much recoil, and the low velocity meant the trajectory was too arched. Despite the rifle's intrinsic accuracy, hitting targets beyond 300m/328yd was not possible. The Type 64 was replaced by the Type 89, which was in 5.56mm.

AR-180

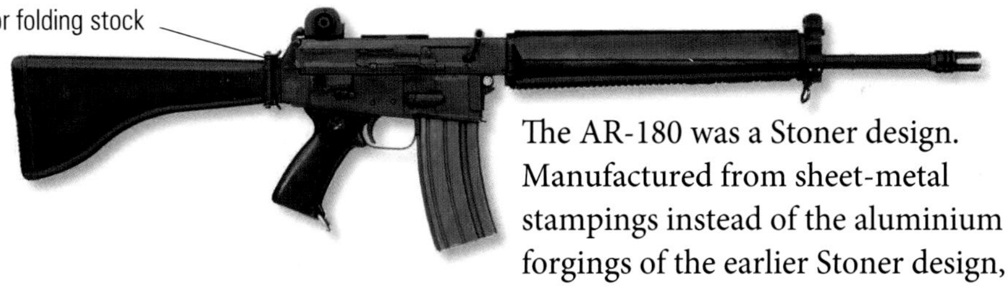

SPECIFICATION

MANUFACTURER Howa
CALIBRE 5.56 x 45mm
MAGAZINE CAPACITY 20 & 30
ACTION Gas operated/rotating bolt
TOTAL LENGTH 940mm/37.0in
BARREL LENGTH 464mm/18.26in
WEIGHT UNLOADED 3.09kg/6.81lb

The AR-180 was a Stoner design. Manufactured from sheet-metal stampings instead of the aluminium forgings of the earlier Stoner design, the M16, the AR-180 failed to compete with the M16 or AK-47. The design did lead to the Singapore SAR-80 and the SA-80, and some elements even appeared in the West German G36. When Japanese law banned the export of rifles that might be used for war, production moved to Costa Mesa, USA and Sterling, UK. Manufacture in Japan lasted from 1968 to 1972, while elsewhere it continued until 1979. While some parts are similar to those of the M16, no parts are interchangeable between the AR-180 and the M16.

Type 89

SPECIFICATION

MANUFACTURER Howa
CALIBRE 5.56 x 45mm
MAGAZINE CAPACITY 20 & 30
ACTION Gas operated/rotating bolt
TOTAL LENGTH 864mm/34.0in
BARREL LENGTH 420mm/16.53in
WEIGHT UNLOADED 3.5kg/7.71lb

Developed by Howa, and a descendant of the AR-18, the Type 89 solves the Type 64's problem of two 7.62mm ammunitions in supply. The Type 89 has a built-in bipod, folding stock and polymer furniture, and is up to date without being a bullpup. To make the Type 89 lighter, designers used aluminum forgings and polymers in place of the steel and wood of the Type 64 it replaced. It is capable of firing rifle grenades. Manufacture and issue commenced in 1989 and continues to the present.

Howa Type 20

Development began in 2014 with the goal of replacing the Type 89. Howa ws chosen over the other options, which were the Steyr AUG, HK416, HK G36, and FN SCA – the latter of which bears some similarities to the Type 20. The first examples were purchased in 2019 and in 2020 the first rifles were given to the Amphibious Rapid Deployment Brigade. Equipped with multiple sections of Picatinny rail, it is Japan's first rifle to come standard with this feature.

SPECIFICATION

MANUFACTURER Howa
CALIBRE 5.56mm NATO
MAGAZINE CAPACITY 30
ACTION Gas operated
TOTAL LENGTH 850mm/33in
BARREL LENGTH 330mm/13in
WEIGHT UNLOADED 3.5kg/7.7lb

Murata Type 22

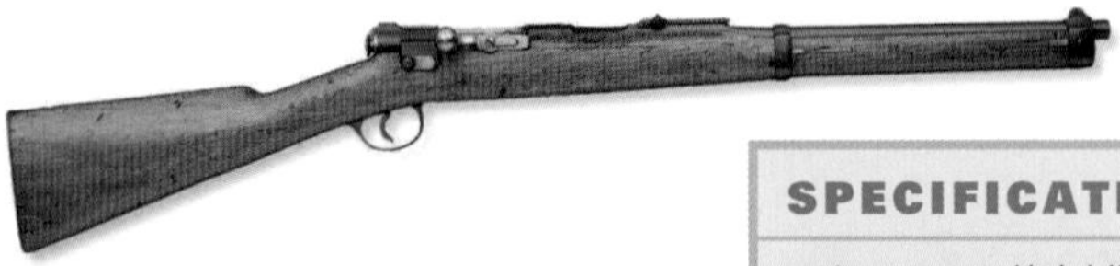

The Murata Type 22, issued in 1889, used a Japanese-designed 8mm rimmed round, and fed from a tube magazine under the barrel. Although Japan's industrial base was centuries behind Europe, this rifle was not particularly backward compared to the magazine-fed repeating rifles that many European countries were adopting at the time. When the Japanese became involved in conflict in China in 1894, they discovered the Gewehr 1888 and learnt about clip chargers and vertical magazines. The speed of reloading the 1888 made it apparent that the Murata was obsolete, and by 1896 it was being withdrawn.

SPECIFICATION

MANUFACTURER Koishikawa
CALIBRE 8mm
MAGAZINE CAPACITY 8
ACTION Bolt action
TOTAL LENGTH 1,206mm/47.5in
BARREL LENGTH 749mm/29.5in
WEIGHT UNLOADED 3.93kg/8.68lb

Arisaka Type 38

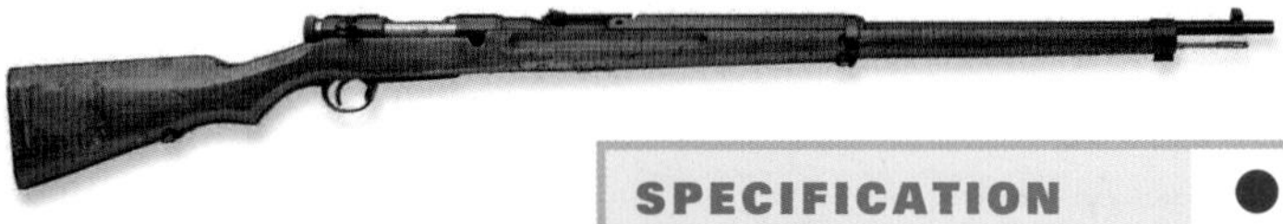

With a split and solid bridge (the bolt handle went ahead of one part of the receiver but behind a solid ring of another) and a circular, rotating safety, the Arisaka Type 38 is distinctive. It is also quite strong. The Arisaka cocks on the forward movement of the bolt, like earlier Mauser designs. Many early rifles were made with receiver covers, which rattled when the bearer walked. The cover was meant to keep dust and debris off the bolt, and moved with the bolt when the action was worked. The Type 38 was manufactured in volume from 1905 to 1945. A sniper version of this rifle was produced between 1938 and 1945, the Arisaka Type 97 Sniper.

SPECIFICATION

MANUFACTURER Koishikawa
CALIBRE 6.5 x 50mm
MAGAZINE CAPACITY 5
ACTION Bolt action
TOTAL LENGTH 1,275mm/50.2in
BARREL LENGTH 799mm/31.45in
WEIGHT UNLOADED 4.11kg/9.08lb

Arisaka Type 99

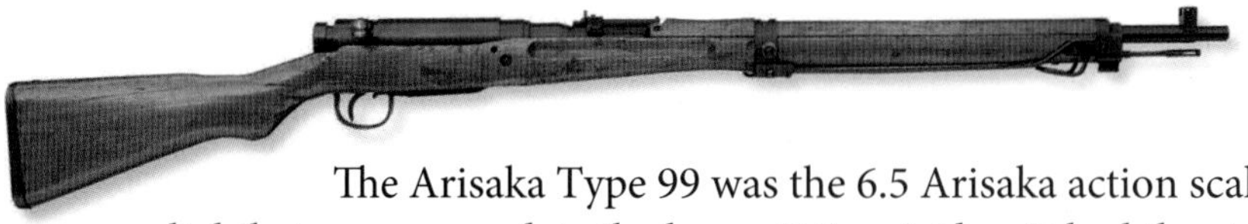

SPECIFICATION

MANUFACTURER Toriimatsu
CALIBRE 7.7 x 58mm
MAGAZINE CAPACITY 5
ACTION Bolt action
TOTAL LENGTH 1,149mm/45.25in
BARREL LENGTH 656mm/25.85in
WEIGHT UNLOADED 3.79kg/8.37lb

The Arisaka Type 99 was the 6.5 Arisaka action scaled up slightly to accommodate the larger 7.7 cartridge. It had the standard sliding dust/mud cover and a wire monopod to aid stability when aiming. Many covers were discarded in the jungles or on the islands to reduce the rattle and prevent revealing the owner's position, or to shed 0.2kg/0.5lb of weight. The wire monopod, while well intended, proved an illusory aid to aiming. Production began in 1939, just before the Japanese war machine turned against the USA, and continued until 1945. The Arisaka Type 2 is the paratroop version of the Type 99.

Type 5 Garand copy

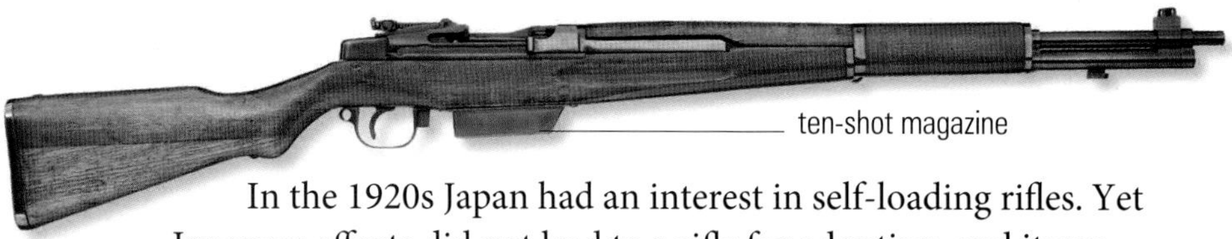

SPECIFICATION

MANUFACTURER Yokosuka Navy Arsenal
CALIBRE 7.7 x 58mm
MAGAZINE CAPACITY 10
ACTION Gas operated/rotating bolt
TOTAL LENGTH 1,098mm/43.25in
BARREL LENGTH 588mm/23.15in
WEIGHT UNLOADED 4.14kg/9.13lb

In the 1920s Japan had an interest in self-loading rifles. Yet Japanese efforts did not lead to a rifle for adoption, and it was left with bolt-action rifles. During World War II, captured Garands were inspected, and a semi-auto rifle produced. However, it was the navy that made the Type 5, not the army. It used an internal magazine charged with two five-round stripper clips, instead of the Garand en bloc clip. Few Type 5s were produced, and most disappeared during the war. Those that still exist are found only in museums. The Type 5 was made only in 1945.

New Zealand

Having little local defence manufacturing, New Zealand purchases weapons from abroad, which allows it to choose the best for its needs. The country has a mixture of British, French, German, Norwegian and Australian equipment. The current primary individual weapon for all three services is the MARS-L.

Charlton conversion

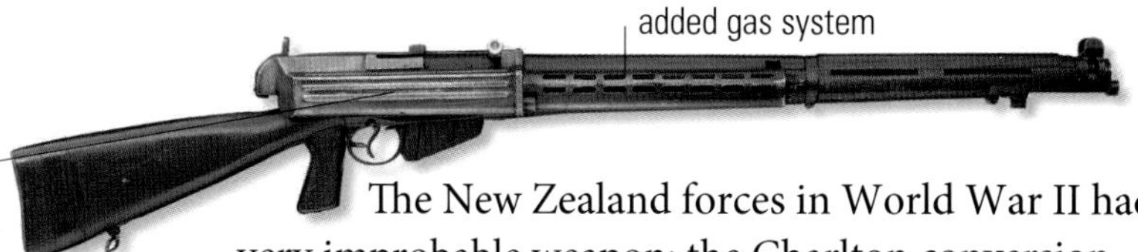

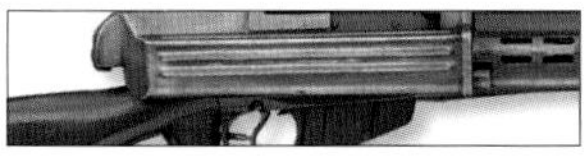

RIGHT The outer housing keeps the firer safe.

SPECIFICATION

MANUFACTURER Charlton Motor Workshops, NZ
CALIBRE .303 British
MAGAZINE CAPACITY 10, 30
ACTION Gas operated
TOTAL LENGTH 1132mm/44.55in
BARREL LENGTH 640mm/25.2in
WEIGHT UNLOADED 7.48kg/16.5lb

The New Zealand forces in World War II had a very improbable weapon: the Charlton conversion. The Charlton .303 Light Machine Gun (LMG) was a No. 1 Mark III* bolt-action rifle converted to a LMG. Besides adding a gas piston, cutting off the bolt handle and putting a sheet-metal cover over a new mechanism, New Zealand devised new magazines of more than ten-round capacity – although the conversion could still use standard rifle magazines. The sheet-metal cover kept the reciprocating parts from grabbing on to the shooter or his assistant. It was remarkable that the device worked at all; in fact, contemporary reports state that it worked well. The Charlton conversion was made only in 1941–2. As soon as BREN guns arrived in New Zealand from overseas, conversion work stopped, and the workshop was switched over to manufacturing Owen submachine guns, of which there was also a pressing need.

LMT MARS-L

MARS-L is an acronym for Modular Assault Rifle System – Light, and it was adopted by New Zealand in 2018. It has ambidextrous controls and charging handle, a flared magazine well, and uses a mid-length gas system.

SPECIFICATION

MANUFACTURER LMT Defense
CALIBRE 5.56mm NATO
MAGAZINE CAPACITY 30
ACTION Direct impingement
TOTAL LENGTH 1,022mm/40.3in
BARREL LENGTH 406mm/16in
WEIGHT UNLOADED 3.4kg/7.5lb

KEY

1 Canada
2 United States
3 Mexico
4 Chile
5 Venezuela
6 Argentina
7 Brazil
8 Portugal
9 Spain
10 UK
11 France
12 Belgium
13 Netherlands
14 Switzerland
15 Germany
16 Italy
17 Norway
18 Denmark
19 Austria
20 Sweden
21 Czech Republic
22 Poland
23 South Africa
24 Serbia
25 Hungary
26 Greece
27 Finland
28 Romania
29 Bulgaria
30 Russia
31 Egypt
32 Turkey
33 Israel
34 Ethiopia
35 Iraq
36 Iran
37 Pakistan
38 India
39 China
40 Thailand
41 Singapore
42 Australia
43 North Korea
44 South Korea
45 Japan

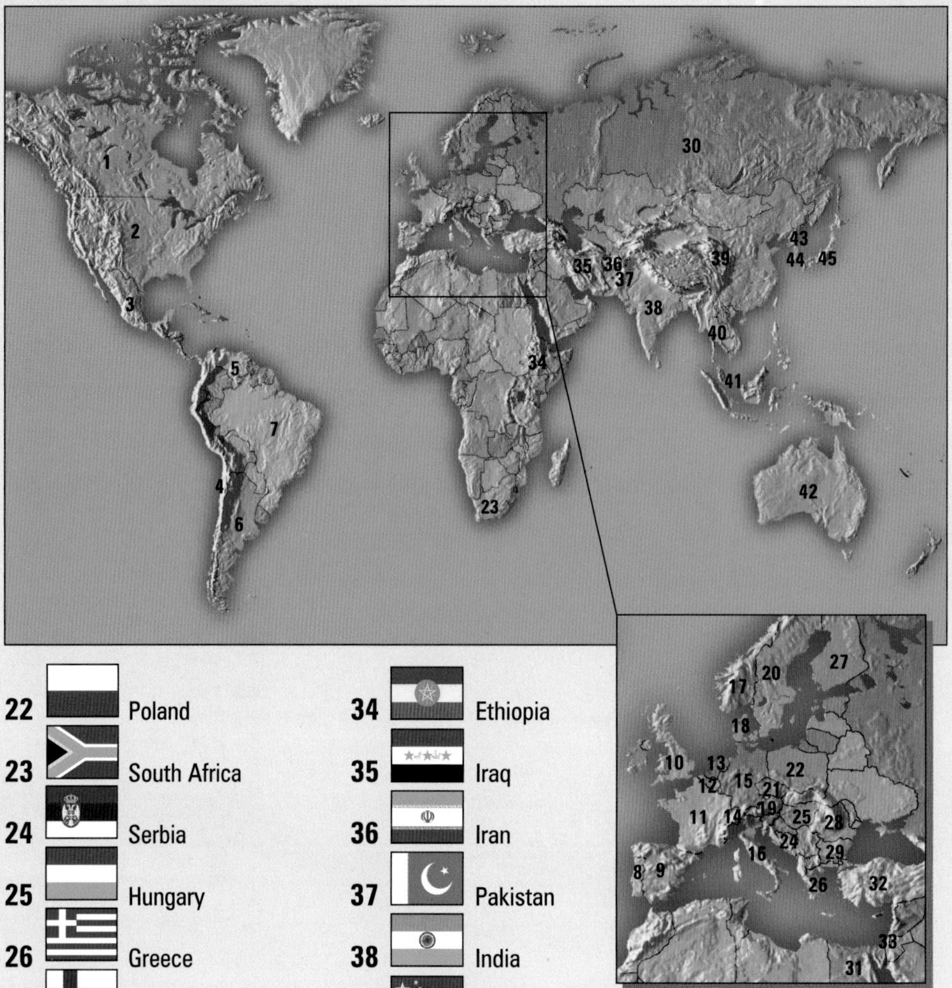

ABOVE The map indicates the countries of the world where machine guns are featured in this section.

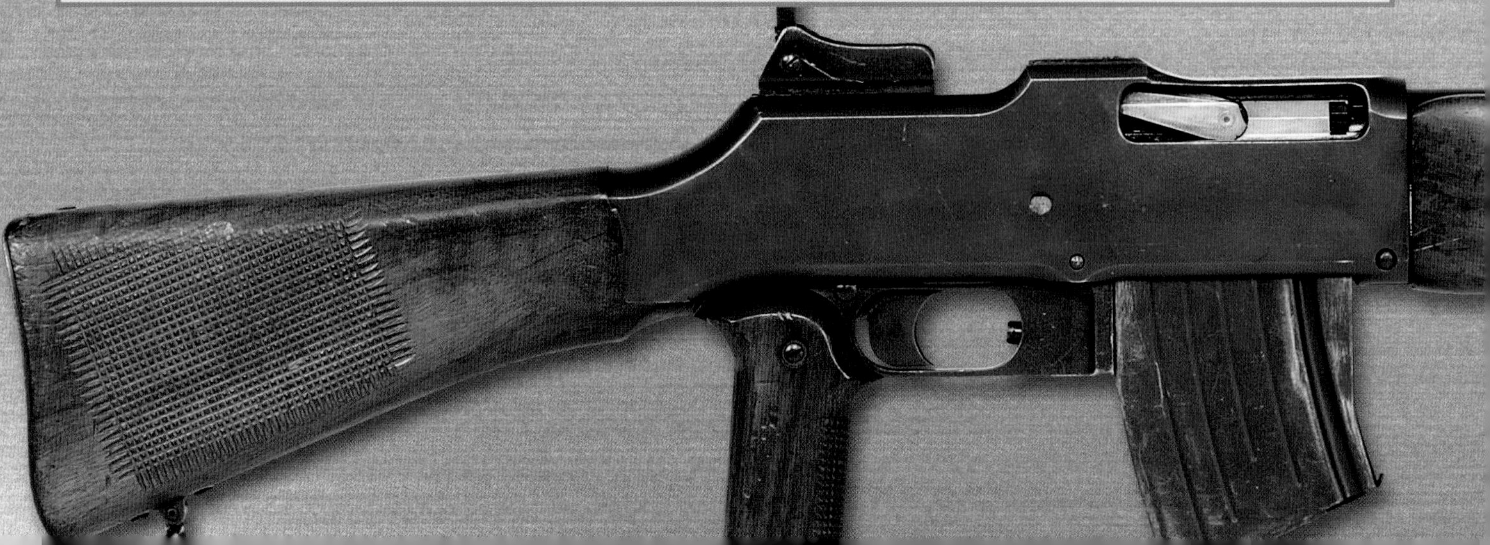

A directory of machine guns from around the world

Machine guns are produced and manufactured across the world – some countries designing weaponry for their own armies, others producing or importing versions of machine guns from abroad, often modified or tailored to the importer's unique needs. This directory takes a look at the weapons from selected countries of the world, travelling from west to east, and details some of the machine guns that are available in those areas. Guns are organized alphabetically by manufacturer, except where their historical development is shown more clearly chronologically, or a company changes its name. Each machine gun has a description and a specification that lists its vital measurements, including length, unloaded weight, calibre, action and magazine capacity.

LEFT While the Hotchkiss Model 1914 had some minor faults, it was sufficient for France to manufacture tens of thousands of Hotchkisses during World War I.

BELOW Too late for more than the last few days of World War I, the Browning BAR Model 1921 was a solid design that sold well around the world, and was later used in all theatres during World War II.

Note on specification boxes: Traditionally guns developed in the United States have been given their calibre in inches, while European countries have designated calibre in metric measurement. Guns have retained this designation in this book. Dimensions refer to the weapon shown, where illustrated. Weights and measurements may be approximate.

Canada

Manufacture of machine guns first began in Canada in 1938 when the Inglis firm signed a contract to manufacture BREN (from BRio/ENfield) guns for both Britain and Canada. Production started in 1940, and by 1943, some 60 per cent of all BREN guns that were being produced came from Inglis.

BREN Mark 2 Conversion

Like so many countries after World War I, when faced with the prospect of converting to the new 7.62mm NATO cartridge, Canada first adapted older designs. Converting the BREN to 7.62mm required only a new bolt, barrel and magazines and it worked well in the new chambering. The most expensive part to make, the receiver, was simply re-marked to show the calibre change. They were only in use from the early 1950s to the early 1960s until replaced by the MAG 58, but were common in Canadian infantry units.

SPECIFICATION	
MANUFACTURER	Inglis
CALIBRE	7.62 x 51mm
MAGAZINE CAPACITY	20
ACTION	Gas operated/tilting lock
TOTAL LENGTH	1,158mm/45.6in
BARREL LENGTH	635mm/25in
WEIGHT UNLOADED	10.51kg/23.18lb

Inglis Experimental

This was a simplified Oerlikon cannon meant for armoured and infantry use. Also known as the "Polsten" (Polish STEN), it was brought to Inglis by Polish engineers fleeing the German invasion. The Inglis was intended to be faster and cheaper to produce. Designed as light tank armament, it quickly became obsolete. Only the Finns found 20mm anti-tank guns transported by infantry to be useful for long. Introduced in 1939, it was quickly outclassed by armour advances, but stayed in service into the 1950s as a direct-fire infantry cannon.

SPECIFICATION	
MANUFACTURER	Inglis
CALIBRE	20mm
MAGAZINE CAPACITY	30
ACTION	Recoil operated
TOTAL LENGTH	2,210mm/87in
BARREL LENGTH	1,397mm/55in
WEIGHT UNLOADED	68kg/150lb

United States

The United States was a power on the world stage before World War I, but the production requirements for World War II turned it into an arms-producing powerhouse, equalled only by the Soviet Union. Every rifle expert selling to the US government had his own machine-gun design.

Stoner 63/Solenoid

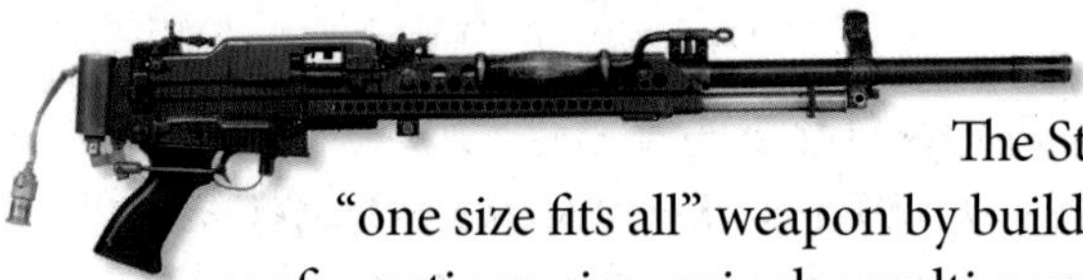

The Stoner 63 was designed to be a "one size fits all" weapon by building the components into the desired configuration using a single, multi-purpose receiver as the "building block". In this way, what was an assault rifle could be built as a belt-fed solenoid-fired fixed machine gun for mounting on a helicopter and fired forward. It could also be used as a top-fed BREN clone, or a belt-fed Light Machine Gun (LMG). The Stoner 63 system was used by the USA Navy's Sea, Air and Land (SEALS).

SPECIFICATION	
MANUFACTURER	Cadillac Gage
CALIBRE	5.56 x 45mm
MAGAZINE CAPACITY	Belt-fed
ACTION	Gas operated
TOTAL LENGTH	762mm/30in
BARREL LENGTH	508mm/20in
WEIGHT UNLOADED	5.25kg/11.57lb

Colt M1895

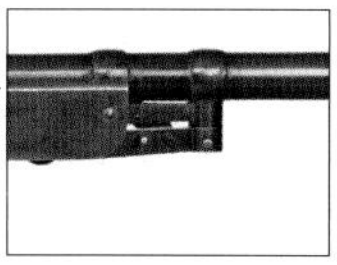

LEFT The Colt gas lever pivots down, and if too close to the ground thrashes the dirt.

SPECIFICATION

MANUFACTURER Colt
CALIBRE .30-06 & .303 British
MAGAZINE CAPACITY Belt-fed
ACTION Gas operated
TOTAL LENGTH 1,035mm/40.75in
BARREL LENGTH 711mm/28in
WEIGHT UNLOADED 15.87kg/35lb

The first Browning machine-gun design to go into production, the Colt used a simple gas system. The gas port, which was drilled into the barrel near the muzzle, threw a hinged lever down and the rod linked to it unlocked and forced the bolt back. Apart from this, it was a normal machine gun, with each round extracted backwards from the canvas belt and then fed forward into the chamber. Potentially, a gas-operated machine gun could be lighter than a recoil-operated one and the Colt was much lighter than the Maxim, Vickers and others, even when the water was left out of them. However, if the Colt gun was mounted too low to the ground the "flapper" would chew the earth, earning the nickname "potato digger". Introduced by Colt in 1895 and used in the Spanish-American War, it lasted to 1918, serving as a training and combat machine gun in World War I.

Benet-Mercie

SPECIFICATION

MANUFACTURER Colt
CALIBRE .30-06
MAGAZINE CAPACITY 24- or 30-round trays
ACTION Gas operated
TOTAL LENGTH 1,232mm/48.5in
BARREL LENGTH 637mm/25.1in
WEIGHT UNLOADED 12.52kg/27.6lb

This was the Hotchkiss light machine gun turned into an automatic rifle. Discarding the tripod for a rather tall bipod, the Benet-Mercié was used in training by the US Army. Between 1900–1914, the US Army owned less than 1,000 machine guns. Between not knowing which was best suited for their needs, and many officers thinking the army did not need machine guns at all, they only bought a few test samples of any one model. The Benet-Mercie was purchased in 1909 and used for training until 1918. It was popular outside the United States as a portable lightweight machine gun.

Browning M1917

SPECIFICATION

MANUFACTURER Colt
CALIBRE .30-06
MAGAZINE CAPACITY Belt-fed
ACTION Recoil operated
TOTAL LENGTH 978mm/38.5in
BARREL LENGTH 610mm/24in
WEIGHT UNLOADED 14.78kg/32.6lb w/o mount

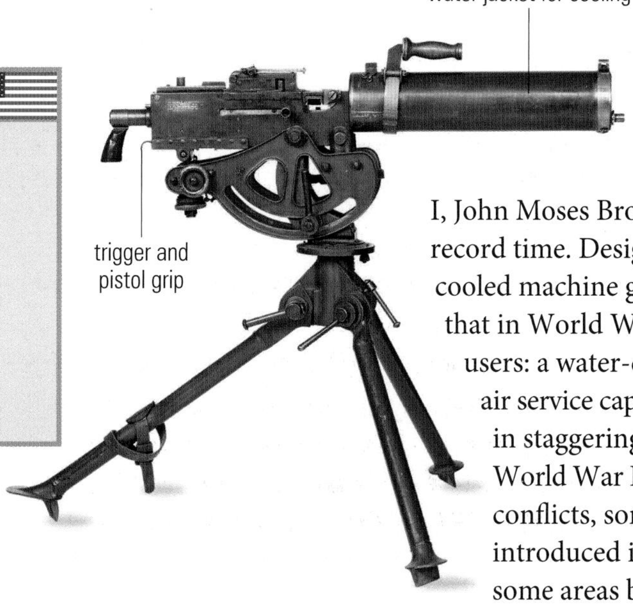

Tasked with designing a new heavy machine gun for the US Army before World War I, John Moses Browning produced this design in record time. Designed as a recoil-operated water-cooled machine gun, it proved so adaptable that in World War II it was all things to all users: a water-cooled, air-cooled, infantry and air service capable machine gun produced in staggering numbers. For decades after World War II it was ubiquitous, found in all conflicts, sometimes on both sides. It was introduced in 1917 and had a service life in some areas beyond the 1960s.

Browning BAR M1918

As a Light Machine Gun (LMG) or Squad Automatic Weapon (SAW), the BAR proved useful enough to still be in service in World War II, Korea and Vietnam. Despite its name, the BAR 1918 went into service just before World War I, and lasted in one form or another to the 1960s. The improvements of the M1918 (the A1 followed by the A2) included the flash hider, bipod and carry handle. Typically, World War II GIs would discard the flash hider and carry handle and some even the bipod from the A2. The barrel is not user-changeable, and by modern standards exchanging magazines is slow. But an adversary armed with a BAR is not to be taken lightly.

SPECIFICATION	
MANUFACTURER	Colt
CALIBRE	.30-06
MAGAZINE CAPACITY	20
ACTION	Gas operated
TOTAL LENGTH	1,214mm/47.8in
BARREL LENGTH	610mm/24in
WEIGHT UNLOADED	8.79kg/19.4lb

Browning M1919A6

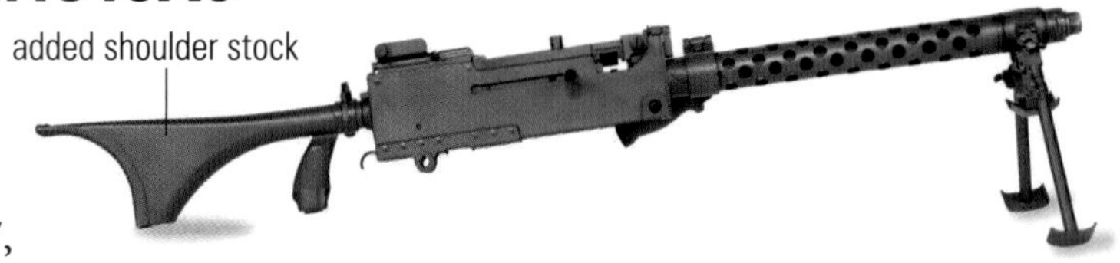

This was essentially the Browning M1917, altered far beyond the designer's mission or intent. It was changed to air-cooled and given a pierced barrel shroud. By adding a shoulder stock to the rear and changing the trigger plate from a spade to a trigger system, the US Army produced a lighter machine gun that could be used by the infantry. Introduced in 1942, it stayed in inventory and in service until the early 1960s. Despite its weight, it was loved for its reliability and durability.

SPECIFICATION	
MANUFACTURER	Colt
CALIBRE	.30-06
MAGAZINE CAPACITY	Belt-fed
ACTION	Recoil operated
TOTAL LENGTH	1,346mm/53in
BARREL LENGTH	610mm/24in
WEIGHT UNLOADED	14.74kg/32.5lb

Chauchat (CSRG) M1918

The Chauchat was designed around the tapered and rimmed 8mm Lebel in 1918. In the .30-06 it was said to be almost as hazardous to the firer as to his target. The long, essentially straight .30-06 case was difficult to extract and the long-recoil mechanism was not up to handling the power of the cartridge, so it was relegated as a training weapon. It was so poor in .30-06 that after the war the army had them all destroyed.

SPECIFICATION	
MANUFACTURER	C.S.R.G.
CALIBRE	.30-06
MAGAZINE CAPACITY	20
ACTION	Long recoil
TOTAL LENGTH	1,143mm/45in
BARREL LENGTH	470mm/18.5in
WEIGHT UNLOADED	8.61kg/19lb

M134 (GAU-2B/A)

The M134 GAU (Gun/Automatic/Unit in US Air Force nomenclature) is the standard weapon on Blackhawk helicopters. It is essentially a multi-barrel Gatling gun powered by an electric motor, in a flexible mount. The firing rate is user-adjustable from 2,000 to 6,000 rpm. The weapon uses linked ammunition, but requires a de-linking feed system. It needs an electrical power supply and chutes to dispose of the links and brass, and thus is vehicular or aircraft bound. Developed in the 1960s and refined by Dillon, it is in use to the present day due to its staggering firepower.

SPECIFICATION	
MANUFACTURER	Dillon Aero
CALIBRE	7.62mm NATO
MAGAZINE CAPACITY	Belt-fed
ACTION	Electrically operated
TOTAL LENGTH	800mm/31.5in
BARREL LENGTH	533mm/21in
WEIGHT UNLOADED	18.8kg/41.44lb w/o mount

Mark 48 Mod 0

SPECIFICATION

MANUFACTURER FNH-United States
CALIBRE 7.62mm NATO
MAGAZINE CAPACITY Belt-fed
ACTION Gas operated
TOTAL LENGTH 1,009mm/39.75in
BARREL LENGTH 470mm/18.5in
WEIGHT UNLOADED 8.2kg/18.1lb

Manufactured since 2000, the Mark 48 was developed to be a lightweight General-Purpose Machine Gun (GPMG) that could be handled like a squad automatic weapon by one operator. Developed for the United States Navy's Sea, Air and Land (SEALs) force, it is not in common use but heavily used by the special operations units that have it. Unlike the MAG 58/M240, the Mark 48 is (for a machine gun) light, handy and responsive. Light for a belt-fed, it is lighter than some models of the BAR, and lighter than the BREN gun.

XM312

SPECIFICATION

MANUFACTURER General Dynamics
CALIBRE .50 BMG
MAGAZINE CAPACITY Belt-fed
ACTION Gas operated, recoil dampened
TOTAL LENGTH 1,600mm/63in
BARREL LENGTH 980mm/38.5in
WEIGHT UNLOADED 19.28kg/42.5lb tripod included

Introduced in 2000, the XM312 was meant to replace the M2HB, but General Dynamics has struggled to make it work. To control the forces of recoil, the XM312 fires each round as the action is moving forward. Recoil must first overcome the inertia of the moving action before the gas system can unlock the bolt and cycle to chamber another round. The design is soft in recoil but complicated, and has a slow rate of fire. Complaints arose during trials about its rate of fire: compared with the sedate 400 rpm of the M2HB, it reportedly fires at the dawdling pace of 240 rpm. It was still being pushed as an M2HB alternative in 2006.

Johnson M1941 LMG

SPECIFICATION

MANUFACTURER Johnson
CALIBRE .30-06
MAGAZINE CAPACITY 20
ACTION Recoil operated
TOTAL LENGTH 1,066mm/42in
BARREL LENGTH 558mm/23.14in
WEIGHT UNLOADED 6.48kg/14.28lb

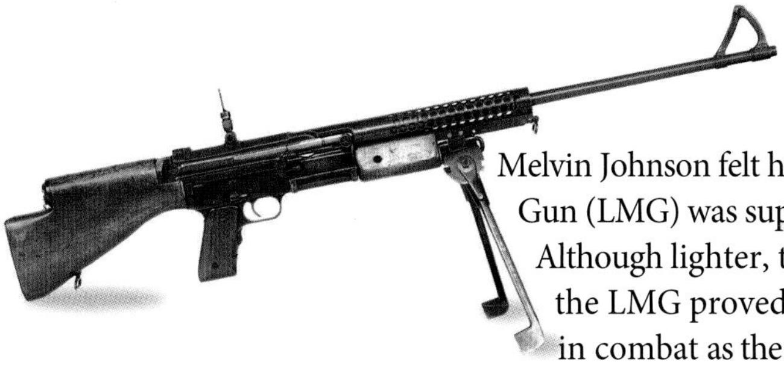

Melvin Johnson felt his Light Machine Gun (LMG) was superior to the BAR. Although lighter, the recoil system of the LMG proved not to be as reliable in combat as the gas system of the BAR, and it only survived in service until 1945. The stock was designed to reduce muzzle rise in recoil, and the magazine could be charged with stripper clips while still in the weapon. While it showed promise in the mid to late 1930s, it was not made in any volume until 1941. It soon proved inadequate, and Johnson's prickly personality made improvements impossible.

M2HB

SPECIFICATION

MANUFACTURER Kelsey-Hayes
CALIBRE .50 BMG
MAGAZINE CAPACITY Belt-fed
ACTION Recoil operated
TOTAL LENGTH 1,656mm/65.2in
BARREL LENGTH 1,143mm/45in
WEIGHT UNLOADED 38.10kg/84lb w/o mount

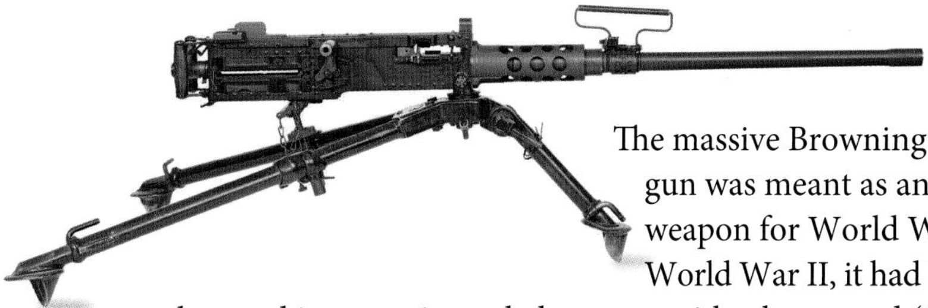

The massive Browning .50 machine gun was meant as an anti-tank weapon for World War I. By World War II, it had been worked over and turned into an air-cooled weapon with a heavy and (for the time) quick-change barrel. Just barely light enough for use by infantry, it could easily be mounted on any vehicle or aircraft. To move the M2HB, a tripod and a useful amount of ammunition would take an entire infantry squad or one jeep. It is so capable and durable that it is still in regular use today around the world, despite decades of work to replace it with an improved model.

M60

Developed by the US Army Ordnance as a General-Purpose Machine Gun (GPMG), the M60 incorporated features of several machine guns combined into one weapon. The bolt and barrel had a short service life because the locking lugs would chip, reducing reliability. Once they were chipped, they would gall the barrel cams. It also had a gas system that could be re-assembled in the wrong way (turning it into a single-shot). Production began in 1960 after years of testing and it remained in service until the late 1990s, when the US Marine Corps persuaded the US procurement system to allow MAG 58s for purchase.

SPECIFICATION

MANUFACTURER Maremont Corp.
CALIBRE 7.62mm NATO
MAGAZINE CAPACITY Belt-fed
ACTION Gas operated
TOTAL LENGTH 1,111mm/43.75in
BARREL LENGTH 648mm/25.5in
WEIGHT UNLOADED 10.43kg/23lb

Marlin M1914

This was the version of the Colt/Browning M1895 produced by Marlin between 1914 and 1918. It was purchased by the US Army for training purposes before and during World War I. As with all air-cooled machine guns, it could overheat if not used judiciously. It was made in two versions. While the first was a copy of the Colt/Browning, the second involved improving the "flapper" design of the Colt to a straight piston parallel to the bore, making it better for use in tanks. Early teething problems almost kept it from service.

SPECIFICATION

MANUFACTURER Marlin-Rockwell
CALIBRE .30-06
MAGAZINE CAPACITY Belt-fed
ACTION Gas operated
TOTAL LENGTH 1,028mm/40.5in
BARREL LENGTH 711mm/28in
WEIGHT UNLOADED 14.74kg/32.5lb

Lewis Mark 6 USN

While the US Army was against adopting the Lewis gun, the US Navy was not. Acquired during World War I, the naval Lewis guns served for years in relative obscurity until the navy gunboats on the Yangtze River were attacked in the early years of World War II, before the United States had even entered the war. As local and light defence weapons, they served well on the gunboats, which were shallow-draft vessels cruising up and down the major Chinese rivers, unlikely to face artillery-class weapons. The high quality of manufacture of the Lewis guns kept them in service into the 1930s, when other machine guns would have been scrapped long before. It is shown here with the 47-round pan magazine.

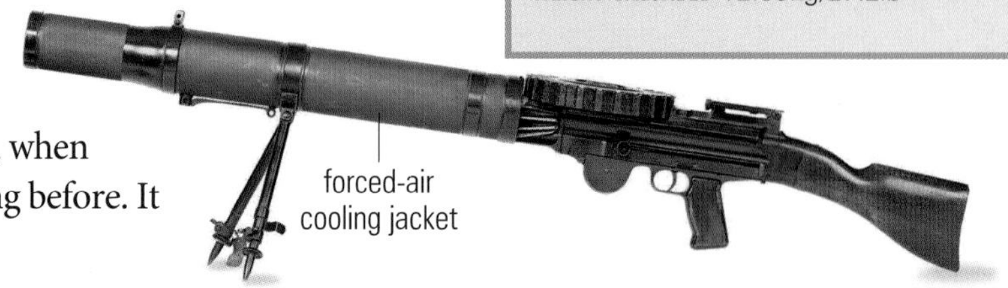

SPECIFICATION

MANUFACTURER Savage Arms Corp.
CALIBRE .30-06
MAGAZINE CAPACITY 47- or 96-round drums
ACTION Gas operated
TOTAL LENGTH 1,283mm/50.5in
BARREL LENGTH 668mm/26.3in
WEIGHT UNLOADED 12.33kg/27.2lb

M73

Developed as a replacement in tanks for the Browning and M60, the M73 turned out to be less reliable than the M60 in training and service, and more expensive than the Browning that the United States already had in inventory and wanted to dispose of. One problematic design feature was the barrel-change method: the barrel could be changed from inside the tank, a requirement that made the design complex, expensive and which decreased accuracy and reliability. It was later removed from (limited) service as unfixable and a waste of effort to continue.

SPECIFICATION

MANUFACTURER Springfield
CALIBRE 7.62mm NATO
MAGAZINE CAPACITY Belt-fed
ACTION Recoil, w/gas assist
TOTAL LENGTH 882mm/34.75in
BARREL LENGTH 559mm/22in
WEIGHT UNLOADED 12.70kg/28lb

Mexico

For a long time, Mexico used imported arms. There were a few designs that Mexican nationals produced, however, and the Mendoza is the most prominent. Mexico licensed manufacture of the Heckler & Koch 21E as its light and General-Purpose Machine Gun (GPMG). It uses the M2HB as its heavy machine gun.

Mendoza RM2

SPECIFICATION

MANUFACTURER Mexico National Armoury
CALIBRE .30-06
MAGAZINE CAPACITY 20
ACTION Gas operated/rotating bolt
TOTAL LENGTH 1,100mm/43.3in
BARREL LENGTH 610mm/24in
WEIGHT UNLOADED 6.39kg/14.1lb

Offset sight
Some say the RM2 was the light machine gun the BAR should have been. A top-mounted magazine needs an offset sight so that the firer can aim.

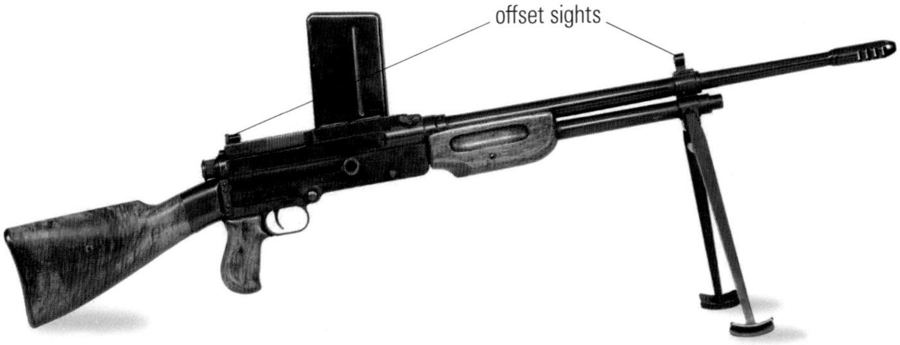

Designed by Raphael Mendoza, while working for the National Arms Factory in Mexico, the RM2 was a refined version of the M1934. During World War II the US government commissioned more weapons, so Mendoza updated his M-1934, changing the calibre to .30-06 and removing the quick-change barrel feature. The war ended before he could fulfil the contract, and in 1947 he submitted 50 prototypes of the RM2 to the Mexican Marine Corps. The Mexican government declined to purchase any. As Mexican law prohibited the export of "instruments of war" he could not sell it outside Mexico. The M1934 served in the Mexican Army into the late 1950s, but the RM2 ended up in museums around the world.

Chile

Many weapons systems in Chile, large and small, reached the end of their useful life at much the same time. From the mid 1960s, Chile's machine gun needs were filled by the Rheinmettal MG3 and the FN M2HB. Since the turn of the century, it has been replacing a lot of equipment, from small arms through to frigates and F-16 fighters.

BAR Model 1925

SPECIFICATION

MANUFACTURER Colt
CALIBRE 7.62 x 63mm aka .30-06
MAGAZINE CAPACITY 20
ACTION Gas operated/toggle lock
TOTAL LENGTH 1,214mm/47.8in
BARREL LENGTH 609mm/24in
WEIGHT UNLOADED 8.79kg/19.4lb

Colt was eager to manufacture and export the BAR, as sales had not met expectations. As a result, they could be found in ones and twos in many armouries, both police and military, before World War II. Used as a Light Machine Gun (LMG) in Chilean service, the only problem would have been in keeping the .30-06 ammunition supply separate from the 7.7mm ammunition for the Nambu. After World War II, the US government gave BARs to any ally who asked for them. It was in service from 1918 until the 1960s.

Madsen M1946

Previous Madsen machine guns purchased by Chile had been in 7 x 57mm. After World War II, ammunition supply was easiest in .30-06, the American service cartridge, due to wartime production, and post- war American Cold War efforts. Chile used the .30-06 until the 1960s, when it adopted the G3 and MG3, both in 7.62mm NATO, the cartridge easiest to procure on the world market. It was in service from 1946 to the mid 1950s.

SPECIFICATION

MANUFACTURER Dansk Industri Syndikat
CALIBRE 7.62 x 63mm
MAGAZINE CAPACITY 20
ACTION Recoil operated
TOTAL LENGTH 1,165mm/45.9in
BARREL LENGTH 477mm/18.8in
WEIGHT UNLOADED 9.97kg/22lb

Nambu Type 3, M1920

This is one of the many Hotchkiss variants made by Japan. Between the wars, business was brisk in weapons, and Japan was active on the Pacific coast in selling. As the Nambu Type 3 was a sturdy, reliable machine gun, the Chilean Army could not have had any complaints about it other than the weight. It was produced between 1920 and 1936.

SPECIFICATION

MANUFACTURER Various
CALIBRE 7.7 x 58R
MAGAZINE CAPACITY 24- or 30-round trays
ACTION Gas operated
TOTAL LENGTH 1,155mm/45.5in
BARREL LENGTH 736mm/29in
WEIGHT UNLOADED 55.33kg/122lb w/ tripod

Venezuela

On the Caribbean coast of South America, Venezuelan forces could count on having to deal with piracy and drug running. Due to oil exports from 1935, Venezuela has had the economic reserves to buy modern weapons. After World War II, they were purchased mostly from FN in Liège, Belgium. Today, Venezuela makes its own AK rifles.

VZ37

The VZ37 was the precursor to the BESA medium machine gun in British service, adapted here to fit on a tripod. As with many earlier designs, it was quite easy to adapt it to any calibre that would fit through the feed tray. For any customer willing to buy, BRio were happy to modify their products to the national calibre. The VZ37 was peculiar in that the pistol grip was the cocking handle to charge the weapon: the gunner would grasp the pistol grip and push forward until it caught the bolt and then draw it back until it stopped. It was bought from BRio at the start of 1937 and remained in service until the late 1950s.

SPECIFICATION

MANUFACTURER CZ, BRio
CALIBRE 7 x 57mm
MAGAZINE CAPACITY Belt-fed
ACTION Gas operated
TOTAL LENGTH 1,104mm/43.5in
BARREL LENGTH 678mm/26.7in
WEIGHT UNLOADED 18.96kg/41.8lb

FN M1950

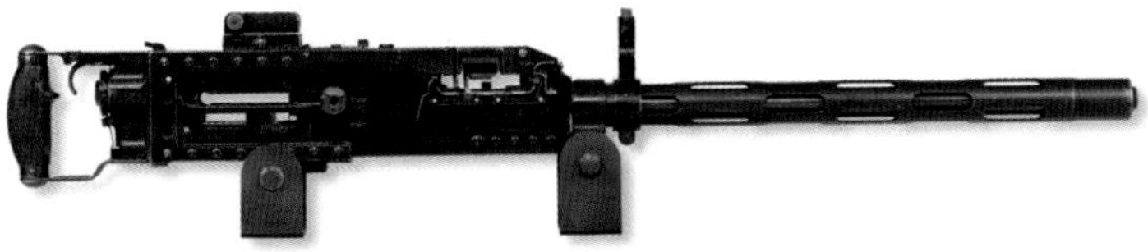

SPECIFICATION	
MANUFACTURER	FN, Liège
CALIBRE	7 x 57mm
MAGAZINE CAPACITY	Belt-fed
ACTION	Recoil operated
TOTAL LENGTH	1,041mm/41in
BARREL LENGTH	609mm/24in
WEIGHT UNLOADED	14.06kg/31lb

The Browning machine gun design was as adaptable to other calibres as any. For FN to produce it in 7mm Mauser was therefore straightforward. By 1950, FN had made improvements to the basic Browning machine gun. The sights had been changed, and the barrel jacket was given larger slots for better cooling. The M1950 also features the FN two-bolt mounting system, which FN have used on all machine guns since then. It was produced between 1950 and the 1960s.

Argentina

After World War II, Argentina licensed manufacture of firepower from FN in Liège, Belgium. The success of a proven design such as the Belgian FN MAG 58 meant that it has continued in service. In the Falklands War, both the Argentine and British sides used licensed copies of FN rifles and machine guns.

FN MAG 58

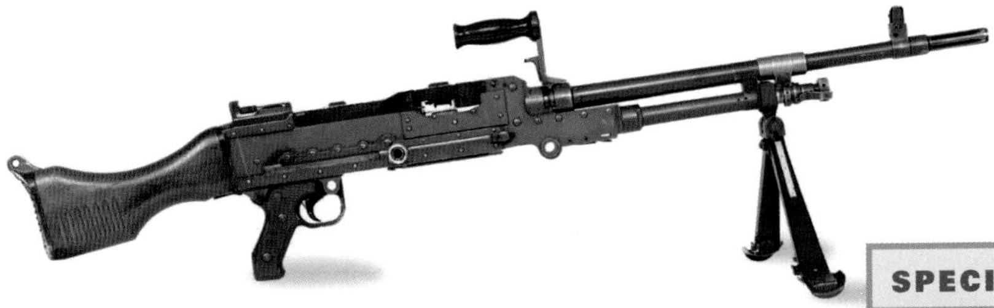

With FN taking over the world's arms markets after World War II, as Mauser had done before World War I, the MAG 58 became nearly ubiquitous. With the adoption of the FAL and MAG 58, Argentina dropped the 7.65mm Mauser cartridge in rifle and machine guns, sold all the older rifles on the surplus market, and adopted the 7.62mm NATO. Observers of the Falklands War commented on how the Argentine and British forces were using identical machine guns. With FN so vigorous in sales and licensing, this has been a regular occurrence since 1958. Argentina adopted the MAG 58 in 1960 and they are still in service today.

SPECIFICATION	
MANUFACTURER	FN, Liège
CALIBRE	7.62mm NATO
MAGAZINE CAPACITY	Disintegrating belt
ACTION	Gas operated/toggle lock
TOTAL LENGTH	1,257mm/49.5in
BARREL LENGTH	544mm/21.4in
WEIGHT UNLOADED	10.88kg/24lb

Maxim M1898

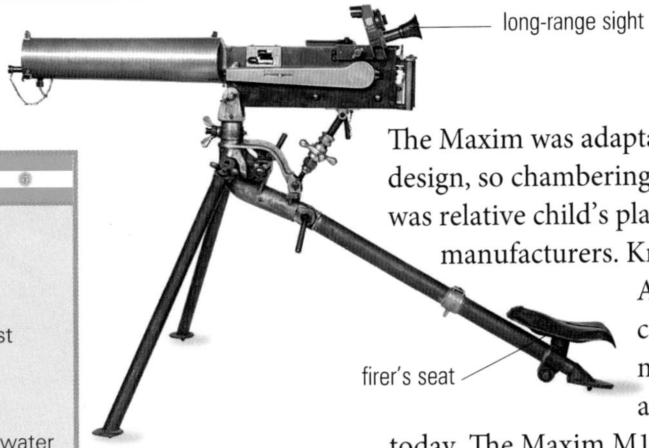

SPECIFICATION	
MANUFACTURER	Simpson & Co.
CALIBRE	7.65mm Mauser
MAGAZINE CAPACITY	Cloth belt
ACTION	Recoil operated, gas boost
TOTAL LENGTH	1,193mm/47in
BARREL LENGTH	711mm/28in
WEIGHT UNLOADED	29.9kg/66lb w/o water

The Maxim was adaptable to almost any cartridge design, so chambering it for the 7.65mm Mauser was relative child's play for the Simpson & Company manufacturers. Known in North America as "7.65 Argentine", the 7.65 x 53mm cartridge is entirely suitable for military use, although little-adopted and thus not common today. The Maxim M1898 was in use from 1898 to the 1920s, when it was replaced by lighter machine guns.

Brazil

Being cut off from suppliers during both World Wars gave Brazil the impetus to form its own arms industry.

Since 1954, Brazil has made sure it is self-sufficient in arms production. Today Mekanika Indutria e Comercio Ltd manufactures the 7.62mm "Uirapuru" for use by the Brazilian Armed Forces.

Madsen M1935

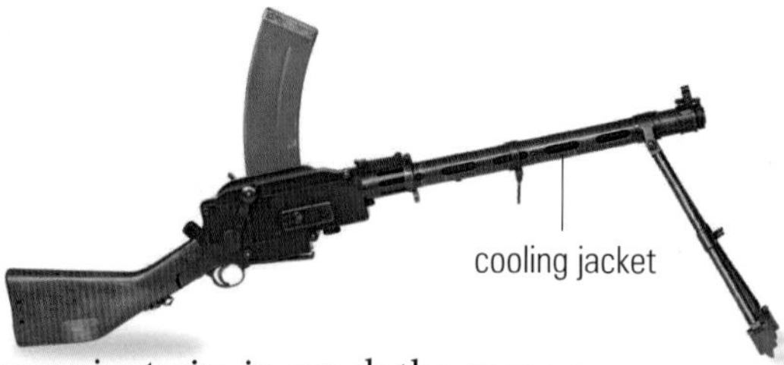

Introduced by Denmark in 1904, the Madsen is the only single-shot rifle action to ever be made into a machine gun. The bolt hinges on a rear pivot pin, in much the same manner as the Martini-Henry rifle. The feed mechanism is activated by a cam shuttling along a track in the side plate and each round is fed down out of the magazine. The Madsen depends on good-quality ammunition, but is essentially low maintenance. In Brazil, the Madsen was used in infantry units and on armoured cars until replaced in the late 1950s by Brazilian-made FALs and MAG 58s.

SPECIFICATION	
MANUFACTURER	Dansk Industri Syndikat
CALIBRE	7 x 57mm
MAGAZINE CAPACITY	30-round magazine
ACTION	Tilting bolt
TOTAL LENGTH	1,165mm/45.9in
BARREL LENGTH	477mm/18.8in
WEIGHT UNLOADED	9.98kg/22lb

Portugal

In World War I, Portuguese infantry fought with France and Britain, equipped with British SMLEs.

INDEP, the Portuguese small arms manufacturer now produces a range of weapons under licence, including a copy of the Heckler & Koch-21 light machine gun (LMG).

Madsen M/956

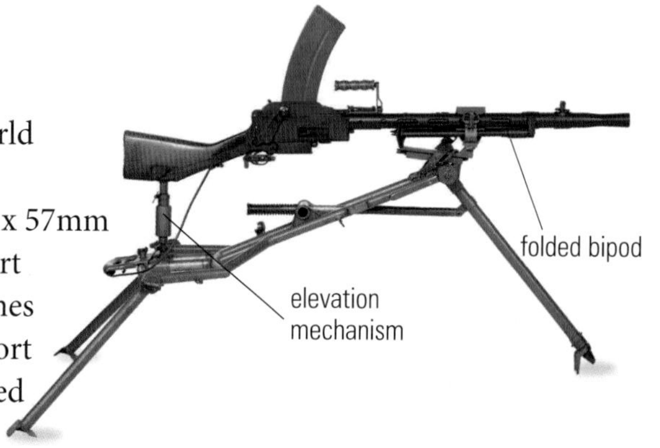

This was simply the post-World War II Danish Madsen Light Machine Gun (LMG) in 7.92 x 57mm chambering, a common export item from Denmark. The Danes must have welcomed the export income, but some have queried the Portuguese decision to buy the Madsen in 1956. It was purchased in 1956 and remained in service until the late 1980s.

SPECIFICATION	
MANUFACTURER	Dansk Industri Syndikat
CALIBRE	7.92 x 57mm
MAGAZINE CAPACITY	30
ACTION	Recoil operated
TOTAL LENGTH	1,166mm/45.9in
BARREL LENGTH	477mm/18.8in
WEIGHT UNLOADED	9.97kg/22lb

SPECIFICATION	
MANUFACTURER	RM&M
CALIBRE	7.92 x 57mm
MAGAZINE CAPACITY	Belt-fed from drums
ACTION	Recoil
TOTAL LENGTH	1,194mm/47in
BARREL LENGTH	622mm/24.5in
WEIGHT UNLOADED	13.15kg/29.2lb

Dreyse M/938

This was a modified Dreyse M1918, used by Germany as the MG13 and sold to Portugal in 1938. A select-fire (rare in an light machine gun) weapon, which can be fired in either semi or full auto settings, it was obsolete even before the Germans sold them. As Portugal was only involved in colonial campaigns, this was not an issue. The Dreyse M/938 was purchased in 1938, but was never used in a conflict.

Spain

Lacking a major industrial base in the first half of the 20th century, Spain did not enter the world market for machine guns as an exporter. After World War II, Spain followed many other countries and began producing small arms for its own use. CETME currently manufactures the MG3 and the Ameli under licence.

Alfa M1944

SPECIFICATION

MANUFACTURER Alfa
CALIBRE 7.92 x 57mm
MAGAZINE CAPACITY Belt-fed
ACTION Gas operated
TOTAL LENGTH 1,448mm/57in
BARREL LENGTH 750mm/29.53in
WEIGHT UNLOADED 12.99kg/28.66lb w/o tripod

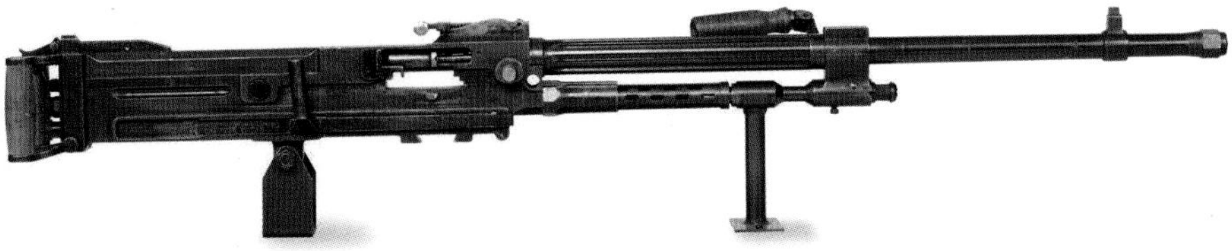

Lacking access to German small arms (particularly machine guns) during World War II, Spain made its own. The Alfa closely resembled the Italian Breda in layout and function but was certainly a solid medium machine gun. Spain even exported a few to Egypt. The Alfa M1944 remained in service until the 1980s.

CETME Ameli

SPECIFICATION

MANUFACTURER CETME
CALIBRE 5.56 x 45mm
MAGAZINE CAPACITY Belt-fed
ACTION Roller-delayed blowback
TOTAL LENGTH 900mm/35.43in
BARREL LENGTH 400mm/15.74in
WEIGHT UNLOADED 5.3kg/11.68lb

Externally a scaled-down MG 42, and internally an HK 21 in 5.56mm instead of 7.62mm NATO, the Ameli has a reputation for being a bit obstinate. Some users report regular malfunctions, while others report flawless reliability. Research suggests that the buffer system may be the main problem and that replacing or rebuilding it turns the Ameli into a spectacularly good Squad Automatic Weapon (SAW). In that role it does not accept the box magazines of any rifle system, only using disintegrating belts. Experience has shown the "feature" of being able to use box magazines far less useful in a SAW than designers had thought. Given the fierce competition from other makers and their designs, the initial problems of the Ameli kept it from gaining market share. The CETME Ameli has been in service since 1982.

HK MG4

SPECIFICATION

MANUFACTURER Heckler & Koch
CALIBRE 5.56mm NATO
MAGAZINE CAPACITY Belt-fed
ACTION Gas operated
TOTAL LENGTH 1,030mm/40.6in
BARREL LENGTH 450mm/17.7in
WEIGHT UNLOADED 8.1kg/17.9lb

The MG4 is a belt-fed 5.56 light machine gun by German firearm manufacturer Heckler & Koch. It was developed in the late 1990s and first seen publicly in September 2001. Spain ordered 2,000 of them in 2007 with delivery spread over four years. The current standard light machine gun for the Spanish Army, it is usually fitted with an ACOG sight.

United Kingdom

The British Army did not take machine guns in any numbers before World War I. But the high rate of fire of British-trained riflemen during the conflict led the Germans to under-estimate the number of machine guns in the British Army. After using one of the heaviest rifle-calibre machine guns (Vickers), after the war Britain adopted the BREN, one of best lightweight rifle-calibre squad automatic weapons (SAWs) ever made.

BESA Mark 2

Developed from the Czech ZB53, the BESA served as armament on tanks. The BESA fired its cartridge while the barrel was moving forward. Thus, part of the recoil was used up in stopping the forward travel of the barrel. This compact design made it useful in the crowded environment of tanks. The design was not changed from the Czech in 7.92mm as the Royal Armoured Corps had its own supply system, separate from that of the Infantry. It was deemed easier to produce and ship 7.92mm ammunition for the tanks than to re-design the BESA to use .303 ammunition. The War Office signed a contract with BRio for licensed manufacture of the BESA in 1936, placing their first order in 1938. They stayed in regular service until 1945, but new tank designs received the L7A1 after the war.

SPECIFICATION

MANUFACTURER BSA
CALIBRE 7.92mm Mauser
MAGAZINE CAPACITY Belts, cloth or disintegrating
ACTION Gas operated
TOTAL LENGTH 1,105mm/43.5in
BARREL LENGTH 736mm/29in
WEIGHT UNLOADED 21.7kg/48lb

Colt M1914

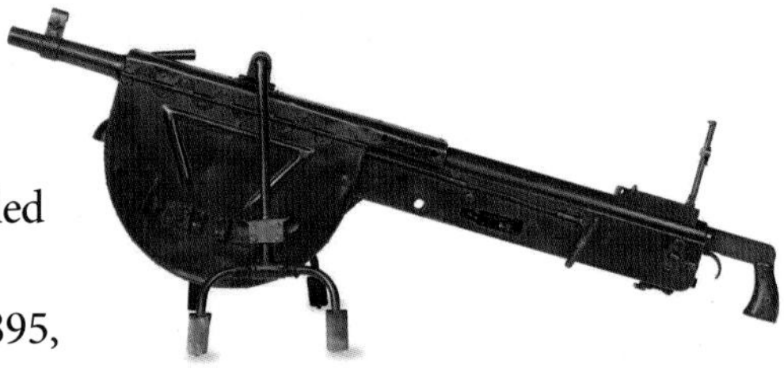

Like the earlier 1895 Colt, this was called the "potato digger" due to the front actuating arm, and was a refined M1895, designed by John Moses Browning. Gas bled off the barrel and pivoted the actuator down. If the gun was too close to the ground, it would dig into the soil. Despite being air-cooled, the Colt had a good reputation for reliability and volume of fire. The slow cyclic rate (400 rpm) kept it cooler than other air-cooled machine guns. Despite its heavier barrel, the loss of the water and jacket made it lighter and more compact than the Vickers or Maxim, and popular with the troops. It was first used in American service in Cuba, but not kept after 1918.

SPECIFICATION

MANUFACTURER Colt
CALIBRE .30-06, .303 British, 7 x 57mm, 7.65 x 54mm
MAGAZINE CAPACITY Belt-fed
ACTION Gas operated
TOTAL LENGTH 1,035mm/40.75in
BARREL LENGTH 711mm/28in
WEIGHT UNLOADED 15.9kg/35lb

Browning Mark 2, Air Service

SPECIFICATION

MANUFACTURER Colt
CALIBRE .303 British
MAGAZINE CAPACITY Belt-fed
ACTION Recoil operated
TOTAL LENGTH 978mm/38.5in
BARREL LENGTH 610mm/24in
WEIGHT UNLOADED 14kg/31lb

The Browning is easily converted from one rifle calibre to another. As long as the cartridge length and rim diameter fit the receiver, the rest of the conversion job is simply detail. Thus, converting Browning machine guns from the American .30-06 to .303 British was easy. Britain purchased many Browning machine guns for air service to arm World War II aircraft. The cyclic rate on aircraft guns was typically increased, with hydraulic buffers and modified springs, from 500 rpm to 1,000 rpm. These guns were quite popular for infantry use. While .303 weapons were desired in 1940, within a few years all aircraft machine guns were .50 BMG.

Browning 1919 A4 conversion

SPECIFICATION

MANUFACTURER Colt, Savage, many others
CALIBRE 7.62mm NATO
MAGAZINE CAPACITY Belt-fed
ACTION Recoil operated
TOTAL LENGTH 1,041mm/41in
BARREL LENGTH 721mm/28.4in
WEIGHT UNLOADED 11.3kg/25lb

Given the durability, near-ubiquity and availability of spare parts for the Browning .30 machine guns in all their guises, it was no wonder than many countries sought to convert them. When NATO switched to the 7.62 x 51mm cartridge, it was easy enough to convert Brownings of all types to the new cartridge. Some conversions even went so far as to change the Browning from cloth to disintegrating belts. However, as soon as the new generation of general-purpose machine guns (GPMGs) were fielded, with their quick-change barrels, all the old Brownings went back into storage and were subsequently scrapped. However, between the adoption of the T65 (7.62mm NATO cartridge) in 1953 and the manufacture of increasing numbers of the Enfield L7A1, it was a machine gun in any inventory, including British.

BREN Mark 2

SPECIFICATION

MANUFACTURER Enfield
CALIBRE .303 British
MAGAZINE CAPACITY 30
ACTION Gas operated/tilting bolt
TOTAL LENGTH 1,158mm/45.6in
BARREL LENGTH 635mm/25in
WEIGHT UNLOADED 10.5kg/23.18lb

A joint development between BRio and Enfield, the BREN gun (a combination of the initials of BRio and Enfield) was adopted in 1937, when production for British use began in Enfield. Experience in World War I had shown that machine guns were an essential part of winning a war, and that troops simply could not move water-cooled guns fast enough to take advantage of any successful attack or breakthrough. The BREN fired from magazines, requiring assistant gunners to keep them fed. But the quick-change barrel allowed a BREN gunner to maintain a substantial rate of fire, for as long as cool barrels were available. The BREN was superbly accurate. In the 1950s many armies converted BRENS to 7.62mm NATO for continued use. From .303 in 1935 to 7.62mm NATO during the 1950s, the BREN was very popular with troops.

L7A1

SPECIFICATION

MANUFACTURER Enfield
CALIBRE 7.62mm NATO
MAGAZINE CAPACITY Disintegrating belt
ACTION Gas operated/tilting bolt
TOTAL LENGTH 1,262mm/49.7in
BARREL LENGTH 629mm/24.75in
WEIGHT UNLOADED 10.88kg/24lb

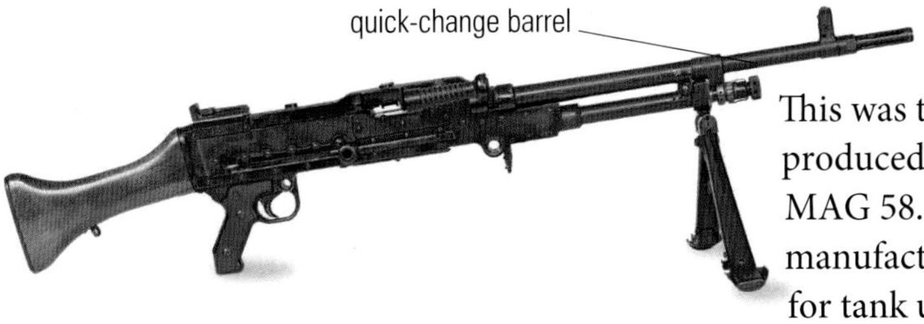

This was the Enfield-produced version of the MAG 58. It was also manufactured in variants for tank use and tested as a fixed-mount aircraft machine gun. The L7A1 went on to aerial service in helicopters, where door gunners could use them to protect the aircraft during landings and takeoffs. It found its way into every infantry, marine and airborne unit as well as coastal craft. Other than the Enfield and British-service markings, it does not differ from the FN version. It was adopted in 1959 and is still in use.

L86A2 HK

The L86A2 Squad Automatic Weapon (SAW) proved as unreliable as the L85A2 individual weapon. Heckler & Koch undertook an upgrade but they were not successful: the L86A2 had the same tactical shortcomings as all other SAWs with only a magazine feed (no belt-feed, thus low sustained fire) and a barrel that was non- interchangeable (limited firepower and fast overheating). The longer barrel gave it more reliability than the similarly upgraded rifle. It was first issued in 1986.

SPECIFICATION

MANUFACTURER Enfield
CALIBRE 5.56 x 45mm
MAGAZINE CAPACITY 30
ACTION Gas operated
TOTAL LENGTH 900mm/35.43in
BARREL LENGTH 646mm/25.43in
WEIGHT UNLOADED 7.3kg/16.1lb

Rexer (Madsen)

The Rexer machine gun company made Madsen light machine guns under licence from Dansk Syndikat until legal difficulties caused Rexer to close their doors in 1910. They managed to fulfil small contracts to Natal, South Africa, and the Indian Army. Except for the markings Rexer machine guns are Madsens, and any user familiar with a Danish Madsen would have no problem using a Rexer.

SPECIFICATION

MANUFACTURER Rexer
CALIBRE .303 British
MAGAZINE CAPACITY 30
ACTION Gas operated
TOTAL LENGTH 1,165mm/45.9in
BARREL LENGTH 478mm/18.8in
WEIGHT UNLOADED 10kg/22lb

Lewis Mark 1

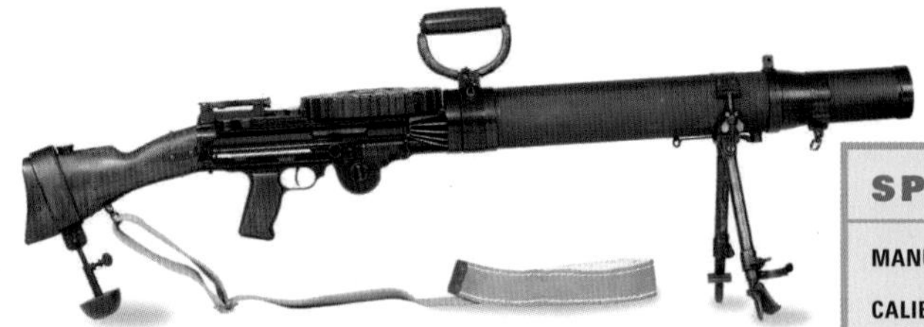

Arguably the best air-cooled light machine gun of World War I, the Lewis was used both as an aircraft gun (fixed and flexible) and an infantry support weapon. Designed in the United States and initially made there and in Belgium, the Lewis ended up being built in quantity at BSA. Nicknamed "The Belgian Rattlesnake" by the Germans in World War I, it was a complex and costly weapon, but very reliable. The pan magazines were high-capacity, without belts to cause feeding problems. It was not widely used after World War I, so its service life was from 1914 to 1918.

SPECIFICATION

MANUFACTURER Savage, FN, BSA
CALIBRE .303 British
MAGAZINE CAPACITY 47- or 96-round drum
ACTION Gas operated
TOTAL LENGTH 1,282mm/50.5in
BARREL LENGTH 668mm/26.3in
WEIGHT UNLOADED 12.33kg/27.2lb

Vickers No. 1 Mark 1, Air Service

A gas-operated Vickers (noted in inventory as VGO), the No. 1 Mark 1 was intended as a defensive weapon on observation planes and bombers. It had a fairly high cyclic rate, 950 rpm. When the Browning machine gun was chosen for that role, the Vickers went off to the Long Range Desert Group of the SAS. There, mounted four or five to a jeep, they were used by scouts looking for the German and Italians. With two or three jeeps positioned to bring all their guns to bear in an ambush, the scouts could fire as many as 1,500 rounds in just over six seconds. The weapons were declared obsolete and scrapped at the end of World War II.

SPECIFICATION

MANUFACTURER Vickers
CALIBRE .303 British
MAGAZINE CAPACITY 60- or 100-round drums
ACTION Gas operated/rotating bolt
TOTAL LENGTH 1,016mm/40in
BARREL LENGTH 508mm/20in
WEIGHT UNLOADED 8.8kg/19.75lb

France

From adopting the Hotchkiss, its first machine gun in 1897, France quickly settled for designs of limited usefulness and consequently suffered in World War I. Using mainly air-cooled machine guns, French troops could not maintain the sustained fire of the Germans, without assembling larger numbers of machine guns. Larger numbers of troops and guns simply meant larger targets for counter-battery machine gun and artillery fire.

Chauchat (CSRG) M1915

SPECIFICATION

MANUFACTURER Bayonne, others
CALIBRE 8mm Lebel
MAGAZINE CAPACITY 20 rounds
ACTION Recoil operated
TOTAL LENGTH 1,143mm/45in
BARREL LENGTH 470mm/18.5in
WEIGHT UNLOADED 8.6kg/19lb

This is a long-recoil design, where the bolt and barrel recoil together down the length of the receiver, then reciprocate forward separately, the barrel first, followed by the bolt. The basic principle was first designed by John Browning and made in the Auto-5 shotgun. In a rifle calibre the parts have to travel a longer distance to avoid harsh internal impact and battering. It was made in massive numbers during World War I, where it was used as a portable, squad-level firepower weapon in trench warfare. The workmanship is at times quite rough, but the weapon was reasonably reliable, at least in 8mm Lebel.

M1931A

SPECIFICATION

MANUFACTURER Bayonne
CALIBRE 7.5mm French M1929
MAGAZINE CAPACITY 36-round magazine and 100-round drum
ACTION Gas operated
TOTAL LENGTH 1,028mm/40.5in
BARREL LENGTH 596mm/23.5in
WEIGHT UNLOADED 12.47kg/27.5lb

This was a tank and fortress gun pressed into service as an infantry weapon after World War II due to a lack of otherwise suitable machine guns. It was replaced by the AAT-52. The M1931A was unsuited as an infantry weapon for several reasons: it lacked a mechanical safety and fired from an open bolt. When unloading, a round would be left in the feed tray, and unless the operating rod was cycled again after removal of the magazine, it would fire a round even after it had been "unloaded". As a fortress gun, it served from 1931 to 1940. As a stop-gap infantry weapon, it was used until the late 1940s.

AAT-52

SPECIFICATION

MANUFACTURER Bayonne
CALIBRE 7.5mm French M1929
MAGAZINE CAPACITY Belt-fed
ACTION Delayed blowback
TOTAL LENGTH 1,166mm/45.9in
BARREL LENGTH 490mm/19.3in light, 600mm/23.6in heavy
WEIGHT UNLOADED 9.8kg/21.7lb light barrel, 10.6kg/23.38lb w/heavy barrel

Made as a General-Purpose Machine Gun (GPMG), the 52 is an amalgam of the MG 42 feed system and a variant of the CETME/Heckler & Koch roller-delayed blowback. With a light barrel and bipod, it is light enough to almost be a Squad Automatic Weapon (SAW). With the heavy barrel and tripod it is suitable as a heavy machine gun. The ejection is rough on empties, extracting them early in the firing cycle and making them unsuitable for reloading. Mangled brass is not usually a problem in military service, except that in the AAT-52 the metal is so abused it is sometimes ripped in half, causing a malfunction. Despite this, it served from 1953 to the late 1950s, when replaced by the AA F-1.

AA F-1

The AAT-52 was chambered in 7.62mm NATO, and used a French adapter to fit the US M2 tripod. Despite the change in chambering it was still harsh on the extracted and ejected brass, and prone to breaking it. To ease extraction and hopefully prevent broken cases leading to malfunctions, troops oiled the belt as it was feeding, but this could create other problems: the oil attracted dust, dirt and other debris, which was then fed into the mechanism. The Mod AA F-1 has been in service from the late 1950s to the present day.

SPECIFICATION

MANUFACTURER Bayonne
CALIBRE 7.62mm NATO
MAGAZINE CAPACITY Belt-fed
ACTION Delayed blowback
TOTAL LENGTH 1,166mm/45.9in
BARREL LENGTH 490mm/19.3in light, 600mm/23.6in heavy
WEIGHT UNLOADED 9.8kg/21.7lb light barrel, 10.55kg/23.38lb w/heavy barrel

Hotchkiss M1914

An updated version of earlier designs, primarily the M1900, the M1914 was the primary machine gun of France in World War I, and was still in service at the beginning of World War II. It was a reliable, if bulky and heavy, air-cooled machine gun. The feed system used stamped steel or brass strips, each holding 24 or 30 rounds. The strips could be linked by the assistant gunner as the weapon fired, to provide continuous fire. In the sustained fire of trench warfare, the barrel would glow red-hot but the Hotchkiss would still work. Once overheated, it had to be left to cool as the barrels could not be changed while hot. Hotchkiss machine guns with worn barrels had to be sent back to rear areas for a new barrel. Production commenced in 1914, and lasted through to 1918, while the weapon itself remained in service until 1940.

SPECIFICATION

MANUFACTURER Hotchkiss et Cie
CALIBRE 8mm Lebel
MAGAZINE CAPACITY 24- or 30-round trays
ACTION Gas operated
TOTAL LENGTH 1,270mm/50in
BARREL LENGTH 775mm/30.5in
WEIGHT UNLOADED 23.56kg/52lb w/o tripod, which added 27.2kg/60lb

The Hotchkiss designs
The Hotchkiss machine guns were based on a design by Captain Baron A. Odkolek von Augeza of Vienna in Austria.

Chatellerault M1924/29

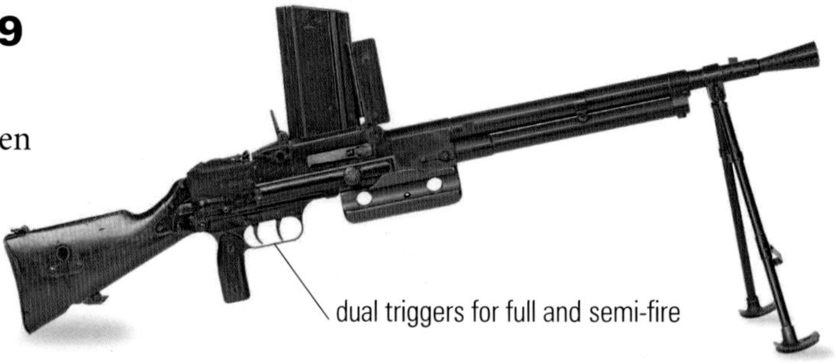

This was the French answer between the wars to the squad need for firepower. The original M24 was chambered in the 7.5mm 1924 cartridge. When the cartridge was redesigned and shortened in 1929, the old machine guns were rebuilt and the old and new alike were known as M1924/29. It had selective-fire, with the front trigger for semi- and the rear for full-auto fire. The M1924/29 was robust, reliable and popular with the troops. Manufactured from 1924 to 1940, it is still found in use in former French colonies. During the occupation, the Germans did not make any for their use, which is surprising. They would have done well to switch it to 7.92mm and produce it as quickly as possible. However, they did use it to arm their occupation troops, thus freeing other weapons for use on the Eastern Front. It was used by the French Army after World War II into the late 1950s.

SPECIFICATION

MANUFACTURER MAC
CALIBRE 7.5 French M1929
MAGAZINE CAPACITY 25 rounds
ACTION Gas operated/linked bolt
TOTAL LENGTH 1,082mm/42.6in
BARREL LENGTH 500mm/19.7in
WEIGHT UNLOADED 11.1kg/24.51lb

St Etienne M1907

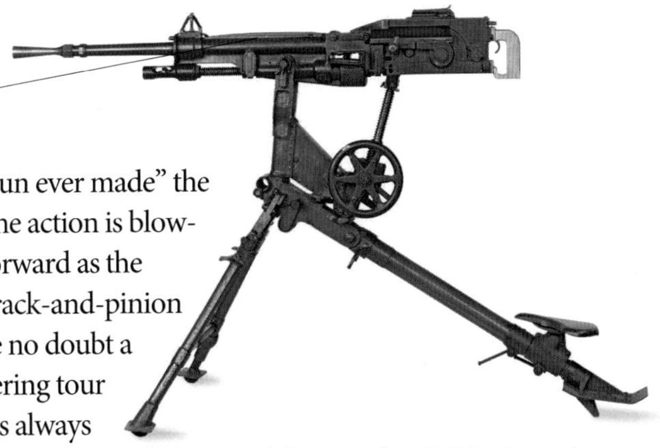

SPECIFICATION

- **MANUFACTURER** St Etienne
- **CALIBRE** 8mm Lebel
- **MAGAZINE CAPACITY** 24 or 30 round strips
- **ACTION** Blow-forward/rack-and-pinion
- **TOTAL LENGTH** 1,180mm/46.45in
- **BARREL LENGTH** 710mm/27.95in
- **WEIGHT UNLOADED** 25.73kg/56.7lb

In a contest of "worst machine gun ever made" the St Etienne is a definite finalist. The action is blow-forward, with the barrel going forward as the action cycles and the bolt (via a rack-and-pinion system) going backwards. While no doubt a design achievement and engineering tour de force, such extra complexity is always bad in a combat arm. The action spring is coiled around the barrel and if the barrel overheats, as it is sure to do in combat conditions, the spring suffers and eventually fails. Despite the urgent need for machine guns in World War I, the St Etienne was so bad it was removed from service and shipped to the colonies.

Hotchkiss

SPECIFICATION

- **MANUFACTURER** Unk
- **CALIBRE** 13.2 x 99mm
- **MAGAZINE CAPACITY** 20-round strips
- **ACTION** Gas operated
- **TOTAL LENGTH** 1,371mm/54in
- **BARREL LENGTH** 686mm/27in
- **WEIGHT UNLOADED** 20.4kg/45lb

Developed between World War I and II, the design was licensed to Japan. The basic Hotchkiss design, while suitable for rifle-calibre cartridges, was strained when it was used in something so large. Curiously, while Hotchkiss was more than happy to license the design to the Japanese, the French Army saw no need for it. In Japanese service it lasted from the late 1930s to 1945. It did not see service in France.

Belgium

With the establishment of Fabrique Nationale (FN) Belgium was well suited to not only equip its own armed forces, but the world's as well. It has succeeded in this task. The Falklands War was not the only conflict waged where both sides used variants (or even identical versions) of FN weapons.

Hotchkiss

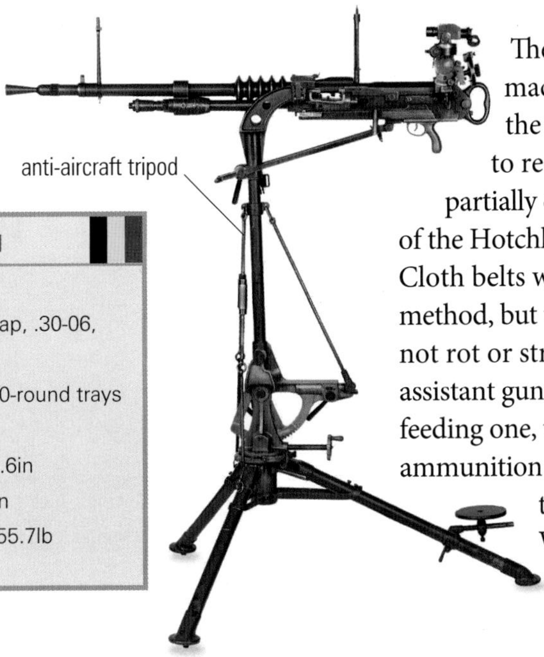

SPECIFICATION

- **MANUFACTURER** FN, Liège
- **CALIBRE** 8mm Lebel, 6.5 Jap, .30-06, .303 British
- **MAGAZINE CAPACITY** 24- or 30-round trays
- **ACTION** Gas operated
- **TOTAL LENGTH** 1,310mm/51.6in
- **BARREL LENGTH** 787mm/31in
- **WEIGHT UNLOADED** 25.26kg/55.7lb

The Hotchkiss was one of the first air-cooled machine guns. Early models used water to cool the barrel, as long bursts could quickly take it to red-hot. The Hotchkiss used cooling fins to partially deal with the heat produced. One peculiarity of the Hotchkiss was the feed mechanism: metal trays. Cloth belts were viewed as a necessary but awkward feed method, but they had drawbacks. The Hotchkiss trays could not rot or stretch. If they froze, they would still work. The assistant gunner could hook each tray on to the end of the feeding one, to keep up a continuous rate of fire, until the ammunition was exhausted or the barrel finally succumbed to the heat. It was made for export before World War I and used from 1896 to 1914, when the Liège plant was overrun.

Hotchkiss Export Model

The Export, also known as the Portative, as well as the M1909, was the Hotchkiss effort at a light machine gun. The locking system was changed to make the weapon more compact, and combined with a reshaped receiver, the weight loss was impressive. So popular as a portable weapon, it even saw use as a Cavalry weapon. The Portative was known in the US as the Benet-Mercie Machine Rifle. The Export could still be found in armoury reserves in 1939, when it was hauled out for yet another war. By 1945 it had been replaced by the BREN and BAR, and fell out of use.

SPECIFICATION	
MANUFACTURER	Hotchkiss
CALIBRE	8 x 50R Lebel, .30-06
MAGAZINE CAPACITY	30-round tray
ACTION	Gas operated
TOTAL LENGTH	1,187mm/46.75in
BARREL LENGTH	597mm/23.50in
WEIGHT UNLOADED	12.25kg/27lb

FN Browning BAR D

In an effort to end the stalemate of trench warfare, the US Army intended to introduce massive firepower into the hands of the infantry. One approach was the Pedersen device, which proved a failure. The other was the BAR, which was not. A select-fire rifle-cartridge weapon that could be carried and used by one man, it proved rugged, accurate, reliable and long-lived. The FN Model D differed from the American version in having a finned barrel for greater cooling, and a pistol grip. As an export weapon, it could be made in any cartridge that fitted the basic BAR platform, and has been seen in eight different chamberings. Many armies had the BAR as their machine gun, a Squad Automatic Weapon (SAW). FN sold a great many between the wars and after World War II, until it developed the FAL and MAG 58. It was a standard export item from the 1920s to 1940, and then again in the early 1950s.

SPECIFICATION	
MANUFACTURER	FN, Liège
CALIBRE	.30-06, 7.92, 7.65, 6.5 x 55
MAGAZINE CAPACITY	20-round magazines
ACTION	Gas operated/toggle action
TOTAL LENGTH	1,194mm/47in
BARREL LENGTH	606mm/24in
WEIGHT UNLOADED	8.93kg/19.7lb

M2HB

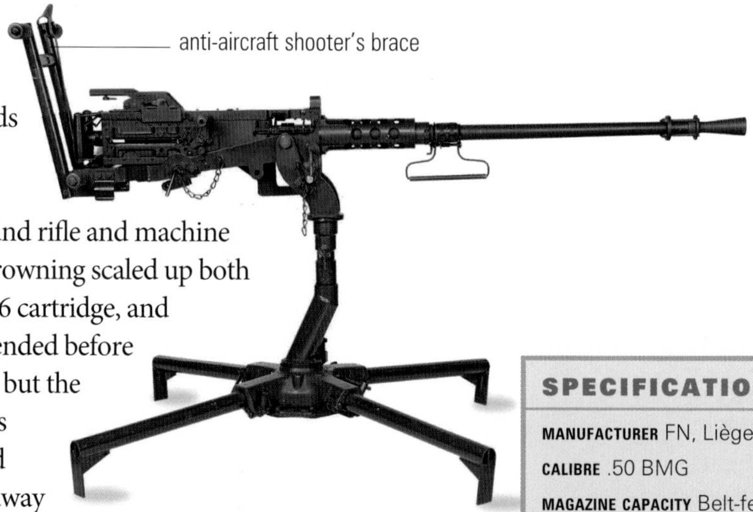

When tanks appeared on the battlefields of World War I, none of the armies involved had the means to deal with them. Artillery was too cumbersome, and rifle and machine guns mostly ineffective. John Moses Browning scaled up both his belt-fed machine gun and the .30-06 cartridge, and produced the .50 calibre M2. The war ended before it could be used on the Western Front, but the M2 has been used ever since. The HB is for "heavy barrel", a thicker-walled and heavier barrel than the original, to do away with the weight of a water-filled cooling jacket. Later FN improvements included a quick-change barrel that did not require adjustment on installation. For over a generation the US Army has been trying to replace the M2HB with something lighter, but all efforts have failed to produce any weapon as rugged, versatile and powerful. Production began in 1946 and continues today.

SPECIFICATION	
MANUFACTURER	FN, Liège
CALIBRE	.50 BMG
MAGAZINE CAPACITY	Belt-fed
ACTION	Recoil operated
TOTAL LENGTH	1,656mm/65.2in
BARREL LENGTH	1,143mm/45.0in
WEIGHT UNLOADED	38.10kg/84lb

FN MAG

SPECIFICATION

MANUFACTURER FN, Liège
CALIBRE 7.62 x 51mm
MAGAZINE CAPACITY Belt-fed
ACTION Gas operated/toggle lock
TOTAL LENGTH 1,260mm/49.60in
BARREL LENGTH 545mm/21.45in
WEIGHT UNLOADED 12.0kg/26.45lb

Designed in the 1950s, the Mitrailleuse d'Appui General (MAG) was meant to be a truly General-Purpose Machine Gun (GPMG), with variants for ground, vehicle and aircraft use. It is an amalgam of designs: a Maxim/Browning-type receiver of riveted plates, the Browning BAR-style bolt as the action and an MG 42 feed mechanism to advance the belt and feed the rounds. It has become near-ubiquitous, and has been adopted by the US Army and Marine Corps as the M240, replacing the American-designed M60. FN L7A2 is the United Kingdom's designation for the FN MAG; in the Netherlands it is used by the Royal Navy, Marine Corps, Royal Air Force and the Royal Army; and in Egypt, the Helwan 920 is a licensed design of the FN MAG. It is air-cooled, has two settings for the cyclic rate and a quick-change barrel.

FN Minimi

SPECIFICATION

MANUFACTURER FN, Liège
CALIBRE 5.56 x 45mm
MAGAZINE CAPACITY Belt and 30-round magazines
ACTION Gas operated/rotating bolt
TOTAL LENGTH 1,040mm/40.94in
BARREL LENGTH 465mm/18.3in
WEIGHT UNLOADED 7.1kg/15.65lb

Almost from the moment of reluctantly adopting the 5.56mm cartridge, the US Army sought to replace it. One avenue explored was to find a Squad Automatic Weapon (SAW) that needed something other than the 5.56mm. After 15 years of experimentation and design dead-ends, the army gave up and adopted the FN Minimi, a 5.56mm SAW that used either belts or M16 magazines. The US Army could not simply adopt it, it had to "improve" it, though such endeavours were in fact digressions. It goes under the designation M249 SAW in the US. The Minimi is now an integral part of many armies at the squad level, where a General-Purpose Machine Gun (GPMG) and the ammunition it consumes would be too heavy. FN sells or licenses the original, not a US Army-improved version. The Minimi, unlike many earlier light machine guns, can be mounted in a tripod as well as used on a bipod. It was introduced in 1982 and is now found worldwide, including the following countries:

Brazil: Guns were purchased directly from FN in 2014 in an effort to standardize equipment used between the Brazilian Army and the Navy, which was already using it.
Chile: 1,225 were purchased directly from FN in 2014.
Portugal: The Portuguese Army began using the gun in 2019, with their Marine Corps following suit in 2022.
France: The French Army has been using guns from FN since at least 2016 alongside the MAG.
Netherlands: The Royal Netherlands Army has elected to use the Minimi in place of the FN MAG in some infantry roles. The Dutch Korps Commandotroepen also use the Minimi.
Switzerland: In Switzerland, the gun is known locally as the Leichtes Maschinengewehr 05, or LMg 05, so designated because it was adopted in 2005.
Norway: Norwegian Special Forces have been using the rifle since the 1980s. Additional contracts for more Minimi guns for their armed forces were signed in 2011 and 2021.
Greece: The Hellenic Army has been using the gun since at least 2011.
Egypt: In Egypt, they use their own locally made version of the gun.
Thailand: The Royal Thai Navy Marine Corps and the Royal Thai Army both use the Minimi.
Japan: Japan was initially making licensed versions of the gun by Sumitomo Heavy Industries, but in 2023, they contracted with FN to purchase directly from them.
Australia: The Minimi has been adopted by the Australian Army as the F89.

Netherlands

The Netherlands adopted the Schwarzlose in 7.92mm rimmed before World War I, opting for a lighter machine gun after the war. Lacking an armoury or manufacturer of their own has not kept the Netherlands from adopting the best rifles and machine guns to be found. They currently field the Minimi and FN MAG.

Lewis M20

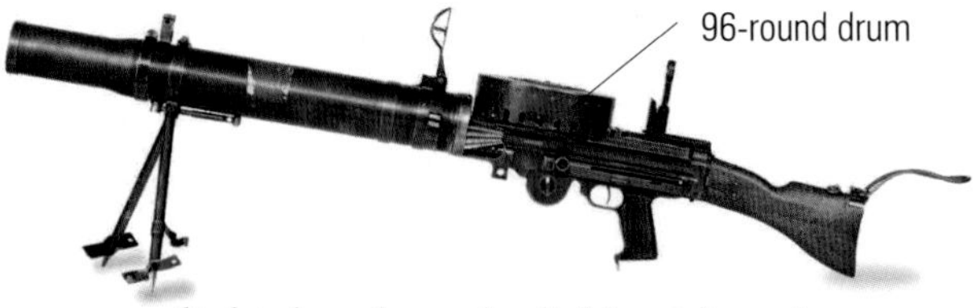

SPECIFICATION

MANUFACTURER FN, Liège
CALIBRE 6.5 x 53R
MAGAZINE CAPACITY 47 or 96
ACTION Gas operated
TOTAL LENGTH 1,283mm/50.5in
BARREL LENGTH 660mm/26in
WEIGHT UNLOADED 12.24kg/27lb

Adopted in 1920, the Lewis gun was light, handy and reliable, although required maintenance. The Lewis was adaptable to many cartridges due to its pan magazine. Modifying the design to use the 6.5 x 53R cartridge probably did not take more than a day for the engineers. With proper maintenance, the Lewis worked under even extreme conditions. It was in use from 1920 to 1940.

Switzerland

Despite a policy of neutrality for several centuries, Switzerland made and exported weapons for most of the 20th century. The mountainous countryside has meant Swiss armed forces have placed a premium on accurate, long-range fire. Switzerland has universal service, where every 18-year-old man goes through recruit training. Machine guns are stored in armouries, while service rifles are kept at home by each adult.

Furrer M1925

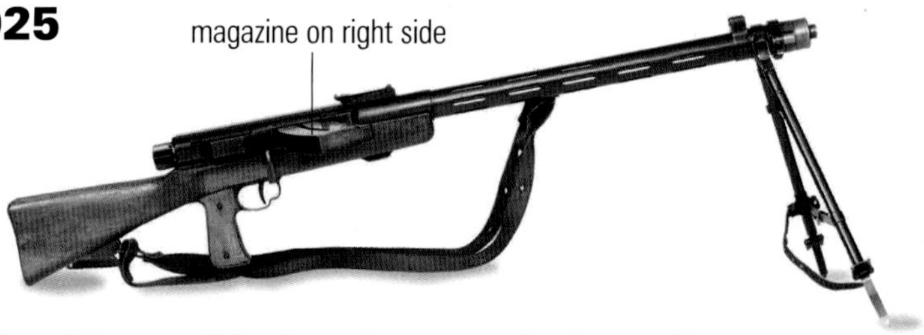

SPECIFICATION

MANUFACTURER Bern
CALIBRE 7.5 x 55mm
MAGAZINE CAPACITY 30
ACTION Recoil operated
TOTAL LENGTH 1,163mm/45.8in
BARREL LENGTH 584mm/23in
WEIGHT UNLOADED 10.74kg/23.69lb

Developed by Colonel Furrer of the Bern Armoury, the Furrer (known as the M25 in Swiss service) uses a side-hinged toggle lock. As a light machine gun (LMG), the odd locking system added cost to production. However, the barrel was easily changed, the selector could be set to full or semi-automatic fire and each spare barrel, when exchanged, also came with a fitted toggle bolt. The side-mount magazine allowed the gunner to acquire a very low prone position. It was manufactured from 1925 to 1946 and remained in service until the 1970s.

Hispano HS820

SPECIFICATION

MANUFACTURER Hispano Suiza
CALIBRE 20 x 110mm
MAGAZINE CAPACITY 25
ACTION Gas-unlocked blowback
TOTAL LENGTH 2,517mm/99in
BARREL LENGTH 1,000mm/39in
WEIGHT UNLOADED 46kg/101lb w/o mount

As vehicles became more common, armour as well as heavy weapons for infantry became bigger. Especially for the Swiss, whose defensive operations called for many ambush and flanking manoeuvres, the 20mm HS820 could be relied upon to inflict extensive work on a vehicular column. It was in service from 1941 to the 1970s.

Solothurn M30

SPECIFICATION

MANUFACTURER Solothurn
CALIBRE 7.92 x 57mm
MAGAZINE CAPACITY 30-round box and 50-round drum
ACTION Recoil operated
TOTAL LENGTH 1,085mm/42.7in
BARREL LENGTH 754mm/29.7in
WEIGHT UNLOADED 12.93kg/28.5lb

Designed by Rheinmetall but rejected by the German Army and prohibited from German manufacture by the Treaty of Versailles, the Solothurn was made in Switzerland. It was later adopted by the Luftwaffe as the MG15 in a flexible mount for bomber defence. The M30 had the option of full-automatic or semi-automatic firing rates, a feature many weapons designers worked on between the wars. It was in service between 1940 and 1945.

Solothurn S3200

SPECIFICATION

MANUFACTURER Solothurn
CALIBRE 7.92 x 57mm
MAGAZINE CAPACITY 30-round box and 50-round drum
ACTION Recoil operated
TOTAL LENGTH 1,085mm/42.7in
BARREL LENGTH 754mm/29.7in
WEIGHT UNLOADED 12.93kg/28.5lb

A light machine gun (LMG) designed between World War I and World War II, the S3200 had many fashionable features. The trigger had two curves on its face. By pressing one curve the shooter could fire in semi-automatic mode. By placing his finger on the other and pressing, full-auto fire was delivered. Such designs were all the rage in the 1930s, despite the added complexity. The partnership of Rheinmetall and Solothurn produced many designs, and while they were all reliable, Switzerland chose to adopt native designs for their own use and sold a few S3200s on the export market.

Germany

In the decades before World War I, Germany was an enthusiastic adopter of the Maxim machine gun. After the war, the Treaty of Versailles greatly restricted the number and type of machine guns German armed forces could have. A great deal of design and manufacturing effort went into weapons that would get around the restrictions. Thus the General-Purpose Machine Gun (GPMG) was developed and first unveiled in the MG 34.

MG08

SPECIFICATION

MANUFACTURER DMW, Spandau, others
CALIBRE 7.92 x 57mm
MAGAZINE CAPACITY Belt-fed
ACTION Recoil operated/toggle lock
TOTAL LENGTH 1,175mm/46.25in
BARREL LENGTH 717mm/28.25in
WEIGHT UNLOADED 18.37kg/40.5lb (bare MG, no water)

Adopting the Maxim gun in 1899, Germany had perfected it for general use by 1908 (and named it the MG08 after its year of adoption). Robust to the point of being unstoppable, the Maxim was water-cooled and could therefore fire continuously until ammunition or water were exhausted. More commonly, the gun crew would be exhausted first. However, the price for that durability and sustained rate of fire was weight. With a water-filled jacket, the first belt of ammunition and a sledge-type mount which was ferried between locations, it weighed close to 68kg/150lb. The MG08 was in use from 1908 until 1918 as a heavy machine gun, and used as a "light" machine gun in fixed positions during World War II.

HK11

Unlike the HK21, which was designed for both belt and magazines, the HK11 was a magazine-fed-only light machine gun. It was to be an improved and updated BAR or BREN for use by the West German Army and for export. However, in the Squad Automatic Weapon (SAW), the trend quickly moved from full-power machine guns of limited capacity to smaller calibres and larger ammunition volumes. The HK11 was manufactured from the early 1960s until the 1990s.

SPECIFICATION

MANUFACTURER Heckler & Koch
CALIBRE 7.62mm NATO
MAGAZINE CAPACITY 20
ACTION Gas operated
TOTAL LENGTH 1,020mm/40.1in
BARREL LENGTH 450mm/17.7in
WEIGHT UNLOADED 6.7kg/14.8lb

HK21A1

This was a development of the CETME and Heckler & Koch G3 series, and built on much the same stamped-steel receiver as the G3 rifle. Firing from the same delayed roller lock as other Heckler & Koch weapons, the 21 has a high cyclic rate for a Light Machine Gun (LMG), stout recoil and brisk ejection of empties. Based on the G3 receiver, it is too light to be a real General-Purpose Machine Gun (GPMG). The A1 had the optional box magazine feed (and attendant parts) eliminated from the standard 21. The HK21A1 was in use from the early 1960s to the 1990s.

SPECIFICATION

MANUFACTURER Heckler & Koch
CALIBRE 7.62mm NATO, 7.62 x 39mm, 5.56 x 45mm
MAGAZINE CAPACITY Belt-fed
ACTION Recoil operated/roller-lock delay
TOTAL LENGTH 1,018mm/40.1in
BARREL LENGTH 575mm/22.63in
WEIGHT UNLOADED 6.66kg/14.7lb

MG 34

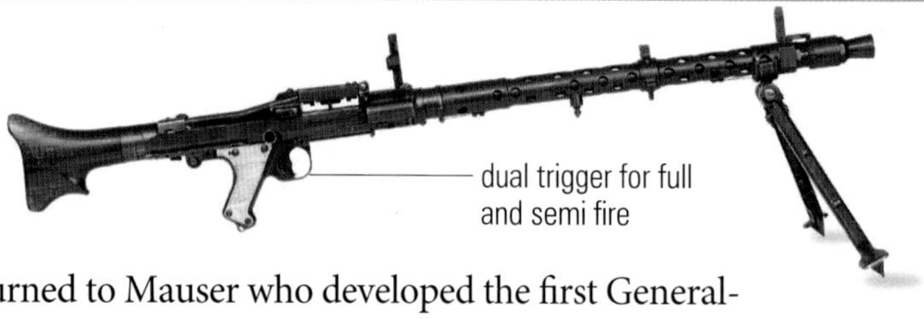

With Versailles prohibiting new Maxims, Germany turned to Mauser who developed the first General-Purpose Machine Gun. It had a quick-change barrel, it was selective fire and used a belt or two different-sized drums, all in a lightweight package. It was not just light by World War I Maxim standards; the weight would be acceptable today. Ultimately it proved too well made and not loose enough for the mud of combat. It also took too much time to manufacture, requiring many precise machining operations. It was in use in Germany from 1934 to 1945.

SPECIFICATION

MANUFACTURER Mauser
CALIBRE 7.92 x 57mm
MAGAZINE CAPACITY Belt, 50- and 75-round drums
ACTION Recoil operated/roller locked
TOTAL LENGTH 1,220mm/48in
BARREL LENGTH 623mm/24.6in
WEIGHT UNLOADED 12.02kg/26.5lb

MG 42/59

SPECIFICATION

MANUFACTURER Rheinmettal
CALIBRE 7.92 x 57mm
MAGAZINE CAPACITY Belt-fed
ACTION Recoil operated
TOTAL LENGTH 1,220mm/48in
BARREL LENGTH 533mm/21in
WEIGHT UNLOADED 11.56kg/25.5lb

The first machine guns produced after the end of World War II, issued to the Border Police, were simply MG42s built on wartime machinery and still chambered in 7.92mm. During the 1950s the design was modified and the calibre changed to eventually become the MG 3. The changes gradually brought down the cyclic rate (as much as 1,300 rpm in the MG 42) and increased durability. It was produced from 1948 to the late 1960s and called the MG42/59. It was adopted by the Italian military in 1959.

MG 08/15

SPECIFICATION

MANUFACTURER Various
CALIBRE 7.92 x 57mm
MAGAZINE CAPACITY Belt or 50-round drum
ACTION Recoil operated/toggle lock
TOTAL LENGTH 1,435mm/56.5in
BARREL LENGTH 716mm/28.2in
WEIGHT UNLOADED 17.7kg/39lb without water

The Maxim MG 08 was a nearly indestructible engine of death in the trench warfare of World War I. What it was not, however, was portable. The MG 08/15 had the sledge removed, a bipod and butt stock affixed and a sling attached. The water jacket was left on, but it was a dull infantryman who failed to drain the water before exiting the trenches on an assault. Even with the reduction in weight, trying to wrestle it across a shell-churned battlefield had to be back-breaking. Still, anything that increased mobility was an improvement. It was used only in World War I from 1915 to 1918. Some were found in World War II in guard towers at armouries and death camps.

MG 42

SPECIFICATION

MANUFACTURER Various
CALIBRE 7.92 x 57mm
MAGAZINE CAPACITY Belt-fed
ACTION Recoil operated/roller locked
TOTAL LENGTH 1,220mm/48in
BARREL LENGTH 533mm/21in
WEIGHT UNLOADED 11.56kg/25.5lb

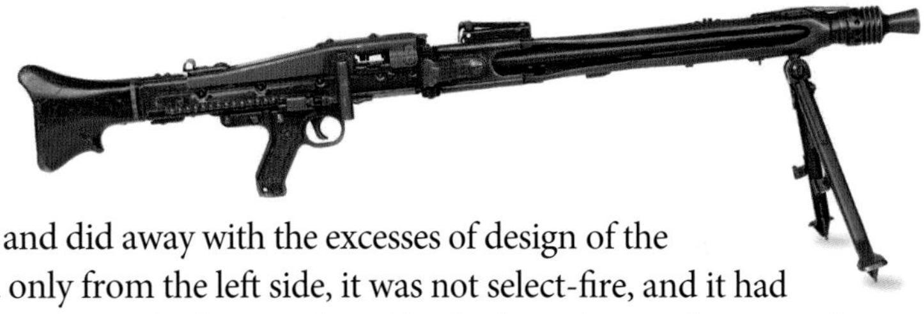

The MG 42 was made primarily of steel stampings and did away with the excesses of design of the MG 34: the 42 fed only from the left side, it was not select-fire, and it had no provision for magazine feed. It used a roller-lock, with a gas boost to the mechanism gained from the adjustable muzzle cone. The cyclic rate was 1,200 to 1,300 rpm, but the quick-change barrel was so easy to change that heating hardly mattered. It was produced in huge volumes from 1942 to 1945 and again after the war both for West Germany and for export.

MG 4

SPECIFICATION

MANUFACTURER Heckler & Koch
CALIBRE 5.56mm NATO
MAGAZINE CAPACITY Belt-fed
ACTION Gas operated
TOTAL LENGTH 1,030mm/40.6in
BARREL LENGTH 450mm/17.7in
WEIGHT UNLOADED 8.1kg/17.9lb

Adopted in 2005, the MG4 is an air-cooled light machine gun similar to the FN Minimi. It feeds from a disintegrating belt with the belt being discarded to the right and spent cases from the bottom. The carry handle doubles as the grip for the quick-change barrel system, which allows the barrel to be swapped when it gets too hot without the shooter needing protective gloves.

HK MG 5

SPECIFICATION

MANUFACTURER Heckler & Koch
CALIBRE 7.62mm NATO
MAGAZINE CAPACITY Belt-fed
ACTION Gas operated
TOTAL LENGTH 1,160mm/45.7in
BARREL LENGTH 550mm/21.7in
WEIGHT UNLOADED 11.2kg/24.7lb

The MG5 is a general purpose machine gun chambered in 7.62mm NATO. While the MG5 is based on the MG4, there are very few interchangeable parts because of the overall size difference between the two due to the calibre differences.

Italy

Italy entered World War I with a motley collection of machine guns. Forces had to contend with machine guns made in two different locally produced rifle calibres (6.5 and 7.35mm) and a large supply of 8 x 50R Schwarzlose guns that were war reparations from Austria. Mussolini's emphasis on production did not help, as much effort went to political favourites instead of a few standard and debugged designs.

Breda M30

A re-introduction of the Breda 1924, the M30 featured an Italian novelty: a permanently attached magazine which fed from the right, and was hinged to open when the gunner pushed it forward. He would recharge an empty magazine by means of a special charger with 20 rounds in it. The delayed blowback system produced a rather violent primary extraction, so the cases had to be oiled as they were fed, via a built-in cartridge oiler. These issues did not discourage the Italian Army from buying many M30s. Breda even exported some in 7 and 7.92mm Mauser. They were in service from 1930 to 1945.

SPECIFICATION

MANUFACTURER Breda
CALIBRE 6.5 x 52mm
MAGAZINE CAPACITY 20
ACTION Delayed blowback
TOTAL LENGTH 1232mm/48.50in
BARREL LENGTH 520mm/20.50in
WEIGHT UNLOADED 10.31kg/22.75lb w/o mount

Breda M1937

The best Italian machine gun of World War II, the Breda 37 was an air-cooled heavy machine gun that tested the supply system by introducing yet another cartridge, the 8mm Italian. Another oddity was the feed system: it used feed trays, but the empty cases were reinserted back into the tray. The gun crews then had to remove these before re-loading the trays with live ammunition for the next engagement. The Breda was in service from 1937 to 1945, and dropped after the war. Had it been built with a regular belt-feed mechanism, in a standard cartridge, it would have been exemplary.

SPECIFICATION

MANUFACTURER Breda Meccanica Bresciana
CALIBRE 8 x 59mm
MAGAZINE CAPACITY 20-round trays
ACTION Gas operated
TOTAL LENGTH 1,270mm/50in
BARREL LENGTH 635mm/25in
WEIGHT UNLOADED 19.41kg/42.8lb

Colt 1914

The 1914 was simply the Colt 1895 chambered in 6.5 Carcano, and manufactured in the early years of World War I. As an air-cooled machine gun it was prone to over-heating in the sustained fire of World War I tactical use. However, the medium-power 6.5 cartridge was a lesser heat source for the barrel, and the Italian guns were probably less prone to overheating than the more powerful .30-06 of the American versions. Despite the success of the Colt, they were not retained after the war, and were replaced by a steady succession of Italian designs of dubious reliability. They were in service during Italy's involvement in World War I, from 1915 to 1918.

SPECIFICATION

MANUFACTURER Colt
CALIBRE 6.5 x 52mm
MAGAZINE CAPACITY Belt-fed
ACTION Gas operated
TOTAL LENGTH 1,036mm/40.80in
BARREL LENGTH 711mm/28.0in
WEIGHT UNLOADED 18.14kg/40lb w/o mount

FIAT-Revelli 1914

As water-cooled heavy machine guns of the World War I period go, the Revelli was relatively lightweight. Chambered in the Italian 6.5mm cartridge, it should have been a steady performer, but any delayed blowback action had the potential to be unreliable with any ammunition that was not perfect. The bolt was not completely enclosed by the receiver, so it would cycle out of the rear, directly toward the firer. Also, the feed mechanism was a bottleneck in any sustained-fire situation. Instead of a belt, the Revelli used a sheet-metal contraption called a cage, holding 50 rounds in ten columns of five. The block of exposed cartridges was inserted into the left side. It would feed each column to the chamber, and then eject the empty feed cage out. The cages were not robust enough to survive many firings. The ammunition manufacturer would have to provide a new feed cage for each 50-round ammunition increment. It is hard to imagine why the designers thought the cage an improvement on a belt-fed system. Desperate for machine guns, the Italians bought the Revelli. After the war, they were put into storage and not seen again.

SPECIFICATION

MANUFACTURER FIAT-Revelli
CALIBRE 6.5 x 52mm
MAGAZINE CAPACITY 50
ACTION Delayed blowback
TOTAL LENGTH 1,181mm/46.5in
BARREL LENGTH 654mm/25.75in
WEIGHT UNLOADED 17kg/37.5lb (no water)

FIAT M35

SPECIFICATION

MANUFACTURER FIAT-Revelli
CALIBRE 8 x 59mm
MAGAZINE CAPACITY Belt-fed
ACTION Delayed blowback
TOTAL LENGTH 1270mm/50in
BARREL LENGTH 654mm/25.75in
WEIGHT UNLOADED 22.6kg/50lb

The Revelli 1914 was quite dated by 1935, so FIAT was asked to update its machine gun. It did so by changing from a water-cooled to an air-cooled barrel. It also increased the calibre, but kept the same delayed blowback action. The result was yet another machine gun that required lubricated cartridges to avoid broken cases and another seized-up machine gun in combat. Additionally, the 8mm cartridge further taxed the Italian production and supply system, which could only be charitably described as disorganized. It was in service only from 1935 to 1945, and immediately scrapped when the war was over.

Vickers Class C

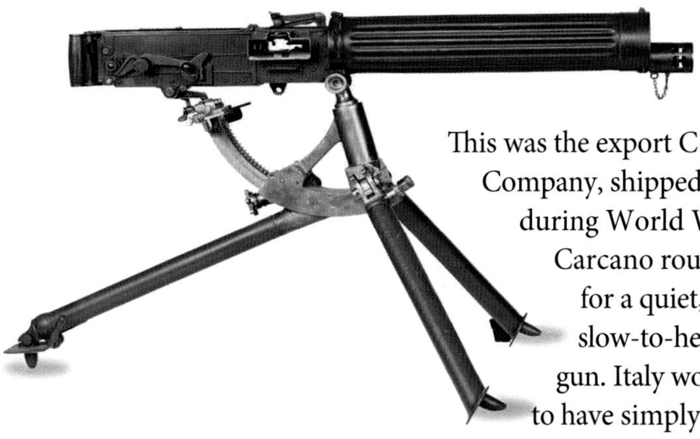

SPECIFICATION

MANUFACTURER Vickers
CALIBRE 6.5 x 52mm
MAGAZINE CAPACITY Belt-fed
ACTION Recoil operated
TOTAL LENGTH 1,100mm/43.3in
BARREL LENGTH 720mm/28.34in
WEIGHT UNLOADED 33kg/72.75lb (no water)

This was the export C model of the Vickers Company, shipped to Italy before and during World War I. The 6.5mm Carcano round would have made for a quiet, low-recoiling and slow-to-heat-up heavy machine gun. Italy would have done well to have simply retained the Vickers in 6.5mm, rather than try other designs such as the later short adoption of the 7.35mm cartridge. But had they stuck with it, their Vickers could have been converted for far less effort than designing and manufacturing a whole new machine gun. It was in service from 1910 to 1918.

Norway

When Norway separated from Sweden in 1905, it went to Denmark and the United States for machine guns: both countries were established and reliable performers. Between the wars, the choice of established machine guns to purchase was limited. It was not that there were many contenders: the list of reliable machine guns was short and Norway was ill-equipped. The Danish Madsen was the standard machine gun and reasonably effective. The Browning MG M29 could be unreliable in cold weather.

Browning MG M29

SPECIFICATION	
MANUFACTURER	Colt
CALIBRE	7.92 x 57mm
MAGAZINE CAPACITY	Belt-fed
ACTION	Recoil operated
TOTAL LENGTH	1,155mm/45.5in
BARREL LENGTH	558mm/22in
WEIGHT UNLOADED	14.9kg/32.5lb

Tripods
After World War I, heavy machine guns were equipped with lighter tripods, as above. While heavier than a modern machine gun, the post-war tripods were light for the period.

Adopted in 1929 as the M29, this machine gun was simply the Colt-manufactured Browning-designed M1917 with the upgrades Colt had made to the design since 1917. The bottom plate was reinforced along with the feed. That the Norwegians elected to increase the calibre of the M29 over that of the light machine gun they chose was also wise. The 7.92mm has greater power and range than the 6.5mm. Chambered in a tripod-mounted, water-cooled machine gun, the extra recoil was of no concern to the crew operating it. During World War II, Norwegian and German units could use each other's ammunition, if not ammunition belts. It was replaced by the MG3 in the late 1950s.

Madsen M1922

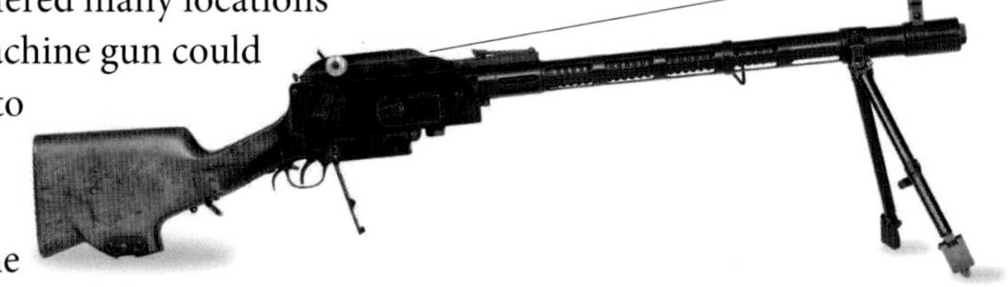

ABOVE The cocking lever on the side betrays the Madsen's age.

While Norway offered many locations where a heavy machine gun could do great damage to an attacker, after World War I, all armies realized the need for a portable machine gun. Norway selected the Madsen. Despite the extra cost of manufacture and procurement, and the odd operating system, the Madsen was a proven reliable performer. Chambered in 6.5mm, the Madsen could use rifle ammunition. That the 6.5mm has mild recoil is also an advantage to the operator, allowing for more-accurate fire. Adopted in the mid-1920s, the Madsen was obviously obsolete after World War II and not replaced. Along with the Browning, it was replaced by the MG3, a General-Purpose Machine Gun (GPMG) that could perform well in both roles.

SPECIFICATION	
MANUFACTURER	Kongsberg Våpenfabrikk
CALIBRE	6.5 x 55mm
MAGAZINE CAPACITY	20, 25 & 30
ACTION	Recoil operated
TOTAL LENGTH	1,168mm/46in
BARREL LENGTH	482mm/19in
WEIGHT UNLOADED	9.97kg/22lb

Denmark

A peninsula in the Baltic, Denmark has a long history of fending off its neighbours, not always with success. Despite little in the way of natural resources, Denmark built a solid firearms production base. After World War II, Denmark left the arms-making field, in the face of increased competition from larger countries.

Madsen M1946

SPECIFICATION

MANUFACTURER Dansk Industri Syndikat
CALIBRE 7.62 x 63mm
MAGAZINE CAPACITY 20, 25, 30 & 40-round magazines (.30-06 were 30-round)
ACTION Recoil operated
TOTAL LENGTH 1,168mm/46in
BARREL LENGTH 482mm/19in
WEIGHT UNLOADED 9.97kg/22lb

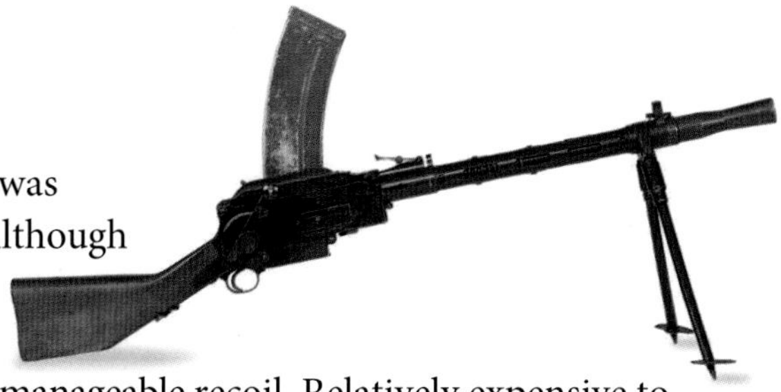

The Madsen light machine gun was distributed widely from 1902. Although awkward in appearance it was easy to handle. The long-recoil design made for brisk, but manageable recoil. Relatively expensive to manufacture, and requiring good-quality ammunition, it worked well when treated well. That, combined with its relative light weight, made it popular around the world. Offered in a host of calibres, the M1946 was made in .30-06 for Denmark. Since it was using the American M1 Garand at the time, keeping the calibre supply simple was wise. It was used from 1946 until Denmark switched to the 7.62mm with the rest of Europe and was replaced by the Madsen-Saetter.

Madsen-Saetter

SPECIFICATION

MANUFACTURER Dansk Industri Syndikat
CALIBRE 7.62 x 51mm
MAGAZINE CAPACITY 50, 7, 100-round magazines, and belts
ACTION Gas operated/rotating bolt
TOTAL LENGTH 1,219mm/48in
BARREL LENGTH 660mm/26in
WEIGHT UNLOADED 11.61kg/25.6lb

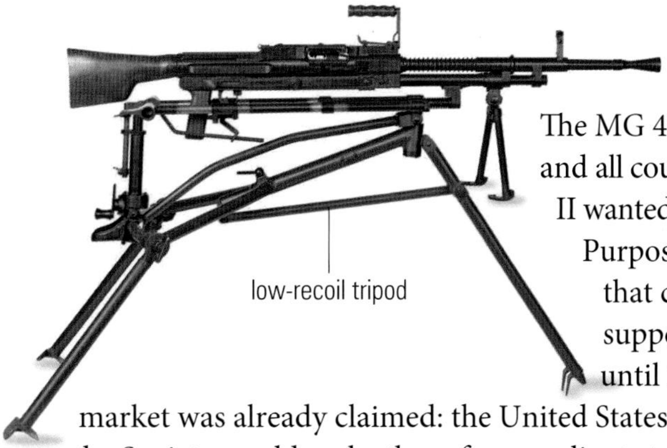

The MG 42 had shown the way, and all countries after World War II wanted an air-cooled General-Purpose Machine Gun (GPMG), that could also serve in the support role. Development took until 1959, by which time the market was already claimed: the United States would make their own, the Soviets would make them for any client state, and FN would sell MAG 58s to the rest of the world. The Madsen-Saetter could be manufactured in any rimless cartridge from 6.5mm to 7.92mm. It fed from either belts or box magazines, unusual for this type of gun. The Madsen-Saetter was never a commercial success and it saw only limited production beginning in 1959.

Vickers Commercial C Model

SPECIFICATION

MANUFACTURER Vickers
CALIBRE 8 x 58R
MAGAZINE CAPACITY Belt-fed
ACTION Gas operated/toggle
TOTAL LENGTH 1,092mm/43in
BARREL LENGTH 721mm/28.4in
WEIGHT UNLOADED 14.96kg/33lb

As good as the Madsen machine gun proved to be, it was not a heavy, support-role machine gun. The only way to accomplish that, before World War II, was with a water-cooled machine gun. Thus, Denmark acquired a supply of Vickers heavy machine guns in the early 1920s. They were chambered in the Danish rifle calibre, 8 x 58R, a simple change for the Vickers Company to have made. Nearly all of them ended up being appropriated to feed the German war machine after the German occupation of Denmark.

Austria

Austrian inventiveness extended to machine guns as well as rifles. As the main supplier of small arms to the Austro-Hungarian empire, Steyr was heavily committed to manufacturing arms. After World War I weapons production in Steyr was next to prohibited, and in 1918, the company faced bankruptcy.

Solothurn Model 30S

This was a licensed Rheinmetall-designed Light Machine Gun (LMG), built in Solothurn, Switzerland to avoid restrictions on machine gun manufacture by Germany as laid down in the Treaty of Versailles. It was one of many contenders for the role of LMG, now called a Squad Automatic Weapon (SAW). Later design modifications in Germany led to the MG 15, a 75-round drum-fed, stockless machine gun for use as a defensive arm in bombers. The Solothurn Model 30S was a commercial export item from 1930, and used in World War II until 1945. After the war there were many LMGs to choose from, so production ceased.

SPECIFICATION

MANUFACTURER Solothurn
CALIBRE 7.92 x 57mm
MAGAZINE CAPACITY 50, beltless drum
ACTION Gas operated
TOTAL LENGTH 1,389mm/54.7in
BARREL LENGTH 754mm/29in
WEIGHT UNLOADED 12.24kg/27lb

Skoda M1893

The 1893 Skoda was patented by Archduke Karl Salvator and Count George von Dormus. It fed on cartridges that were hand-laid into the feed chute by the assistant gunner. Blowback designs and rifle-calibre cartridges do not mix, so we also owe these two for the concept of the cartridge oiler. Oiled cartridges extract more easily, but the oil attracts dust and grit, causing malfunctions. A pendulum adjustment in the trigger mechanism allowed the operator to select the cyclic rate, from 180 to 250 rounds per minute. Upgraded marginally in the M1902, and greatly in the M1909. The 1893 lasted just long enough to reportedly be used in the Boxer Rebellion in 1900, before making its way into museums.

SPECIFICATION

MANUFACTURER Steyr
CALIBRE 8 x 50R
MAGAZINE CAPACITY N/A
ACTION Delayed blowback
TOTAL LENGTH 1153mm/45.4in
BARREL LENGTH 621mm/24.4in
WEIGHT UNLOADED 16.78kg/37lb

Schwarzlose M07/12

Adopted by several other countries, the Schwarzlose was used extensively during World War I by Austro-Hungarian empire units. It has a straightforward blowback mechanism. The bolt was not mechanically locked to the barrel or receiver when the chambered cartridge was fired. There was a lubricating pump in the original M07 to lubricate each cartridge for ease of extraction. The M07/12 update and rebuild changed the extraction timing and removed the need for the pump but the weapon still relied on a heavy bolt and very strong recoil spring. As with all World War I-era machine guns, the mount can weigh as much as or more than the weapon. The 8 x 50R was adopted in 1912 and used until the 1920s when it was replaced with locked-breech machine guns.

SPECIFICATION

MANUFACTURER Steyr
CALIBRE 8 x 50R
MAGAZINE CAPACITY Cloth belt
ACTION Blowback
TOTAL LENGTH 1,066mm/42in
BARREL LENGTH 527mm/20.75in
WEIGHT UNLOADED 19.95kg/44lb w/o mount

Steyr AUG A1 LMG

SPECIFICATION	
MANUFACTURER	Steyr
CALIBRE	5.56 x 45mm
MAGAZINE CAPACITY	30 or 42
ACTION	Gas operated/rotating bolt
TOTAL LENGTH	900mm/35.4in
BARREL LENGTH	621mm/24.4in
WEIGHT UNLOADED	4.9kg/10.80lb

Belt-fed General-Purpose Machine Guns (GPMGs) are considered too heavy to be used as the integral weapon for a squad. Usually chambered in 7.62mm NATO or an equal, the GPMG needs a multi-man team to operate it. To increase the firepower of squads, the Squad Automatic Weapon (SAW) was re-invented near the end of the Cold War. The AUG A1 is the firepower base for the Austrian Army squad and is simply an AUG with a longer and heavier barrel and a bipod. The box magazine limits firepower, but the ease of barrel changes makes the AUG A1 a much more viable SAW than other assault rifles pressed into this role. The Steyr Aug has been used by the Austrian Army from 1985 to the present day.

Sweden

By the 20th century Sweden's Baltic empire was long gone, but all countries need Armed Forces to defend themselves from would-be invaders. With a solid industrial base with world famous companies like FFV and Carl Gustav, Sweden had no problems with local manufacture, but also purchased guns from abroad.

Browning M1936

SPECIFICATION	
MANUFACTURER	Carl Gustav
CALIBRE	7.92 x 63mm
MAGAZINE CAPACITY	Belt-fed
ACTION	Recoil operated
TOTAL LENGTH	1,008mm/39.7in
BARREL LENGTH	610mm/24in
WEIGHT UNLOADED	14.51kg/32lb w/o mount

The M1936 was a water-cooled heavy Browning, chambered in the special Swedish heavy machine gun cartridge – the 7.92mm – which delivered a larger and heavier bullet than the 6.5mm, at a higher velocity. As a static machine gun in the kind of defensive positions found in World War I, a water-cooled machine gun in a heavier calibre makes sense. It remained in service to the late 1950s until it was replaced by the MAG 58.

Browning BAR M1921

SPECIFICATION	
MANUFACTURER	Colt
CALIBRE	6.5 x 55mm
MAGAZINE CAPACITY	20
ACTION	Gas operated
TOTAL LENGTH	1,118mm/44in
BARREL LENGTH	670mm/26.4in
WEIGHT UNLOADED	8.71kg/19.2lb

This was bought from Colt and supplied to them in the Swedish calibre. The 1921 Swedish requirements added a pistol grip and dust covers over the ejection port and magazine port. Otherwise it was quite similar to the M1918 BAR. The M1921 served in Swedish Army units and Reserves between 1921 and the late 1950s.

SAV Model 40

This was an odd light machine gun, built by the Swedes and used by some Waffen-SS units as the MG 35/36. The distinctive loops of the gas system made it easy to identify. It was unpopular with every unit it was issued to. Eventually it was withdrawn from regular Swedish service and sent to the Home Guard units, who also hated it. It was replaced after a short service life between 1940 and 1945 by the M1921 Browning.

SPECIFICATION	
MANUFACTURER	SAV
CALIBRE	6.5 x 55mm
MAGAZINE CAPACITY	20
ACTION	Gas operated
TOTAL LENGTH	1,257mm/49.48in
BARREL LENGTH	685mm/26.96in
WEIGHT UNLOADED	8.5kg/18.73lb

Czech Republic

After World War I, the Austro-Hungarian Empire was divided into countries of similar ethnic backgrounds, with the Czechs and Slovaks amalgamated into a new country known as Czechoslovakia. After World War II, the country was a Warsaw Pact ally. With the fall of the Soviet Union, the two groups went their separate ways. With many natural resources and a manufacturing history, it is little wonder Czech designs are common.

VZ26

One of the first light machine guns, now called a Squad Automatic Weapon (SAW), the VZ26 (also ZB26) was popular enough to be made on three continents and used by two dozen countries. As a milled-receiver magazine-fed weapon, it was relatively easy to produce in any cartridge that fitted the basic receiver/bolt dimensions. When built on contract, it could be delivered in a variety of chambering choices. It was quickly improved and upgraded. The VZ26 was the design and tactical forerunner to the BREN gun. Production began in 1926 and it was used until the late 1940s.

SPECIFICATION	
MANUFACTURER	CZ BRio
CALIBRE	7.92 x 57mm, 6.5mm Jap
MAGAZINE CAPACITY	20
ACTION	Gas operated/tilting bolt
TOTAL LENGTH	1,163mm/45.8in
BARREL LENGTH	602mm/23.7in
WEIGHT UNLOADED	9.65kg/21.28lb

VZ37

The forerunner to the British BESA machine gun, the VZ37 (also ZB37) was a heavy machine gun meant to be used from a tripod. The barrel moved fore and aft and the cartridge was chambered and fired during forward movement. The recoil of firing had to thus overcome the forward inertia of the barrel. It was compact for a heavy machine gun and used a pair of side-grasping/firing handles that were pitched downwards. The Czechs manufactured them from 1937 until Germany invaded, and then for the Germans until 1945. After the war, there were many other designs found in greater numbers, so production ceased.

SPECIFICATION	
MANUFACTURER	CZ BRio
CALIBRE	7.92 x 57mm
MAGAZINE CAPACITY	Belt-fed
ACTION	Gas operated
TOTAL LENGTH	1,105mm/43.5in
BARREL LENGTH	678mm/26.7in
WEIGHT UNLOADED	18.96kg/41.8lb

VZ60

SPECIFICATION

MANUFACTURER CZ BRio
CALIBRE 15mm
MAGAZINE CAPACITY 25-round belt
ACTION Gas operated
TOTAL LENGTH 2,050mm/80.75in
BARREL LENGTH 640mm/25.2in
WEIGHT UNLOADED 56.9kg/125.5lb

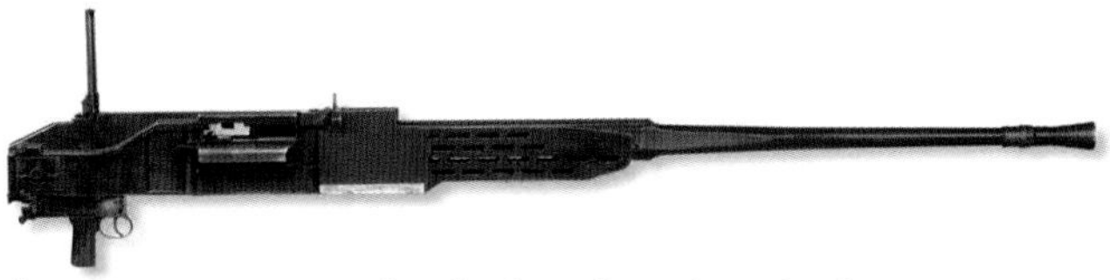

Basically a scaled-up ZB37/BESA, also meant for use in armoured vehicles, the VZ60 had an extra feature not usually found on machine guns: semi-automatic fire. The selector had three settings: safe, repetition and auto. It was also used primarily in British armoured vehicles during World War II. As a scaled-up BESA, training and maintenance would have been very easy for the Royal Armoured Corps. It was manufactured from 1940 and declared obsolete in 1949.

VZ52/57

SPECIFICATION

MANUFACTURER CZ BRio
CALIBRE 7.62 x 39mm
MAGAZINE CAPACITY 25-round box, 100-round belt
ACTION Gas operated/tilting bolt
TOTAL LENGTH 1,041mm/41in
BARREL LENGTH 541mm/21.3in
WEIGHT UNLOADED 7.98kg/17.6lb

A new and improved post-war ZB26/30 or BREN gun, the VZ52 was designed to be fed from a belt or box magazine. Complex and sophisticated, it pre-dated the current SAWs such as the M249 or Minimi that also fed from either box or belt. As a bonus, it featured a quick-change barrel. The VZ52 was chambered in the new Czech intermediate cartridge, the 7.62 x 45mm. The 52/57 was the designation given to the original light machine gun rebuilt to use the Soviet M43 cartridge, the 7.62 x 39mm. The Czechs began making it in 1952 and, after the calibre change, continued to manufacture it into the late 1960s.

UK 59

SPECIFICATION

MANUFACTURER CZ BRio
CALIBRE 7.62 x 54R
MAGAZINE CAPACITY Belt-fed
ACTION Gas operated/tilting bolt
TOTAL LENGTH 1,217mm/47.9in
BARREL LENGTH 693mm/27.3in
WEIGHT UNLOADED 19.23kg/42.4lb w/heavy barrel, on tripod. 8.66kg/19.1lb in bipod

This was the Czech answer to the desire for a General-Purpose Machine Gun (GPMG) that could be used on a bipod for squad use and on a tripod for support fire. The feed mechanism is basically that of the ZB37 combined with the quick-change barrel design of the ZB52. Chambered for the Soviet rimmed .30, the 7.62 x 54R, it was manufactured from machined forgings, and was thus somewhat heavy and expensive to manufacture. While production was still underway, it was altered slightly (and the name changed to UK68) when re-chambered for 7.62mm NATO. It is in current use with both the Czech and Slovak armies.

Schwarzlose VZ7/24

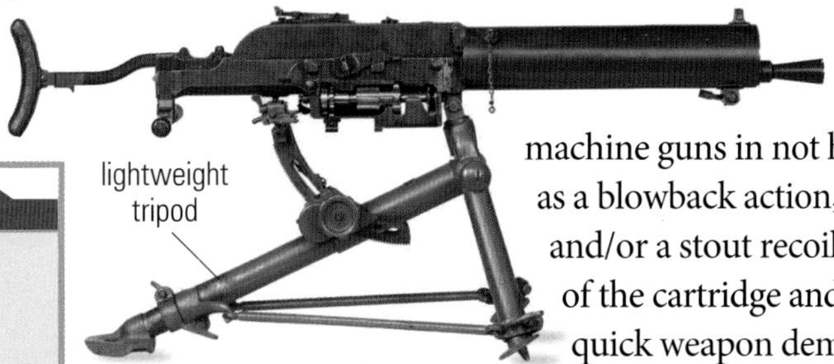

SPECIFICATION

MANUFACTURER Steyr
CALIBRE 7.92 x 57mm
MAGAZINE CAPACITY Belt-fed
ACTION Blowback
TOTAL LENGTH 1,066mm/42in
BARREL LENGTH 527mm/20.75in
WEIGHT UNLOADED 19.95kg/44lb

The Schwarzlose is perhaps unique in belt-fed rifle-calibre machine guns in not having a locked breech. Known as a blowback action, the design needs a heavy bolt and/or a stout recoil spring to contain the power of the cartridge and to prevent battering and quick weapon demise. The Schwarzlose has both. Germany used Schwarzlose machine guns in World War I and World War II, the latter chambered in the standard 7.92mm cartridge. The M07/24 was common enough to have specialized equipment such as belt loaders and training manuals printed for use by Wehrmacht troops in World War I. Production began in 1907. It was rebuilt as the VZ7/24 in 1924, and used in German service until 1945.

Poland

Regaining independence after World War I, Poland did not have long on the world stage. Crushed between the Germans and Soviets in 1939, it was then fought over in the Russo-German war of 1941-5. Once it became a member of the Warsaw Pact, Poland supplied armaments and personnel to support the Red Army.

Browning BAR M28

Simply the American version in the German calibre, the Polish BAR was a vast improvement over its previous light machine gun, the Chauchat. It was purchased in 1928 and was in service until 1939.

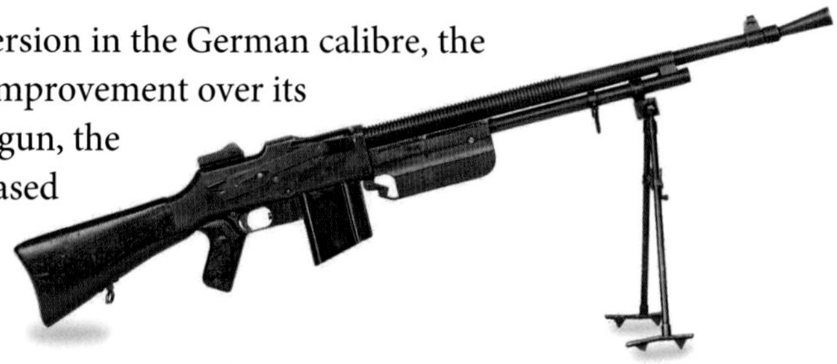

SPECIFICATION

MANUFACTURER Colt
CALIBRE 7.92 x 57mm
MAGAZINE CAPACITY 20
ACTION Gas operated/toggle lock
TOTAL LENGTH 1,214mm/47.8in
BARREL LENGTH 610mm/24in
WEIGHT UNLOADED 8.79kg/19.4lb

Goryunov WZ43

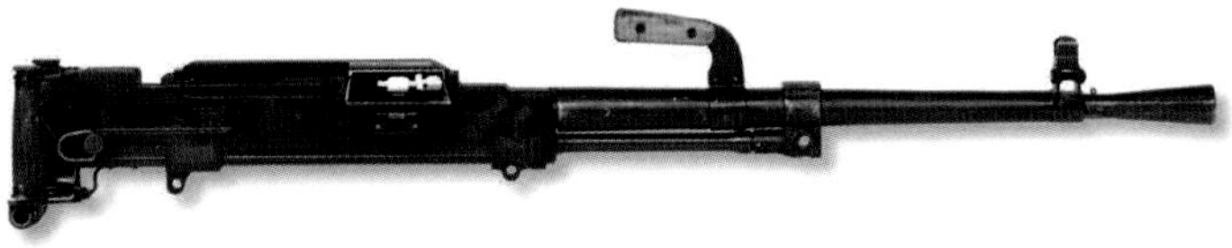

This is the reliable, if heavy, Soviet-designed medium machine gun. After World War II, all Soviet client states converted to the Soviet pattern of small arms and produced weapons for their own use as well as for the Red Army. The Goryunov would have been issued to Polish infantry and mechanized infantry units, who were expected to be reserves to their Soviet and East German comrades for any offensive into Western Europe. It was replaced by the PKM in the mid 1960s.

SPECIFICATION

MANUFACTURER Radom
CALIBRE 7.62 x 54R
MAGAZINE CAPACITY Belt-fed
ACTION Gas operated
TOTAL LENGTH 1,120mm/44.1in
BARREL LENGTH 719mm/28.3in
WEIGHT UNLOADED 13.15kg/29lb w/o mount

DSHK M38/46

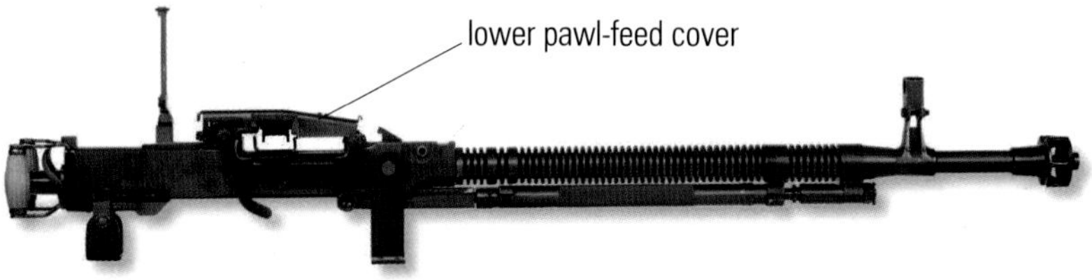

The standard Soviet heavy machine gun, the 38/46 variant is a design improvement on the M38, where the rotating feed block is replaced with a conventional feed pawl to advance the belt. While rotating feed blocks or "spools" are seen by designers as an improvement, in the field the advantages are often illusory. Pawls and dog-leg shaped action tracks work just as well, as seen on the MG42 and other machine guns. Much as the American M2HB has outlived its replacements, the DSHK has outlasted lighter, "better" heavy machine guns. It was first placed into service with the Soviets in 1946, and with the Polish in the early 1950s, and is still in service to the present day.

SPECIFICATION

MANUFACTURER Radom
CALIBRE 12.7 x 108mm
MAGAZINE CAPACITY Belt-fed
ACTION Gas operated
TOTAL LENGTH 1,588mm/62.5in
BARREL LENGTH 1,070mm/42.1in
WEIGHT UNLOADED 36.28kg/80lb w/o mount (approx 118kg/260lb)

Replacement for DSHK
With Poland entering NATO, the DSHK may be at the end of its service, replaced by an even older heavy gun; the M2HB.

Kalashnikov PK

SPECIFICATION

MANUFACTURER Radom
CALIBRE 7.62 x 54R
MAGAZINE CAPACITY Belt-fed
ACTION Gas operated/rotating bolt
TOTAL LENGTH 1,199mm/47.2in
BARREL LENGTH 658mm/25.9in
WEIGHT UNLOADED 7.48–9.52kg/16.5–21lb

The Soviet General-Purpose Machine Gun (GPMG), the PK (Pulemyut Kalashnikov) is a Kalashnikov design with an additional belt-feed, scaled up to accept the larger 7.62mm Tsarist/Soviet cartridge. While the RPD has use at the squad level, the PK is meant for heavier work. In addition to the heavier cartridge, the PK has a quick-change barrel for use in sustained fire. It is a very versatile, dependable and long-lived GPMG, having been rebuilt in 7.62mm NATO and showing no signs of retiring. It was originally fielded in the late 1950s and is still going strong.

Chauchat CSRG

SPECIFICATION

MANUFACTURER St Etienne
CALIBRE 7.92 x 57mm
MAGAZINE CAPACITY 20
ACTION Long recoil
TOTAL LENGTH 1,143mm/45in
BARREL LENGTH 470mm/18.5in
WEIGHT UNLOADED 8.61kg/19lb

Barely adequate in the French Lebel chambering and a disaster in the longer and more powerful .30-06, the Chauchat could not have been any better when chambered in 7.92 x 57mm than the .30-06. The long-recoil action had the bolt and barrel travelling the full cyclic distance backwards together, then the barrel recoiling forward, followed by the bolt as it chambered the next cartridge. When properly designed and built, it could be a reliable model. However, the Chauchat design was marginal at best: many were hastily assembled during World War I to dubious quality standards, and Polish use was entirely unsuited to the 7.92mm cartridge. Even a small amount of firing has been known to break the welded assemblies of the receiver. It was bought in 1920 and used until the late 1930s.

South Africa

South African troops were involved in both world wars on the side of the British empire. Arms embargoes gave South Africa the impetus to build its own arms industry following the wars, eventually turning it into an arms exporting powerhouse. It manufactured and exported everything up to self-propelled artillery.

Vector SS77

SPECIFICATION

MANUFACTURER Lyttelton
CALIBRE 7.62 x 51mm
MAGAZINE CAPACITY Belt-fed
ACTION Gas operated
TOTAL LENGTH 1,155mm/45.47in
BARREL LENGTH 550mm/21.65in
WEIGHT UNLOADED 9.6kg/21.16lb

The SS77 was designed and built in South Africa as a General-Purpose Machine Gun (GPMG). With the examples of all other designs to draw from, and decades of experience in combat, the Vector SS77 is as good as any. The minimalist fore grip saves a pound or two of weight. Production commenced in 1977 and continued to the early 1990s. The SS77 is still in service.

Vector Mini SS

The Mini SS is the SS77 receiver built in 5.56mm calibre. The Mini SS is also found as a parts or conversion kit, containing all the parts needed to rebuild a 7.62mm SS77 that uses 5.56mm ammunition. As a result it is only a bit lighter but cannot be less durable than the larger calibre general-purpose machine gun (GPMG). While 8.26kg/18.21lb is fairly heavy for a squad automatic weapon (SAW), which is what most 5.56mm machine guns are, the durability of such an approach cannot be faulted. Conversions began in 1994 and the Mini SS is presently in use.

SPECIFICATION

MANUFACTURER Lyttelton
CALIBRE 5.56 x 45mm
MAGAZINE CAPACITY Belt-fed
ACTION Gas operated
TOTAL LENGTH 1,000mm/39.37in
BARREL LENGTH 515mm/20.27in
WEIGHT UNLOADED 8.26kg/18.21lb

Vickers conversions

Not only were the Vickers rebuilt to 7.62mm by the South African forces, the weapons were updated to the new calibre in the 1960s and served for several decades. The conversions required new barrels, altering the feed system for the shorter cartridge, and exchanging action springs. The Vickers would be fine for vehicular or fortification use, but it was by no means a portable weapon in the modern sense. Once a replacement was named, the machine guns were dismantled and the parts were sold as surplus.

SPECIFICATION

MANUFACTURER Vickers
CALIBRE 7.62 x 51mm
MAGAZINE CAPACITY Belt-fed
ACTION Recoil operated
TOTAL LENGTH 1,158mm/45.6in
BARREL LENGTH 724mm/28.5in
WEIGHT UNLOADED 14.96kg/33lb

Serbia

As Yugoslavia, prior to the dissolution into five independent countries in the 1990s, this region produced many small arms for use by other Warsaw-Pact or communist-aligned countries. It also went further with the Kalashnikov design, chambering it in calibres not found in the Soviet Union.

Maxim MG08

As part of the Austro-Hungarian Empire before and during World War I, it would be natural to find Maxim machine guns in Yugoslavia. Except for the markings required by Yugoslavian purchase, they would not have varied from German-issue heavy machine guns of the period. They also would have been turned against the army of their former manufacturers when Germany invaded Yugoslavia in 1941. The Maxim MG08 was in service from 1908 to 1945.

ABOVE The Maxim has more than just an ejection port because a lengthy cloth belt had to be expelled. The exit tray is to control the belt to keep it from catching in the ejection port.

SPECIFICATION

MANUFACTURER Spandau
CALIBRE 7.92 x 57mm
MAGAZINE CAPACITY Belt-fed
ACTION Recoil operated
TOTAL LENGTH 1,175mm/46.25in
BARREL LENGTH 717mm/28.25in
WEIGHT UNLOADED 18.37kg/40.5lb w/o water or mount

Sarac M53

SPECIFICATION	
MANUFACTURER	Zastava
CALIBRE	7.92 x 57mm
MAGAZINE CAPACITY	Belt-fed
ACTION	Recoil operated
TOTAL LENGTH	1,219mm/48in
BARREL LENGTH	533mm/21in
WEIGHT UNLOADED	11.56kg/25.5lb

This was the MG 42, built in Yugoslavia, and offered for export. While the 7.62 x 51mm version would be expected to work faultlessly, the proposed but never-seen .30-06 version probably would have had problems. It did not matter, as there were plenty of buyers and lots of ammunition available for the 7.92 x 57mm version. Buyers who were locked into the 7.62 x 51mm cartridge would find the Sarac altogether reliable. Manufacture of the M53 began in 1953 and continued until the dissolution of Yugoslavia in the 1990s.

M72 Kalashnikov

SPECIFICATION	
MANUFACTURER	Zastava
CALIBRE	7.62 x 39mm
MAGAZINE CAPACITY	30 or 40
ACTION	Gas operated
TOTAL LENGTH	1,040mm/40.94in
BARREL LENGTH	591mm/23.26in
WEIGHT UNLOADED	5kg/11.02lb

Interchangeable parts
All parts of the RKP can be used with the AK or AKM, making the unit armourer's job easier.

This is simply the Yugoslavian RPK, in the standard Soviet chambering. The Yugoslavian manufacturing and design process of the M72 created a distinctive bulge in the receiver, caused by the bulged trunnion inside (the steel block securing the barrel and receiver). The longer barrel added little muzzle velocity but did add a significant sighting radius. The bipod was necessary, as the M72 (and other RPKs) were commonly issued with 40-round magazines. The bipod kept the magazine off the ground, although it also made the firer a slightly taller target. It was manufactured from the 1960s to the 1980s.

M84 PKM

SPECIFICATION	
MANUFACTURER	Zastava
CALIBRE	7.62 x 54R
MAGAZINE CAPACITY	Belt-fed
ACTION	Gas operated
TOTAL LENGTH	1,173mm/46.18in
BARREL LENGTH	658mm/25.90in
WEIGHT UNLOADED	8.99kg/19.81lb

Modern Kalashnikov
PKM means "Machine-gun Kalashnikov Modernized".

The M84 was a clone of the Soviet PKM with very few differences. While the Soviet Union exported firearms at times for ideological reasons, the Yugoslavians did so only for cash. The Yugoslavian M84, like all PKMs, fired from an open bolt, and the cartridges must (the rims dictate it) be extracted rearwards from the belt on each firing cycle, before then being fed forward into the chamber. It was manufactured from the early 1960s to the 1990s.

Hungary

Prior to World War I, Hungary was a province of the Austro-Hungarian empire, and as such used the arms the Empire required. After World War I, with a communist revolution suppressed and territory lost, Hungary slowly allied itself with Germany. When Germany invaded the Soviet Union, Hungary became a full Axis ally. As with all countries occupied by the Soviet Union after World War I, Hungary adopted the Soviet pattern machine guns. They were manufactured at FÉG, the national arms factory.

PKM

Occupied by the Soviets after World War I, Hungary switched over to Soviet-pattern small arms. The PKM was made in Hungary, and except for markings denoting location of manufacture, it was identical to the Soviet version. The PKM was introduced in the early 1960s and remains in use to the present day. As with all ex-Warsaw Pact countries, Hungary is looking to upgrade her small arms, so the PKM may be replaced, or it might simply be made in a new version in 7.62mm NATO.

SPECIFICATION

MANUFACTURER FÉG, Budapest
CALIBRE 7.62 x 54R
MAGAZINE CAPACITY Belt-fed
ACTION Gas operated
TOTAL LENGTH 1,173mm/46.18in
BARREL LENGTH 658mm/25.9in
WEIGHT UNLOADED 8.99kg/19.81lb on bipod

Goryunov

The medium machine gun of the Soviet Union during Word War II, it was adopted by Hungary after the war. It was replaced by the PKM as supplies became available. It was in service only from 1945 until the mid 1960s.

SPECIFICATION

MANUFACTURER FÉG, Budapest
CALIBRE 7.62 x 54R
MAGAZINE CAPACITY Belt-fed
ACTION Gas operated
TOTAL LENGTH 1,150mm/45.27in
BARREL LENGTH 720mm/28.3in
WEIGHT UNLOADED 13.8kg/30.41lb (gun only, not carriage or shield)

Solothurn M31M

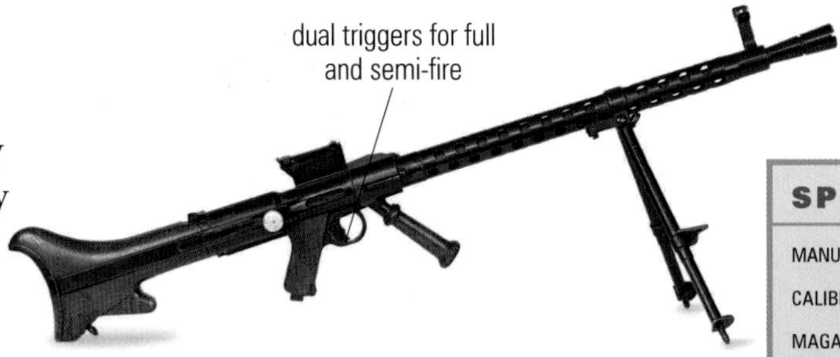

Denied possession of heavy machine guns by the Treaty of Versailles, Germany investigated light machine guns. Designed by Louis Schmeisser at Rheinmettal, the Solothurn M31M was rejected by the German Army, but produced in Switzerland and Austria for export. It was in use in Hungary from 1930 until 1945. Although the Hungarian Army served alongside German units on the Eastern Front and was often directed by German commanders, it retained its own small arms and calibre.

SPECIFICATION

MANUFACTURER Steyr-Daimler-Puch AG
CALIBRE 8 x 56R
MAGAZINE CAPACITY 30
ACTION Short recoil
TOTAL LENGTH 1,170mm/46.06in
BARREL LENGTH 600mm/23.6in
WEIGHT UNLOADED 9.5kg/20.93lb

Greece

After separating from Turkey, Greece re-armed with "modern" small arms when it would have done well to retain the German small arms that Turkey had used. Between the wars, Greece tried to remain neutral to ensure her security. When World War II broke out and this was no longer possible, Greece sided with the Allies.

Hotchkiss M1926

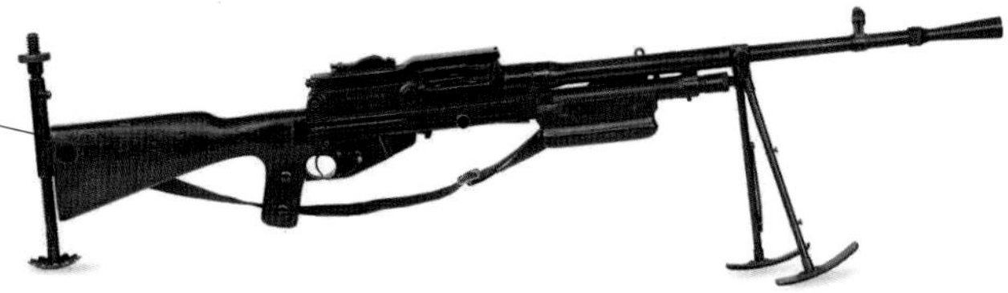

SPECIFICATION	
MANUFACTURER	St Etienne
CALIBRE	6.5 x 54mm
MAGAZINE CAPACITY	Belt-fed
ACTION	Gas operated
TOTAL LENGTH	1,180mm/45.5in
BARREL LENGTH	597mm/23.5in
WEIGHT UNLOADED	9.97kg/22lb

The Hotchkiss firm did not stop between the wars, and developed light machine guns for export. The Model 1926 for Greece was a belt-fed light machine gun that was greatly refined from the 1909 Portative. Hotchkiss could not find other export markets for such a well-made light machine gun due to the intense competition within the arms market between the wars. That competition, combined with the huge volume of surplus arms, made it a difficult time to make a living selling machine guns. They were only in service until World War II – after the war, Greece converted to American small arms and ammunition.

Finland

Bristly about the independence it painfully acquired in 1917-1918, Finland has struggled to remain free of Russian control since. It sided with the Germans against the Soviets in World War II at its cost. To protect its arms production capacity, it supplied maps without firearm-producing towns for decades.

SPECIFICATION	
MANUFACTURER	Tula, Russia
CALIBRE	7.62 x 54R
MAGAZINE CAPACITY	Belt-fed
ACTION	Recoil operated/toggle lock
TOTAL LENGTH	1,110mm/43.7in
BARREL LENGTH	720mm/28.3in
WEIGHT UNLOADED	24.0kg/52.9lb (tripod adds 27.6kg/60.8lb)

Maxim M09/21

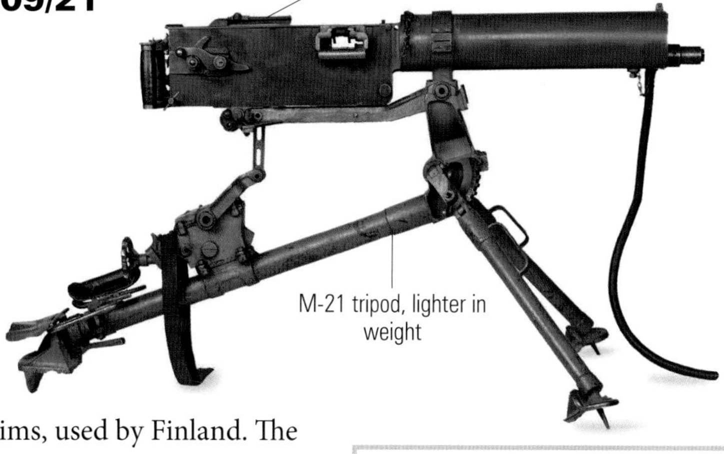

This was one of three heavy machine guns, all Maxims, used by Finland. The 21 part of the model designation refers to the tripod. All Finnish heavy machine guns were Maxims, wrested from Russia or captured from armouries during Finland's break from the Russians. The M09/09 used the original wheeled mount whereas the 09/21 model used a tripod modelled after a pre-World War I Maxim tripod design, saving over 8kg/17.6lb from the 09/09 weight. From independence in 1918 to weapons retirement or upgrades in 1945, the Finnish Maxim could be counted on to keep Finnish borders intact.

Russian-based arms
It was not only logical that Finland's smaller army would use Russian-based small arms, it was also predictable that high-quality manufacturing standards would have been sought.

Valmet M-60 type B

Where it differs from the AK-47, the Valmet M-60 improves on it. The handguards are sturdier and actually protect the hands from heat (the AK and AKM hand-guards can get quite hot in sustained firing.) The rear sight is on the receiver cover, for better accuracy. The stock is a steel tube, stronger than the laminated wood of the AK. As an early rifle or Squad Automatic Weapon (SAW), it was a better rifle. Production began in 1960 and samples are still in use to the present day.

SPECIFICATION

MANUFACTURER Valmet
CALIBRE 7.62 x 39mm
MAGAZINE CAPACITY 30
ACTION Gas operated/rotating bolt
TOTAL LENGTH 914mm/35.9in
BARREL LENGTH 420mm/16.5in
WEIGHT UNLOADED 4.3kg/9.47lb

Lahti M39/44

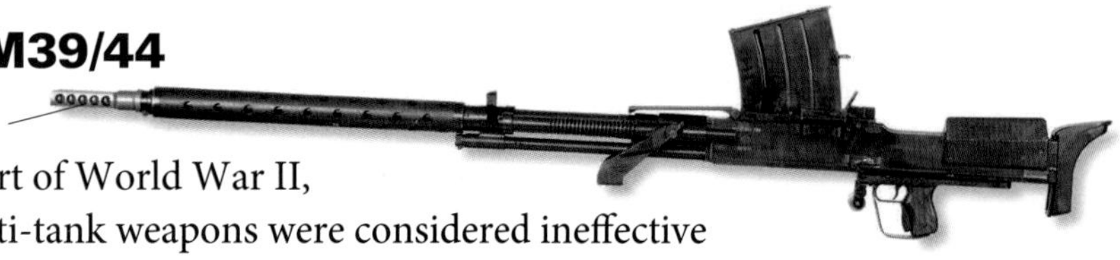

At the start of World War II, 20mm anti-tank weapons were considered ineffective against all but the lightest tanks. The M39 was, however, a relatively portable weapon that the Finns put to good use besides shooting armoured vehicles. The 20mm explosive projectile did well on bunkers and the vehicles of supply convoys. The M39/44 was a full-auto variant that proved less successful in its designated role as an anti-aircraft gun: the receiver simply was not stout enough for full-auto fire. Original models were produced in 1939, the full-auto version five years later in 1944, lasting to retirement at the end of the war.

SPECIFICATION

MANUFACTURER VKT
CALIBRE 20 x 138mm
MAGAZINE CAPACITY 10
ACTION Gas operated/tilting lock
TOTAL LENGTH 2,240mm/88.1in
BARREL LENGTH 1300mm/51.1in
WEIGHT UNLOADED 55.9kg/123.2lb

Sampo L41

This was a prototype machine gun: an attempt to produce a weapon lighter than a Maxim, fielded at the beginning of World War II. Only 50 were reported to be made. Some were sent to the front, for testing and to provide much-needed firepower to infantry units. At least one was captured by the Soviets, and is reported to be on display in the St Petersburg Artillery Museum. It required more work and, since existing designs worked as well, Finland used it for only a short time then dropped it from consideration.

SPECIFICATION

MANUFACTURER VKT
CALIBRE 7.62 x 54Rmm
MAGAZINE CAPACITY Belt-fed
ACTION Gas operated
TOTAL LENGTH 1,180mm/46.45in
BARREL LENGTH 500mm/19.6in
WEIGHT UNLOADED 14.9kg/32.8lb

Valmet KvKK 62

This is a Finnish-designed and produced light machine gun in the Squad Automatic Weapon (SAW) role. Unfortunately it is a heavy weapon and lacks a quick-change barrel, and even as a squad weapon this limits its firepower. Barrel overheating can be a problem even in the sub-zero climate of Finland. Despite local design and manufacture, it may soon be replaced with something with more power and greater reliability (such as the PKM). The Valmet KvKK 62 was first issued in 1966 and is still in use today.

SPECIFICATION

MANUFACTURER VKT
CALIBRE 7.62 x 39mm
MAGAZINE CAPACITY Belt-fed
ACTION Gas operated/tilting bolt
TOTAL LENGTH 1,080mm/42.5in
BARREL LENGTH 475mm/18.7in
WEIGHT UNLOADED 8.3kg/18.3lb

Romania

Newly independent after World War I, Romania found itself allied with Germany at the beginning of World War II. Romanian troops fought on the Eastern Front, where much of the army was destroyed at Stalingrad. When the Soviets rolled west, they invaded Romania and found a newly victorious pro-Soviet government waiting. From Austro-Hungarian Empire, to independent country, to Soviet client state in a generation, Romania had much the same rollercoaster ride that other Eastern European countries had.

PKM

SPECIFICATION

MANUFACTURER State Armoury
CALIBRE 7.62 x 54R
MAGAZINE CAPACITY Belt-fed
ACTION Gas operated
TOTAL LENGTH 1,173mm/46.18in
BARREL LENGTH 658mm/25.90in
WEIGHT UNLOADED 8.99kg/19.81lb

The standard post-war General-Purpose Machine Gun (GPMG) of the Soviet Bloc, the PKM (Pulemyot Kalashnikova Modernizirovanniy) is still in production. The PKM is the updated version of the PK. As with so many ex-Warsaw Pact countries, Romania must decide if it will change the PKM to 7.62mm NATO, leave it as it is, or replace it entirely. It has been in service from the late 1960s.

RPK

SPECIFICATION

MANUFACTURER State Armoury
CALIBRE 7.62 x 39mm
MAGAZINE CAPACITY 40 (can use standard magazines)
ACTION Gas operated/rotating bolt
TOTAL LENGTH 1,040mm/40.95in
BARREL LENGTH 591mm/23.26in
WEIGHT UNLOADED 5.0kg/11.02lb

This squad automatic weapon (SAW) was nothing more than an AK with a longer barrel, strengthened receiver, altered buttstock and larger magazine. Lacking a quick-change barrel, it had limited firepower before overheating. However, as a cost-effective means of getting a bit more firepower into a squad, the RPK made some sense. It was issued from the early 1960s until the to early 1980s.

RPK74

SPECIFICATION

MANUFACTURER State Armoury
CALIBRE 5.45 x 39mm
MAGAZINE CAPACITY 45 (can use standard magazines)
ACTION Gas operated/rotating bolt
TOTAL LENGTH 1,060mm/41.73in
BARREL LENGTH 590mm/23.25in
WEIGHT UNLOADED 5.0kg/11.02lb

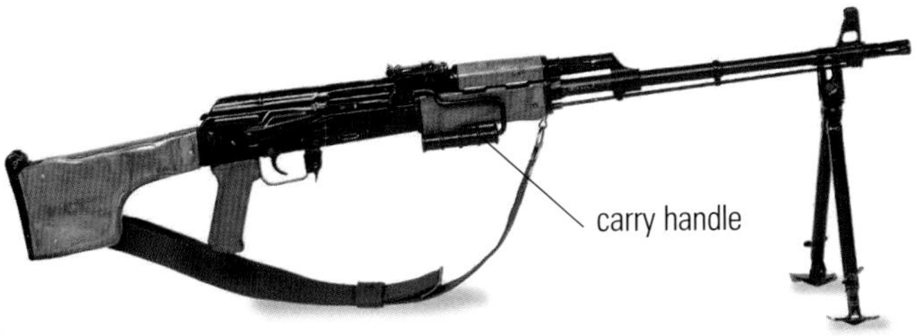

This was the successor to the RPK with a new Soviet calibre and minor changes such as polymer furniture, manufactured and issued from the early 1980s to the present day. Many AK-74 variants, including the RPK74, have an optics mount as a side rail. The 5.45mm cartridge is slightly less prone to overheating than the 7.62 x 39mm. If the RPK74 is issued with an optics mount, it would serve well as a squad-level sniper rifle (also known as the Designated Marksman Rifle). When Romania is fully a member of NATO, the AK-74s in 5.45 x 39mm will likely be withdrawn and replaced with AK-74s in 5.56 x 45mm calibre.

Bulgaria

After World War I, Bulgaria found itself with less land than previously. In the years leading to World War II, they reluctantly worked more and more with Germany. After World War II, and a member of the Warsaw Pact, they manufactured Soviet-pattern rifles. Today, the army is undergoing a series of changes.

BREN ZB39

The ZB39 (made in 1939) was a BREN variant chambered in 8 x 56R. The cartridge was the standard Austro-Hungarian service round, the ZB39 from Czechoslovakia. The combination worked quite reliably. Hungary accepted the first ZB39 light machine guns in 1939. In 1941, Germany was at Bulgaria's border, and Bulgaria reluctantly accepted Germany's aid in recovering lost territories ceded after World War I. The ZB39 was used both by Bulgarian government troops and partisans until the end of World War I. After the war, Bulgaria reluctantly became a signatory of the Warsaw Pact, and began using Soviet-pattern machine guns.

SPECIFICATION

MANUFACTURER CZ BRio
CALIBRE 8 x 56R
MAGAZINE CAPACITY 20
ACTION Gas operated
TOTAL LENGTH 1,041mm/41in
BARREL LENGTH 541mm/21.3in
WEIGHT UNLOADED 7.98kg/17.6lb

Russia

Whether Tsarist, Soviet or as a Federation, Russia has always had a big army. Keeping it supplied means either a large purchase programme, a large number of arsenals at home and occasionally both. Under the Tsars they had both, but the Soviets insisted on home production. When Germany invaded in World War II, Russia packed up the arsenals that were too close to the front and shipped them to the Urals, where production continued.

Maxim M1905

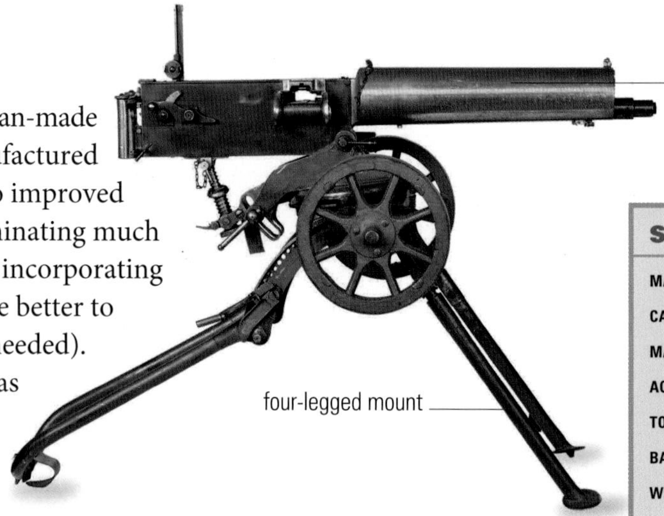

This was a copy of the German-made Maxim which Russia manufactured in large numbers. They also improved it in the 1910 upgrade, eliminating much of the expensive brass, and incorporating a large water entry port (the better to shovel snow inside, when needed). The shield on the mount was a feature of the Russian Maxim throughout World War II. Nearly indestructible, the Maxim, given decent maintenance, will work forever. Introduced in 1905, in one form or another, it remained in service until 1945.

SPECIFICATION

MANUFACTURER Maxim, Tula
CALIBRE 7.62 x 54R
MAGAZINE CAPACITY Belt-fed
ACTION Recoil operated
TOTAL LENGTH 1,107mm/43.6in
BARREL LENGTH 721mm/28.4in
WEIGHT UNLOADED 23.81kg/52.5lb w/o mount

Lewis LMG, Russian pattern

SPECIFICATION	
MANUFACTURER	Savage Arms
CALIBRE	7.62 x 54R
MAGAZINE CAPACITY	47-round drum
ACTION	Gas operated
TOTAL LENGTH	1,282mm/50.5in
BARREL LENGTH	668mm/26.3in
WEIGHT UNLOADED	12.33kg/27.2lb

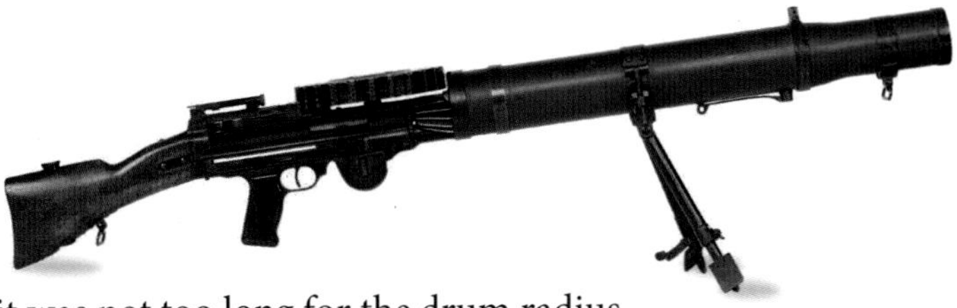

Using a drum, the Lewis was adaptable to almost any cartridge, as long as it was not too long for the drum radius. Adapting it to the Russian cartridge was a minor matter of drum shape, bolt face and recoil springs. Despite the complexity and cost, the Lewis LMG was so well made that it proved remarkably long-lived. While the Lewis guns were made for and shipped to Tsarist Russia in 1917, they may still be in warehouses in the Russian Federation as they use the standard 7.62mm rimmed cartridge.

DP

SPECIFICATION	
MANUFACTURER	Soviet State arsenals
CALIBRE	7.62 x 54R
MAGAZINE CAPACITY	47-round drum
ACTION	Gas operated
TOTAL LENGTH	1,295mm/51in
BARREL LENGTH	604mm/23.8in
WEIGHT UNLOADED	9.29kg/20.5lb

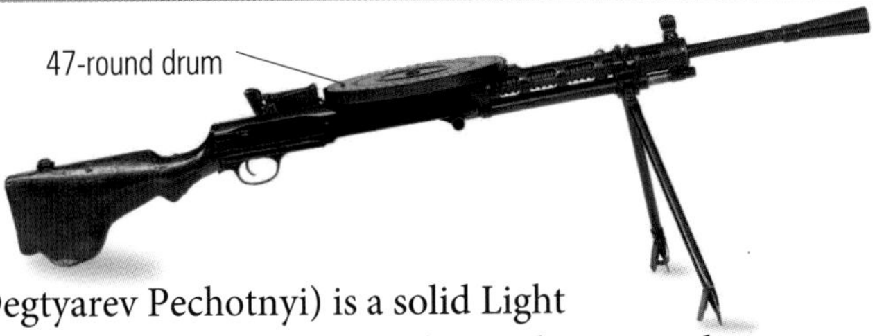

Using the firing pin to actuate the locking flaps, the DP (Degtyarev Pechotnyi) is a solid Light Machine Gun (LMG). The feed pan is a necessity due to the rimmed cartridge and the first versions had the recoil spring around the barrel. Heat could cause problems with the spring temper, it was slightly redesigned in 1943-44 to move the spring away from the heat. It was named the DPM ("M" for modernized.) In 1946, a DP built for belt-feed was unveiled, called the RP-46. This and the DP served from 1928 to the late 1950s.

DSHK Model 1938

SPECIFICATION	
MANUFACTURER	Soviet State arsenals
CALIBRE	12.7 x 108mm
MAGAZINE CAPACITY	Belt-fed
ACTION	Gas operated
TOTAL LENGTH	1,587mm/62.5in
BARREL LENGTH	1,069mm/42.1in
WEIGHT UNLOADED	36.28kg/80lb w/o mount

This was the Soviet heavy (large calibre) machine gun in service since 1938. The cartridge is so robust that the DSHK was designed and built with a muzzle brake to reduce felt recoil, but at the cost of increased blast to the gunner. The Soviets have tried unsuccessfully to replace their heavy machine gun with an improved, lighter version for decades. The Model 1938 was the original belt-fed version with a rotary feed mechanism. It was upgraded in 1946 with a regular pawl and dogleg track feed system.

Goryunov SGM

SPECIFICATION	
MANUFACTURER	Soviet State arsenals
CALIBRE	7.62 x 54R
MAGAZINE CAPACITY	Belt-fed
ACTION	Gas operated
TOTAL LENGTH	1,120mm/44.1in
BARREL LENGTH	718m/28.3in
WEIGHT UNLOADED	13.15kg/29lb w/o mount

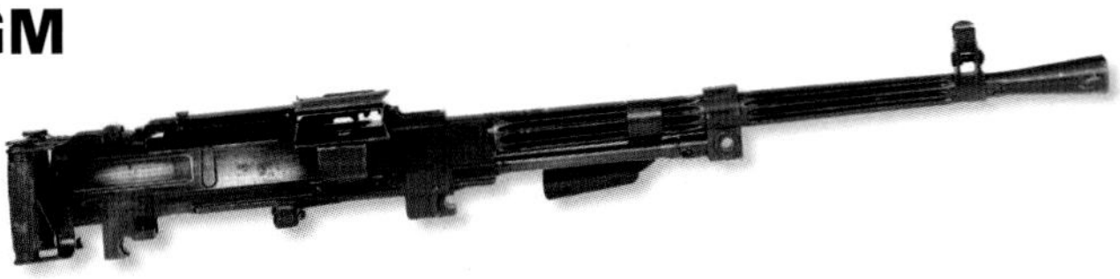

The Goryunov SGM ("M" for modernized) was intended as the wartime replacement for the Maxim. It ended up not being much lighter in combat-ready condition due to the various heavy mounts it was placed on. The standard Soviet/Tsarist wheeled mount weighed 27kg/60lb without the shield, so the end result was a medium, air-cooled machine gun that did not weigh much less than the Maxim. However, the Goryunov was made in large numbers. It entered service in 1943 where it remained until the late 1950s.

PKM

Only with the arrival of the PK did the Soviets have the General-Purpose Machine Gun (GPMG) they desired. The original PK was modified to the PKM with a few mechanical changes, and a smooth barrel instead of the fluted (and thus more costly) barrel it began with. With the quick-change heavy barrel and mounted in a tripod, it can be used in support. The lighter barrel and bipod weighs only 0.5kg/1lb more than an RPD (a much less effective weapon), and is far more mobile for use by infantry units. It has been in service since 1969.

SPECIFICATION

MANUFACTURER Soviet State arsenals
CALIBRE 7.62 x 54R
MAGAZINE CAPACITY Belt-fed
ACTION Gas operated
TOTAL LENGTH 1,198mm/47.2in
BARREL LENGTH 658mm/25.9in
WEIGHT UNLOADED 7.48kg/16.5lb

RPK

Designed as a Squad Automatic Weapon (SAW), the Ruchnoi Pulemet Kalashnikova (RPK) is an AK with a stiffer receiver, longer barrel and a larger magazine. However, the AK itself overheats too quickly, so the RPK is not nearly as useful as it might first appear. As an interim weapon to supply the squad with more firepower, it was an obvious step in the mid 1950s. That it continued in service until the 1970s can only be attributed to either parsimony or extreme need. For a little more weight, the RPD is far more useful to an infantry squad. However, even the RPD overheats too quickly.

SPECIFICATION

MANUFACTURER Soviet State arsenals
CALIBRE 7.62 x 39mm
MAGAZINE CAPACITY 40 rounds
ACTION Gas operated
TOTAL LENGTH 1,039mm/40.9in
BARREL LENGTH 589mm/23.2in
WEIGHT UNLOADED 5.58kg/12.3lb

RPK-74

This was the RPK automatic rifle translated to the AK-74 and its new 5.45mm cartridge, which does not overheat the RPK quite as quickly as the 7.62mm does. The end result is still the same: the small-unit commander has to work with an inefficient system. The RPK would be more useful if issued with optics, and used as a squad designated marksman rifle, delivering accurate semi-automatic fire at close-to-medium range. It has been in service from 1974.

SPECIFICATION

MANUFACTURER Soviet State arsenals
CALIBRE 5.45 x 39mm
MAGAZINE CAPACITY 45 rounds
ACTION Gas operated
TOTAL LENGTH 1,060mm/41.73in
BARREL LENGTH 590mm/23.22in
WEIGHT UNLOADED 5kg/11.02lb

Pecheneg

A modernized and improved PKM, the Pecheneg features forced-air cooling, a concept not used since the Lewis gun of World War I. The gas pressure of cycling the mechanism also forces air down the covering of the barrel, cooling the barrel with each shot. The designers are so sure of its function that the barrel is not one with a quick-change design built in. Only severe testing or field experience will show if the manufacturer's assertions are true. Offered as a replacement for the PKM and for export, production began in the late 1990s and continues today.

SPECIFICATION

MANUFACTURER TNTM
CALIBRE 7.62 x 54R
MAGAZINE CAPACITY Belt-fed
ACTION Gas operated
TOTAL LENGTH 1,145mm/45.07in
BARREL LENGTH 600mm/23.6in
WEIGHT UNLOADED 8.2kg/18.07lb

Egypt

Until receiving Soviet machinery, Egypt did not have an indigenous arms making capacity for machine guns and had to buy them elsewhere. The Husqvarna machinery used to make the Hakim only provided a service rifle for a short time. Since the late 1950s Egypt has been able to produce arms for itself and even export some.

Alfa

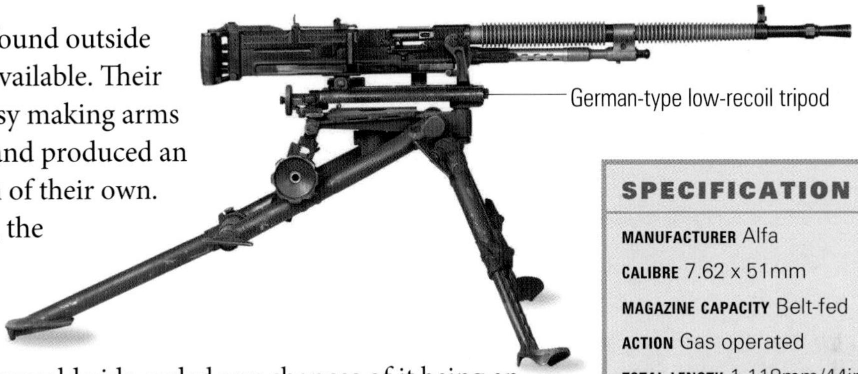

During World War II, Spain found outside sources for machine guns unavailable. Their previous suppliers were all busy making arms for the war, so they designed and produced an air-cooled heavy machine gun of their own. Initially produced in 7.92mm, the Alfa was later manufactured in 7.62mm NATO. Not surprisingly, fierce competition for post-war sales worldwide ended any chances of it being an export success. Egypt bought a few, but soon after this, they began to convert to Soviet-pattern small arms and did not need Spanish machine guns. The Alfa was produced in Spain from 1943 and used in Egypt from 1953 to 1962.

SPECIFICATION

MANUFACTURER Alfa
CALIBRE 7.62 x 51mm
MAGAZINE CAPACITY Belt-fed
ACTION Gas operated
TOTAL LENGTH 1,118mm/44in
BARREL LENGTH 610mm/24in
WEIGHT UNLOADED 14.96kg/33lb

Goryunov Aswan

SPECIFICATION

MANUFACTURER State Factory 54
CALIBRE 7.62 x 54R
MAGAZINE CAPACITY Belt-fed
ACTION Gas operated/side-tipping bolt
TOTAL LENGTH 1,150mm/45.27in
BARREL LENGTH 720mm/28.34in
WEIGHT UNLOADED 13.8kg/30.42lb

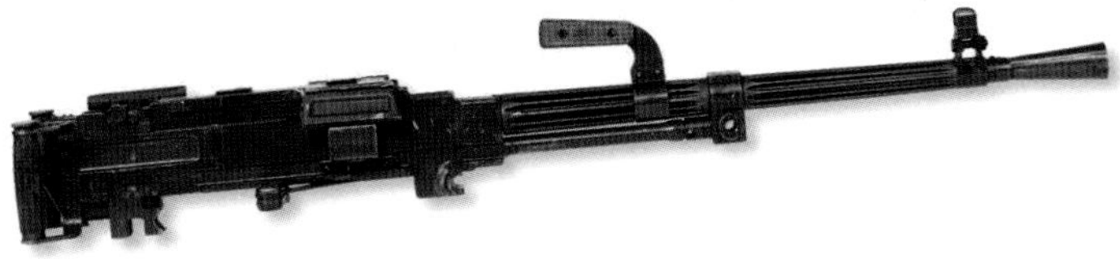

An air-cooled heavy machine gun built on Soviet-supplied machinery, the Aswan is simply a 1960s-era Goryunov SGM. Soviet charity had nothing to do with it; they were planning to replace the SGM with what would become the PK series and giving away tooling was simply smart politics. The Egyptians had nothing like it, so the tooling was a double blessing for them: they could both equip their army, and create jobs. The SGM is durable enough to have lasted from the early 1960s to the present day.

VZ26 copy

SPECIFICATION

MANUFACTURER Unk
CALIBRE 7.92 x 57mm
MAGAZINE CAPACITY 20
ACTION Gas operated/tilting bolt
TOTAL LENGTH 1,163mm/45.8in
BARREL LENGTH 602mm/23.7in
WEIGHT UNLOADED 9.65kg/21.28lb

Given the history of the area, it should come as no surprise that something as common as a VZ26 or a copy of it should be found in Egypt. Despite being a British protectorate before and during World War II, weapons could come in from all points of the compass.

Turkey

Despite being aligned with Germany, Turkey bought small arms from many sources, including France, where there was a large volume of surplus weapons available after World War I. The resulting mix of German and French machine guns and calibres could not have been easy on the Turkish supply system.

Hotchkiss MA4

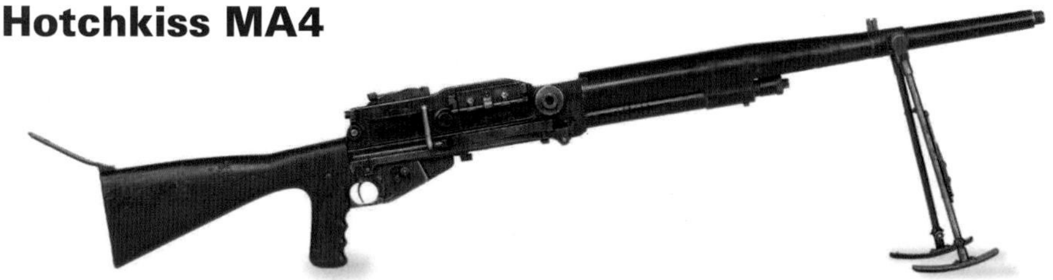

In the 1920s, Hotchkiss developed what could have been a viable General-Purpose Machine Gun (GPMG), ten years before the German MG34. The Model 1922 (called the MA4 in Turkish service) could be manufactured to feed from a vertical box magazine, a belt or the peculiar Hotchkiss feed trays. For Turkey, Hotchkiss made it in 7.92mm calibre, but it could also be made in others. Unfortunately Hotchkiss only sold a few, mostly to Greece and Turkey. The model was scrapped after World War II.

SPECIFICATION

MANUFACTURER Hotchkiss at CIE
CALIBRE 7.92 x 57mm
MAGAZINE CAPACITY 24- or 30-round trays
ACTION Gas operated
TOTAL LENGTH 1,310mm/51.6in
BARREL LENGTH 787mm/31in
WEIGHT UNLOADED 25.27kg/55.7lb w/o tripod

MPT-76

The first prototypes were built in 2008 and chambered in 5.56mm NATO. Turkish soldiers gave it bad reviews, so the calibre was changed to 7.62mm NATO. The design was based on the AR-15, but the gas piston system was influenced by the HK417. The first batch was delivered in 2017. There is an option to mount an under-barrel shotgun or grenade launcher.

SPECIFICATION

MANUFACTURER MKEK, Sarsilmaz, and Kalekalip
CALIBRE 7.62mm NATO
MAGAZINE CAPACITY 20 or 30
ACTION Gas operated
TOTAL LENGTH 920mm/36in
BARREL LENGTH 406mm/16in
WEIGHT UNLOADED 4.2kg/9.3lb

SAR 240

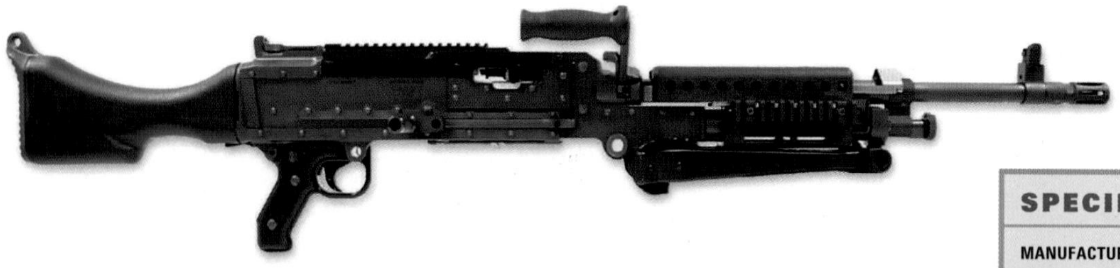

The SAR 240 is an indigenously-produced machine gun that began development in 2018. Prototyping began in 2020, but the pandemic slowed progress. The first batch of rifles were delivered in 2021. The body of each of the SAR 240 rifles is designed to fire at least 50,000 rounds, while the lifetime of the barrel is at least 25,000 rounds.

SPECIFICATION

MANUFACTURER Sarsilmaz
CALIBRE 7.62mm NATO
MAGAZINE CAPACITY Belt-fed
ACTION Gas operated
TOTAL LENGTH 1,200mm/47.2in
BARREL LENGTH 547mm/21.5in
WEIGHT UNLOADED 12kg/26.4lb

Israel

Israel had to start out with managing with whatever could be obtained from the miscellaneous collection of German and British small arms before independence. Only after establishing a sufficiently large production base could Israeli Military Industries manufacture what was both needed and desired.

Browning

Tripod advantages
By using the control knobs on the traverse and elevation mechanism, the shooter can fire to extreme distances with accuracy, or return the gun back to a previous setting, to resume fire at a particular extreme range.

SPECIFICATION

MANUFACTURER Colt, others
CALIBRE 7.62mm NATO
MAGAZINE CAPACITY Belt-fed
ACTION Recoil operated
TOTAL LENGTH 1,041mm/41in
BARREL LENGTH 610mm/24in
WEIGHT UNLOADED 14.06kg/31lb

During World War II the Browning air-cooled machine gun was to be found everywhere and performed well. The basic weapon is so durable and versatile (although heavy) that it can be used in almost every role where the weight can be withstood. Inevitably, Israel converted it to 7.62mm. It was used in the War for Independence (1947–48) and can still be seen on vehicles to this day. Lighter machine guns than the Browning may be available, but few have had a longer service life.

Negev

SPECIFICATION

MANUFACTURER IMI
CALIBRE 5.56 x 45mm
MAGAZINE CAPACITY 30, and belt-fed
ACTION Gas operated
TOTAL LENGTH 1,020mm/40.15in
BARREL LENGTH 460mm/18.11in
WEIGHT UNLOADED 7.6kg/16.75lb

The Negev is the Israeli answer to the need for a Squad Automatic Weapon (SAW) in its modern army. The Negev looks a great deal like the FN Minimi. Like the Minimi, the Negev uses either linked belts of ammunition, or can be fed from magazines. The Negev magazine is the same as the Israeli Galil, and IMI makes adapters for the Negev allowing it to use M-16 magazines. Unlike other armies, Israel plans to replace all belt-fed machine guns with the Negev, retiring all their MAG-58s in service. Its advantages are its weight and lighter ammunition; its disadvantages are its lack of range and power. The Negev was first issued in the mid-1990s and is in use to the present day.

DROR (Johnson)

After World War II, Israel purchased the tooling for the Johnson light machine gun. The DROR is listed in references as having been re-designed to use .303 British ammunition. However, there are samples of the DROR in existence in .30-06, so the Israelis clearly manufactured both. As both calibres were common, and easily purchased, having weapons in both ensured Israel was able to acquire ammunition for the Israeli Defence Force.

SPECIFICATION

MANUFACTURER Johnson/Israeli
CALIBRE .303 British,.30-06
MAGAZINE CAPACITY 20
ACTION Recoil operated
TOTAL LENGTH 1,070mm/42.12in
BARREL LENGTH 560mm/22.04in
WEIGHT UNLOADED 10kg/22lb

Ethiopia

A backwater in world events, Ethiopia still had to defend itself from its neighbours, and later, the aspirations of Italy under Mussolini. With no indigenous arms manufacturing, it had to import everything. That it chose the VZ30 should come as no surprise: it was the best at the time and would still be a good choice today.

VZ30

SPECIFICATION

MANUFACTURER CZ BRio
CALIBRE 7.92 x 57mm
MAGAZINE CAPACITY 20
ACTION Gas operated/tilting lock
TOTAL LENGTH 1,163mm/45.8in
BARREL LENGTH 602mm/23.7in
WEIGHT UNLOADED 9.65kg/21.28lb

An improved VZ26, the VZ30 only added to the sales and lustre of CZ and the reputation of their products. It was purchased by Ethiopia in the early 1930s, and used for decades until stocks were exhausted. Ethiopia wisely declined to design a proprietary cartridge. As the standard export light machine gun, the VZ30 in 7.92mm could be fed ammunition from any source of reliable and common 7.92 x 57mm.

Iraq

In the Cold War struggle for dominance of the Middle East and its oil, Iraq elected to go with the Soviets for small arms, military vehicles, and command and staff structure. This did not keep Saddam Hussein from accepting Western aid in the Iran-Iraq War, something Iran has not forgiven. While still purchasing weapons from non-aligned countries, the basic small arms stock was Soviet, although locally produced.

Al Quds

This was a local version of the RPD. Iraqi small arms tended to have a glossier finish than their Soviet counterparts, whether an aesthetic selection or simply a result of the steel stock selected for use is unknown. As with all belt-fed squad automatic weapons lacking a quick-change barrel, the Al Quds overheats if not used carefully. Given the extreme desert environment, over-heating and weapons maintenance was an ongoing problem for Iraqi soldiers. Also, trying to deal with Iranian MG 3s, while armed with an Al Quds in 7.62 x 39mm, had to be a real challenge. The Iraqi soldiers were out-ranged, and did not have the sustained fire capability of the MG 3. Manufacture began in the 1970s and the Al Quds can still be seen in use to the present day.

SPECIFICATION

MANUFACTURER Iraqi armouries
CALIBRE 7.62 x 39mm
MAGAZINE CAPACITY 30, 40 or 75
ACTION Gas operated
TOTAL LENGTH 1,037mm/40.8in
BARREL LENGTH 520mm/20.47in
WEIGHT UNLOADED 7.4kg/16.3lb

Magazines
The Al Quds accepts 30 and 40 magazines, but has been seen with 75-round drum magazines.

Iran/Persia

Persia was useful to Europe (and Britain) primarily as a block to Russian attempts to gain a warm-water port. However, the discovery of oil made it a much larger player on the world stage. During World War II, Iran was a transportation route for materials to the Soviets from the United States. So it did, for a brief time, have a warm-water port. With the post-war oil boom, Iran became a power in the Middle East. However, the revolution, followed immediately by the long war with Iraq, kept them isolated until recently.

MG 3

When Iran purchased Heckler & Koch G3 rifles in the early 1970s, it made sense to only purchase machine guns in the same calibre. They replaced their US .30 and .50 Brownings and the ZB 30 light machine guns they had on hand with the updated German MG42, aka the MG 3. One of the updates to the MG 3 was the ability to use disintegrating belts as well as the German continuous ones. Those machine guns no doubt went on to serve in the Iran-Iraq War in the early 1980s. The MG 3 was purchased in the early 1970s and has remained in service to the present. As they are entirely serviceable and nearly indestructible, they will probably remain in service for quite some time.

SPECIFICATION

MANUFACTURER Rheinmettal Borsig
CALIBRE 7.62mm NATO
MAGAZINE CAPACITY Belt-fed
ACTION Recoil operated
TOTAL LENGTH 1,219mm/48in
BARREL LENGTH 533mm/21in
WEIGHT UNLOADED 11.56kg/25.5lb

Pakistan

As part of the pre-war British Indian Empire, Pakistan had the same selection of rifles, machine guns, spares and training as India. After independence from India, Pakistan has had almost continual friction with its neighbour, having both the border to patrol, and its own fractious north-west provinces to oversee.

MG 1A3

SPECIFICATION

MANUFACTURER POF
CALIBRE 7.62mm NATO
MAGAZINE CAPACITY Belt-fed
ACTION Recoil operated
TOTAL LENGTH 1,219mm/48in
BARREL LENGTH 533mm/21in
WEIGHT UNLOADED 11.56kg/25.5lb

Belts
The MG 1A3 accepts disintegrating and non-disintegrating belts.

The MG 1A3 is an improved (by Germany) MG 42, built under licence from Rheinmettal. The "1" denotes conversion to the NATO standard rifle cartridge of 7.62mm NATO, while the "A3" indicates the minor changes which collectively increase durability, reliability and service life of the already exemplary design. Typically, MG 1 machine guns can be made or issued with two bolt-buffer combinations. One produces a cyclic rate of 1,100 to 1,300 rpm, while the other produces 700 to 900 rpm. The MG 1A3 has been produced in Pakistan from the mid 1950s, with manufacture continuing to the present day.

India

When India was still a British colony the British set up armouries to make British-pattern small arms for their own use. After independence, India kept the armouries open, while upgrading to designs it saw fit for its own needs. In the first quarter of the 21st-century India has greatly increased initiatives to modernize India's arsenal with advanced weaponry manufactured within the country.

BREN Model 1B

SPECIFICATION

MANUFACTURER Enfield
CALIBRE 7.62 x 51mm
MAGAZINE CAPACITY 30
ACTION Gas operated/tilting lock
TOTAL LENGTH 1,156mm/45.5in
BARREL LENGTH 635mm/25in
WEIGHT UNLOADED 10.03kg/22.12lb

As with many countries post-war, converting BREN guns from .303 to 7.62mm was an attractive proposition. For a small investment, India could keep its existing weapons going long enough to find a better replacement. It has been in use from 1953 to the present day, although all conversions were completed within a few years of the start of the process. Given the wide-open spaces of India, and the long distances from one ridgeline to another in various border skirmishes, the superb accuracy of the BREN had to be an asset. Along with the BREN, India made a copy of the MAG 58. The BREN is destined to be retired as soon as the INSAS Light Machine Gun (LMG) is fielded.

Negev NG-7

The Negev NG-7 was adopted by India in 2020 and the order was delivered by Israel Weapon Industries (IWI) in 2021. It is a gas-operated selective fire light machine gun that uses propellant gases from the barrel to cycle a short-stroke gas piston operating system under the barrel and a rotary bolt locking mechanism.

SPECIFICATION

MANUFACTURER Israel Weapon Industries
CALIBRE 7.62mm NATO
MAGAZINE CAPACITY Belt-fed
ACTION Gas operated
TOTAL LENGTH 1,100mm/43.3in
BARREL LENGTH 508mm/20in
WEIGHT UNLOADED 10.03kg/22.12lb

China

By the modern era, China had suffered the indignity of being apportioned between the occupying powers. Combined with internal strife from competing warlords, pre-World War II, Chinese small arms lists could only be described as "eclectic". Warlords and the central government bought arms from whomever they could or whichever sales agent offered the best bribes. What could not be bought was made. With Mauser vigorous in sales, most rifles and light and medium machine guns were chambered in 7.92 x 57mm. After the revolution, China had a huge army and People's Militia to equip. It chose Soviet-pattern weapons, built at home. The volume of its production made export an attractive prospect once the Cold War had thawed somewhat.

MG Browning

SPECIFICATION	
MANUFACTURER	Colt
CALIBRE	7.92 x 57mm
MAGAZINE CAPACITY	Belt-fed
ACTION	Recoil operated
TOTAL LENGTH	1,041mm/41in
BARREL LENGTH	610mm/24in
WEIGHT UNLOADED	14.06kg/31lb

The Browning machine gun was a natural for the Chinese market. All it needed was a supply of barrels chambered in 7.92 x 57mm and the receiver would work forever. While making one in a local workshop would have been a daunting task, Colt found it easy to produce a model in that calibre. It was made by Colt from 1919 to 1939, and used until 1949.

VZ26 copy

SPECIFICATION	
MANUFACTURER	Unk
CALIBRE	7.92 x 57mm
MAGAZINE CAPACITY	20
ACTION	Gas operated/tilting lock
TOTAL LENGTH	1,163mm/45.8in
BARREL LENGTH	602mm/23.7in
WEIGHT UNLOADED	9.52kg/21lb

The progenitor of the BREN, the VZ26 would have been a natural choice to copy once imported. Light, handy and reliable, it would have been the centrepiece of any warlord's armoury. While China did not have a large industrial base prior to the 1960s, it did have a lot of local armouries and workshops before World War II. The design of the VZ26 is not so complicated that it could not be copied. From its introduction in 1926 to the Communist takeover in 1949, a workshop could have produced quite a few.

Manufacturing challenges
The barrel and magazine are the two hardest parts of an automatic weapon to be made. Drilling a barrel needs costly machinery or excruciating labour and magazines must be bent out of sheet steel.

Maxim Type 24

SPECIFICATION

MANUFACTURER Various
CALIBRE 7.92 x 57 & 7.62 x 54R
MAGAZINE CAPACITY Belt-fed
ACTION Recoil operated
TOTAL LENGTH 1219mm/48in
BARREL LENGTH 605mm/23.8in
WEIGHT UNLOADED 23.8kg/52.5lb w/o mount

Robust design
Given the lack of maintenance any weapon could expect in Chinese service, the Maxim was a good choice. Short of allowing it to rust, anyone could keep a Maxim running, once they had been given a day's instruction.

The Type 24 was both purchased from Germany, and Chinese-manufactured copies of the Maxim. The Type 24, like all Maxim-type machine guns, is heavy by the standards of today, but when reliability matters the Maxim can hardly be faulted. The originals were doubtless made in 7.92mm, but converting each to 7.62 x 54R would have been a simple operation when time for an overhaul. They were first purchased in 1924 and in use throughout the 1950s.

VZ26

SPECIFICATION

MANUFACTURER Various
CALIBRE 7.62 x 39mm
MAGAZINE CAPACITY 20
ACTION Gas operated/tilting lock
TOTAL LENGTH 1,156mm/45.5in
BARREL LENGTH 635mm/25in
WEIGHT UNLOADED 10.03kg/22.12lb

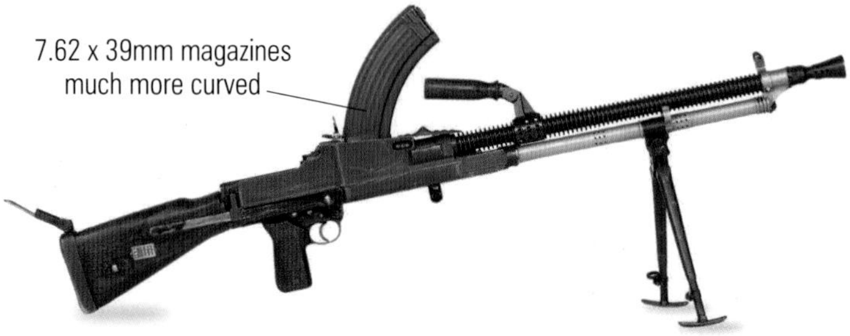

Faced with equipping an army in the millions and a People's Militia, China sought to upgrade older weapons to the new calibre. The real problem when converting a VZ26 gun to 7.62 x 39mm is that designing and producing new magazines would have been extremely difficult. It might have done better to leave the VZ26 alone and to have simply made 7.92mm ammunition for it. The conversion was made in the early 1950s, and became instantly obsolete.

DSHK Type 54

SPECIFICATION

MANUFACTURER Various Chinese heavy industries
CALIBRE 12.7 x 109mm
MAGAZINE CAPACITY Belt-fed
ACTION Gas operated/locking flaps
TOTAL LENGTH 1,587mm/62.5in
BARREL LENGTH 1,069mm/42.1in
WEIGHT UNLOADED 35.6kg/78.5lb

After the revolution, China made its own small arms, either based on or exact copies of Soviet designs. The DSHK Type 54 is the Soviet and Chinese heavy machine gun, chambered in the Soviet equivalent of the .50 Browning. The feed mechanism uses a sprocket, rotating the belt and cartridges to the chamber. A sprocket is more robust and less complicated than a pawl and dog-leg channel to move the belt, but a sprocket makes the receiver taller. Given even the least amount of care, the DSHK is completely reliable. It is typically manufactured with a muzzle brake that produces a ferocious back-blast. The DSHK Type 54 has been made from 1954 to the present day.

Degtyarev Type 56

SPECIFICATION

MANUFACTURER Various
CALIBRE 7.62 x 39mm
MAGAZINE CAPACITY Belt-fed
ACTION Gas operated/locking flaps on bolt
TOTAL LENGTH 1,037mm/40.8in
BARREL LENGTH 520mm/20.8in
WEIGHT UNLOADED 7.2kg/15.9lb w/o mount

This Chinese-built Soviet RPD is an air-cooled belt-fed machine gun that fills the role of the squad automatic weapon (SAW). The belt is held in a drum attached to the receiver. Belts can be used without the drum. Lacking a quick-change barrel, the gun can and will overheat if not fired with restraint. Overheating will cause myriad problems, including failure to extract or runaway firing. Otherwise the Type 56 it is quite reliable, relatively light, portable and quite formidable when used properly. In production since 1956 to the present day, it faces replacement by the new Chinese small arms family.

Chinese Type 57

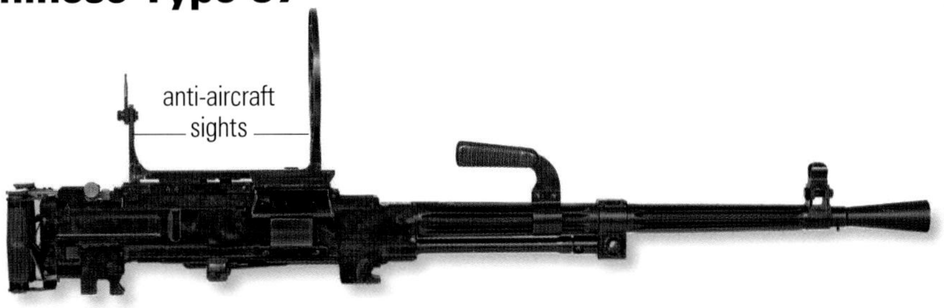

SPECIFICATION

MANUFACTURER Various
CALIBRE 7.62 x 54R
MAGAZINE CAPACITY Belt-fed
ACTION Gas operated, side-shift bolt-lock
TOTAL LENGTH 1120mm/44.09in
BARREL LENGTH 720mm/28.35in
WEIGHT UNLOADED 13.83kg/30.5lb w/o mount

As with so many other small arms, the Communist Chinese took advantage of the manufacturing and combat experience of their Russian counterparts. The Type 57 was simply the Goryunov SG43/SGM built in China. While it was certainly adequate as a war-time medium machine gun in World War II, by the late 1950s, it was clearly not ageing well. The Goryunov was relatively light for a medium machine gun when it was designed in 1943. By 1958, when it was adopted by the Chinese, it was portly. In addition, it could not be used without a mount, the lightest of which weighed another 20kg/44lb. Despite its age, the Type 58 served until replaced by the Type 80 in 1980.

Kalashnikov Type 80

SPECIFICATION

MANUFACTURER Various
CALIBRE 7.62 x 54R
MAGAZINE CAPACITY 20
ACTION Gas operated/rotating bolt
TOTAL LENGTH 1,192mm/46.9in
BARREL LENGTH 605mm/23.8in
WEIGHT UNLOADED 12.6kg/27.8lb

Based on the Soviet PKMC 7.62 general-purpose machine gun, the Type 80 was adopted in 1980 and issued in the early 1980s. In the Soviet Union, the PKM replaced a slew of medium machine guns. In China, the Type 80 replaced the locally designed Type 67, which had proven less than satisfactory. Simple in design, tough as an anvil, and not requiring special alloys to be constructed, the Chinese PKM did not hurt the weapon's reputation for reliability. It was first made in 1980 and there are no plans to replace it.

Thailand

One of the many customers of Dansk Syndikat, the Kingdom of Thailand simply bought what it needed.

In the post-war period, the US and China have been Thailand's main source of military equipment. Russia, the Czech Republic, Spain, and Sweden are its European arms suppliers.

Madsen

SPECIFICATION

MANUFACTURER Dansk Industri Syndikat
CALIBRE 7.92 x 57mm
MAGAZINE CAPACITY 30
ACTION Gas operated
TOTAL LENGTH 1,168mm/46in
BARREL LENGTH 482mm/19in
WEIGHT UNLOADED 9.97kg/22lb

This was the standard export version of the Madsen, in the standard calibre, for customers who did not insist on their own proprietary cartridge. As with all export models, customers could have their order in any calibre, kitted out with any accessories they wished. Except for the markings denoting Thai ownership, the Thai Madsen could be any other Madsen. It was in service from the 1920s, through to World War II, where it may well have been used against the Japanese.

Singapore

As a centre of heavy industry in the modern world, it has not been a problem for Singapore to invest in arms production in the modern era. Attracting designers is also straightforward. Its efforts in getting designs adopted abroad have not met with great success due mostly to the huge volume of small arms available.

CIS Ultimax 100

SPECIFICATION

MANUFACTURER Chartered Industries of Singapore
CALIBRE 5.56 x 45mm
MAGAZINE CAPACITY 30, 100-round drum
ACTION Gas operated
TOTAL LENGTH 1,024mm/40.31in
BARREL LENGTH 508mm/20in
WEIGHT UNLOADED 4.9kg/10.80lb

The Ultimax 100 is a Light Machine Gun (LMG) or Squad Automatic Weapon (SAW) that reduces felt recoil by a simple method: the receiver is long enough internally to prevent the cycling bolt from striking the rear of the receiver. The firer only feels the spring compression, never the bolt bottoming out against the rear of the receiver. As a result, it is very smooth in operation. Manufacture began in the early 1980s and continues to the present day.
The Ultimax is a regular contender in SAW and LMG trials, but has yet to see much acceptance outside Singapore.

CIS .50

SPECIFICATION

MANUFACTURER Chartered Industries of Singapore
CALIBRE .50 BMG
MAGAZINE CAPACITY Belt-fed
ACTION Gas operated
TOTAL LENGTH 1,670mm/65.74in
BARREL LENGTH 1,141mm/44.92in
WEIGHT UNLOADED 30kg/66.13lb

This is another contender to try and throw the Browning M2HB off the throne. The CIS .50 has dual-feed, right and left. The feed is selectable, and the firer can switch from one to the other and use either type being fed. It is lighter than the M2HB. The barrel is a quick-change design, and the firing mechanism offers semi- and full-auto firing. The bolt rotates to lock, and features 24 small locking lugs, arranged in three rows. The advantage of such a design is that it allows for a more compact receiver, as the bolt is kept to the minimum size needed for safe function. It was introduced in the 1990s.

Australia

Australia did not have its own government rifle factory until the establishment of the Lithgow Arsenal in 1912. Production of Vickers began in 1925, and subsequently that of BREN guns in 1938. Once World War II was underway, the Lithgow Arsenal worked day and night to meet demand.

BREN Mark 1

Manufactured by Lithgow, for Australian use during World War II, the BREN gun in Australia served long past the cartridge it was originally made in – the .303. Considered heavy now for a squad automatic weapon, it was thought a marvel in 1937. With its quick-change barrel and a deserved reputation for superb accuracy, the BREN could easily be pressed into the support role, or used for long-range fire fights. From adoption in 1938, it was used by the army until it was replaced by the MAG 58.

SPECIFICATION

MANUFACTURER Lithgow
CALIBRE .303 British
MAGAZINE CAPACITY 30
ACTION Gas operated/tilting lock
TOTAL LENGTH 1,155mm/45.5in
BARREL LENGTH 635mm/25in
WEIGHT UNLOADED 10.0kg/22.12lb

Vickers Mark 1

In 1925 the Lithgow plant was expanded and tooling installed to begin production of the Vickers machine gun, in addition to the manufacture of Lee-Enfield rifles. With the extra weight of the tripod (50lb), and water in the jacket, a World War I-era machine gun is not exactly a portable weapon. However, neither jungle operations nor amphibious assaults in the Pacific were exemplars of fluid warfare. A completely dependable, if heavy, machine gun, it was highly valued. It was adopted in 1925 and used (along with the BREN) until it was replaced by the MAG 58.

SPECIFICATION

MANUFACTURER Lithgow
CALIBRE .303 British
MAGAZINE CAPACITY Cloth belts
ACTION Recoil operated, water cooled
TOTAL LENGTH 1,092mm/43in
BARREL LENGTH 721mm/28.4in
WEIGHT UNLOADED 14.96kg/33lb w/o water

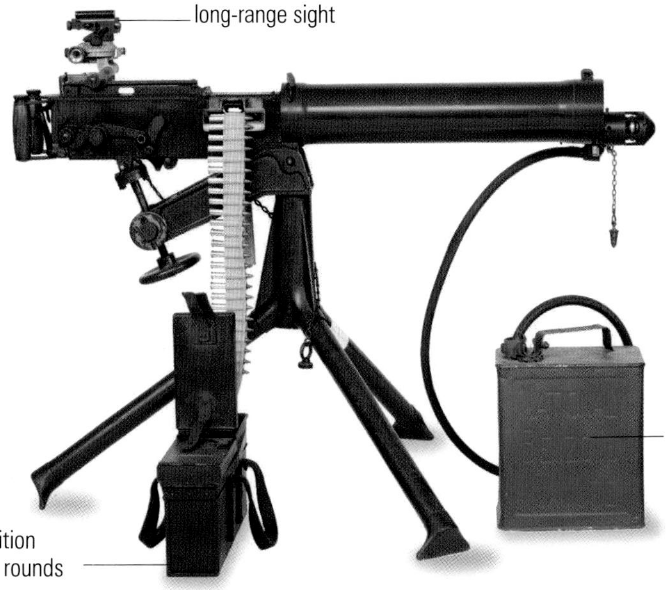

Water-cooler can
The can that is often seen with a water-cooled machine gun is the condenser. In addition to supplying additional water for cooling, it cools and condenses the steam produced by the heat of firing. Without it, the machine gun could be quickly spotted by the plume of steam coming out of the water jacket vent.

SPECIFICATION

MANUFACTURER Lithgow
CALIBRE 5.56 x 45mm NATO
MAGAZINE CAPACITY 30 and belt-fed
ACTION Gas/rotating bolt
TOTAL LENGTH 1,038mm/40.9in
BARREL LENGTH 465mm/18.3in
WEIGHT UNLOADED 6.90kg/15.2lb

F89

This was the Australian-built version of the FN Minimi, adopted in 1989 and still in use today. The F89 has a picatinny rail on which can be mounted a 1.5 power optic sight. The combination allows a gunner to engage targets at the extreme range of the 5.56mm cartridge, and the rail allows the gunner to mount night-vision optics if necessary. The F89 uses either belted ammunition in 100 and 200-round disintegrating belts, or 30-round M-16 magazines.

North Korea

North Korea makes copies of the standard Soviet arms. The Korean People's Army (KPA) was expanded during the 1970s and 1980s from half a million men to its present size of 1.2 million men, and a force that large needs many arms. Given the extremes of climate and terrain, simple but durable guns are a wise choice.

SPECIFICATION

MANUFACTURER N. Korea Arsenal
CALIBRE 7.62 x 39mm
MAGAZINE CAPACITY Belt-fed
ACTION Gas operated
TOTAL LENGTH 1,036mm/40.8in
BARREL LENGTH 520mm/20.5in
WEIGHT UNLOADED 7.07kg/15.6lb

RPD

The quality of manufacture of North Korean small arms is reported to be quite good internally, even if the exteriors are reported to be rough. The roughness may be more a matter of a harsh service environment, and the rigours that led to their capture, than a lack of concern for exterior finish. Other than the Korean markings, this weapon is a standard RPD, with all the strengths and weaknesses of the gun. It has been manufactured from the late 1950s to the present day.

South Korea

In 1950 the North invaded, and since the stalemate of 1953 Korea has been divided between North and South. The South Korean Army is only half the size of the KPA facing it from the North, but determined to resist an invasion. Daewoo is an an industrial giant; makers of a wide variety of products besides small arms.

SPECIFICATION

MANUFACTURER Daewoo
CALIBRE 5.56 x 45mm
MAGAZINE CAPACITY M-16 magazines & belt-fed
ACTION Gas operated
TOTAL LENGTH 1,030mm/40.55in
BARREL LENGTH 533mm/21in
WEIGHT UNLOADED 6.85kg/15.10lb

Daewoo K3

An aspirant for the Squad Automatic Weapon (SAW) market and clearly inspired by the FN Minimi, the Daewoo K3 is a solid light machine gun in use by the South Korean Defence Forces. It has not yet been accepted elsewhere but, as large as Daewoo is, contending with FN is not an easy task. Issue to South Korean Army units began in 1990 and the K3 remains in service in Korea, if not elsewhere. With a quick-change barrel and able to use either belt or box magazines, the K3 would serve as well as the FN Minimi. The fact that the FN Minimi was on the market first should not be held against the K3.

Japan

Not only did Japanese machine guns use 6.5 and 7.7mm cartridges, there were further complications: some were rimmed, some were semi-rimmed, and none were interchangeable. Add to this a few foreign makes such as the Japanese-made Lewis Gun in .303 British, and the fact that the Army, Navy and Air Force selected models without consulting each other, then supplying troops with ammunition must have been very challenging.

Nambu Type 11

Another modified Hotchkiss, the Nambu Type 11 used the same 6.5mm cartridges as Japanese rifles and the same stripper clips. The feed "system" was a hopper that held the stripper clips. The operator would lift the hinged feed paddle and drop loaded stripper clips in, horizontally, and point forward. He would also have to operate the cartridge oiler. The machine gun would feed the rounds off the stripper clips, and eject empty brass and stripper clips. Contemporary shooters say that the oiler system was effective. The Type 11 was introduced in 1922 and used until 1945.

SPECIFICATION

MANUFACTURER Kokura Arsenal
CALIBRE 6.5 x 50mm
MAGAZINE CAPACITY 25
ACTION Gas operated
TOTAL LENGTH 1,104mm/43.5in
BARREL LENGTH 482mm/19in
WEIGHT UNLOADED 10.20kg/22.5lb

Hotchkiss-designed Type 93

Licensed from the French (who never built any), the | Hotchkiss-designed Type 93 met a need the Japanese experienced after their invasion of China: long range and power. The 6.5mm machine guns that they had were not up to long-range machine gun duels, but the Type 93 with its powerful 13mm cartridge solved that problem. Built in the late 1920s and early 1930s, it was not made in particularly large numbers and served until the end of World War II.

SPECIFICATION

MANUFACTURER Tokyo Arsenal
CALIBRE 13 x 99mm
MAGAZINE CAPACITY 20-round trays
ACTION Gas operated
TOTAL LENGTH 2,413mm/95in
BARREL LENGTH 1,651mm/65in
WEIGHT UNLOADED 96.61kg/213lb w/ tripod

Lewis Type 92

This was a Japanese-built copy of the Lewis for flexible mounting in aircraft for use by the Japanese Imperial forces. It is not be confused with the Nambu/Hotchkiss Type 92. Curiously, the copy was also made in British .303, rather than the Japanese 7.7mm, which the Lewis mechanism could easily have handled. Consequently, the Imperial Air Force added yet another calibre to the ammunition supply chain. It was manufactured for the Air Force from 1924 until 1945.

SPECIFICATION

MANUFACTURER Tokyo Arsenal
CALIBRE .303 British
MAGAZINE CAPACITY 47- or 96-round drums
ACTION Gas operated
TOTAL LENGTH 940mm/37in
BARREL LENGTH 660mm/26in
WEIGHT UNLOADED 9.97kg/22lb

Type 89

SPECIFICATION

MANUFACTURER Tokyo Arsenal
CALIBRE 7.7 x 58mm
MAGAZINE CAPACITY Belt-fed
ACTION Recoil operated
TOTAL LENGTH 1,051mm/41.4in
BARREL LENGTH 686mm/27in
WEIGHT UNLOADED 16.78kg/37lb

This was a copy of the Vickers machine gun, which had a reputation for being solid and reliable. The Type 89 was close enough as to almost have interchangeable parts. It was used as an aircraft gun and also would have been pressed into use on the ground. At least infantry units using salvaged Type 89 machine guns could count on them using the standard 7.7mm rifle cartridge, as long as they saved the belts and reloaded them. It was manufactured and used from 1928 until 1945.

Type 92

SPECIFICATION

MANUFACTURER Tokyo Arsenal
CALIBRE 7.7 x 58SR
MAGAZINE CAPACITY Tray feed, 30 rounds each
ACTION Gas operated
TOTAL LENGTH 1,156mm/45.5in
BARREL LENGTH 731mm/28.8in
WEIGHT UNLOADED 28.12kg/62lb (tripod another 27.21kg/60lb)

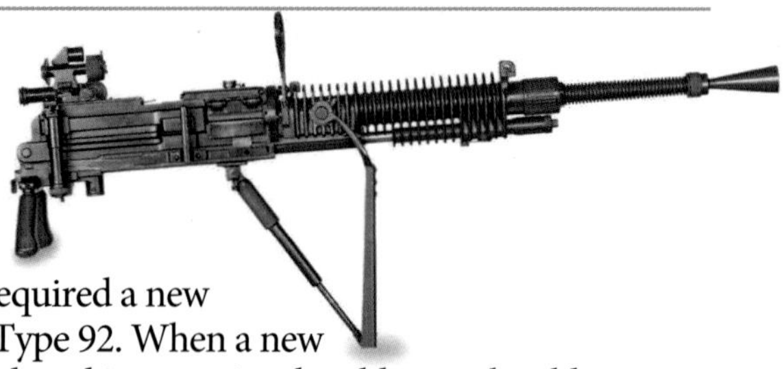

The Type 92 is a heavy machine gun of Hotchkiss-type design, that required a new cartridge – a semi-rimmed 7.7mm: Type 92. When a new cartridge and machine gun are introduced into service the old ones should be withdrawn. The new Type 92 ammunition was more powerful than the 7 .7mm, and rifles could not fire it. Conversely, the Type 92 could fire rifle ammunition. The tripod was fitted with sections of pipe, allowing it to be carried, stretcher-like, for short distances. It was introduced in 1932 and remained in service until the end of World War II.

Nambu Type 96

SPECIFICATION

MANUFACTURER Tokyo Arsenal and others
CALIBRE 6.5 x 50mm
MAGAZINE CAPACITY 30
ACTION Gas operated
TOTAL LENGTH 1,054mm/41.5in
BARREL LENGTH 552mm/21.75in
WEIGHT UNLOADED 9.07kg/20lb

The Type 96 is reported to be an improved Type 11, but it is simply the Czech ZB in 6.5 x 50mm, built for the Imperial Navy. Doing away with the cartridge oiler, the hopper feed of the Type 11 and changing to a quick-change barrel and magazine feed, the Type 96 is a much superior Light Machine Gun (LMG) to the Type 11. The Type 96 often had a 2.5x optical sight attached to the receiver, a first for an LMG. It entered service in 1936 and lasted until 1945.

Nambu Type 99

SPECIFICATION

MANUFACTURER Tokyo Arsenal
CALIBRE 7.7 x 58mm (could also use 7.7 x 58SR)
MAGAZINE CAPACITY 30
ACTION Gas operated
TOTAL LENGTH 1,187mm/46.75in
BARREL LENGTH 549mm/21.6in
WEIGHT UNLOADED 10.43kg/23lb

This was another Czech ZB copy, in 7.7mm rimless for use at the squad level. The fact that the Type 99 looks very much like the Type 96 only increased the confusion over ammunition (and in this case, magazine) supply. The Type 99 and Type 92 both used 7.7mm ammunition, but with different rim diameters on the case heads. The Nambu Type 99 was an excellent model, but the Japanese never had enough of them. Initially built for the army, it also entered service with Naval garrison units, often mistakenly called "Marines". Production began in 1939 and lasted to 1945.

Manufacturers

Here are details of the manufacturers whose arms are featured in both directories, where information is available.

CANADA

Diemaco Diemaco produces the Canadian version of the Colt M16 and M4, for use in the Canadian armed forces and for export. In 2005 Colt purchased Diemaco, re-naming it Colt Canada.

Inglis A marine engine and water pump company at the beginning of World War II, Inglis produced a huge number of rifles, pistols and BREN guns during the war. After the war they transitioned completely into manufacturing household appliances.

UNITED STATES

Armalite The original Armalite was a division of the Fairchild Aircraft Company, and developed the AR-15. They sold the rights of that rifle to Colt. The current Armalite company makes AR-15, AR-180 and AR-10 rifles.

Barrett This company was established to manufacture and sell the Barrett Light Fifty (known as the M82A1 in military use.) The company now also makes Ar-15 rifles in 6.8mm, and a prototype semi-automatic 20mm grenade launcher.

Cadillac Gage An automotive manufacturer, Cadillac Gage made small arms components during World War II, and was still trying to market small arms 20 years later. The Stoner was their final attempt. They continued making armoured cars.

Colt Established in 1836 by Samuel Colt to manufacture his handgun design, Colt went on to automatic rifles, pistol and machine guns, and produced huge volumes of all for the US military in World War I and II, Korea and Vietnam. Colt is the main producer of the M16 and M4 today.

Dillon Aero A new manufacturer to the small arms business, Dillon Aero re-designed and manufactured new parts for existing miniguns, and then went on to produce new ones when the US government found there were not enough of the old ones.

FNH-USA US Government regulations require that any producer of small arms have production facilities in the United States. So FN opened a business office, plant and hired staff in the US to be able to manufacture for the government.

General Dynamics A huge defence manufacturer, mostly in the heavy industrial sector (vehicles, aircraft, naval vessels) G-D has sought small arms contracts for decades with small success.

Johnson Arms Formed to manufacture and market the rifle and light machine gun of Melvin Johnson, Johnson Arms was in existence only for a few years during World War II, manufacturing the rifle and machine gun.

Kelsey-Hayes During World War II, every machine shop, large or small, made something for the war effort. Kelsey-Hayes was an automotive components manufacturer that produced heavy machine guns.

Knight's Armament The largest manufacturers of AR-10 type rifles (known as the SR-25 in US service) Knight's huge plant is so busy with military orders they cannot fulfill all their commercial requests.

LMT Defense Lewis Machine and Tool Company is an armaments company founded by Karl Lewis, in 1980. Their products are used by the military forces of the United Kingdom, New Zealand, Estonia and the United States.

Maremont Corp. A diversified manufacturing corporation that had a speciality division to manufacture the M-60 machine gun for the US armed forces.

Marlin A sporting arms manufacturer, Marlin stepped up to produce small arms during World War I and II.

Remington Established in 1816, Remington manufactured military rifles for both US and foreign contracts in both World Wars.

Savage Arms Founded in 1894. As with many sporting goods manufacturers, Savage manufactured weapons for the war effort, in both World War I and World War II. Their primary product in peacetime was (and still is) a lever-action hunting rifle, although they produce arms for other activities such as law enforcement.

Springfield Armory Established in 1794 as the official government arsenal, Springfield was closed in 1968 when then Secretary of Defense Robert McNamara changed the government acquisition process from government-designed weapons to private industry.

Stevens The hunting rifle and shotgun manufacturer fulfilled contracts in both World Wars for military arms for the US.

Sturm, Ruger & Co. The late Bill Ruger was a weapons' designer in World War II. He founded his firm in 1949, and pioneered the use of stampings and investment castings.

CUBA

Unión de Industrias Militares Founded in 1988, the UIM is the state-owned military-industrial complex in Cuba composed of 12 different companies.

MEXICO

Fabricas Militares Begun in 1918, Mexico currently has 17 manufacturing areas, distributed in Military Fields Nos. 1–D, Tecamachalco, State of Mexico; 1–F, Santa Fe, Mexico City and 25–E, Oriental, Puebla.

Productos Mendoza Formed to produce the LMG designed by Mendoza himself, it produces firearms and accessories for the Mexican military.

CHILE

Las Fábricas y Maestranzas del Ejército (FAMAE) Founded in 1811, Fábricas y Maestranzas del Ejército manufactures licenced copies of the FAL, as well as the Swiss SG540, in 5.56mm and 9mm. They also produce a 7.62mm variant, called the SG542.

DOMINICAN REPUBLIC

Armeria San Cristobal Begun in 1950, the Armeria produced the Model 2 carbine. After the assassination of Trujillo in 1961, the government of the Dominican Republic decided to leave the armaments business. By 1966, production had ceased and the factory closed.

ARGENTINA

FMAP One of the Argentine arsenals, devoted to small arms. FMAP produced a licence-built FN-FAL until it became necessary for Argentina to use the 5.56mm cartridge. In the 1980s they developed their own rifle.

BRAZIL

Indústria de Material Bélico do Brasil (IMBEL) Manufactured under licence FAL rifles for the Brazilian Army. They have also fulfilled contracts elsewhere in the Western hemisphere. When the 7.62 fell from favour, they re-engineered the FAL into the MD-2 and MD-3. They also manufacture copies of the M-1911 pistol, and an impressive array of cutlery.

PERU

Servicios Industriales de la Marina S.A Since Peru makes very few of the firearms that they use, production is carried out by SIMA, which is actually a state-run shipyard established in 1950.

PORTUGAL

Fábrica Militar de Braço de Prata One of the major armaments manufacturers in Portugal. It produced the Heckler & Koch G3 under licence.

Indústrias Nacionais de Defesa (INDEP) The main ordnance factory in Portugal, which produces a wide range of equipment, including mortars, artillery and small arms.

SPAIN

CETME The Spanish Design and Manufacturing Centre, set up after World War II, refined the Vorgrimmler lock system to become the HK G3.

Fabricas de Armas Oviedo was Spain's main armoury and manufacturing site for the first half of the 20th century, overtaken after World War II by CETME.

UNITED KINGDOM

Birmingham Small Arms Company (BSA) This company was founded in 1861 in the Gun Quarter of Birmingham. During World War I, the gun business grew exponentially. In World War II, production was focused on the Lee Enfield rifle as well as on military folding bicycles and on motorcycles. In 1986 BSA Guns was liquidated and now trades as BSA Guns (UK) Ltd.

FNH UK Ltd. Known as Manroy Engineering until 2017, it is the UK-based subsidiary of FN Herstal.

Royal Ordnance This was formed as a public corporation in 1985 but its roots in the Royal Ordnance factories extend back to the middle of the 16th century. The company was bought by British Aerospace, later BAE systems, and became part of BAE Systems Land and Armaments.

Royal Small Arms Factory, Enfield Founded in 1804 as one of the factories of the Board of Ordnance. Privatized in 1984 as part of Royal Ordnance Plc. Production included Bren and Sten guns as well as a modified version of the Webley service revolver.

FRANCE

Giat Industries Begun in 1973, GIAT Industries is a government-owned weapons manufacturer, based in Roanne, Loire. The name was changed to Nexter Systems in 2007.

Hotchkiss et Cie. This company was set up by Benjamin B. Hotchkiss of the United States in 1867 to produce a wide range of weaponry for both the French and the American armed forces. By the the beginning of the 20th century, Hotchkiss was also manufacturing cars.

Manufacture d'Armes de Châtellerault (MAC) Founded 1819 on the banks of the River Vienne. Initial production was of tools and swords. In 1822 the factory began to produce firearms and this was to continue until 1968.

St Etienne One of the first French armories to convert to the system of interchangeable parts (during the Napoleonic era) St Etienne manufactured small arms through World War II.

Tulle One of the main French armories, kept busy for decades starting with the manufacture of the Lebel 1886 rifle.

BELGIUM

Fabrique Nationale (FN) Herstal In 1888 the Belgian government offered a contract for 150,000 rifles, if a Liège firm could be found large enough to fulfill the order. The arms makers of Liége organized a corporation which would be large enough, and filled the order. Thus began one of the largest arms manufacturing companies in existence.

NETHERLANDS

Artillerie Inrichtigen This company had a brief period of success with the AR-10. When contracts failed to appear they went back to heavy equipment.

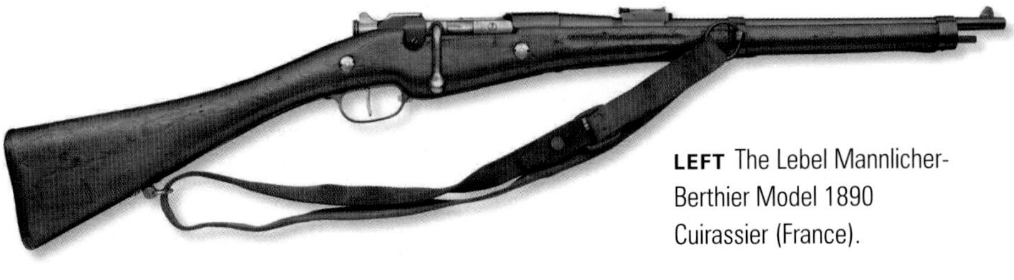

LEFT The Lebel Mannlicher-Berthier Model 1890 Cuirassier (France).

SWITZERLAND
SA Hispano-Suiza While primarily an aircraft engine manufacturer, Hispano-Suiza worked on various small-arms designs.

SIG Formed in the middle of the 19th century, SIG has produced small arms for Swiss use and export ever since.

GERMANY
Carl Walther Waffenfabrik GmbH. This business was first founded in 1886 by Carl Walther to make hunting and target-shooting rifles. The first semi-automatic pistol was produced in 1908.The factory closed at the end of World War II and re-opened again in West Germany.

Heckler & Koch GmbH. This firm began business in January 1950 and was first concerned with making parts for bicycles and sewing machines. In 1956 the company won the bid for the new West German general service rifle, the G3. In the mid-1960s, the MP5 was developed. In 1991 the company was bought by British Aerospace/ Royal Ordnance. It produces the whole range of small arms, from pistols to grenades and machine guns.

Waffenfabrik Mauser AG. Founded in 1811 as a royal weapons factory in Oberndorf. In 1867 Wilhelm and Paul Mauser developed a rifle with a rotating bolt system. In 1912 the company started producing pistols. In 1897 the factory became Waffenfabrik Mauser AG. It supplied rifles to the German Army through both World Wars. The factory was dismantled by French authorities at the end of World War II. The firm was re-established in the 1950s. In 2004 Mauser-Werke Oberndorf Waffensysteme GmbH incorporated into Rheinmetall Waffe Munition, GmbH. Mauser is highly regarded in the field of hunting rifles.

ITALY
Fabbrica d'Armi P. Beretta SpA. One of the oldest manufacturing firms in the world, Beretta has been making sporting and military weapons since the 16th century.

Fabbrica Nazionale d'Armi Brescia
A cooperative of gunmakers, located in the north of Italy, and beginning manufacture of military small arms in 1935. Bought in 1955 by Beretta.

GREECE
Hellenic Arms Industry The main arms manufacturer since 1977.

DENMARK
Dansk Industri Syndikat
A manufacturing conglomerate, of which small arms was a small part. Despite the success of the Madsen light machine gun, the post-war rifles were not greeted with enthusiasm, and in spite of good engineering and design, by 1963 there was no market share left to be had, and small arms production ceased.

AUSTRIA
Steyr Founded in 1864, the firm entered the military market with their breech-loading Werndl rifle of 1867. From then to the end of World War I, Steyr supplied small arms to the Austro-Hungarian Empire. Afterwards they supplied them to anyone in the market for small arms. Today they make select-fire rifles, sniper rifles and submachine guns.

SWEDEN
Carl Gustaf Arms Co. Formed as part of the original agglomeration of small arms producers that began in 1620 and centred on certain designated towns. The company itself dates from 1812. It is now part of Bofors.

Husqvarna Vapenfabriks AB. The company was founded in 1689 to produce muskets.

CZECHOSLOVAKIA (FORMER)
CZ-Brno Located in Strakonice, Czechoslovakia, the CZ Brno factory produced Mauser-pattern rifles after World War I, and through World War II. After World War II, the bolt-action rifles were produced for the sporting market while CZ-Brno developed and produced military rifles.

POLAND
Fabryka Broni Radom Founded in 1922, the company became independent in 2000.

Zaklady Mechaniczne Tarnów
Defense manufacturing company based in Tarnów that produces handguns, assault rifles, sniper rifles and anti-air guns.

CROATIA
HS Produkt Founded in 1991, HS Produkt is best known for the design and production of the HS2000 and XDM series of semi-automatic pistols, which are sold in the United States market by Springfield Armory, Inc., under their XD, XD-S, XD-M and Hellcat brandings.

RH-Alan In addition to the APS-95, RH-Alan manufactures pistols, submachine guns, grenades and mortars.

SERBIA
Zastava Arms Co. Founded in 1853 to manufacture cannons. Although it mainly produces cars, it is the sole arms producer in Serbia and Montenegro, with production largely based around Kalashnikov designs.

HUNGARY
Fegyver es Gepgyar (FÉG) Founded in 1891, the company produced Frommer pistols and also hunting and sports weapons. In 2003 the company was privatized and continues to produce small arms.

FINLAND
Valmet The State-owned weapons manufacturer, Valmet produced Kalashnikov-based weapons for the Finnish Defence forces from the early 1960s to the mid-1990s. The company now makes machinery for handling paper products. Before the 1960s, it was known as VKT; State Rifle Factory.

ROMANIA
Cugir Arsenal This State Arsenal located in Transylvania has manufactured small arms from 1799 to the present day. It is now known as the Romarm National Company, or just ROMARM.

BULGARIA
Arsenal Co. A government arsenal until 1999, when it was sold to the employees as part of the Bulgarian privatization programme, Arsenal is a vigorous exporter of small arms.

Long Branch Established to produce No 4 rifles during World War II to augment the production of other factories. Long Branch also produced STEN sub machine guns. Rifle production continued through the 1950s, switching to FAL production. After the Canadian army was converted to the FAL the plant was closed, and decades later the buildings torn down.

RUSSIA
Izhmech The State-owned Izhevsk Mechanical Plant, now manufacturing Kalashnikov-pattern small arms.

Tula Established in 1712 by Peter the Great, the Tula arsenal has produced small arms ever since.

UKRAINE
Zbroyar A privately owned weapons manufacturer that specializes in the production of high-precision sports and hunting rifles.

TURKEY
Kalekalip A group of Turkish factories that provides military products to the Turkish Armed Forces.

Makina ve Kimya Endüstrisi Kurumu (MKEK) The Mechanical and Chemical Industry Corporation was established in 1950 and is a reorganization of the government-controlled group of factories that supplied the Turkish Armed Forces with military products.

Sarsilmaz Founded in 1880 in the Ottoman Empire, it is a privately owned small arms manufacturer based in Düzce,Turkey, and is the largest small arms manufacturer in the country.

EGYPT
State Factory 54, "Aswan"
Established in Port Said to produce small arms for the Egyptian Army, Factory 54 began with the production of the Ljungman rifle. The tooling, bought from Husqvarna, armed the Egyptian Army and gave the factory production experience. Then, they went on to manufacture their own design, the Rasheed, then Soviet designs in the Goryunov and AK-47.

SOUTH AFRICA
Lyttelton Engineering Works For decades this has been a small arms and artillery manufacturing centre.

ISRAEL
Israel Military Industries (IMI)
IMI was formed as a State-owned company to manufacture weapons. The small arms division was privatized in 2005 and renamed Israel Weapon Industries.

IRAN
Defense Industries Organization
A conglomerate of companies founded in 1981 and run by the Islamic Republic of Iran to provide the armed forces with the necessary manufacturing capacity.

INDIA
Ishapore Located outside Calcutta, this was converted from a powder factory to a rifle factory in 1902. From SMLE to L1A1 rifles, the Ishapore factory now manufactures the INSAS rifle.

AUSTRALIA
Lithgow Established in 1909, production began in 1912 to produce the SMLE No.1 Mk III rifle for Commonwealth use. Production of BREN guns and Vickers (1937 and 1925, respectively) machine guns meant the Lithgow plant was able to supply impressive numbers of weapons in World War II.

CHINA
205th Arsenal Formed in 2002, the 205th Arsenal is part of the Armaments Bureau, which is part of the Ministry of National Defense of the Republic of China.
Norinco Also known as China North Industries Corp, Norinco is the exporter of Chinese-made small arms to the world. They offer military as well as non-military firearms.

State Factories Chinese State factories are only known by their factory number. Thus, the "location" of manufacture can often only be noted as "Factory 26" "Factory 36" or "Factory 66".

INDONESIA
Pindad Founded in 1808, Pindad provides armaments and munitions to the Indonesian National Armed Forces and other uniformed agencies.

SINGAPORE
ST Kinetics Formerly known as Chartered Industries of Singapore, this company grew from a small arms manufacturer to a heavy-industry and integrated defence manufacturer.

SOUTH KOREA
Daewoo Founded in 1967, and an industrial giant, the corporation manufactures cars, ships, heavy construction and weapons.

JAPAN
Howa In the larger sense, Howa is a Japanese machinery manufacturer, but it is known internationally for the production of military and civilian firearms.

Kokura This factory began in 1935. It was such a hub of production it was selected as the second target for atomic bombing, but bad weather brought the alternate city, Nagasaki to the history books.

Nagoya Opened in 1923, closed in 1945. It was not reopened after World War II.

ABOVE The HK-CETME Prototype (Germany).

Glossary

ABOVE The FN SAFN M-1949 (Belgium).

Air cooled Using ambient air as the cooling medium to deal with the heat of cartridge combustion.
Ammunition A supply of fully assembled cartridges ready for firing, sometimes abbreviated to "ammo".
Aperture sight Also a "peep" sight. The rear-aiming element of the sight is a device with a circular hole through it. The eye automatically centres the field of view in the middle of the aperture. The shooter then places the tip of the front sight in the centre of the view, and thus aims correctly.
Armour-piercing A bullet made with a hard core, used to penetrate light armour and chance obstacles.
Arquebus An early matchlock that preceded the musket, the forerunner of the rifle and other shoulder-fired weapons.
Assault rifle An automatic or semi-automatic rifle with a magazine feed now commonly firing small calibre ammunition.
Assault weapon A class of firearm which is a shoulder-fired, select-fire individual weapon chambered in a moderate-power cartridge.
Automatic A firearm with only one firing mode; where the weapon fires at its cyclic rate until the trigger is released. Also known as full-auto.
Backblast The backward blast created by igniting the propellant in a weapon designed to be as recoilless as possible.
Barrel The metal tube of a gun. The bullet, shot or projectile accelerates through it when the gun is discharged.
Battle rifle A self-loading rifle that uses full-power cartridges.
Bayonet A knife or spike that attaches to the muzzle of a weapon, for use in combat. Some are attached semi-permanently, and hinge into place while others are removable.
Beaten zone The area in which a burst of bullets fired from a machine gun will fall.
Belt A series of cartridges, parallel to each other, in a feeding mechanism. Belts can be reloaded with fresh ammunition and re-used. Metal belts can be continuous and disintegrating.
Blowback A breeching system that depends on the weight of the bolt and the force of the recoil spring to keep the bolt closed when the cartridge is fired.
Blowout vent Recoilless weapons dampen recoil by venting the gases of combustion to the rear, as well as launching the projectile forward.
Body The part of the weapon containing the bolt and return spring. The barrel is located forward of the buffer, and the end cap at the rear. In the US, it is known as the receiver.
Bolt A mass of metal that feeds the round from the magazine into the chamber and supports it during firing.
Bolt-action The locking mechanism that works much like a deadbolt on a door. The firer lifts the bolt handle, pulls it back, then pushes it forward and turns the handle down.
Bore The inside of a barrel of a gun excluding the chamber. It is the channel through which the projectile passes when the gun is discharged.
Breech The open rear part of a firearm's barrel.
Breech loader A gun that is loaded via the rear or breech.
Bullpup A rifle design that has the trigger (and usually a pistol grip) forward of the magazine and receiver.
Burst-fire Either a set number of rounds fired by a mechanism designed to limit fire, or a small number of rounds fired by the operator.
Butt or stock The rear part of a firearm that may be made from wood, polymer or a metal frame that fits against the firer's shoulder.
Calibre Used both to describe the diameter of the bore, and a descriptor of the cartridge itself (in metric or imperial measure). The original Russian rifle cartridge of the Mosin-Nagant is both .30 calibre and the 7.62 x 54R calibre.
Carbine A shortened rifle. When rifles were bolt-action or large-calibre semi-automatics, a carbine was created by shortening the barrel and otherwise making the rifle lighter.
Cartridge A self-contained unit, comprising case, powder, primer and bullet. Each cartridge can be fed into the chamber, discharged, and the empty one extracted.
Centrefire A cartridge with the primer in the centre of the base.
Chamber The area of a gun where the round rests prior to firing.
Change lever The lever that controls the mode of fire i.e. single shot or automatic.
Clip Used correctly, a reloading tool, or an essential part of the mechanism. Used incorrectly to describe a magazine.
Closed bolt A design that when ready to fire has the bolt closed and locked, and a round chambered. Each cycle typically ends with the bolt closed on a fresh cartridge.
Cocking lever (or handle/retracting handle) A lever used to draw back the bolt in an automatic weapon.
Cook off The ignition of the propellant charge due to heat conducted from the chamber walls.
Combat/effective range The distance at which rounds are effective against a human target.
Cyclic rate The rate at which an automatic weapon fires (this is measured in rounds per minute).
Direct fire Firing at a target the operator can see. The operator can see the effect and correct fire himself.
Direct gas impingement The gas tapped off the barrel is not directed against a piston, but is ported via a tube directly to the bolt carrier. The carrier is pushed by the gas, and rotates the bolt, then reciprocates. Also called the Stoner system.
Discharge To cause a firearm to fire. A negligent discharge or ND is the accidental firing of a weapon.
Disconnector A part of the mechanism that intercepts the hammer or striker, preventing full-auto fire.
Disintegrating link Interlocking metal clips that hold machine gun ammunition. Upon firing the links separate and fall from the weapon.
Double-barrel A firearm with two barrels, which may be side by side or over/under. Used in shot guns.
Drop safety A safety device that prevents a weapon firing if it is accidentally dropped.
Dum dum/hollow point A bullet where the lead core has been exposed to cause the bullet to expand when it hits soft tissue.
Ejection port The opening normally on the side of the receiver through which spent cartridges are ejected after the bullet as been fired.
Ejector The spring-loaded plunger, or tab in the receiver, that ejects the cartridge from the mechanism when the action is cycled.
En bloc clip A package of cartridges in a metal clip. The firearm feeds the rounds when cycling, and ejects the clip when ammunition is exhausted.
Extractor A way of removing a cartridge by grasping the rim and pulling it rearward to remove it.
Feed tray On a belt-fed weapon,

flat section of the feeding area that the belt rides over as it enters the receiver. On the Hotchkiss design of machine gun, the flat sheet metal trays that hold cartridges.
Firing cycle The eight steps necessary for a mechanism to function. They are: feed, chamber, lock, fire, unlock, extract, eject, cock. Not all designs use all eight, but they do all use them in that order.
Firing pin The mechanism that strikes the percussion cap on a cartridge.
Flash hider A device attached at the muzzle to diminish the visible incandescent gases produced when firing to assist in concealing the user.
Flintlock The action of early firearms where a sliver of flint was held by a cock. When the trigger was pulled the spring-loaded cock holding the flint struck the steel "frizzen" producing sparks that ignited powder in the flash pan adjoining the "touch hole". The flash from the exploding powder passed through the hole to ignite the main charge in the barrel.
Fluted chamber A chamber manufactured with longitudinal slots, called flutes, to assist extraction.
Folding stock Normally a metal shoulder piece that folds back against the main body of the weapon when not in use. Stocks may also be telescopic.
Foresight A small blade or pillar above the muzzle. It may be adjusted laterally and sometimes vertically for "zeroing".
Frizzen The metal arm of a flintlock. The flint strikes the frizzen to create sparks in the flash pan.
Fullering Longitudinal grooves pressed into the magazine body to increase strength and let dirt drop to the bottom.
Gas The flame produced by an exploding cartridge – the pressure generated by the gas can be used to operate automatic weapons.
Gas operated A mechanism that utilises some of the propellant gases to activate the mechanism. Typically, gas is bled out of the barrel via a port, which then pushes a piston, attached to the carrier or bolt.
GPMG General purpose machine gun. A design intended to be versatile enough that it could be used in support, as an infantry weapon or as an aerial weapon.
Grenade launcher A weapon that fires or launches a grenade to longer distances than a soldier could throw by hand. Modern grenade launchers are separate tubes mounted under the rifle barrel, firing self-contained grenades.
Grip/spade/pistol The handle on a weapon. A pistol grip is behind the trigger. There are two spade grips with the button trigger between them.
Grooves The series of helical spirals cut into the bore of the barrel.
Hammer A spring-loaded, usually pivoting part of the mechanism, used to strike the firing pin and initiate the firing sequence.
Hammer-forged barrel A method of barrel making where a very hard mandrel, which is the exact shape and dimension of the desired bore, is inserted into the reamed and polished "blank". Powerful hydraulic hammers peen the blank down around the mandrel, shaping the interior so closely to the mandrel as to produce rifling.
Handguards A resting place and insulation against the heat of the barrel.
HMG Heavy machine gun. In the early years, a heavy machine gun was any that used water as a cooling method. With the development of the GPMG and larger calibres, "heavy" came to mean a larger-calibre machine gun.
Hold-open device A device operated by the magazine, to hold the breech block to the rear after the magazine is emptied.
Indirect fire The operator cannot see the target himself or the effect of his fire. The use of radios has made artillery so effective that machine guns are no longer used in this way.
Lands The raised portions between the grooves of the rifling. The jacket of the bullet is engraved by the lands to provide spin and stability and to prevent gas escaping past the bullet.
Link The metal clips holding machine gun ammunition.
LMG Light machine gun. When machine guns were new, any model that did not require water as a cooling medium was considered a "light" machine gun. Later, the designation shifted to cover those fed from a box magazine instead of a belt.
Long recoil In the long recoil design, the bolt and barrel stay locked together after firing. They recoil, locked together, for a distance greater than that of the loaded cartridge length. Then, the mechanism unlocks and the barrel returns to battery followed by the bolt. Movement of the bolt and barrel activates the feed mechanism.
Lug/locking lug The shoulders of the bolt that lock into or against a surface on the receiver.
Magazine Either a sheet-metal box external to the firearm containing a cartridge lifter or follower and a spring, or a design internal to the rifle.
Mainspring/return spring The source of the energy required to fire a gun. The helical spring, generally behind the bolt, is placed under compression as the bolt moves to the rear. The compression is used to drive the bolt forward again.
Malfunction An unwanted interruption in the firing cycle.
Match A length of cord soaked in saltpetre, which was used to ignite gunpowder in early firearms.
Matchlock Early firearms fitted with an S-shaped metal lever holding a smouldering match. The lever can be operated to tip the smouldering end of the match into the powder in the priming pan and set off the main charge via the touchhole.
Musket A muzzle-loaded smoothbore weapon fired from the shoulder.
Muzzle brake A device attached to the muzzle of a weapon to re-direct the flow of the muzzle blast.
Muzzle climb The upward movement of a weapon as a result of recoil. A significant problem with automatic weapons.
Nose cap The steel or brass reinforcement at the front end of a stock, to support the stock and provide a bayonet-mounting attachment point.
Open bolt A design where the mechanism, cocked and ready to fire, has the bolt held back from the chamber, and the chamber is ready. When fired, the bolt will be pressed forward by the action spring, feed a round, close, fire and then retract, extracting the case and ejecting it.
Open sight A sighting system where the rear element is a notch, V-shaped, U-shaped or a rectangular slot.
Operating handle/rod The grasping handle or knob the firer uses to hand-cycle the action.
Optics Previously, magnifying optics used as an aiming aid. Now, red-dot optics, using a view screen and a reflected laser dot as an aiming aid.
Pan The small container located on the side or stop of a matchlock, wheel-lock or flint-lock firearm used to hold the priming powder.
Parabellum One of the terms used to describe the 9 x 19mm cartridge; it is also known as the 9mm Luger.
PDW Personal defence weapon. A compact weapon designed for close-quarters defence, rather than assault.
Percussion system A system in which a substance such as sodium chlorate is detonated by the impact of a hammer, setting off the main charge.
Percussion cap A small soft metal cup containing explosive that is placed over the nipple of a percussion firearm. In the days of muzzle loaders it allowed a gun to be loaded in all weathers. In breechloaded cartidges it was a primer.
Picatinny rail A type of mounting platform used to attach accessories such as scopes, lasers and bipods to firearms.
Pinfire cartridge A 19th-century cartridge where a pin would ignite the priming mixture and the explosion would cause the brass sheath containing the gunpowder and ball to expand, closing the breech.

LEFT The Armalite AR-18 (United Kingdom).

Pistol grip A grasping structure, looking much like the butt of a pistol that projects below a shoulder weapon. It is there solely to locate the firing hand near the trigger.
Primary extraction A movement of the bolt that frees the case from adherence to the chamber walls, but does not move the case out of the chamber.
Proof-mark Official mark placed on a firearm after the barrel has been tested by a proof house.
Propellant The charge of chemical energy which when burnt, produces a large volume of hot gas to force the bullet up the bore.
Quick-change barrel A design that allows an operator to change barrels to cool an overheated air-cooled machine gun quickly.
Rail attachment A rail either fixed onto the firearm or integral to the frame to which telescopic sights, laser pointers or lights can be attached.
Rear sight A "V" or an aperture placed over the breech, which with the foresight, allows aligning of the barrel.
Receiver The heart of a firearm. The receiver is the structure to which all other parts of the firearm are joined.
Recoil The rearward movement of integral parts of a gun as a result of the explosive force of the cartridge.
Reload To recharge a weapon with a fresh supply of ammunition. Also, to take empty cartridge casings and replace the consumed portions: primer, power and projectile.
Rifling A series of helical grooves cut in the interior of the barrel to give the bullet the required spin needed for stability in flight.
Rim The edge on the base of a cartridge case. The rim is the part of the case that the extractor grips in order to remove the cartridge from the chamber.
Rim-fire A cartridge that has its primer located inside the rim of the case.
Rimless Not truly rimless, but called so. The rim of the extractor groove (where the extractor grasps the cartridge) is not larger in diameter than the base, or head, of the cartridge case.
Rimmed Where the rim of the cartridge is larger in diameter than the base, or head, of the case it is on.
Round One shot fired by a gun. It is also one complete unit of ammunition or a cartridge which has all the parts required to fire one shot.
Sear A lever/catch connected to the trigger that holds back the firing pin.
Selector The lever that sets the rate of fire for a weapon from safe, through single shots to automatic.
Select-fire A firearm where more than a single firing mode may be selected.
Semi automatic A firearm where each pull of the trigger produces only one shot, but the mechanism operates to eject the empty and feed a fresh round into the chamber. Also known as a self-loading rifle (SLR).
Short recoil In a short recoil firearm the movement of the bolt and barrel are locked together, to actuate the mechanism. The distance moved is less than the cartridge's overall length. When the barrel movement stops, the bolt continues rearward enough to activate the feeding mechanism.
Sidemount A mount secured to the side of the receiver for designs that do not allow optics to be mounted above the bore.
Silencer or suppressor A device attached to a gun's muzzle that suppresses the sound of firing. Also known as a moderator or "can".
Single shot A gun mechanism without a magazine that requires rounds to be loaded manually.
Smooth bore A firearm with a bore that is not rifled, now only found with shotguns.
Sniper A trained precision marksman who uses a rifle of above-average accuracy to engage high-value targets or individuals at extreme range. In slang, anyone who takes a pot-shot at an individual or group.
Sniper rifle A rifle built or tuned for use as a sniper's tool. Typically it is a bolt-action rifle, and full-calibre (.30) or larger.
SAW Squad automatic weapon. A machine gun of moderate calibre, used by one or two men as an integral part of a squad.
Squad designated marksman An individual of above-average skill, tasked with precision marksmanship in service at the squad level.
Straight-line recoil To control semi and full-auto firing, the stock is placed directly behind the bore. The forces of recoil have no leverage, and the muzzle does not rise when fired.
Straight-pull bolt action Instead of the operator needing to lift the bolt handle, he just grasps the handle and pulls it directly to the rear. Camming surfaces machined into the bolt unlock the bolt from the receiver, and lock it again when the bolt is shoved straightforward.
Stampings/pressings A firearm's receiver made from stampings is created by large hydraulic machines pressing sheet steel into shape. By selecting the correct alloy, the steel is strengthened.
Stripper clip Also known as a charger, and used to quickly reload magazines. The clip is only a sheet metal strip that attaches to fresh cartridges on the rims.
Submachine gun A select-fire rifle or carbine, chambered in a calibre typically considered a pistol cartridge.
Sustained fire In the early days, this meant the native cyclic rate of the weapon until a stated time period or number of rounds were fired. These days, it is the firing rate at which the weapon will not overheat, but which is needed at that moment.
Telescopic sight An optical sight attached to a firearm that magnifies the user's view of a target.
Telescoping stock A design that is made smaller for transport or storage by having the stock collapse in on itself, without the need for a hinge.
Tilting bolt A bolt that cams to lock and unlock, by means of the rear being tilted up or down into the locking recess.
Toggle lock A hinged lock, identical in operation to the human knee. When the hinge is in line or over-rotated into battery, it is incredibly strong. A small lateral force will pivot the hinge out of line, and the bolt then unlocks and collapses.
Tracer A bullet manufactured with a hollow base, which is filled with a combustible compound. The heat of firing ignites the compound, which burns with a visible light.
Water-cooled A cylinder filled with water to cool the barrel of early machine guns. This allowed for incredible sustained-fire volume but the weight made movement prohibitive.
Wheel lock An early firearm mechanism. Developed in the early 16th century it was the next major development in firearms technology after the matchlock. A spring-loaded wheel with serrated edges spins against a piece of iron pyrites producing a stream of sparks into the pan, and so igniting the powder.
Windage The adjustment or adjusting mechanism that moves the projectile's point of impact along the horizontal plane.
Zeroing The adjusting of sights to ensure that each of a firer's shots coincide with the point of aim.

Index

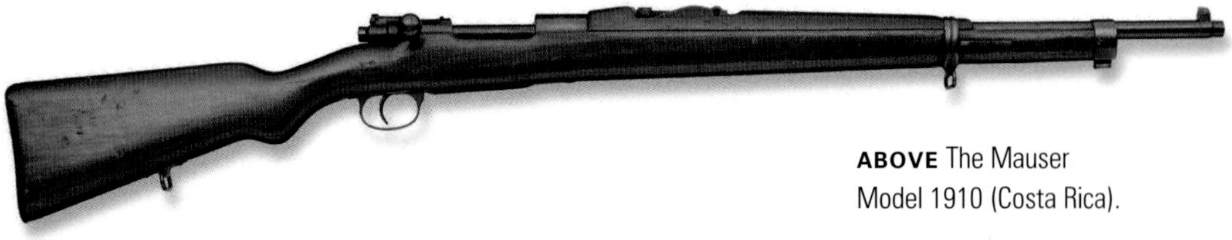

ABOVE The Mauser Model 1910 (Costa Rica).

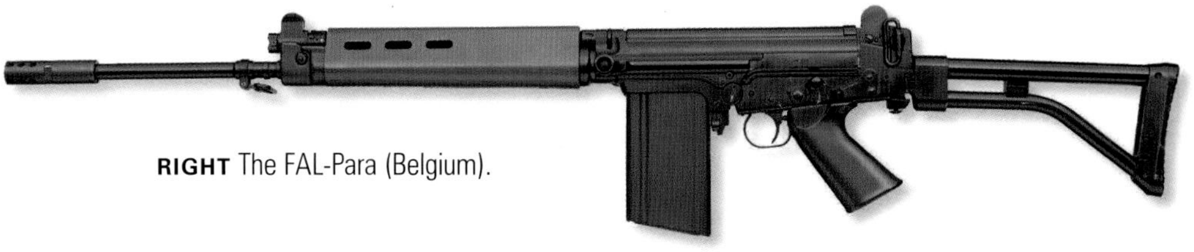

RIGHT The FAL-Para (Belgium).

ABOVE The Mondragon Air Service (Switzerland).

Picture credits

The publisher would like to thank the following for supplying photographs: Cody Images/TRH Pictures: 34b, 45t, 46t, 47, 49t, 58b, 78, 79b, 86b, 88b, 90b, 92b, 94t; David Ezrets: 175 (www.israeli-weapons.com); The Lordprice Collection: 6t, 11, 18t, 65t, 68t, 90t; Peter Newark: 7t, 8t, 13t, 14b, 15, 18b, 20, 22, 23, 25, 26b, 27, 29, 32, 33, 34t, 36, 37, 38t, 41b, 52t, 53t, 61, 63t, 64, 65b, 67t, 70b, 84t, 93; Royal Armouries Picture Library: 10, 14t, 17, 21, 26t, 30c, 51b, 54, 55b, 58t, 76b, 89b; TopFoto: 12, 13b, 28, 35, 53b; Will Fowler: 30t, 39, 41t, 43, 44, 46b, 51t, 52b, 57t, 71, 72, 79t, 81b, 82, 84b, 85, 87b, 89t, 91, 94b, 95b.

All other images are commissioned. With thanks to the Royal Armouries, Leeds in England for allowing access to their extensive collection of firearms.

All commissioned pictures by Gary Ombler. All artwork by Peters & Zabransky Ltd.

Every effort has been made to obtain permission to reproduce copyright material, but there may be cases where we have been unable to trace a copyright holder. The publisher will be happy to correct any omissions in future printings.